Critical praise for *Don't Tread On Me*

"Perelman handled the American language the way a virtuoso piccolo player plays 'The Stars and Stripes Forever.' " — Kurt Vonnegut, Jr.

"Almost without exception, the pieces are imaginative and hilarious. . . . Perelman's satirical hyperbole reveals truths that seem otherwise inaccessible or inexpressible." — *San Francisco Chronicle Book Review*

"His letters are charming, flirtatious, buffed to a high sheen." — *The Wall Street Journal*

"There is a lot to savor in this collection." — *Cleveland Plain Dealer*

"The Perelman who emerges from this selection of his correspondence simmers with volcanic pressures: sometimes passion, sometimes disgust, but most often creative energy." — *Business Week*

"A treasure . . . Perelman polished his correspondence as carefully as his formal work." — *Newsday*

"Perelman was an original. At once subversively funny, surreal, and a polyglot, armed with a surprising vocabulary that sent me diving for my dictionary more than once . . . He was superb at what he did." — Mordecai Richler, *The New York Times Book Review*

"The letters proper are highly revealing and suggest tantalizing interpretations." — *The Boston Globe*

PENGUIN BOOKS

DON'T TREAD ON ME

Prudence Crowther was S. J. Perelman's close friend at the very end of his life. Her pieces have appeared in *The New Yorker*, *The New York Review of Books*, and *The Atlantic Monthly*.

Don't Tread on Me

The Selected Letters of S. J. Perelman

EDITED BY

Prudence Crowther

PENGUIN BOOKS

PENGUIN BOOKS
Published by the Penguin Group
Viking Penguin Inc., 40 West 23rd Street, New York, New York 10010, U.S.A.
Penguin Books Ltd, 27 Wrights Lane, London W8 5TZ, England
Penguin Books Australia Ltd, Ringwood, Victoria, Australia
Penguin Books Canada Ltd, 2801 John Street, Markham, Ontario, Canada L3R 1B4
Penguin Books (N.Z.) Ltd, 182–190 Wairau Road, Auckland 10, New Zealand

Penguin Books Ltd, Registered Offices: Harmondsworth, Middlesex, England

First published in the United States of America by Viking Penguin Inc. 1987
Published in Penguin Books 1988

The editor gratefully acknowledges permission from the following sources to reprint letters from
their archives:

Rare Book and Manuscript Library, Columbia University, for use of the Random House, Leah
Salisbury, and Daniel Longwell papers; Special Collections, Mugar Memorial Library, Boston
University, for letters to Karl Fortess and Victor Wolfson; Harry Ransom Humanities Research Center,
University of Texas at Austin, for letters to Ogden Nash; American Academy and Institute of Arts and
Letters for a letter to Felicia Geffen; Princeton University Library, for use of the Philip Wylie papers
and the archives of Story magazine (Whit Burnett); Cornell University Library for letters to E. B.
White; Houghton Library, Harvard University, for a letter to L. E. Sissman; Collection of the
Historical Society of Saratoga Springs for letters to Frank Sullivan; Collection of American Literature,
Beinecke Rare Book and Manuscript Library, Yale University, for letters to Edmund Wilson; Brown
University Library for letters to Arthur Rosen and S. D. Cohen; Nathanael West Collection,
Huntington Library, San Marino, Calif., for letters to Jay Martin; Manuscript Division, Library of
Congress, for letters to Groucho Marx.

LIBRARY OF CONGRESS CATALOGING IN PUBLICATION DATA
Perelman, S. J. (Sidney Joseph), 1904 – 1979.
Don't tread on me.
Includes index.
1. Perelman, S. J. (Sidney Joseph),
1904 –   — Correspondence.   2. Authors, American —
20th century — Correspondence.   3. Humorists, American —
20th century — Correspondence.
I. Crowther, Prudence.
II. Title.
PS3531.E6544Z48   1988   818'.5209   [B]   87–32805
ISBN 0 14 00.9482 2

Printed in the United States of America by
R. R. Donnelley & Sons Company, Harrisonburg, Virginia
Set in Times Roman   Designed by Camilla Filancia and Prudence Crowther

Preface

In the summer of 1983 I went to London to find sources for this book, and among the many people there who helped me was the British foreign correspondent Clare Hollingworth. She'd known S. J. Perelman in London and New York and in Hong Kong and Tokyo. They occasionally dined together at the Foreign Correspondents Club in Hong Kong, and one evening when she fetched him at his hotel room, Perelman asked how her day had gone. She said she'd worked up a number of leads in the morning, had lunch with a source, sent several telexes, and filed two stories that afternoon. And Sid? "I've written one postcard," he said sheepishly. Indeed, his room was littered with half-written cards. As he put it, "I am an introvert nail-chewer who has to lock himself into an iron maiden, preferably sound-proofed, to even answer a dunning letter." He suffered, he thought, "from *mot-juste* poisoning arising from the way I make a living."

Yet as this collection proves, he was detoxified often enough to write many free and unlabored letters. He used his correspondence as a kind of companionship, and as he was good at that, the letters read accordingly.

Don't Tread on Me is an alternate title Perelman proposed to Bennett Cerf for a collection that was ultimately published as *Crazy like a Fox*, in 1944: "It seems to characterize the general mood of many of my pieces." The motto beneath the serpent on the flag of the thirteen rebel American colonies, it characterizes many of his letters as well.

His other moods are less well represented here. Given his temperament — the book could also have been titled *Jaundice vs. Jaundice*, or *Miasma, and Welcome to It* — that's perhaps unfortunate. Tenderness, for example, gets short shrift; so does ribaldry. He could be eloquent in both, but to gain the cooperation of certain correspondents I have acceded to some editing by other hands.

Even so, there is plenty left to constitute a species of autobiography, starting in 1928 and ending only with Perelman's death. For that reason, I have kept the biographical notes in the introduction below as brief as possible.

To collect Perelman in this way is to define him, however lively, wayward, revealing, or obscuring his letters may be. Following the biographical outline, I have attempted to sketch lightly for the reader the Perelman I knew, offering by indirection some perspective on my work as editor.

Those already familiar with Perelman's life will note the absence of letters to some seemingly obvious correspondents. Some, of course, have chosen not to contribute. Good friends frequently received only postcards, written in a telegraphic style based on inside jokes and gossip; editors were often consulted over the phone or in person. Other relationships were too formal to prompt an exchange of interest to any but the academic reader. In even the most perfunctory letters, however, Perelman was apt to lay a small gold egg: "I recently spent five days in Tunisia—transportation, hotel, etc.—at a total cost of 25 pounds, or $62.50. Even a weekend in San Diego, with a case of crabs thrown in, would cost you more than that." To avoid publishing an overlong book, I have culled only a sampling.

Although I know that Perelman wrote to Robert Benchley, Nathanael West, F. Scott Fitzgerald, Dorothy Parker, Somerset Maugham, and Lillian Hellman, I have turned up nothing to them. Perelman saved virtually none of his own letters, and there is some reason to think that he or he and his wife, Laura, as executors of West's estate, destroyed the bulk of whatever correspondence remained at West's death. Perelman once told me that T. S. Eliot made him promise to send along anything he could find on baton twirling; what surfaced instead were comparatively dry notes written in a dry season. Additional letters to Raymond Chandler are held by the Bodleian Library at Oxford, and the terms of their bequest stipulate that they not be released until they are catalogued. The late David Maurer, master of criminal argot and a friend of Perelman's since the forties, undoubtedly had a rare correspondence with him. Maurer's *The Big Con* was an early slang bible for Perelman (he gave copies to Eliot, Maugham, and V. S. Pritchett), and Maurer in turn credited Perelman with influencing his own style. Late in life, he told me, he burned his immense files, including Perelman's letters, to protect his underground sources.

There are similar tales behind many of the gaps. Even so, although I have tried to elicit and pursue the most obscure leads, I have undoubtedly left some strongboxes unturned. I urge anyone who knows of such material to get in touch with the Brown University Library, which has the largest and most important Perelman holdings.

Not surprisingly, Perelman was nearly as fastidious in his correspondence as in his pieces. Most of his letters are neatly typed and take few shortcuts of any kind; the "letterhead above" he occasionally refers to is that of *The New Yorker*. I have corrected obvious errors and only occasionally regularized spelling and punctuation. Perelman was, of course, known for his wide-ranging allusions. With some key assists from Max Wilk, I have made an attempt to ground them, as obvious as they will seem to many, for younger readers.

Perelman's parents spoke Yiddish; he did not, although he used it fairly frequently in his writing (Israel Shenker called it "the Yiddish he never got quite right but never entirely wrong"). I have not tinkered with his spellings, which are often his own, nor have I offered any translations. There's a hoary old story about always keeping on hand the makings of a martini. If you get lonely, start to fix one, and someone will be sure to come up behind you and say, "That's not how you make a martini." As I discovered, you could accomplish the same thing by translating Yiddish. There was nothing arrogant in Perelman's use of recondite words; they are a mark of respect for his readers, whom he trusted were not too feeble or bored to head for the dictionary.

I have made many cuts in the letters. Some were requested, most are my own doing. Periods in the text that run together without spacing are Perelman's own (....); spaced ellipses are mine (. . .). Large cuts, of a paragraph or more, are marked by a space of a line and three centered dots. Not all these deletions, of course, represent delicacy on my part or someone else's. Perelman had many occasions to give roughly similar accounts of himself, especially when traveling; I have included what I thought were the best and have felt free to drop the dull along with the indiscreet.

I have sometimes been offered preedited material that I found more frustrating than illuminating to read. While I appreciate the desire or need for privacy, the result is sometimes an instance of too little learning. I have tried not to pass on any inadvertent coyness, and I hope correspondents will not feel ill-served.

In hunting for letters I have followed a trail that goes from Ava Gardner to the zoo in Basel. Perelman made enemies, real and imagined (he suffered not from sheer but from run-proof paranoia—easier, he said, to rinse out in the shower); he also had a truly extraordinary range and number of friends, people who harbored no illusions about him and yet who cherish and miss him to this day, particularly when they open the morning paper. I can't take the space to list even the fraction I've had the privilege to meet and know.

To assemble a collection like this is to be a pest of the worst sort. I am grateful to those who responded to my importuning, and to those who made it unnecessary. They include, for starters, all the correspondents who appear in these pages. I offer this book as partial thanks.

My time in England was made more profitable by Challice Reed, of the BBC archives, and far more pleasurable by Mel Calman, John Hillaby, and Chaim Raphael. In New York, Perelman's longtime lawyer and friend James Mathias showed me early courtesy. Dorothy Herrmann, whose *S. J. Perelman: A Life* was published by Putnam in 1986, passed on many letters and leads I would not otherwise have known about—her openhandedness has been uniquely helpful. The Writers Room gave me a cheap desk and tolerated my solitary cackling in a room full of industry. For bolstering and good judgment from the start, I thank Nancy Meiselas Berner and Janet Sternburg; for her equanimity, my agent and the agent for the Perelman estate, Liz Daranshoff; for her seminal idea, Barbara Epstein.

I have had an embarrassment of moral support and *sachel* of every stripe from more folk than I can name, but chief among them are Mary Blume, Marion Meade, Paul Pavel, Caskie Stinnett, William Zinsser, and my incredulous family, in particular my sister, Beverly, who roots for two. I've enjoyed the back-and-forth with my editor, Gerry Howard, whose steady enthusiasm helped rouse me after some dispiriting interruptions.

For a prolonged and rigorous exhortation to find Blake's truth "in minute particulars," I am happily beholden to Albert Goldman. Except for this sentence, the front matter was edited and the "cut velvet" copyedited by Roslyn Schloss, my best friend.

In Bucks County, where I've been able to work since 1982, I have benefited from the kindness of Perelman's friends Joan and Denver Lindley. The devotion and example of Allen Saalburg, whom I met through Perelman himself, will sustain me for a long time.

Copyright on the letters is held by Abby and Adam Perelman. They have done better than take a leap of faith in allowing me to make this selection — they have not taken it but have instead labored to see the thing done right according to their lights. The brightest of these is the loving presence of Ruth Goetz, diplomat without portfolio, ebullient counselor. Adam has helped put critical materials within reach; Abby has answered relentless queries with alacrity, good will, and the honesty of her reservations. No editor could have had a fairer shot or a more gratifying project, and I hope their trust has been repaid.

Introduction

Sidney Joseph Perelman was born in Brooklyn on February 1, 1904, to Russian Jewish immigrants. He was an only child. The family soon moved to Providence, Rhode Island, where his father, Joseph, opened a dry-goods store, earning a parlous living that did not improve after a switch to poultry farming ("to this day I cringe at the sight of a gizzard," Perelman wrote in a letter in 1966). He characterized his milieu as "lower middle bourgeois." His parents were not religious; Joseph was a socialist. In 1959, Sid told a panel of BBC interviewers:

> There was no particular persecution or pressure brought upon me because of my racial background. It just didn't exist. We were an extremely polyglot crowd. . . . The circumstances of my boyhood were, in fact, quite enjoyable in every way. . . . I never had any sense of being alienated from my background or culture whatever.

He claimed to have had the normal boy's ambitions but most wanted to become the rear driver on a hook and ladder fire truck. From an early age, he began drawing and cartooning. He received a solid public-school education and often worked after class.

In 1921 Perelman entered Brown University in Providence, where he met Nathanael ("Pep") West of New York City. West became his closest friend and, in 1929, his brother-in-law, when he married Laura West, who was eighteen. Perelman was made editor of the college humor magazine, *The Brown Jug*, his senior year. He left Brown without graduating, having failed the math requirement, and moved to Greenwich Village in 1924.

There he joined the staff of *Judge*, a weekly humor magazine, and the captions for his drawings began to grow into the singular style that characterized his life's work. Perelman also contributed to *College Humor*, until its demise in 1934. *That Old Gang o' Mine: The Early and Essential S. J. Perelman*, edited by Richard Marschall (Morrow, 1984), offers substantial and delightful evidence of his skill as an artist in the school of Ralph Barton and John Held, Jr., and as a well-advanced parodist and dementia praecoxswain, to turn Robert Benchley's phrase for the kinds of pieces they were both then writing.

Perelman went abroad for the first time in 1927 and again, on his honeymoon, in 1929, the year *Dawn Ginsbergh's Revenge*, a collection of his magazine pieces, was published by Horace Liveright. It was noticed by Groucho Marx, who soon latched onto Perelman as a writer. The movies *Monkey Business* (1931) and *Horse Feathers* (1932), both written in collaboration, show his handiwork. In December of 1930, he began his nearly half-century association with *The New Yorker*.

Although working with the Marx brothers provided him with inexhaustible storytelling capital — written and oral — over the years, Perelman often felt that the glamour of the connection upstaged the value of his work. In a 1976 letter to Deborah Rogers, his British agent at the time, he responded to a publisher's request to include extracts from his Marx brothers scripts in his next book:

> I am fucking sick and tired of my endless identification with these clowns. If it is not yet apparent after 50 years of writing for publication in the U.S., Britain, and elsewhere that my work is worth reading for its own sake; if illiterates and rock fans (synonymous) can only be led to purchase my work by dangling before them the fact that I once worked for the Marx brothers, then let us find some other publisher.

Over the next decade the Perelmans shuttled back and forth between coasts. In Hollywood they wrote as a couple for films; back East, for the stage. *All Good Americans* and *The Night before Christmas* were both produced and made into films. By himself, Perelman wrote radio and theater sketches and continued to collect his magazine pieces: *Strictly from Hunger* appeared in 1937, *Look Who's Talking!* in 1940. With their two young children, Adam and Abby, the Perelmans lived in the Village and on their farm in Bucks County, Pennsylvania — purchased in 1932 with West, whom they later bought out. West intended to settle there as well, but in December 1940, during one of his own screenwriting stays in Hollywood, he and his wife of eight months, Eileen McKenney, were killed in a car accident.

Hollywood, with its "ethical sense of a pack of jackals" and producers who "had foreheads only by dint of electrolysis," was the place Perelman most loved to loathe. He did time there strictly for money, and as soon as he could afford to escape, he did. In 1943 he teamed up with Ogden Nash to write the musical *One Touch of Venus* (music by Kurt Weill), a Broadway smash that enabled him to end his servitude in the studio system. Not that he was set up for long: between private-school tuition, support of his mother (his father died in 1926), periodic psychiatric help, his determination to travel, and the costs of two households and an office, staying solvent was a frequent anxiety.

Hoping for another big score, Perelman wrote the musical *Sweet Bye and Bye* with his friend Al Hirschfeld in 1946 (songs by Vernon Duke). In the wake of its closing out of town, the editor of *Holiday* magazine proposed that Perelman and Hirschfeld go around the world. The accounts of that trip, with illustrations by Hirschfeld, were collected in *Westward Ha!*, brought out in 1948 by Simon and Schuster (Perelman's publisher from then until his death).

Perelman's passion for travel soon became inseparable from his search for copy. "The humorist," he said, "has to find himself in conflict with his environment. . . . He has to pretend that he's sublimely unhappy in most places, but that's a very small price for me to pay for the pleasure I derive from being in Africa or Asia." *The Swiss Family Perelman*, also illustrated by Hirschfeld, describes a second global trip in 1949, this time undertaken by the whole clan.

In 1955, the producer Mike Todd — "an ulcer no larger than a man's hand" — hired Perelman to write additional dialogue for his extravaganza *Around the World in 80 Days*. Much as Perelman professed to despise the job and the man, both together inspired him. At the point of maximum tension between his values and Todd's, he wrote some of his most ecstatic letters.

Perelman won an Oscar for the picture and parlayed the acclaim into a series of writing assignments for television. For the cultural series *Omnibus* he wrote "The Big Wheel," a tribute to burlesque starring Bert Lahr, and "Malice in Wonderland," three sketches about Hollywood. In 1962 he again wrote for Lahr, this time a star turn in *The Beauty Part*, a well-received play that had the ill luck to open — and close — during a printers' strike against the city's newspapers.

Toward the end of 1969, the Perelmans went to England for three months. In January they returned to Bucks County with the flu. Laura, in fact, was also suffering from a recurrence of breast cancer; she died in April of 1970 at the age of 58. Unable to work and claiming to find the States intolerable, Perelman fell back on his habitual recourse with a vengeance. He sold the farm in Bucks, auctioned off nearly all of his and Laura's possessions, and announced his decision to move to England.

In an autobiographical reflection for *The New Yorker* that never ran, Perelman wrote:

> I clearly envisioned myself ripening there in the afternoon of life,
> a mellow old philosopher with an endearing twinkle, a familiar
> and beloved figure in the neighborhood. (How this transforma-
> tion would be accomplished, I wasn't quite sure, but no matter.)

No sooner was he settled in than he again took off around the world, this time in imitation of Phileas Fogg's journey in the original Jules Verne story. On his return to London, he was lionized a little while longer before beginning to experience a more normal life. By the second year, it had palled. He was lonely; he was out of touch with his idiom. He found English life both "too couth" and too boorish. He told Alan Brien of *Punch*:

> I was talking in the street with a friend of mine, a real Cockney with a real Cockney accent. An upper-class Englishman I knew chanced by and I introduced them. I could see him looking at me and at my friend. He didn't say anything, of course. But I could see him altering his attitude toward me and wondering why I was mixing with people of that sort. I couldn't stand that. A barrier rang down.

By May of 1972, he was back in New York. He continued to travel and write. *Vinegar Puss* (his twentieth book) appeared in 1975; *Eastward Ha!*, an account of yet another global swing (his sixth), in 1977. The following year, when he was 74, he proposed to the editor of the London *Sunday Times* the idea of recreating, in reverse, a famous 1907 road race.

In the fall of 1978, Perelman was driving his 1949 MG from Paris to Peking in company with an English friend, Eric Lister, and Sydney Beer, an MG specialist. He was looking for trouble for the last time, and finding more of it than he wanted. Although on the trip Beer bitterly accused him of being "a word man," Perelman gave up writing about the trip after finishing only 38 pages—the first and last assignment he ever failed to complete. By September 30, however, the drive was not yet the debacle it would become. From Pakistan he writes: "Thus far the high point of the trip (in every sense) was Afghanistan—the people are the nicest, most colorful, and filthiest."

At the time I was also in a colorful and filthy place, or two of them: Manhattan and the production studio of *The New York Review of Books*, where I was setting type by day and by night working tentatively on my first piece of writing. After six years in New York, I was still burdened by naïveté and the feeling that my life was faintly absurd. Even so, I had a few preoccupations and thought that if I could express them, I would find some relief, if not a starting point. I was 30.

One evening, an editor at the *Review* saw that I was working on something of my own and asked to see it. Since I wasn't sure yet what I was up to, I hoped her remarks would be brief. She said simply, "I think you should send this to Perelman."

As a teenager in Oklahoma City, my father, himself an exceedingly funny man, read Perelman's early work in *College Humor*, reprinted from *The Brown Jug*. By the time Dad became editor of the MIT *Voodoo*, Perelman had published *Dawn Ginsbergh's Revenge*. Dad's recollection of "How to Fall out of a Hammock," from that book, was nearly reverent. Lest he think he had any more influence over me than he already had, I'd never read it. Somehow I'd also never become aware of Perelman as a public figure. I was raised to think of him as living in the Pantheon, not in an apartment, much less fifteen blocks from where I lived.

Of course you could write to him in care of *The New Yorker*. But what could you say that wouldn't be a gross presumption? As he wrote E. B. White, the standard fan letter is so obnoxious it generally ends in a request for a small loan until Easter.

As a first exercise in sedulous aping, I paraphrased the youthful Heinrich Heine's first letter to Goethe, then 72. I identified my source and tried to allow for the fact that I was not one of Germany's great lyric poets but instead probably one of the simpler people in town. I was pretty sure the letter would go straight into the wastebasket with the rest of that day's pile of unsolicited piety.

After reaching Peking, minus his car and companions but with a case of pneumonia, an exhausted Perelman flew home to New York in December and settled back into his modest apartment in the Gramercy Park Hotel.

Nobody suffers from future shock around Gramercy Park. *Michelin* calls it "one of the spots in New York which most recall the past," and indeed there are few signs of the present. The park is bounded by one of the city's earliest apartment buildings and by nineteenth-century townhouses, pristine classical revivals in several styles. Number 16 to the south is the Players Club (Perelman was a member), founded by the actor Edwin Booth in 1888. Next door is the National Arts Club, the handsome old home of a former governor: bas-relief heads of Shakespeare, Milton, Goethe, and Dante surround that of Ben Franklin on the wall outside. To the west are three-story red brick homes framed by wisteria and black cast-iron balconies. Perelman had a writer friend at number 4 and also occasionally visited number 19, Ben Sonnenberg's fine mansion to the southwest. Residents have keys to the kempt park, with its hearty trees and large black urns full of red geraniums. In the middle, an undefiled Edwin Booth rises from a throne chair as Hamlet, hand on heart.

From Room 1621 in the Gramercy Park Hotel, if Perelman stood at the window he could see just enough of the pretty parts to remind him of London. But the hotel is also on an axis that took him back to his earliest days in New York: two blocks north, at 23rd Street and Lexington Avenue, is the Kenmore Hall Hotel, where between 1927 and 1932 Perelman used to visit his brother-in-law, Nathanael West, the assistant manager. West was already practicing the largess that he became better known for later at the Sutton, uptown. From the Kenmore, they could wander to the Village, nearer Perelman's digs, for a meal at Siegel's on Sixth Avenue — dinner was 85¢. Perelman introduced West to the columnist known as Susan Chester there one night; West used the letters she showed him as the basis for *Miss Lonelyhearts.*

In 1979 the Gramercy Park Hotel was also reasonably cheap, and convenient to Perelman's essential haunts. Within a mile-and-a-half's walk were *The New Yorker*, the Mercantile Library, where he subscribed, the Coffee House — in its day an offbeat club frequented by editors and writers, like his beloved Robert Benchley — and the Century Club, to which he also belonged. Even handier were the Second Avenue Deli on 10th Street and Hammer's Dairy Restaurant on 14th. Right around the corner, at Walsh's Chop House on 23rd, he could dine on one of his favorite standbys — a ham steak with raisin sauce and sweet potatoes. Shops were a block away on Third Avenue. The cost of a danish at the Gramercy Pastry Shop (since 1932) served as Perelman's consumer price index, and a jump seemed to alarm him more than a stock slide might. Three doors down was the Gramercy Park Flower Shop, where every Christmas he ordered a dozen yellow spider mums sent to "the two most angelic people in America," his old screenwriting friends Frances and Albert Hackett. If he was visiting Al Hirschfeld on 95th Street, he could hop on the Third Avenue bus. As he wrote a friend in England, "Where I'm living there's an affable Chinese to whom I take the laundry; a discount store for drugs; and a bakery with seeds in the rye. What more do I need?"

The hotel itself gave no sign of its distinguished occupant, unless you thought to take Saul Steinberg's famous *New Yorker* cover, framed in the lobby, as a clue. Other than that, most of the color was provided by the rock'n'roll clientele, putting up close to their gigs in the Village and nearby. If you'd asked them who wrote *The Road to Miltown*, they'd probably have guessed the Rolling Stones.

After catching up on his mail, Perelman answered my letter in January, 1979. We wrote some more, and in the middle of March he invited me to meet for dinner. I was keen, of course, but also wary. As Perelman's friend Raymond Chandler wrote: "Never Meet a Writer if You Liked His Book." I girded myself for the possibility that fame had warped him, and spent the afternoon seeing the last of a silent film series as insurance against having nothing to say.

Perelman told me to meet him at Sal Anthony's, a two-story family restaurant on Irving Place, south of Gramercy Park. Outside the entrance, on the second floor, is a plaque that says O. Henry once lived there and wrote "The Gift of the Magi" in "two feverish hours." Perelman, who could spend a day on a paragraph, must have snorted at that.

Remembering a description of him from *Time* (and forgetting he'd written it himself as a parody of *Time*-ese), I expected a "tall, stooping figure," suave and self-important. Instead I saw, stylishly but unself-consciously posed at the bar, a small man, quietly but beautifully dressed. He had freckled skin, cheeks mapped with spidery blood vessels, and light blue walleyes, large and expressive behind gold wire-rim glasses.

One eye found me, then the other followed; his stare was never quite dead-on. His hands were graceful, whether miming, smoothing his hair, or characteristically resting one finger across his mustache—a gesture both elegant and slightly protective. For a satirist he seemed fittingly, if barely, stigmatized: the index fingers curved gradually in opposite directions. His voice was pleasantly croaky, and his Rhode Island accent gained distinction as it stamped his precise and delightful speech.

Perelman was one of those people who make you feel as charming as they are. I talked about the Chaplin I'd just been watching; he *knew* Chaplin. I talked about Beerbohm; he'd once escorted Elizabeth Taylor to Oxford (she was consulting a doctor) and seen the undergraduates react just as violently as they had to Zuleika Dobson's first visit. He was dazzling company and yet completely modest—naturally so, and never as a point of style.

After dinner we walked back to the hotel, and Perelman excused himself for a minute—"I have to go to the sandbox." He never said anything in an ordinary fashion, but every spin was spontaneous. We had a nightcap in the bar, and I ordered an unusually stiff liqueur. Depression followed: the audience would shortly be over, and I'd probably live another forty years. He put me into a cab and said he hoped we'd become good friends.

I wrote Sid a follow-up note and included two articles from the *Times*, one concerning a snake heist, the other a university in Ohio that was giving college credit for delivering children by the Lamaze method. When I met him again for dinner he showed up with his own sheaf of clippings, plus a small gift—a seam-ripper that doubles as the perfect tool for clipping items from a newspaper.

No longer Sid's guest, I insisted on paying for myself. He protested ("I mean to speak to you about this conceit"), but we split the tab thereafter. That may be why I never saw evidence of his putative stinginess, although once when he was giving me change and I said, "Are you sure you're not giving me too much?" he answered, "No, I have the soul of a bookkeeper." To me he seemed generous. There was a marked appropriateness about his gifts or gestures that gave them their value. Clare Hollingworth once told me about the time Sid took her to have her first pizza. I laughed, and she said, "Oh, but it was a *superior* pizza." No doubt it was.

His best gifts, of course, were his enthusiasms, and in spite of everything, one of them was still New York. Like a Kafka character, the New Yorker is "constantly on trial for something the nature of which he doesn't understand," he told Mary Shenker. The steady smell of garbage and the paucity of good slang were more recent complaints. But as he'd discovered in London, he needed New York for his work, and my own relative ignorance of the city may have served to resurrect some of his excitement about it. There was scarcely a block in the city, the Village especially, that didn't speak to him.

One night early on I was walking home late from a ballet class — "twirling," Sid called it — and swung by his hotel. I thought of phoning him from the lobby but hesitated, picturing him in the middle of a more or less permanent salon in his rooms, which I hadn't yet seen. After circling the block once I finally dialed and asked him what he was doing. "I'm poised here looking like I'm about to make an epigram, and all I've got in my head is butterscotch." I asked if he wanted to go have some dessert, and he sounded overjoyed to be sprung from his solitude. That was my first inkling that his life was not exactly the Olympian bower I'd imagined. He looked very sharp as usual, like an old artist, and wore a plaid shirt with a dark tie.

That night I borrowed a copy of *Dawn Ginsbergh's Revenge*, inscribed to his wife, Laura, "who is funnier than Jimmy Durante." He spoke of her infrequently but easily, with deference and affection. We talked about other books as well — a natural way for cautious people to reveal themselves and begin catechizing each other. Was I right in assuming he was a polymath along the lines of an Edmund Wilson? He gave an embarrassed laugh (he never pretended to the erudition critics attributed to him) and, by way of answering, said the most learned people he'd known were Wilson, Ogden Nash, and Aldous Huxley. He showed me his signed copies of *The Waste Land* ("Inscribed for Sid Perelman by T. S. Eliot in homage") and *On Poetry and Poets* ("Some people think my books are funnier than yours") and talked about Chandler, whom he was rereading at the time. He was in the middle of V. S. Pritchett's *The Living Novel*, as well as Karl Menninger's *Love and Death*. I also carted off Flann O'Brien's *At Swim-Two-Birds* and *Hand-Made Fables* by George Ade. Sid was particularly keen on "The Fable of the Waist-Band that was Taut up to the Moment it gave way" (it figures in a note to E. B. White). I got hooked on that, and sentences such as "Effie was just at the Age when a Girl has to be Deformed to prevent her from being a fairly Good Looker" and "Like all high-class Boarding Houses, it was infested by some Lovely People" (one Ring Lardner must have liked). The only passage Sid had marked, however, was from "The Civic Improver and the Customary Reward":

The Plain People are worth dying for until you bunch them and give them the cold Once-Over, and then they impress the impartial Observer as being slightly Bovine, with a large Percentage of Vegetable Tissue.

He talked about his other favorites: Beerbohm's *Seven Men*, Zola's *Au Bonheur des Dames*, which he loved for its mastery of department-store culture, and the Goncourt brothers' journals. This last brought him to a sore point about his own work, in particular the autobiography he'd long since contracted to do — he'd already cannibalized his life more than anybody realized. He said the trouble with old writers was that they repeated themselves, and in trying to mine the past for something new he just couldn't remember it right. The tediousness of having to dredge up period material — he was rereading the magazine *Snappy Stories* on microfilm in the public library — made him wish he'd kept even the skimpiest diary to jog his memory. The only advice he ever presumed to offer me about writing was that I keep a journal.

Sid read to feed his fancies, and even when he read more seriously he wasn't systematic. If he saw himself as part of a tradition, he derived no solace from identifying with his peers in an earlier age. (I once asked him if it was reassuring to read his praises, and he said wryly, "Yes, every night.") He told me his two unachieved goals were to speak perfect French and play jazz piano.

In mid-April we had dinner at Sweet's on Fulton Street — another part of New York I'd never been to and a section Sid specially liked. In the cab downtown he said he'd had dinner the night before with Lillian Hellman and was finding her increasingly difficult to take. "Theirs was a very ambivalent relationship," a friend of his told me: "He detested her and she detested him." That night he said Lilly had once given him a play of hers to read and asked him to really lay it on the line. He demurred at first, but she insisted she could take it. When he went ahead, she didn't speak to him for a year and a half. All the same, in old age they vacationed together in Florida with other friends, and a card from her inside his copy of *The Hite Report* reads: "A testament to how young I think you are."

He mentioned that he'd agreed to have lunch with Dashiell Hammett's biographer, Diane Johnson, and was in a quandary as to what to tell her. After all, he had his own autobiography to think of, or as he put it: "Macy's doesn't tell Gimbel's." He alluded darkly to a tale involving Nathanael West (it found its way to her book anyway, through another source), but his own buttoned-up memoir of West in *The Last Laugh* doesn't mention it. West had saved Hammett by giving him free board at the Sutton Hotel while Hammett wrote *The Thin Man* and, as Sid told it, when West was on his uppers in Hollywood, the now-famous Hammett pointedly said that West could expect no financial help from him.

The story still galled Sid, as did another that concerned West. Sid claimed that within days of West's death in a car crash, Bennett Cerf called to ask for the return of the advance on West's next novel, a matter of about $150. When they next encountered each other, taking refuge under an awning during a rainstorm, Sid pounced on him. In Sid's version, Cerf was wearing a white suit that ended up covered in mud.

As fresh as his indignation over an old insult could be, Sid was too good a storyteller to be merely sore. His outrage was vigorous and entertaining. He told a story about a war-bond tour in the forties that took him and several other writers as far as Texas. After the bond pitch, Stanley Marcus guided him personally through Neiman-Marcus in Dallas. After showing off a fine jewelry display, Marcus said with an air of noblesse oblige, "Surely there's something here your wife would like—earrings, a brooch . . . ?" Sid considered. "Well, yes, I think she'd like these earrings here." Marcus snapped his fingers at the saleswoman behind the counter, told her to wrap them up, and left. The woman said, "That'll be $1,200."

Sid had a highly polished repertoire of stories that he delivered as if they were brand-new, but even the new ones came out perfect the first time. When you realized how flawlessly he spoke and how slowly he wrote, you began to appreciate the standard he held himself to in his work.

At Sweet's I talked about the seder I'd just been to, in particular about the plague of frogs. Sid said, in earnest (I say that for readers who assume such a writer must be a relentless put-on artist, which he wasn't), that he'd read a book about the plague once and that in fact they were very tiny frogs. A short pause. "Blue points," he added. "Delicious."

Sid was a fanatic for dessert and ordered blueberry pie. The topping looked like spackling compound and a good bit of it somehow ended up plastered on his cuffs. Walking around the Village later, he said he wanted to find another restaurant so he could finish off the rest of his suit. Apropos the dry-cleaning problem, I mentioned having read that the curator Henry Geldzahler had once worn a porcelain bow tie to an art opening. Sid asked me if I'd be embarrassed if he wore a ceramic hat to the theater; I said fine, as long as it wasn't earthenware. He said thoughtfully, "In that case, maybe I'll wear my Spode vest." Then his hat blew into the street, and although he occasionally betrayed his age by shuffling slightly, he streaked after it as nimbly as a stunt man. He said it was the seventh time it had happened that day.

It seemed proper that Sid should live in a hotel, where he stood a greater chance of being abused in a stimulating way than if he'd lived entirely by himself. He wasn't a kvetch, as I knew him; his crotchets were comic, and while he was certainly capable of real rage, he could also feign an antic apoplexy. He complained that the morning maid (whom he calls Isosceles in a letter) was filching some special pencils he'd brought back from Japan and that she had stopped tucking in his bedclothes on the grounds that he was a "tousler." One morning he called, ostensibly beside himself, to say that after shaving he'd headed for the living room in his shorts and bumped into a couple standing there with suitcases. They insisted it was their room and were unimpressed by his claim to have lived there six years. When he phoned the desk, the clerk said the couple must have taken the wrong key. As Sid was pleased to point out, from the registration counter to the room keys is a reach of about six feet.

Sid said happiness was "a brown paper bag of possessions and a room in the Mills Hotel" (or Dixie, sometimes), and for a cosmopolite he'd come close to his ideal. His apartment consisted of two moderate-size rooms and a kitchenette, equipped with a hot plate and a counter oven, restaurant-style stainless steel for two, a sweet potato, and a rubber fried egg from Japan. In the living room, among a small but very personal collection of art works, was Saul Steinberg's *Egypt Still Life*, a collage whose focal motif is a wrapper of Chinese toilet paper with the happy brand name of Kapok. (Screenwriting, Sid wrote, was "an occupation akin to stuffing kapok in mattresses"; the air in New York was "like kapok twice-breathed.") Steinberg hadn't let him buy it but accepted in exchange Sid's offer of a copy of *Ulysses*, inscribed by Joyce. The set and costume designer Aline Bernstein, Thomas Wolfe's mistress, had given it to him.

Except for a Victorian swivel chair, the furniture was largely the hotel's, which made it all the more appropriate, somehow, that on his dresser were a number of Steinberg artifacts—a false matchbox, notebook, and fancifully labeled wine bottle, all gifts. Why so many tokens from the artist? Steinberg was indebted, he said, to anyone who saved him time, and when he arrived in America in 1942 and encountered Sid's work, his first experience of "the popular native avant-garde," it gave him an invaluable shortcut to the clichés of American culture.

At the time I met Sid, he was no longer so sure he had the inside track on those clichés. *The New Yorker* was hanging onto his pieces, and he said he'd recently got back a set of galleys edited by an unidentifiable hand. I asked him why he didn't try to find out the reason, and he said that, unlike Thurber, he'd never been able to be pushy about his work. "You know me, Patient Griselda. Can't you just see me in my pinafore?" He was anxious that his readers would think he'd stopped writing—they no longer sent him the oddball clippings that gave him ideas. I came over once just after he'd seen

Robin Williams do a bit on a talk show, and he was both baffled and distressed. If people wanted to be bludgeoned to death by maniacs, where did that leave him?

In spite of such discouragement, Sid indulged himself very little in backward looks and not at all in self-pity—he had too much nerve and too much industry. He continued to examine his world as keenly as he knew how and, as far as I could tell, expected as much of himself as he ever had—that is, far more than most do. And reasonably or not, he still felt the financial necessity of working. If he occasionally thought he'd become an artifact—that literacy had outlived its day—his readers set him straight. Earlier in the day, he told me once, someone had called out to him as he was crossing the street in the middle of the block, "Be careful—we need you." This astonished and moved him.

When I was still thinking that Sid was probably used to a diet of high culture, I got tickets to the New York City Ballet. It was performing Vivaldi's *The Four Seasons*, which Sid had said was the only classical music he knew, as well as Stravinsky's *Agon*. In the cab to Lincoln Center I read him Lincoln Kirstein's synopsis of the Stravinsky: "Behind its active physical presence there was inherent a philosophy; *Agon* was by no means 'pure' ballet 'about' dancing only. It was an existentialist metaphor for tension and anxiety." Sid asked: "On the part of the audience?" He said the lights in the theater were the largest zircons he'd ever seen, and waited quietly for what he called "the resistance piece." When "Spring" came, he asked if the corps was supposed to be corn.

The mockery of superstition has been a hallmark of the satirist, and you could say that insofar as Sid dealt with cultural superstitions—that wealth confers character, say—he was true to his métier. At the same time, his fascination with the occult had a serious side, not always concealed by his also genuine desire to exploit the subject for comic purposes. (In his letters, for instance, he interprets one particular séance three ways for three separate correspondents.) That evening, Sid brought the subject up for the first time, so casually that I felt free to say something dismissive. At that he claimed he didn't put any credence in it either but simply liked to keep his hand "on the throttle of the future." He said he thought I'd like the language of the tarot even so, and when I went to London that summer, he gave me three addresses: his bookseller (Heywood Hill), his favorite candy dealer, and his "psychic surgeon." (I lost the note.)

Sid complained that our dining was getting too "Mimi-Sheratonesque." I was content to give it up, since finding places quiet enough—that is, empty enough—for him to hear well was getting difficult. I proposed cooking at my place and asked my mother to send me a tablecloth. I don't know why I thought that would help, but when the evening rolled around, Aunty Con's double damask covered my unpainted trestle table clear to the floor. I seated Sid formally at one end, me at the other, and served a white fish with a white sauce that was hard to see on the plate. Some weeks later, I heard Sid express puzzlement that hostesses had stopped serving beef at parties and were now trying to fob off things like chicken as entrees. But that night, with a characteristic blend of shy grace and invention, he said only, "I feel like Marion Davies at San Simeon."

Not long after that he introduced me to the Second Avenue Deli, a genial place where the maître d' treats you like family, barley counts as a second vegetable, and the waitresses call everyone "honey." I once overheard one of them declare that there were fifty Hebrew words that were cognate in Gaelic, a claim Sid nearly made credible in *Eastward Ha!* ("Pech-and-Schwebyll of that Ilk," "Ichvaisnit Grange, the fief of Gornicht Kinhelfinn"). He admired the fact that you could actually buy a sandwich-and-a-half there, prorated.

My next and last attempt at mutual uplift was to get tickets for *Happy Days* at the Public Theatre. I figured Beckett was close enough to Joyce, and we both liked the actress, Irene Worth. Sid said she had the décolletage of a young woman; he'd seen it once at a dinner party in London.

Unfortunately he didn't hear much of the play, and to salvage the price of the tickets we took a window seat at Lady Astor's across the street and ordered some cake. Sid forthrightly, but with no particular confidence, addressed the question of the gap in our ages, which he felt "was so great as to be ridiculous." I said I didn't see what the problem was, since he'd spent his whole life making the ridiculous into the sublime. It sounds too tidy now, but it seemed obvious, and he accepted it. As a friend of mine put it, "Yeah, too bad you couldn't have met when you were 26 and he was 70 — or when he was 30, and your parents hadn't met yet." He seemed to be generally preoccupied about what his future would bring and appeared to put stock in Yevtushenko's prediction, made on Sid's last trip to the Soviet Union, that he'd live eight more years.

A friend of his had recently told him about a psychic, and he suggested that for the fun of it we should go separately, not letting on that we were acquainted, and compare prophesies to see if we were slated to figure in each other's lives. I think Sid liked to entertain the notion that some things were simply out of his hands, even while he was busy trying to influence them.

In May, then, I made an appointment with a character whose card identified him as a "humanistic astrologer" who read the tarot and practiced something called "TRANS formative counseling." A bachelor who worked out of his apartment, he gave me a cup of coffee and from a series of casual questions established that I was going to London that summer and was trying to write.

Finally we turned to the tarot, and he began laying out the themes of my life as he saw them. The "humanistic" part seemed to mean that, whenever my expression indicated a reading was farfetched, he would change it—if necessary, to its opposite. As the session wore on, his desire to appear credible began to get the best of him, until he suggested, rather tentatively, that a trip to London might be in the offing, as well as some kind of creative work—writing, perhaps. More to the point, by the time we were done I was quite sure, from his detailed narrative, that Sid had inadvertently tipped him off: the King of Swords was all but identified as a 75-year-old humorist with strabismus. He concluded by reading my palm and redeemed his integrity, after a fashion, by seeing in it a future completely unrelated to the one just foretold by the tarot, including a spell in a convent and the assurance that I would not have a hysterectomy. He was a harmless and well-meaning person and pretty clearly a psychotherapist manqué.

When Sid and I met to swap notes he was quite keyed up and showed a credulity that seemed odd in such a relentless student of scam; that it might have been a willful suspension only made it more intriguing. In any case, we had an occasion to talk about ourselves without getting too confessional, and with a good deal of amusement. (The astrologer had begun by asking Sid what his chief value was, to which he answered, "honesty.") My debunking account bothered him not at all.

As the summer approached, Sid pressed on doggedly but futilely with his Paris-Peking saga. Even so, he got around quite a bit and was not so isolated or bereft as his sometimes woebegone expression could suggest. Bette Midler sought him out to see if they could work together on cabaret patter (he felt they couldn't); he met London *Sunday Times* editor Harold Evans at the Century and turned down a proposal to revisit Hollywood, as a possible substitute for the China material. He scouted the charms of a new screen goddess, Laura Antonelli, and an old one, Louise Brooks in *Pandora's Box.*

William Shawn called to have lunch at the Algonquin ("you know, where the guests have those special swiveling heads"), and Perry Howze, an aspiring cartoonist he'd met after she too had written him a fan letter, took him to tea. He trained his usual sharp eye on the latest advertising bilge (one enclosure reads: "Pru—If you were a girl, wouldn't this be the man you'd most want to marry?") and kept stirring what he called his "vats" full of marinating ideas—he had several files full. He hiked up four flights of a walk-up to have dinner with my friend Roslyn, five flights to visit his friend Irene Kemmer, and six flights to come to my birthday party. (He brought a clipping from *The Observer* on "the pinching Lord of Fowey," who pleaded guilty to three cases of gross indecency—"Do you suppose there's such a thing as a 'net' indecency?")

In August we went to see "The Treasures of the Kremlin" at the Metropolitan, and after staring at the cases, Sid said he was going to have his boxer shorts sewn all over with tiny pearls. A trip to the Museum of Natural History was less stimulating—I think we saw a film about lava—but Sid got an idea for a book jacket, showing him typing inside either a mummy case or the black-bear diorama.

The September 10, 1979, issue of *The New Yorker* carried its last contribution by S. J. Perelman. "Portrait of the Artist as a Young Cat's-Paw" describes his first trip to Europe in 1927 and how he got shanghaied into smuggling a conjugal bed from Paris back to the U.S. He's captured himself at age 23, before the evolution of his worldly and world-weary persona:

> In the spring of 1927, I occupied a wee studio on West Ninth Street
> in the Village, where I drew cartoons that ultimately lowered the
> circulation of a weekly named *Judge* to the vanishing point. . . .
> It was on the sixth floor of a building equidistant from the Athens
> Chop House and a restaurant run by the Siegel brothers, and, what
> with my meagre sustenance and my constant toiling up those five
> flights, I became so thin that a Siegel brother inadvertently stuck
> me in a jardiniere, mistaking me for an umbrella.

I hadn't known this piece was in the works and came upon it by surprise in the subway one morning on the way to work. It was the only piece of his that appeared while I knew him, and I was amazed to think he'd been able to confect anything so perfect without letting on. I called him from work and said his phone must be ringing off the hook. Rather wistfully he said no and suggested we each take a door-to-door canvass to find out what people thought. I said, "Then what?" "We could hold hands."

Sid once advised the young Heywood Hale Broun, "No one ever laughed a girl into bed. What do you think they're always talking about Gary Gooper for?" I don't know if Sid ever took his own advice, but when I asked him once why his hands were so cold he said, "They've been insufficiently osculated." Something Gary Cooper would never have said.

Sid was a boon companion to women for many reasons. One was his attractive lack of swagger and proprietariness. As his friend Israel Shenker put it, Sid was "a collection of modesties, lightly worn and easily displayed," although when it came to flattering others, he never hung back. He favored the oblique ("Who does your burnishing?") and the hyperbolic remark. Out-

rageousness only made his compliments more delightful: since they were patent-
ly false, you could enjoy them without having to dimple. He regarded women
as another species altogether—a view that may have accounted for his con-
scientiousness and lack of presumption. For him, certainly, it heightened their
exoticism. One evening I wore a thrift-shop dress that had a peplum (an over-
skirt at the waistline), and Sid was enchanted to be reacquainted with the word,
one of the few he was no longer able to retrieve. He could be immensely playful,
and I suspect he found it easier to be so with women.

Sid also had an instinctive and sharp sense of the underdog. Once when
we were riding a bus back from Pennsylvania, a woman he knew slightly came
to say hello and perched on the armrest of my seat. She said things like, "Sid,
you old card you," bragged about her how-to manual on tax evasion, and
wound up by professing to find my work as a typesetter fascinating and enviable. After she'd returned to her seat, Sid rounded on me with a fuchsia
face and said in a voice choked with indignation: "Did you see how she
patronized you?"

As September came on, Sid heard the call of the foliage and began to
get nostalgic about Bucks County, his home for forty-odd years. After Laura
died in 1970, he said, his women friends told him not to "burn the wigwam"
but to save something for when he recovered himself. He felt that he'd been
impetuous in selling the farm—that grieving people ought to be locked up for
a year to protect them from their mad behavior.

He suggested we take a bus out and pick up his old MG, which a
mechanic in Pipersville was converting back to meet local inspection, and head
southwest to see the Amish country. In the event, the mechanic was confounded
by the English wiring, and we ultimately made the trip in a rented car. We
saw Sid's old house and visited his painter friend Allen Saalburg; saw fabled
farmland, horses and buggies, a cloister, a kosher chicken farm. The absence
of glamour didn't seem to trouble Sid; he was content to ramble, and I saw
no sign of the petulant persona from his work. The more bum the territory,
the more inventive he became—his romanticism was sui generis.

In October, Morley Safer of 60 Minutes brought a crew to Sid's apartment to do a segment focusing on his travels. ("Unlike Las Vegas, which I
very much like, Hollywood has very little charm. I think that anybody who
wants to wrap up a four-year course of sociology has only to walk from Vine
Street to La Brea to get a swift kind of pastiche of the worst that has been
thought and said in our century.") Sid claimed the filming improved his status
at the hotel immensely, although the program never ran.

On the first Saturday in October, Sid and I took the train up to Rhinebeck
to see Clermont, a stately home on the Hudson open to the public. It was
a spectacular day; Sid suspected the lawn had been professionally dappled.

We toured the house and on the way out studied an *objet* decorated with a frieze of Apollo in a chariot drawn by butterflies. I said the motif might be another good one for a book jacket, Sid drawn by wasps—"yes," he added, "or drawn and quartered by Anatole Broyard." It was warm enough to eat lunch on the grass, overlooking the river, and as we heard a whistle in the distance, Sid said: "We need never leave here. We can steal vegetables from the passing trains."

The travel section of the October 14 Sunday *New York Times* ran an article on cruise liners with an addendum on freighters, their itineraries, and the cost of passage. Sid had recently been talking about the wonders of Hong Kong and said the ideal way to get there was by tramp steamer—twelve passengers maximum and no doctor on board. On his second global trip, in 1949, he wrote Leila Hadley: "I prefer the previous way I girdled this ocean, viz., a cargo ship which gave you some sense of accomplishment." American President Lines had several vessels that sailed east every two weeks from Oakland, California. Sid and I hadn't girdled much of anything, apart from each other, but so far the companionship looked promising. Undaunted by his last punishing venture, he clipped the schedule and began scheming how he could pay for the trip by writing.

The morning of October 17, a Wednesday, I was wandering down Madison Avenue and spotted in the window of a fancy hardware store a rather good-looking carryall—something I figured I ought now to have. I bought it and walked to work, wondering what winter in New York would be like knowing someone like Sid. An idle thought, but I remember it because that afternoon, as we were closing pages of the *Review*, the woman I worked with heard on the radio that S. J. Perelman was dead.

This book was a search for a man I did not know well but was certain I wanted to know better. I've not been disappointed; I hope others will not be. The letters do not describe a happy life: "I alternate between violence and despair when I consider what faces anybody who wants to really write as well as he can." How much more astonishing, then, the work it produced. "You can be as deeply moved by laughter as you can by misery," Sid wrote Abby. Whether this book bears him out, I'd like to dedicate my share of it to the memory of my father, with whom it really began.

I . J . K A P S T E I N *

180 Madison Avenue
New York City
June 14, 1928

Dear Kap,

Here are the 18 steps by which the harmless clod becomes the actively disagreeable outlaw, as we discussed it a couple of weeks ago:

Pischer	Schlemiehl
Pachechlick	Schmuruck
Nebich	Schnorrer
Dapess	Pascudnick
Chnyoch	Pascudnyack
Schmielitzik	Pascudstveh
Schmendrick	Schvantz
Schlepper	Schmuck
Schmegeggie	Pötz

I think you will agree that there is a beautiful and mounting anger as it goes along. Herewith also some by-products, in case you need a sudden epithet:

Hooligán	Parch (soft "ch")
Chazer	Schikker
Grubyán	Kalikeh
Bohlván	Laimineh gaylim
Besyák	Nahfkeh

Gephonpheter (a beauty, meaning an old crumb whose speech is bumbling)

Kochleffel (cooking-spoon, therefore a busybody)

I hope this holds you for a while. I couldn't find the program of the Charles Angoff play, worse luck.

It was good seeing you again, and I hope next time is sooner.

Yours,

*Israel James Kapstein (d. 1983) was a classmate of Perelman's at Classical High School and Brown University. Before Perelman's marriage in 1929 they twice shared apartments in Greenwich Village. A novelist and Hebrew scholar, Kapstein was also a distinguished professor of English at Brown until 1969.

PHILIP WYLIE*

64 West 9th Street
New York City
April (?), 1929

Dear Phil,

The lucky gal and myself have decided to inch up on the matrimonial institution and consequently will probably "take the step" (ha ha!) around July 1st, scramming for France shortly afterward. We thought of going to Bandol sometime during July; if I remember you were there then. Is it too warm during the summer months? And would it be too much trouble for you to scribble a few lines of introduction to the local Boniface, old Man-with-the-Inn-Pitched-on-the-Cliffs or whatever his name is?

Nothing around here to make the blood hammer at one's temples. I signed a contract with the Gimlet of West Forty-Eighth Street, Horace Liveright, for three books, the first to appear this fall, a collection of drawings and drool which have appeared in *Judge*. The second book is the novel another bloke and I have been writing for the past two years, *Whiskey Sours*.† What the third will be is beyond me; maybe a book on cheese-making or one of those quaint slabs of ointment like *Through Camelot on a Bicycle* or *The Inns and Sins of Old Provence, by an Old Inn-and-Outer*. You know the type of garbage.

Well, my best to Sally, and strike me pink if I'm not at home when you ring my bell. Do that the very next time you're in town, hey?

Sincerely,

P.S.   That was one swell bit of dental floss Mary Rennels calked into the *Telegram* last Saturday about you. What sort of dame is she anyway? She's one bet the torch-slayers have been overlooking, if you ask me.

*American novelist (*Generation of Vipers*, etc.), essayist, and short-story writer (d. 1971).
†*Parlor, Bedlam and Bath*, written with Quentin Reynolds (d. 1965) and published in 1930.

PHILIP WYLIE

64 West 9th Street
New York City
c. May 6, 1929

Dear Phil,

I press your paws for your prompt reply, and render the lady's and my thanks for the letters of introduction to Crouan et Bowles. We also want to signify our pleasure of accepting your invitation to walk barefooted with you before God the week-end of the twenty-fourth. Do I understand you right:

we are to arrive late Friday afternoon of the twenty-fourth, first letting you know the train? If this is O.K. just drop me a line to confirm it. Check. O.K. Right. Sign on the dotty line. O.K. Check back. Yes, Miss Oberholster, take a letter to Niles Bros. and Nussbaum. Gentlemen: In re yours of the sixth inst., beg to advise that we have shipped the carload of antipasto F.O.B. Wagram and she had on the pair of stockings Myles Crawford gave her for the dance at Hely's.......laugh all this nonsense off, I've just spent a couple of hours reading the Walpurgisnacht scene of *Ulysses* and I'm all of a pother.

I'm spinning around like a teetotum trying to grab off passports, staterooms, etc. "Are you a native-born cistern?" "No, I was born in Nanking." "And how is the nanking there now?" "Oh boy, why only yesterday the man next door caught a nank about two feet long, etc." A flock of dumber barnies than the clerks at the Sub-Treasury I never met. We'll probably get booked in on the destroyer *Maryland* bound for Thursday Island. And oh, the whistle of the wind in the cordage, the creak of the hawsers, and the salt tang! . . .   Sincerely,

HORACE LIVERIGHT*

64 West 9th Street
New York City
June 11, 1929

Dear Mr. Liveright,

[Jack] Shuttleworth, the editor of *Judge*, reminded me yesterday that he had not yet received a request from your office for reprint permission on the material in *Dawn Ginsbergh's Revenge*. Might I suggest that this be done soon, as they expect it and might stir up a No. 5 youth's-size pother if they didn't get it?

I understand, by the way, that you care for the sentimental oil painting I sent up the other day. Please accept it with my compliments and let the little blonde gal always watch benevolently over your household.

Sincerely,

*Publisher, Horace Liveright, Inc. (d. 1933).

KATHARINE and JOSEPH BRYAN III*

Monte Carlo
c. July, 1929

Dearies,

Flash! Have just broken the Greek syndicate, crippled the Syrian Syn-

*Bucks County neighbors. Joseph Bryan was associate editor of *The Saturday Evening Post*.

dicate, mangled the Irish syndicate, and, well, you ought to see Rockefeller. He just wishes he had *your* stomach.

They serve a very good 4-course dinner here, but the wine is extra (so is the dinner). I've been here 10 days now and it's only cost me a trifle over twelve million dollars.

Sailing N.Y. late Sept. and looking forward to seeing you both —
Love!!

E D M U N D   W I L S O N *

Paris
September 2, 1929

Dear Wilson,

Your good letter fell like manna on the American Express Company. I wanted to see you before I left but my feet were awash in lilies of the valley and my head bowed down with tons of bridal net. In a word, I was being married. And you should have heard the pretty squeals of my bridesmaids as I threw them my bouquet of fresh cucumbers with Russian dressing! It was a veritable fairyland.

Well, the book is out and, one hears, has sold out its first printing. I cannot say much for the jejune advertising — "Priceless $2.00" — "This book does not stop at Yonkers" — and suchlike, but what would you, as they say here. So far I haven't seen any reviews except a bushel of whimsy from the *Charleston Gazette* which reveals the fine Italian hand of H.L. I was somewhat peeved to note that Liveright had omitted all my drawings, a little dedication I had prepared, and had turned the thing out in a generally cheap fashion. But the usual plaintive cries of a beginner can't have much interest. Let them apply their Rivington Street methods as long as they sell the damn thing.

The usual flock of compatriots lounge before the Dome, the Rotonde, and the Select; the Coupole, the new and garish cafe here, houses all nationalities, just one big family under their berets. We spent several weeks at a place called Bandol on the Mediterranean which Phil and Sally Wylie recommended and had a good time in spite of some of the fellow-countrymen. The *Republic* sails from Cherbourg the 21st of the month with us below hatches, and it will not be long before you will be having dinner with us. Please bear my regards to Gilbert Seldes and Mrs. Seldes and stroll down Broadway for me some evening.
Sincerely,

*At the time, associate editor of *The New Republic* (d. 1972).

4

I. J. KAPSTEIN

92 Grove Street
New York City
October 9, 1930

Dear Kap,

Can't either one of us smear a little medicated ointment on that large chancre in the groin of Life — no hitting below the parables, mind you — and start the balls rolling again? This Hatfield-McCoy stuff is boloney. Why should I shoot you from ambush? I would hardly recognize you, I haven't seen you in so long, and even if I did shoot, I'd probably bump off your brother Johnny, he must be older than you by this time. Throw away your Krag-Jorgenson and take off your beard, Floyd Collins, I know you.

I often feel that after all Life is only a stage and we are all only players, here to speak our brief piece and then bow off at the command of the Great Showman. Only in this case, I am not a player, I am one of the piccolo-players in the pit, and piccolo-players are notorious sons-of-bitches. For one thing, I am s.o.b. enough not to have got together enough coin to be able to live permanently in Europe, instead I bake my nuts in Sodom here and no Proust to chronicle me or even hand me a glass of poisoned water if I were dying in the street. You know how the elderly Yid ladies put it: *Darf men hauben kinder? Or darf men gayan in collitch?* Of course, college is valuable in making contacts, do not you often feel this, my Armenian friend?....Speaking of that lousy mutton-smelling race, a swell girl friend of ours who unfortunately is compelled to make a living in Paris and thus is far away tells this gag: Party of people sitting around in front of the Dome, one of the usual Armenian rug-peddlers pestering everybody in the group to buy his carpets. Too tiresome, my dear. Finally one gent more bored than the rest lifts his conk from a glass of mixed schmaltz and pernod and says: "I'll tell you, fella, *The Green Hat* was o.k., but that last book of yours was LOUSY." Build your own blackout....I'll never forget that Armenian line of yours which went "Come up my room — coffee-cake?"

The babe and I have settled down with our schnozzles to the grandstand at 92 Grove Street for the winter and are wondering what's delaying the wolf, he should have arrived a week or so ago. Myself, I am through with *Judge*, free-lancing for *College Humor* and trying to write a skit for the Marx Bros. to play picture-houses with in the middle west. Between these various things we manage to eke out bread and eke. The bread is mouldy and the eke worse, but we always have enough to visit the Fifth Avenue Playhouse and see *In Gay Madrid* with Ramon Novarro, a short film dealing with the way the sea anemone catches its prey, and a Fox newsreel for Sept. 14th showing gigantic

5

fires in Fall River and waves demolishing the breakwater at Short Ass, Massachusetts.

Well, Hime, you pitch the next inning. Paint me a word-picture of life under the elms, how soon are you going to scram from that place and join our breadline? Or have you got a novel in you, as they say at Liveright's quite seriously. Sometime when I get a week off I am going to sit down and write you a letter telling you about that place. I can match you bastard for bastard you'll name at Knopf's.   Ever the Staten Island wonder girl,

I . J . K A P S T E I N

92 Grove Street
New York City
October 31, 1930

Dear Io,

I have been so busy birching my ass trying to squeeze out my monthly stint — I said *stint* — for *College Humor* that I haven't had a chance to even pay my bills, much to my own delight. However the pissy thing is finally finished and it's the last time I ever try to write anything with beach-combing lingo in it — you know, "Foreign devil like look-see peachum white girl? Make number one wifey allee samee alongside you, heap long pig yum yum," that stuff. I got the idea from reading Frank Buck's *Bring 'Em Back Alive*, Simon and Shoestore's latest. You probably read it serially in the *Post*; if not borrow and read the bit where the Maharajah of Matzador or somebody has a tiger's claws pulled out by the roots and his lips sewed with surgical thread, then turns six dogs loose on him. Reminds me of the general treatment we used to get from Herman Hunkins.

Before I forget it, have you read Vincent van Gogh's letters (two vols. Houghton and Mifflin)? Don't know if you care for painter's talk, but it's a Slice out of a Life. Also maybe you haven't run across *Letters of Paul Gauguin to Emile Bernard*? Liveright published, also *Intimate Journals of Gauguin*, published by latter also. I came as near to bawling as I have in years reading Gauguin's letters to Bernard. Jesus, guy, if you haven't read it, get ahold of it.

An old acquaintance swam into our steaming ken a couple of days ago. . . . She is turning — if she hasn't done so already — into a tight-lipped and horribly repressed kind of New England spinsterish dame. Really pretty terrible, I can't describe what I mean but it's plenty obvious that what she needs is Richmond's old recipe, a sub-cutaneous injection of hot apple-sauce. Imagine going to your grave virgo intacta. She lives in an institution called the Milbank Home for Girls down on Tenth Street here where they have fancy Spanish grill-work on the door and also on the external lower orifices of the

6

tenants to protect them from roving codpeckers. Some night I'm going to sneak in there and hang up over the fire-place the following motto embroidered in blue worsted yarn "Give a woman enough rape or she'll hang herself."

I see Orleans occasionally, he has become a much better guy; there are still momentary flashes of that curving sneer around the fringes of his puss but they are rare, thank God. He must have been through lean times, by all accounts, he's thin enough to read a paper through him on a clear day.....Your genial memories of Feingold, etc. acted like a physic on a stomach bound up for three days, I flew to the cabinet and remained there hoist by my own petard over the throne for one of the greatest little touchdowns in the history of the establishment. Empty your slop-jar over any of that crowd you see and don't give them my regards. Good old Dave Brodsky! Hardly a day passes that I don't think of Ernie Shein.....with revulsion.

As for the Scotchman who found a fifty-cent piece (but wouldn't give her telephone number to anybody) the less said about him the better. So we can pass right on to that old one — stop me, try and do it — about the gent caught short in Central Park, slips into the bushes and lets down the galluses. Just finishing the job when he spies a flatfooter approaching. Quick as a flash he claps his derby hat over it and stands there. "What's going on here?" demands officer. "I just caught a canary under this hat but I haven't got a cage," blubbers the mook. "Oke, I'll stand here and guard the hat while you run get a cage," offers the shommus. Well, after fifteen minutes waiting for the guy, along comes a sergeant mad as hell. Bawls out cop for being off his beat, cop explains the lay, sergeant suggests they capture the bird. "Fine," says Sarge. "You lift the hat when I've counted three and I'll grab him. Ready? One — two — THREE!" "Did you get him?" hollers the cop. "No," puffs the sergeant, "but I scared the shit out of him!"

Don't wait as long as I did to answer this. The babe transmits her best to both yourself and the girl friend, and enclose my own with that. I look forward to splitting a bottle of zoolak with you in December.

Six Who Pass While The Lentils Boil,

BETTY WHITE JOHNSTON*

St. Moritz Hotel
New York City
October 17, 1931

Dear Betty,

Well, you J.J. Shubert southerner, you Georgia neocracker you, what

---

*Hired by Paramount in 1931 to write a screenplay for her own book, which had won a college contest. She chose not to renew her contract and moved to Alabama with her husband.

7

the hell you mean giving me that Hollywood routine? With stomach swollen with sowbelly and grits, with old Uncle Cudgo bending over your ivory-white shoulder fanning midges away from you, you boll-weevil hell out of me for selling my corpse to a lot of lousy yid producers. But who's crying now? There you sit in your steaming bayou with malaria in both lobes and up to your ass in wood-whittlers . . . and me high and dry in NEW YORK. I admit, it's six of one and half a dozen of the other and I'm heading back to Vine Street and its wistful beauty in six or eight weeks, but at least it's a respite.

Your too, too welcome letter reached me the morning I left California after a six weeks' sentence at Warner First National, which was furthest north in horror. I never hope to work for Columbia and Tiffany, but if Warner's isn't a prep-school for it, nothing is. A flock of beetle-brained wind-suckers with necks hinged so they can yes Darryl Zanuck, walking on their heels lest they talk out of turn, a covey of the most inept mental stutterers it has yet been my grief to encounter—arrgh, I *earned* that dough.....You thought that Par[amount] was bad. What do you think of a place where you're supposed to be in at nine and out at six, where you can't call outside on your phone, where you can't receive newspapers or magazines, where the commissary closes immediately after breakfast so's you won't sneak in for a cup of coffee ON THE COMPANY'S TIME, where the COMPANY owns everything you've got including your cerebrum, testicles, and spleen? All right, they can have mine for all the good they do me in that misbegotten flea-pit called Hollywood.

Europe was swell—the French were nastier than ever, short-changing, snarling, cursing, and generally unpleasant. The Germans were desperately poor and consequently more decent than they like to be ordinarily. We were in Paris, Munich, and Saint-Malo. . . .

At present I'm here for the new Marx nonesuch, the lineup being Johnstone, myself, Kalmar and Ruby (the songsmiths).* There will probably be seventeen or eighteen others before we get through. We stay here six to eight weeks, return by boat via Havana, Colon, and Panama. Out there we'll finish the picture and shoot it. The same thought goes for Arthur Sheekman— fortunately he is not in the picture thus far, but I know my luck....I suppose you may have heard that *Monkey Biz* is breaking records everywhere, personally I think it is much inferior to *Animal Crackers*. Laura just burst in with the information that she would give my left nut for a Schiaparelli model she saw twenty minutes ago. She sends her best....Are you coming up here before Dec. 12th? Ah sho would admire to see you if you do. Meanwhile write me about how you spend the time among the apple-knockers, although I'll

*__Horse Feathers__ (Paramount, 1932), written in collaboration with Will Johnstone, Bert Kalmar, and Harry Ruby.

warn you that I take Wm. Faulkner's word as gospel. Do write, you nice person.

Best,

BENNETT CERF*

Erwinna, Pa.
September 15, 1936

Dear Mr. Cerf,

I understand that you are including a piece by James K. McGuinness in your forthcoming *Kalmar and Ruby Song Book*. If this is correct, please omit the piece I wrote and return it to me, as I have no intention of singing in the same choir as this distinguished fugleman of the late Mr. Thalberg.†

In passing, I should like to add that the actions of Messrs. Kalmar and Ruby subsequent to my writing the piece for them cancel out whatever esteem I had for either. Perfidy apparently is no national characteristic confined to the Irish.

Sincerely,

*Founder and editor-in-chief, Random House, Inc. (d. 1971).
†Film producer Irving Thalberg, along with Jack Warner and Louis B. Mayer, formed a spurious union called the Screen Playwrights in an initially successful effort to crush the Screen Writers Guild, founded in 1933. The National Labor Relations Board intervened, and in 1938 the Guild won an election giving it the right to represent screenwriters in eighteen studios.

BENNETT CERF

Erwinna, Pa.
September 24, 1936

Dear Mr. Cerf,

I should like to put on my most winning smile and tell you to go ahead and run that piece for the Ruby book; but without going into the intricacies of the Screen Writers Guild fight, I should like to say that the actions of the group of which Ruby was a member culminated in a particularly obscene and tragic sell-out. I was on the ground throughout and happen to know that the pandering sons-of-bitches who scuttled the Guild deserve no tendernesses — let alone eulogies from my hand. This is no *boy-scoutisme* on my part; both Kalmar and Ruby knew what the issues were and consciously aligned themselves with the *Schutzstaffl* led by the strikebreaking Mr. McGuinness.

So, to take up your time no further, I must insist that my piece be omitted from your collection. Please oblige me by returning it to the address below. As for my previous letter (and this one), you may forward them to Ruby if you wish. I hope that our next meeting takes place under better auspices.

Sincerely,

9

BENNETT CERF

154 East 56th Street
New York City
February 8, 1937

Dear Bennett,

Would you please hand over the manuscript of *Strictly from Hunger* to the messenger boy who bears this note (retaining with yourself the new stuff I brought in today)? I will chop it up and let Pell* read it, and by God, it'll be a book that only a dreamer and a visionary would want to publish. Thanks a lot.   Sincerely,

*The Perelmans' dog, possibly named for Arthur Pell, then treasurer of Horace Liveright, Inc.

I . J . K A P S T E I N

154 East 56th Street
New York City
March 1, 1937

Dear Kap,

God damn it, man, this is the third letter I've started to you. And the minute I finish the salutation and get into the body of the letter, in accordance with Snead's *English Letter-Writing for Jews and Other Foreign Bodies*, some member of my harem wraps her arms around my neck and before you know it, it's touch and go. She touches and I go.

Let alone writing a letter, I've been on the point of coming up to see you a number of times, but there's always been some tiny nodule to prevent. You may have heard through the grapevine that Adam sneaked into our lives after a successful preview; at the present time he is tipping the beam at a little over eighteen pounds and is so long that we are looking around for some sort of reverse bed of Procrustes. We've tried giving him nicotine and beating him around the head and ears with rubber hammers, but he still keeps growing. No record of giantism in either family, so he'll have to take the rap himself. He's four months and a week old and looks like neither of us as much as like Pep* — which conjures up some pretty interesting speculations. I'll have to get that $1.98 edition of Krafft-Ebing and reread that chapter.

What do you say? How are you? You'd think that the Andes extended sideways between Providence and New York, to judge by the frequency with which we see each other. Maybe we ought to wear clothes made out of llama skins to keep up the illusion; llama skins at that would be an improvement

*Nathanael West, Laura Perelman's brother.

10

over this faded number I've got on with pee on the fly and old Baby Ruth bars in the pockets.

I myself am fairly happy and healthy—with that I'll probably crumble like a cigar ash, but let's live only in the moment, shall we? Let's be desperately gay and terribly modern, shall we? No matter what heartbreak lies beneath, let's drink cocktail after cocktail and hair streaming behind us in the wind, our throttles open, ride headlong down the old Merrick Road and go in nude bathing. Wait till I stop at this drug-store and pick up a tin box of nudes.

We stayed in town most of the summer after I saw you, working away on that jerk-off musical and hating it more and more; finally finished it and sawed ourselves off around the first week last August. Then down to the farm for a while till Laura had to come in for the surgical high jinks. (Incidentally, had an easy time and insists on raising a brood.) Since then we have been living in the city; I've got two acts of a new play done in collaboration with a girl named Beatrice Mathieu (who oddly enough was the girl on whom we founded the character of the leading lady of *All Good Americans*). It's strictly with the laughter and heart-throbs, and is aimed at making a little money.... Beyond that, I have sort of gotten into the swing of doing pieces again and have an arrangement with *The New Yorker* for a while to give them a set number. It's the only thing I enjoy doing in any kind of writing and if I can combine self-indulgence with an occasional check, who's to say me nay? For relaxation, Benny Goodman and his orchestra—about whom you know, of course. If *not*, lose no time getting his records, particularly of the quartette. We spend whatever increment there is a couple of nights a week at the Pennsylvania Hotel, where he plays, and then go up to the maestro's room and sway like boogies while he plays recordings of his broadcasts. Listening to things like "Whisperin'," "Bugle Call Rag," and songs of that vintage carries me back to dim parlors adjacent to Candace Street Grammar School where we used to do the camel walk with immature hussies in formfit sweaters. Maybe I'll wind up being the Proust of the small boulevards off North Main Street.

Pep is out on the Coast still, getting gray in the service. He's planning a trip back here as soon as he finishes up a contract he has with a studio, as he has a book nearly done (I think I told you that).* Apart from all this, not much news; the Laughing Eagle was supposed to come to the house one night with Brounhoff, and we both wanted to see him, but at the last minute either the water-main broke or he developed encephalitis, because he didn't show up. Incidentally, do you remember Ben Clough, or it may have been Percy Marks, delivering some sort of words to the effect it was a pity that words like "syphilis" had acquired unpleasant connotations, as they were poetic

*The Day of the Locust (pub. 1939).

11

or rhythmical in themselves? I came across a phrase in *Time* a few weeks ago which certainly falls into that sphere — "post-abortal septicaemia." Roll that around a bit — am I wrong?

My very best to Stella and the twiglet, who must be a big gal by now. And sit yourself down with that goose-quill and parchment, and give out with the facts. And say hello to anybody you think won't be revolted by the mention of my name.

DONALD KLOPFER*

> 154 East 56th Street
> New York City
> March 5, 1937

Dear Donald,

Enclosed one of the contracts, with my signature witnessed as I believe you wanted it. I hope this is the beginning of a lovely and profitable friendship eventually ripening into marriage (or at least a pleasant rape).

> Sincerely,

*Perelman's editor at Random House after Cerf.

BENNETT CERF

> Erwinna, Pa.
> June 11, 1937

Dear Bennett,

Under separate cover I'm sending the corrected galleys of *Strictly from Hunger*, together with the two galleys of the additional pieces you had set up, "Seedlings of Desire" and "Black Pearl — White Girl."

I think you're okay about "Seedlings of Desire" and if it must be included to pad out the length, the best position for it is as the very last story in the book. But "Black Pearl — White Girl" I don't care for, it's very similar in type to one or two of the others, and I really feel it would be a mistake to include it. If you don't feel that "Seedlings" is enough to pad it out, I honestly think the best other choice would be "Poisonous Mushrooms — Are We at the Cross-Roads?" which I should say would fit in best between "Strictly from Hunger" and "A Farewell to Omsk." I'm sorry that this has to happen after "Black Pearl" is set up but I got a note only several days ago from Saxe telling me that it had been sent through.

Otherwise I think everything is in order, as far as I can see — I included an acknowledgment to various publications, also indicated a dedicatory page

12

which seemed to have been left out. Is it true that a mysterious veiled lady has already placed a private advance order for fourteen thousand copies to be bound in crushed Oscar Levant?   Sincerely,

S A X E   C O M M I N S *

Erwinna, Pa.
June 11, 1937

Dear Saxe,

Herewith the galleys corrected in my beautiful Spencerian hand. . . .

If the Morgan Library calls you up and tries to buy the entire first edition, please be civil to them but quite firm. I know they'd love to own it in its entirety but I'd rather have it circulated among the general public. After all, collector's item or no, we have a duty to the buying public, haven't we?

Sincerely,

*Senior editor, Random House.

B E N N E T T   C E R F

Erwinna, Pa.
July 23, 1937

Dear Bennett,

Forgive me for not writing before about *Strictly from Hunger*, but a splinter got into my ping-pong table and infection set in, and well, all in all we had quite a time pulling it through. But the crisis is past and now we can look forward to many an innocent romp together.

I think you did a really swell job on the book and everyone who has seen it (and some people have seen it down here who have never seen a book before) agree with me. I particularly liked the sobriety and restraint of the book; as I told you in town there is some kind of notion abroad that because a book is humorous the publisher has to be funnier and madder than hell in marketing it. I had to be quite firm with Liveright when they got out the other one, they wanted to bind it in a sow's ear or something...Another valuable point is that it doesn't look like a collection particularly, looks more like a book of short stories and two dollar's worth.

In short, you certainly did *your* part, and now, if there is anything I can do, like canvass the neighborhood and tell the housewives that I get a magic lantern with every fifty copies I sell, just let me know. Or maybe you would

13

go for a parade with floats up Fifth Avenue, with me astride a captive balloon.

. . .

Sincerely,

B E N N E T T   C E R F

Erwinna, Pa.
July 29, 1937

Dear Bennett,

Thank you for sending down the enclosed reviews; the one in the *Satur-day Review* I thought was pretty fancy. As for the man on the Flint *Journal*, he should live so that those pieces are "the outgivings of a long bout with Bac-chus." I am a Jewish Puritan, one of the old strait-laced, non-drinking, hard-riding, Talmud-toting variety, just as sure as Jehovah made little green apples.

I have a subscription with Romeike but must say you run a much faster clipping service. What are your rates? And do you prune apple trees? I have a hell of a problem down here, with no rabbis within fifty miles, and me an orthodox young Jew in a greasy caftan.　　　　Ever,

B E N N E T T   C E R F

Erwinna, Pa.
August 3, 1937

Dear Bennett,

Enclosed one of a series of photographs taken by Ralph Steiner which your publicity department might be able to lodge with a review or article about *Strictly from Hunger*. A companion photo of this one was included in last year's *U.S. Camera*. . . .

Drop me a line in your inimitable vein (the big one in the back of your neck) and let me know how (a) the publishing business is going (b) the farm outlook for 1938; and — most important of all (c) what are the prospects for nooky this fall and winter?　　　　Lovingly,

E D M U N D   W I L S O N

Hotel Fairfax
116 East 56th Street
New York City
February 9, 1939

Dear Edmondo,

I got back from the country to find your card sparkling like a jewel in

14

a diadem of unpaid bills, poison pen letters, and rusty old telephone messages. We would like very much to see you but there is no earthly reason why you should have to bend over a hot stove (with flushed cheeks, occasionally tucking up a wisp of hair on the nape of your neck) to prepare dinner for us. I think it would be much better if Mrs. Wilson and you came in and had dinner with us. This invitation does not extend to your baby, who I understand has a tendency to fall asleep about six o'clock after gorging himself, belching and generally behaving in the worst possible taste.

Do you have a sitter whom you could call in for the occasion? A father of two since I saw you last, you will find my conversation studded with references to Snuggle-duckies, pablum, and strollers. But why depress you in advance?

We look forward to seeing you just as soon as possible.

Ever,

FRANCES and ALBERT HACKETT*

Erwinna, Pa.

July 4, 1939

Dear Frances and Albert,

The less excuses the better. I know I've been a beast. You'd think I would have the decency to reply at least to that letter Albert sent me fully four months ago enclosing the advertisement he got from a Philadelphia tailor. Oh no — not me. I'm the surly kind who spits on your shoes when you try to do him a favor.

In any event, the copies of *Strictly from Hunger* winged in from Brentano's, or from the publisher or somebody; I signed them and returned them post-haste, and they should reach you in plenty of time for the auction.

We have been on the usual rapidly-revolving merry-go-round ever since being in the country; you find that you start off well in advance of the weeds, moles, and grubs in April but by midsummer they are beating your ears down and you retire to the moist cool darkness of the living-room mumbling "To hell with the forsythia appendulata. If it won't grow by itself, I say to hell with it." Anyway, it has been a miserable summer as far as the elements are concerned; drought, tent moth, and pestilence succeed each other and give place to drought, tent moth, and pestilence. And pretty soon it will be fall and none of us any younger, you may be sure.

*Frances Goodrich (d. 1984) and Albert Hackett, screenwriters considered by Perelman as among his oldest and closest friends (*Westward Ha!* is dedicated to them). Their Broadway and Hollywood credits are cited by him in the course of the letters.

15

Myself, I have been creaking along on this radio program, hating it more and more and wondering where it and I will end up.* Last night our guests were Vicki Baum and Bayard Veiller. Baum was very good, I thought, but you can't tell a thing sitting right there in the refrigerator. We have had several good programs, Moss Hart and George Kaufman were fine, and so was Dotty Parker, who was a guest twice before they both went to Europe. Their play is finished and everyone says very good. It is supposed to go into rehearsal Sept. 1st.

The kids seem to be thriving in the country, Abby has started walking lately and runs around through the poison ivy at top speed. Adam has been at me to let him plow the north forty, but I think there is time for that, don't you? Laura is also learning how to walk; she has been doing a lot of creeping and if we can only get her to stop crying and listen to us (of course the poor thing is making teeth like mad) perhaps she can be left alone to play with Abby and Adam.

We often used to think how nice it would be if you could be persuaded to buy a place in Pennsylvania, and we are still saying so. There's nobody we'd rather have living near us, you cunning things. Well, very recently we ran across a place which has just been put up for sale. I thought so much of it that I was practically signing on the dotted line when Laura hid my checkbook. Anyhow, it's really about as extraordinary a bargain as we've ever seen. I took the enclosed pictures on one of my trips there (it's about twelve miles from us) and I'm sending them along to show you. . . . If you are interested, you must see it when you come East.

And when will that be? We would like to see you right this afternoon, or tonight at the latest. Why don't you take a year or eighteen months off, come east and see the fair, buy this place and live on it a few months this fall or winter, write a play, and make everyone happy, especially yourselves? Answer me — don't sit there all hands and feet!

Love from all of us —

P.S. If you have no use for the enclosed snaps, would you turn them over to Pep? I shouldn't like them to get around and have the place fall into the hands of someone who didn't deserve such a bargain. Or maybe you'd like to buy it in partnership with Pep and all three settle down there. Then, after you got it fixed up, Laura and Abby and Adam and my mother and her mother and all your relatives could move in. God knows it's big enough.

*Perelman was quizmaster on "Author, Author," which featured a panel of fiction writers charged with making up mystery plots out of material sent in by listeners.

16

JOSEPH BRYAN III

Erwinna, Pa.
October 1, 1939

Dear Joe,

Do you remember that little Devonshire lass you left behind with eyes like clotted cream and a neck nowhere to be found but in a Maillol sculpture? Well, Joe, I don't want to knock you off your pins, but we're married now — just Maillol and me, and baby makes three. And there'll always be a haggis a-smoking on the a-stove for good old a-Joe a-Bryan. Ah, balls.

Anyhow, it's good to have you back in Eastern Pennsylvania for more than one reason (by the way, a man who once went to Fordham recently told me about the philosophy professor or somebody up there who used to stalk around the campus in his long soutane and accosting a freshman would bark "Take your hand out of your pocket for many reasons!").

During your absence I started writing a book in collaboration with a friend and neighbor down here, which will be called *Home Is Where You Hang Yourself*.* It's intended to be a kick in the pants to this rhapsodic school of return-to-the-land, farm-remodelling school of literature. I believe it would be very much at home in the pages of the *Post*, and I am enclosing the first chapter, which runs about 4200 words. I wonder if you would be kind enough to put it through the mill and let me know as soon as you can how it fits. *The New Yorker* is waiting to see it, also Kyle Crichton on *Collier's*, but naturally I would rather place it with you — in the words of the Jesuit father — for many reasons.

If you are interested, the ensuing chapters will discuss the remodelling of the house, servants in the country, relatives, farming for amateurs, the home-made swimming pool, and a host of related subjects, all treated in the same vein.

Meanwhile, we would like to see you and hear about the big top. We came very near to blowing ours while you were away, what with drought, boredom, and the war. Can you come over and see us? Or vice versa?

*Eventually published by Perelman alone as *Acres and Pains* (Reynal and Hitchcock, 1947). "Home Is Where You Hang Yourself," by Augustus Goetz, ran in *The New Yorker* (May 10, 1941).

BETTY WHITE JOHNSTON

Hollywood Knickerbocker Hotel
Hollywood, Calif.
December 3, 1939

Dear Betty,

You are an old peach, a langorous middle-aged peach, and a slender,

17

lissom young peach to think of one who has worn you all these years as a bright diadem in his hair. And to think of him so kindly that you can part with a magazine as irreplaceable as *The Poultry Item*—well, it made my glasses cloud over with a suspicious moisture.

The only thing I can't forgive you is waiting so long to do it. I had been living in the East all this year, most of it on our farm in eastern Pennsylvania, and got your note the day before entraining back to This Place. I came back here several times to drink out of the poisoned well after you did, with rather long intervals between, but this time there seemed to be no other way of paying for that new screened-in porch and repainting the barn. Judging from your absence, you married more money than I did.

Meanwhile, this is to remind you that I have a rain check and that when the geese start north again we'll pledge each other in a bumper of Madeira. Start saving up now for your prettiest hat, and I'll start saving for my prettiest pair of pants. I'm sure everybody at Le Pork Rouge will say "Isn't that young couple made for each other?" (The clientele at Le Pork Rouge speak very ungrammatically, as you can see.)

Until then, a squeeze for sending me the poultry bulletin, and if I can endorse your note at the Morris Plan or any similar little service, don't hesitate to call on me.   Yours ever,

R U T H and A U G U S T U S   G O E T Z *

Hollywood Knickerbocker Hotel
Hollywood, Calif.
December 4, 1939

Dear Kids,

You know all that shit about "we'd rather go by car any day" and "pfoo on airplanes and trains"? Well, disregard it.

Not that we had a bit of mechanical or tire trouble. Except for a whole day of driving snowstorms in the New Mexican mountains and half a morning of impenetrable fog thereafter in Arizona, the weather was good enough. But the food and the hotels and the endlessness of it — sometimes we thought we must go mad, and mad we went.

It took us exactly eight days, starting from Erwinna at 10 o'clock Friday morning and arriving the following Friday afternoon at five. The car held up like a trouper, and without our conscious knowledge, the fact that it had a heater and a de-icer for the windshield saved our lives in the snowstorms, because the snow kept freezing on the windshield as it fell.

*Playwrights (*The Heiress*, etc.) and Bucks County neighbors (*Acres and Pains* is dedicated to them). Augustus Goetz died in 1958.

Items encountered en route which might interest you are two. In Vinita, Oklahoma, we passed the Silver Dollar Cafe, the *specialité de maison* of which was blared out in big neon letters "Nigger Chicken." The town happens to have a good share of negro residents, who must feel corking when they shuffle by the Silver Dollar. The other item was a lunch we had in Sayre, Okla. It was captioned "Virginia Ham Roll," which set our taste buds working like pistons. The ham roll consisted of greasy pie dough of the sort contained in five-cent pork pies. Imbedded rubber-like in this were strips of fried ham tasting slightly of kerosene. Over the pasty lay an inch of Dole's Hawaiian shredded pineapple. The vegetables were a stone-cold, glass-hard roast potato, some billiard-green string beans out of a can and floating in a water sauce, and two spoonfuls of tuna-fish salad using hemp instead of lettuce.

I don't know why I silhouette this particular meal when it was typical of all the food we had, but the hotels in three instances were even more horrendous. The first night, unable to make Wheeling, where we had stayed previously and knew there was a decent hotel, we stopped over at something called Greensburg, Penna. We got there after dark and barely managed to get up to our room, a filthy affair in the town's leading hotel called the Penn-Albert. Steam pipes ran through the room so we were unable to regulate the heat, and after dinner, we fell into bed. Immediately a roar of band music rose from the street. The town was having its annual Christmas shopping parade and turkey bingo. Thirty drum-majorettes were practicing under the windows, directed by a man's voice on a public address system. We closed the windows and were stifled, we opened them and were deafened. The hotel hung over the Reading station and every fast freight in the country passed through that night. The parade and shouting kept up till almost three the following morning, and you can imagine what we looked and tasted like the next morning.

At Tucumcari, New Mexico, we had a room in the Randle, a matchboard hotel with people clearing their throats all night and peeing into cuspidors. The worst horror was the Beale in Kingman, Arizona, which had a coating of fine gray fur over everything as thick as Gurke's coat.* Men walked up and down an alley contiguous to our room and three women in the next room came in about four and tried very hard to vomit up their drinks without much success.

Here we are cached for the time being in the Hollywood Knickerbocker, where every prospect pleases and only price is vile. It is the kind of place that I imagine Mrs. Goetz and Mrs. West and other ladies with iron-gray permanents flock to; they're all sitting on a glassed-in porch downstairs listening

*Gurke was the family schnauzer.

19

to their veins cracking like ice in a Maine pond. Every so often a Cadillac shlurrs up to the door and a chauffeur lifts out somebody's mother and gives her the fireman's carry to a wicker chair. After she gets her breath, she starts bragging about how much money her son makes a year.

The kids and Lula got here in fine shape and are comfortably installed at Laura's brother's house, but he doesn't mind the noise because he's working at a studio, which is a great insulation against noise and worry. The Campbells* seem to be in similar good shape, Alan is delighted to be out here and is chirruping like a Kentucky cardinal, Dotty is a little less delighted and most of her improvisations on the four-letter words are already familiar to you. Otherwise the whole god damned place smells exactly like a laundry and the people have the fierce deranged stare of paretics. Coming back to the hotel from lunch in the only Hebe delicatessen in town with Laura, I just saw a lady of sixty strolling down the boulevard wearing a pair of shiny black silkateen pajamas with a lace collar and a brooch at the throat. She obviously wanted to tell me how much money her son was making, but I beat her to a stop light and hid behind a bougainvillea.

The temperature is about ninety-eight and everybody says we are in for another hot spell. The only thing Laura and I have accomplished thus far is to decide that this is *really* our last trip here, forever. If we can get the dough to make those changes in our house and repair that buckled bank balance, we hope to blow taps over our glorious career in this branch of the entertainment world. If our estimates are right and we have only one life to lead, it isn't going to be led here.

And here I am rattling away about poor little me and not a word about you. How is everything on Featherbed Lane in Keller's Church and Hicks Street in Brooklyn? Come on, give. Laura, of course, sends you her dearest locked inextricably with mine.

*Dorothy Parker (d. 1967) and Alan Campbell (d. 1963).

AUGUSTUS GOETZ

Hollywood Knickerbocker Hotel
Hollywood, Calif.
January 27, 1940

Dear Gus,

We didn't reply to those last letters of yours and Ruth's out of a combination of growing desperation and the mañana fever that grips one after being out here a few weeks; though strictly speaking there is no such thing out here as a few weeks, it's just one lifeless eternity. As one week faded into the next, we found out that whatever else the picture business was looking for, it wasn't writers. Either the actors were making up the lines as they went along (a very good possibility) or the executives had decided that perhaps people could sit in a theater and look at different facial angles of Don Ameche for ninety minutes without getting jumpy.

However, yesterday—which was eight weeks to the day since we pulled in here—James Roosevelt, who is starting to make pictures out here at United Artists and is therefore completely inexperienced, decided to play all the angles and hire himself a couple of writers for his first picture—the man's obviously a visionary fool—and signed us on to do *The Bat*. We're starting there Monday and if our luck holds out, should be finished by Wednesday. Boy, when we work, we work.

> •   •   •

The Campbells are as usual, with an added touch of hysteria caused by Alan's contracting a light case of influenza of the gut. He held several levees we attended; a light collation was served, with small canapes, tequila—the Mexican equivalent of applejack—and nails bitten to the quick. Dotty kept sneaking Laura into the entresol to whisper "I'll kill him, the cross little man, I really will, the shit" and I was left alone with the Pride of Richmond, whose voice in repose now has the mellow screech of a Nicholson file. Ruth will want to know, I'm sure, that I'm still the butt of the same sort of ill-natured badinage because I insist on eating before 11:30, and that it's very rare indeed when we sit down to break bread before 10:30....They had Johnson draw up some plans for the porch they are also thinking of adding to their house (you recall the one with the electric barbecue or vaginal oscillator or whatever it was) and Johnson designed what Alan calls a late Plantagenet conservatory. From all accounts it really is a horror; Johnson is very fond of stone piers and flying abutments, and it seems that in his drawings he showed several figures dotted about the grounds, such as a woman in Colonial costume, hoopskirt, panniers, etc. Well, you can imagine what the Campbells had to say about that. I had the feeling that Alan may fly East just to scratch Johnson's eyes out.

The children are well, and I was about to say, contented, except that nobody has bothered to ask them whether they are or not. They are still staying at Laura's brother's house and have just recovered from colds which swept them and Lula alike. Their uncle, Mr. West, has been flat on his pratt the last few weeks with a battery of doctors peering up his pecker hunting for a stone of the Triassic period that got lodged in the tubes. They have finally dynamited it, somewhat in the fashion of a log jam, with a musical chorus of wails furnished by Laura's mother, which, combined with two growing children, made the premises reminiscent of Donnybrook Fair.

Laura herself is scuppers awash with sore throat and cold, but definitely on the mend. . . . We are planning on moving out of this hotel as soon as we can find a house and collect the far-flung branches of our little brood. Gurke has been sitting in a kennel since December 1st wondering what the hell life is about—as who hasn't.

I need not comment (a) on Ruth's picture of life in Buffalo, which sounds almost as bad as this place, and (b) your plan to move into the Cooper Union on 39th Street. All I can say is that you almost had a couple of depressed Jews in the next flat, who love you and wish you would write at once. And so, a pinch of the claws from one and all. In writing, address this hotel and it will be forwarded.   Ever,

B E N N E T T   C E R F

                                        Hollywood Knickerbocker Hotel
                                        Hollywood, Calif.
                                        February 4, 1940
Dear Bennett,
     I busied myself the last couple of weeks over our little non-fiction best-seller of next fall and mailed it out to you yesterday. I have found a title I like very much and everyone who has heard it has shared that opinion, but just to keep your taste buds working, I'll leave it for you to savor when the ms. reaches you.*

     I believe we can rate a good thwacking blurb when the time comes from Alec Woollcott, who has told Dotty Parker several times that mine is the only stuff being written which makes him laugh out loud. I'm sure Dotty also will oblige, as well as Scott Fitzgerald, who has been saying some very complimentary things. (I apologize for my immodesty, but I suppose these things are the life-blood of commerce.)

     Please plant a passionate kiss on the foreheads of Don and Saxe Commins, and do write your little school-fellow.
                                        Sincerely,

*Look Who's Talking!

A U G U S T U S   G O E T Z

                                        1710 Angelo Drive
                                        Beverly Hills, Calif.
                                        February 26, 1940
Dear Gus,
     This stationery ["Samuel Goldwyn Inc., Ltd."] should awaken a damp, boozy nostalgia in Ruth. I am opposed to all Goldwyn anecdotes but it seems fitting that I enclose at least one to go with the stationery, so here it is. Goldwyn

22

was voicing his satisfaction with some script or other in a conference and shouted "I'm so happy I could dance a jigsaw!"

This is a rainy Monday, four weeks to the day since we started over here, and incidentally our last day of employment. It's been one of those usual Hollywood hippodromes; Roosevelt is a very pleasant, affable young man with not the slightest comprehension of pictures, hedged around by several broken-down ancients all at odds with each other. *The Bat*, when we first appeared on the scene, was one of several pictures the company was going to produce; the others were abandoned within ten days of our arrival, leaving everybody free to concentrate on us, chivvy, advise, interfere, goose, and otherwise drive us nuts. The pressure was unbelievable; we turned out 108 pages of screen play within three and a half weeks, pretty nearly a record in the industry. Now it looks very much as if the whole picture was to be shelved and the papers all say that the company is about to produce miniature films for distribution in saloons, toilets, etc. When we leave tonight, there will remain only one moody writer as a remnant of the writing staff we found here, and he is working on a gem called *The Life of Horace Mann*. Your guess is as good as ours about Mr. Roosevelt's movie career.

The Campbells are as usual, which means that they are getting on as badly as ever. I have been on the point of hitting him with a Mack truck practically every time I see him and have only been restrained by Laura, who has some quaint theory that we would all curl up and blow away if we stopped seeing them. They are still eating at two-thirty in the morning; let's not eat right away, shall we, let's have another of these delicious creolin cocktails.

We are living in a modified Andalusian rancho at the address you will find at the bottom of this letter; it's a rather pleasant house, the pleasantest feature of which is a three-month's lease so that if we run into a stretch of unemployment we can scram out quickly. . . .

I have been conducting an animated correspondence with that noted architect and designer, Carlisle Johnson, whose estimate on our remodelling I mentioned in my last letter. His letters are full of good creamy jokes left over from the Izzy Herk burlesque wheel and very little information. As things stand now we will shortly pay him a sum equivalent to the Finnish debt (oops, Ruth, sorry) and put off the building until 1975, when everybody tells me things are going to be a lot better. Meantime we can all live in the cow-stable.

There was a feverish bit of activity out here a few days ago in reply to Martin Dies's brilliant forensics in *Liberty* about Communism in Hollywood;* great talk of organized effort to show him up for the cornpone Hitler he is,

*Congressman from Texas (d. 1972) who in 1938 established the Committee to Investigate Un-American Activities, of which he was chairman. Its charges of Communist infiltration of organized labor, Hollywood, etc., prefigured the witchhunting of the McCarthy years.

but it seems to have died down. The producers, courageous as ever, are now whining that "Hollywood, which always adored Martin, is deeply shocked, etc." (actual quote from *Hollywood Reporter*). All in all, it would shrivel your guts.

Well, kiddies, it's lunchtime; chopped liver on white twist, a slab of strudel, two cups of coffee. On the way back we will stop at the Guild circulating library where we will take out *Fanny Kemble, A Portrait of an Eminent Victorian* and *The Corpse with the Burning Pancreas*. We will then return to the office and Laura will call up her mother and fight with her while I stand moodily at the window and watch the secretary across the way adjust her garter.

For Christ's sake, WRITE. What do you think we're paying you for? Best from Laura....

BENNETT CERF

1710 Angelo Drive
Beverly Hills, Calif.
March 3, 1940

Dear Bennett,

The drumming of your pulses as you read *Look Who's Talking!* came to me across the Great Continental Divide as a soft subdued murmur. When your letter arrived, however, I realized that it was only the hum of the cement-mixer on that new one-story taxpayer across the street I had been hearing.

Lest you become unjustly depressed about the book's possibilities, however, I bid you be of good cheer. To mount the dunghill for a moment, I feel that a good many more people would want to read it than the potential audience which greeted *Strictly from Hunger*, if for no other reason than that two years have elapsed. Judging from the reception each successive piece gets as it appears in *The New Yorker* and the very flattering personal réclame on "Author, Author" (you may have seen Winchell's orchid about my abilities several days ago), we aren't dropping a pebble down a disused well with *Look Who's Talking!* Mind you, it may not out-sell *The Woodcarver of 'Lympus* but it should certainly earn you a better percentage on your money than allowing those piastres to rust away in the chilly vaults of the Bankers Trust Company.

And thus, by a very neat glissando, into the subject of money so revolting to two men of integrity and principle like ourselves. I am afraid that the $250 advance is mandatory; after fourteen months of life on my Sabine farm, I have practically no worms to drop into the bills of my young and the movie business isn't helping to any degree. I think it would be even more foresighted of you to honor me with a check for three hundred, as you did on the previous contract, as you will only have to pay it out in royalties eventually. Come now, coz, don't you think it would be better business to send me back to my typewriter with a happy grin and a high heart? What are you going to do with that money anyway, leave it to the Ellin Speyer Hospital?*

Well, dear, call in Swaine, Cravath, deGersdoff & Wood and draw up those tortuous contracts. I'll have Samuel Untermyer go over them (I pay him fifty or sixty thou a year just to handle my book contracts) and send them on without delay. And don't be a pinch-penny; look what it got Stephen Girard — a measly two hundred million.   As always,

*A dog and cat hospital on the Lower East Side, overseen by the founder.

A U G U S T U S   G O E T Z

1710 Angelo Drive
Beverly Hills, Calif.
March 8, 1940

Dear Gus,

As you see from the masthead above ["Metro-Goldwyn-Mayer Pictures"], we are keeping company with thieves. The motto girdling the lion's head may be paraphrased to read "Fars Gratia Fartis." Although art is its own reward, we are glad to report that we took no cut in salary. All this happened right after I wrote you last; we left Mr. Roosevelt to his new production plans, which embrace making 3-minute films for pay stations and public toilets, and came on here to work for an aged poop named Edgar Selwyn. The current drek is named *The Golden Fleecing*. It's a play on words, as you can see, but it's strictly the story of our lives here. However, we have no faith in its lasting, and by the time the desk-clerk will have handed you this letter we will probably be free to have our nails done and our hair cut on our own time.

First, a high-class joke I made up yesterday at the luncheon table in the commissary. You must understand that I am usually a very silent and reserved party who buries his nose (or that portion of it I can bury) in the double-strength chicken soup, leaving the epigrams to my juniors. But one of my confreres addressed me squarely yesterday as follows: "You must have hated the idea of leaving your place in Pennsylvania, maestro. Was it much of a wrench?" Without pausing my ingestion, I replied like a flash, in a hilarious Hebrew dialect: "No, it was just a little farm with maybe twenty thirty chickens."...Well, maybe it was the way I said it.

·   ·   ·

We got a letter yesterday from Mrs. Art Williams in Erwinna retailing news of the district; Mrs. Hager, a very nice lady down by the covered bridge, was gathered to her fathers, and Mrs. Williams, on jury duty in Doylestown, saw Sonny Bryan, who had been made assistant jailer and is as sleek and fat as the best Cloverdale butter. If you want me to put you up for membership in the jail I may be able to use my influence with him. It's probably the beginning of a distinguished political career. I can see Sonny stretched out in the firelight like the young Lincoln, reading Parson Weems' *Life of Washington* and doing his lessons on a shingle. They do say he is intending to read for the law in Harry Able's office in Frenchtown. The Erwinna Fee-Splitter, one might say.

Dotty is her usual self, also That Man. His voice is now permanently in the upper register and their brawling may be heard in Catalina on a clear day. I am afraid he is Just an Old Scold. They are coming to a plain little New England dinner tonight, just scraps really, and we will sit down about 1:30 tomorrow morning. Last night we were out with some people named Benchley, and also Dotty and Alan, so you may judge who we see constantly these days. Tomorrow night I think we are seeing Dotty Parker and Alan Campbell, and Sunday we are going down to the beach with the Campbells. Laura has promised me that if I am a good boy she will introduce me to a completely unknown citizen named Kratzfuss, he is in the insurance game and has never read a book in his life.

Speaking of books, have you and Ruth read Elizabeth Bowen's *The Death of the Heart*? I am queer for it, please read it if you haven't done so already....Our mouths are watering at the thought of you people being able to see two French films, *The Baker's Wife* and *The Human Beast*; as you can imagine, it takes six months for a picture to get out here.

Laura begs that when you get down to the country you will skip on over to our joint and send us a report about its condition. We are very homesick and a simple description of the manure pile would throw us into sobs.

I in turn beg you to examine this letter and guide yourself accordingly. We rolled on the floor two days with laughter after your last one (me on top of Laura, of course), but when we came to add up the information we'd gleaned, we found you had been playing your cards inside your vest. How about the old lady? What's new along the Tohickon, chez Pratt, etc.? Neglect no detail and remember, *"We Will Not Be Undersold!"*

Louis B. Mayer just went by the window, Hedy Lamarr on one arm and leprosy on the other. It's time for lunch, and if I can only get somebody else to ask me about leaving Pennsylvania, I will retain the title.

Squeeze Cuddles for us, and write reams.

Your loving,

RUTH and AUGUSTUS GOETZ

1710 Angelo Drive
Beverly Hills, Calif.
April 10, 1940

Dear Fellow Bucks-County-ites,

I hope you don't vomit at the above salutation but that's what I was called and there's no reason why you shouldn't be made to suffer as well. The occasion was last Sunday; we had gone around to a Molotov-for-President caucus at the home of a friend and I was listening to B. Goodman beating the brains out of his clarinet when a hoarse voice rasped out "Hello, Fellow Bucks-County-ite!" Turning I discerned the schmaltz-ridden features of Aben Kandel, our new neighbor up there on the plateau in Lodi. Enough people had overheard to start that crimson tide welling up the alabaster column of my neck. He then drew me into a corner, patronized me — "You're in that little place over in Erwinna, aren't you?" — and gave me a brief lesson in remodelling. And here's the payoff. It seems he has a stone hut a few feet away from his house, probably a summer kitchen from the description. Well, he's turning it into a Russian steam bath à la Rivington Street. Gus, you and I'll have to go over there one of these days with Ernie Schaible and have ourselves flogged with a bundle of witch-hazel. If either of us had a grain of business sense we'd quick grab off the Uhlerstown agency of Barney Greengrass, the Sturgeon King. I understand George Eddy has wired his harness-maker to rush him thirteen gross of phylacteries.

. . .

We spent this morning sobbing over your report on the country, as you may well imagine, and we smother you with kisses for your clear-cut, evocative prose. We toiled with you step by step on your tour of inspection, grinned at each new bud, blenched at every mole-hill, and even went with Gus to take a pee behind the barn. I hope that the flora and fauna in Keller's Church came through the winter as successfully as ours seems to have. How about that big dogwood you transplanted? Please be sure and let me know about this, won't you? You know they are said to be very hard to move, and it would be a triumph to transplant one that size. I moved one about six feet high, bushy, but of course very much smaller than yours, just before we left, and I wonder whether it pulled through. It's in that row of young trees that flank the lane, on the lower left-hand side as you come up, right next to a tulip tree I also moved.

Dotty has just emerged from a two-day hospitalization, she caught a cold on top of a lot of brandy (or maybe she just had to get away from Alan, that could be). There have been but heap big fireworks chez Campbell, some really spectacular quarrels. Dotty has been heard to say very freely that this is the end, etc., etc. I am sure you were with us, in spirit at least, one evening not long ago when we spent an evening with them and Janet Flanner and a group of spectacular bull-dikers of the Elsa Maxwell set. The talk was strictly concerned with H.R.H. the Nizam of Hyderabad who dresses up as a faun in a tiger-skin and chases his cicisbeos around the conservatory with bull-whips. Alan was in a sheer tizzy, and although the figures have not yet come in from the outlying districts, *on dit* he came three times. Dotty had a slight cold that evening which did not impede the flow in the least, and in a voice which could be easily heard in Altadena described her husband's brief career in the New York theater. It seems that he was among those present in Keith Winter's *The Shining Hour*, when he made his entrance through French doors in a canary-colored pullover, tennis racket grasped in one hand and a lime squash in the other, with the speech "Cheehio—who's for teddis?" Alan greeted this exposé of his past with a charming but somewhat glassy smile, but I venture to say he beat the living urine out of her when they got home...I shouldn't wonder that by the time this gets to you Dotty and Alan will have made up their mind to return to Pipersville. They have finished their picture—yes, dears, 22 weeks—and if Dotty can make up her mind to come to grips with her mother-in-law, who apparently has been buying real-estate hand over hand, they'll be winging back.

Charlie Freedman, whom you have mentioned, it seems to me, is working on the MGM lot, we have lunch with him every day and he seems very nice. Also Vincente Minnelli, who arrived here several days ago to work on musicals. Seen at a table together in the commissary today: Geo. S. Kaufman, who has become some kind of producer at Warner's.

Of the international set-up, let us say the least. Unless I am in a front-line listening post by September first, we will be back. We're just finishing up this foolish little film and hope to be put on another foolish little film right away so's we don't miss a beat, but that is in the lap of L.B. Mayer, which is a thought for today. From this morning's paper I glean the glad news that Germany has conquered Denmark, ¾ of Norway, and is moving on Sweden; also that Norma Shearer will play the Countess in *Escape* and that Robert Taylor will play the boy. I guess it's enough just to stay alive.

As a final thought, Laura asks me to inquire how badly the collar and armpits on Ruth's fur coat wore this winter. It must look pretty shoddy by now, is her thought. (I don't know what the hell this all means, Gus; sounds like dike talk to me.)

The phone has started exploding with requests for us to go and scratch our producer's ass, so this'll have to be quits. We all of us send our love, and if our replies are belated from time to time, don't be harsh on us. Your letters are a joy.   Ever,

AUGUSTUS GOETZ

1710 Angelo Drive
Beverly Hills, Calif.
April 26, 1940

Dear Gus,

My eyes misted over with a suspicious moisture at yours of even date, which on analysis turned out to be composed as follows:

32 m. chicken fat (also called "beggar's schmaltz")
2 gr. fritto misto
17% Turkey Pee
Fish-hooks, peasants, soldiery, etc.

In case you have summoned up a vision of sunny California with full-bosomed mermaids laying around in huaraches, here is a weather report. The sun has shone twice in the last eight days. As I write, a row of poplars over on Chevy Chase Drive were just uprooted and flung into the sea at Carmel (about 360 miles from here) and two associate producers' hats were blown off at Paramount — but by whom it is hard to say. The children both have had colds since February 19th and there is a smell of white pine and tar around like a Georgia turpentine camp. Also, their father and mother are unemployed.

It wouldn't seem that things could be much worse but they were the early part of this week when I went out and bought a bloodhound. She was three months old and was about half a hand smaller than your Rosie. Her feet were the size of an indoor baseball and when she sat up straight there was an odor in the room like six mastiffs breaking wind. I carried this Shetland pony across the threshold and spent the next 48 hours figuring ways to stifle the baying without actually breaking the skin. Gurke took to her like a brother, the way Cain took to Abel. Most of the time she was skulking in the shrubbery because the children were running after her with a croquet mallet, and the balance was spent stripping the flounces off the chairs and biting holes in the carpet. The first night I got five hours' sleep, but the next I had only two, as there was a full moon and she must have smelled an escaped body-servant. At seven that morning she was back with her brothers and sisters. Do you know where I can pick up a Mexican hairless?

Laura's brother up and married Ruth McKenney's sister Eileen last week and there has been a lot of talk out of them about buying a place in Penna., so if you see anything likely, let us know. He is interested in getting something with a certain amount of water on it (isn't he cute?) and would be satisfied with a piece of Tohickon Creek, or the equivalent. Judging from the real estate ads I read out here in the N.Y. Sunday *Times*, property down our way is booming. But Pep isn't very particular; it doesn't have to be a wooden house, it can be made out of tailored stone, it can have as many as four levels, but shouldn't have too many fireplaces (five will be enough), and he'd just as soon not have new trees, old ones will do just as well.

As regards our homecoming, it doesn't look as if we would get back much before late September or early October. The bankroll has the rickets bad, and it isn't being helped any by the current layoff. We have just renewed our lease on this stucco rabbit-warren for a period expiring Oct. 8th, and what we would like to do if possible is work here till then and return to the country and work on this musical we started when we first got here, say until Jan. 1st, and then move into town. We think we have a good show, with a lot of comedy and plot, and if we could get such a show on in January might make a few rugs and enable us to stick around for a real while. By then the country will be at war and everything will be hunky-dory. Laura will be sent to Plattsburg and I'll sew bandages for the Red Cross.

Why don't you answer my questions? I asked you repeatedly how that big dogwood of yours moved and whether it is in leaf. And why don't you send me a locket containing some of your pubic hair? What do you think I'm made of—stone? And if so, on how many levels?

WRITE WRITE WRITE WRITE WRITE WRITE

BELLE BECKER *

1710 Angelo Drive
Beverly Hills, Calif.
May 12, 1940

Dear Miss Becker,

I hope by this time you have received the correct ms. and copy of *Look Who's Talking!* If it hasn't yet passed out of your hands, or if the change can possibly still be made, I should like you to make one small correction for me. In the piece "Boy Meets Girl Meets Foot," you will find a sentence (I am quoting from memory) which reads something like: " . . . without even a 'What do you say to Paganini at the Albert Hall tonight, Watson?' " The word "Paganini" should be changed to read "Sarasati," as Paganini had been dead for almost fifty years when Holmes said this to Watson. Please see if you can catch this.

•   •   •

. . . In sending a review copy to *The New York Times, please* try to make sure Robert van Gelder doesn't review it, if such a thing can be done. His review of *Strictly from Hunger* was so savage that I'd rather not have a copy of this one sent to that paper at all if he's going to get it. I happen to have made a little study of Mr. van Gelder, who doesn't like any kind of humor too well

*Editorial assistant, Random House.

30

anyway, and happens to loathe anything I write. This is a small detail except that it's possibly the most important review in the country, and if it can be swung to Charles Poore, who really has some verstammt, we can save ourselves a headache. I will consider it a personal favor if you call this to Bennett's attention as well as to Saxe's.

Thanking you very sincerely for all this complicated embroidery.

Sincerely,

AUGUSTUS GOETZ

1710 Angelo Drive
Beverly Hills, Calif.
May 23, 1940

Dear Gus,

I've been doing the same thing you have the past couple of weeks (no, you evil-minded thing, from that comes baldness and mopery): namely, hanging over a radio listening to our stout fellows being pushed into the English Channel. However, one can't resist a murmur of admiration at their strategic retreat; if they can only retreat to that patch of woods in back of Queensland, Australia, I think they will show Hitler "what for." All the same, I think it was rash to remove Chamberlain before he had had a chance to fight back. You know, it takes an Englishman a long time to become angry, but when he does, "watch out."

Well, dear, it begins to look as though your shabby genteel friends from Geigel's Hill over in back of Art Williams' store are coming back, as there isn't a frigging job in sight and we are up to here with boredom and lack of the ready. About all that has kept us here the last two weeks is the fact that we are trying to sub-let this house — you don't know anybody offhand who wants to pay $275 a month plus $15 for gardener, do you? What about Mr. Sassaman in Ottsville or Quintus Lerch? Where are they planning to summer?

We have set the end of next week more or less definitely as a deadline (June 1st), and unless some miraculous job comes along, our little parcel of fun-loving rascals should be winging over the road-bed of the Union Pacific then. . . .

.   .   .

Our love to Ruth, and we count the days.

RUTH and AUGUSTUS GOETZ

1710 Angelo Drive
Beverly Hills, Calif.
May 29, 1940

Dear Old Things,

There is nothing like a letter from the Goetzes to warm the cockles of
the heart, unless it is two letters, and there is a smell of frying cockles around
here that would curl your hair. Need I go into any petty bourgeois exclama-
tions of gratitude for your efforts *in re* Gulden, Petzel, et al?* Or shall I get
down to business, which is starkly the fact that we are all set to pull out of
here this next Monday night, June 3rd? That would bring us into the last ditch
(not a bad name for our place with our present prospects) on Thursday, the
6th. I can't tell you how delighted we will be to get back; you must always
remember that you can at least turn off the radio and go outdoors to find
Pennsylvania, whereas here it's strictly with the ratty palm trees and advanced
unemployment. We have had our share of this latter goody to a degree we
shall not soon forget, and if we don't tumble off the train bleeding from self-
inflicted knife wounds, we'll eat it. Eat what? Dirt probably.

.   .   .

The war I won't even discuss with you; I'll arrive in time to be gathered
up in the first draft and Laura can pull a plow over the fields. We've accumulated enough fat to see us through the next ten years, and I shake all
over like a chocolate pudding when I walk...Funny, but I can already see myself
sitting in the pingpong room staring hopelessly at our checkbook. . . .

All our love,

*Concerning some minor remodeling of their house.

RUTH and AUGUSTUS GOETZ

Bedford Hotel (?)
118 East 40th Street
New York City
c. July, 1940

Dear Ruth & Gus:

Thanks for sending along the *New Masses* review. The next voice you
hear will be that of J. Edgar Hoover, asking a few pointed questions.

The prospect of Harvey's plus the Eastern Shore in the autumn is lovely, but untenable. The family bank balance has shrunk to a wizened condition hitherto only approached by my genitalia, and we really had to stick with
(a) the play,* and (b) the budget. The sooner the one, the quicker the other,

*The Night before Christmas.

32

or something. As soon as the play is written, rewritten, cast, opens, and flops, we will be in a position to talk turkey.

I hope this finds you both in pocket and high spirits, whether in Keller's Church or Buffalo. If in the former, please come and see us chez nous (Monday or Tuesday, as you prefer). Meanwhile,

Love & kisses,

S . D . C O H E N *

Erwinna, Pa.
September 2, 1940

Dear Mr. Cohen,

With respect to our connection with *Sweethearts* and its producer, Mr. Hunt Stromberg, the statement below approximates the facts as closely as we are able to remember them at this time.

We arrived in Hollywood about September 23, 1937, and entered Mr. Stromberg's employ, I believe, on October 15, 1937. Mr. Stromberg thought we might adapt *Arms and the Man* by Bernard Shaw for the screen, and we read it, but the project was abandoned after some discussion. We then read one of John van Druten's plays with the same idea in mind, but nothing came of that either. He then asked us whether there were any plays we might be interested in adapting; we suggested one, *At Mrs. Beam's*, which had been done by the Theater Guild in the late 'twenties. We re-read this, told Mr. Stromberg its salient points, but he felt it was not an important enough idea. The foregoing consumed between two and three weeks.

During this period, on one or two occasions, Mr. Stromberg asked whether we would be interested in doing a musical picture for Jeanette MacDonald and Nelson Eddy. (I believe this duo was also suggested for *Arms and the Man*.) When the possibilities above seemed to have fizzled out, Mr. Stromberg again returned to the idea of a musical for MacDonald and Eddy. He gave us the script of the old musical hit *Sweethearts* to read and played us several records of the songs it had contained. It was his notion that the curse might be removed from this ancient vehicle somewhat as follows: MacDonald and Eddy to be depicted as the twin stars who had been appearing in *Sweethearts* for five or six years on Broadway; married to each other and outwardly happy; but the constant strain of working together, the deadly routine, eventuating in ultimate dissension and strife. He felt that the picture might open with the fifth- or sixth-year anniversary performance, a gala affair to which the composer, producer, and lyric-writer return after years of

*Cohen was investigating a plagiarism charge for MGM.

33

fat living abroad. Following the performance we would show all the principals of the company, as well as producer, composer, lyric-writer, etc., adjourning to a magnificent banquet given in honor of MacDonald and Eddy, where the stars would again be called on to render songs they had been singing for the past five or six years. We would further show them, following this party, at their home in the suburbs, where their respective families were battening off their largesse and interfering in their connubial relationship and so forth. It was Mr. Stromberg's idea that the musical numbers and songs of the old hit *Sweethearts* were to be interwoven and scattered through this modern framework.

We returned to our office glowing with energy and determined to justify the proud motto on the escutcheon of Metro-Goldwyn-Mayer, "Ars Gratia Artis." Taking the above elements, we wove them into a narrative, or treatment, into which we introduced the character of a psychoanalyst for complications (a part we felt was ideally suited for Mischa Auer*). We dictated this to a stenographer from the script department during the period roughly covered by the dates November 10th, 1937, to November 28th or 29th, and handed it in on December 1, 1937. Mr. Stromberg at first was quite enthusiastic, but on reflection decided that he hated our concept of Nelson Eddy's character, and eventually decided that we had departed from his original idea. He explained this again at length. Having been employed for some years in motion pictures, we realized that Mr. Stromberg was determined to produce his conception of the story rather than any variations we might suggest. After a number of parleys and conferences, we then wrote a second treatment during the last two weeks of December, 1937, and the first week of January, 1938, which we handed in, I believe, January 6, 1938. This second treatment was practically word for word as we understood Mr. Stromberg wished the story, embodying situations he had outlined in conference. It was Mr. Stromberg's habit, following these conferences, to send us notes taken down by his secretary during our meetings with him as well as inspirational matter he dictated to her after we had left. We used these notes to refresh our memory during preparation of the second treatment, as I recall, and also received further notes of this type after handing it in.

About January 10th, 1938, we had begun trying to attract Mr. Stromberg's attention to the fact that it would be necessary for Mrs. Perelman to leave his employ, as she was about to become a mother. In the heat of producing *Marie Antoinette*, it was only natural that Mr. Stromberg was somewhat distracted, but finally we managed to flag him, and Mrs. Perelman was allowed to leave the lot on, I think, January 15, 1938. The baby was born February 9,

*Popular Russian-born supporting actor (d. 1967), usually in comic roles (*My Man Godfrey*, etc.).

34

1938, and is today a happy and healthful child showing no visible signs of the mental or physical anguish sustained by her parents previous to her birth.

I remained on with Mr. Stromberg after this date, and shortly Dorothy Parker and Alan Campbell arrived from New York and were assigned to the picture. We had several conferences with Mr. Stromberg, and immediately thereafter Mr. and Mrs. Campbell began work on the screen-play. Mr. Stromberg assigned Mr. Ogden Nash and myself thereupon to construct an original story for the screen based on Dale Carnegie's *How to Win Friends and Influence People*. On approximately February 12, 1938, he informed us that it was necessary for him to go to New York and he wished to put our story into abeyance for the time being. I was transferred to Mr. Harry Rapf's unit, where I was invited to work on a story called *Broadway Goes to College*. I felt that my talents were insufficient to do justice to this epic and on February 15, 1938, terminated my engagement at Metro-Goldwyn-Mayer.

I may add that throughout the above engagement our agent was Mr. George Frank, 1626 North Vine Street, Hollywood, California, whose books will reveal the commissions paid by us during that period and thus particularize dates.

Neither Mrs. Perelman nor I had ever heard of Barney Gerard until July 3, 1940, when your legal staff communicated with us. We had, of course, seen Mr. William Anthony McGuire around the Metro lot during the various times we worked there, but we have never met him either socially or professionally. As for Mr. Gerard's story, which he alleges to have been infringed, neither of us has at any time, either previous to our association with Mr. Stromberg or since, ever heard it. The major story points, identity of character, and plot development, were just as Mr. Stromberg told them to us and himself amplified them. Finally, we received no screen credit; had we been offered it, we were prepared to refuse, as we felt most definitely that it was totally Mr. Stromberg's story and that he himself was justly entitled to any credit which might ensue.

Very truly yours,

JOSEPH BRYAN III

Erwinna, Pa.
September 8, 1940

Dear Joe,

Nothing would be finer than to take a stratoliner off to New Hope (to hell with it, it won't scan any further) next Wednesday night. But the plaintive fact is that we are going into town Tuesday to get some work done on a five-act tragedy on the order of Stephen Phillips' *Marpessa*.* Everybody tells us this would be a great time to bring in a five-act tragedy on the order of Stephen Phillips' *Marpessa*.

If you are kicking around town and care to spend an evening with two middle-aged, shabby genteel people straight out of George Gissing, give us a blow of phone at the Dryden, East 39th Street. . . .

Ever,

*Phillips (d. 1915) enjoyed a vogue as the would-be savior of English poetic drama, although his work is now dismissed as derivative and archaic. *Marpessa* was a poem based on Greek legend.

JOSEPH BRYAN III

"Boiling Diapers"
Erwinna, Pa.
October 22 (?), 1940

Dear Joe,

As you see from the appended message, transcribed in the fine Presbyterian hand of our postmaster, I got your message — but unfortunately about three hours ago, or, I judge, roughly five days after you sent it. Perhaps I didn't explain with any degree of intelligibility in my last letter, but my doxy and I are spending five days a week (Wednesday–Sunday) in NY hammering out a dramatic piece.* Your wire must have arrived shortly after we left last week, and with their usual brisk perception, the locals decided to hold on to it until I got back rather than forward it to NY. Also, as if to further puzzle my poor aching head, somebody had to add some message in the code of the Dancing Men.† I have more than a suspicion that Hosmer Angell may be back of this dastardly thing. . . .

Would there be anything in a picture of a cop in a restaurant, napkin tucked in at his throat and halfway through stuffing himself on a smoking goose, saying to his superior officer (who has just surprised him at his feast): I JUST CAME IN FOR A QUICK GANDER, FALTERED THE FLATFOOT.

Yrs.

*The Night before Christmas.
†An allusion to "The Adventure of the Dancing Men," by Arthur Conan Doyle.

JOSEPH BRYAN III

Erwinna, Pa.
December 16, 1940

Dear Joe,

This Friday, the 20th, would be a dream night for us, and we'll be on deck at seven. In a program I caught on the radio last night, the Vogt scrapple people assured me that from Ardmore to Cynwyd, from Overbrook to Merion, smart hostesses are slicing Vogt's scrapple and frying it on electric grilles right on the table. "Even the guests," continued the announcer, "chip in briskly and aid the hostess in toasting Vogt's nonpareil scrapple to a golden brown." Please tell Katharine we will help to the utmost. Laura's bringing along a mop and pail and will wash the upstairs bedrooms, and I shall varnish the foyer floor.

And lest this turn into a wholesale varnishing, perhaps we'd better leave Monsignor [John] O'Hara out of the proceedings. Unless you feel you must have him, in which event I'll put a horseshoe in my glove.

Best regards, and we'll see you Friday at 7.

JOHN SANFORD*

Erwinna, Pa.
January 11, 1941

Dear Scotty,

Thank you for your note, and as well for your very kind wire to Laura.† Believe me that I appreciate your asking me to do a piece about Pep, and the reasons for the choice. But I am really so very close to the whole thing that I believe almost anyone who knew Pep well would be better equipped. I haven't any perspective about him, just a dull sense of unreality and shock which I am afraid will be a long while in disappearing.

I think that exclusive of his qualities as an individual, Pep's artistic measure is summed up in one sentence of a letter Edmund Wilson wrote to Laura recently, and if you would like to include it in any tribute you run in the *Clipper*, I feel sure Pep would have liked nothing better. "It is at least consoling to remember," Wilson said, "that he left two books more finished and complete as works of art than almost anything else produced by his generation."

Sincerely,

*Writer and close friend of Nathanael West at Brown.
†West and his wife, Eileen McKenney, were killed in a car crash on December 22, 1940.

BETTY WHITE JOHNSTON

Beekman Tower
3 Mitchell Place
New York City
February 26, 1941

Dear Pen Pal,

Lymphatic elderly party though I am, I believe I can match whatever

37

wit and gaiety you might encounter at Buzzard's Roost, N.C. The epigrams may not be as salty as those you are accustomed to at Bagnigge Wells and Brighton, but I think that over a hot bird and a cold bottle we can iron out a number of problems.

The schedule is something like this. I hope to go into rehearsal with our side-splitting new farce *The Night before Christmas* on either Monday, Tuesday, or Wednesday of next week, which means we'll be here in town rehearsing for 3½ weeks. Following that, we go out of town for ten days previous to the New York opening. Hence it's a cinch I'll be here until approximately March 25th. So I urge you very strongly to buzz up as early in March as you can. Don't wait for the dogwoods; you don't think they'd wait for *you*, do you?

If you insist on wearing that formal, I suppose I can always put on that blue serge jacket and white flannel pants. (And we can both eat parti-colored brick ice-cream out of paper plates.) Whatever the terms, it's exciting to think I'll be seeing that handsome, cynical puss again.

Always,

BETTY WHITE JOHNSTON

New York City
April 19, 1941

Dear Bess,

Thank you for your wire on the occasion of our shabby little entertainment, and I hope you weren't cut by any of the flying glass. Despite the press-agent's hurried whisper to me "Take to the hills!" and the shouts of the enraged citizens pursuing us with brush-hooks and scythes, the show persists in remaining open. Perhaps with a little artificial resuscitation, the Cheyne-Stokes breathing may subside into a rhythmic and measured snore, and ultimately into a picture sale.

I expect to linger in these parts some two weeks more before going down to Pennsylvania for the spring planting, and would like to see you. Why don't you grab the midnight special this next week and buy yourself those Delman shoes? New York is at its maddest and if you have any desire to see *The Night before Christmas* (de gustibus non est disputandum, dear), you'd better make it fast before it snaps shut in your attractive face.

Besides which, I've worn out the crease in two pairs of pants waiting for you. Who the hell do you think you are — Ninon de l'Enclos?*

Ever,

*French lady of fashion (1620–1705), famous for her wit, beauty, salon, and distinguished lovers.

38

BETTY WHITE JOHNSTON

Erwinna, Pa.
June 6, 1941

You minx you,

You really must stop behaving like a combination of Madame de Montespan* and fresh-water eel. Every time I think I've pinned your shoulders to the mat, you wriggle off to your "mother" in Chicago or a "labor dispute" in Cody, Wyoming. And never mind throwing those harpoons into your loyal friend. Not only has he no intention of returning to Hollywood, but he is sitting here less than ninety minutes from New York chewing a straw and thinking about a mercurial little witch in Norfolk.

Now then, you deceitful baggage, pull yourself together and face facts. Your clothes are hopelessly out of date, your shoes worn paper thin, and your hats démodé. If you don't get up to New York pretty soon, the Navy will tow you out to sea and use you as a target. I'm offering you a way out; why not try our convenient budget plan? I'll fill you with food and listen to your oldest anecdotes without a whimper. I'll be a big brother to you (or at least that's what I'm pretending until the fifth Manhattan).

Acceptez, ma chère, les assurances de fidélité les plus distinguées, etc. A letter in your crabbed hand will always find me here.

Love,

*Mistress of Louis XIV.

JOSEPH BRYAN III

151 East 83rd Street
New York City
October 8, 1941

Dear Joe,

Neither Roget nor the Pocket Oxford have words to describe how happy we'd be to join your little seminar this weekend. BUT — we have just finished moving our troupe into New York and we're completely disorganized. I'm writing this with a mouth full of upholstery nails (you thought I was using a typewriter, didn't you?) and every so often I pluck one out and try to hammer it into the drapes with the heel of an evening slipper.

Our address, if there can be said to be any permanence these days, will be 151 E. 83rd Street for a while. . . . Please ring us when you get into town, and meanwhile a friendly chuck under the chin from both of us for Katharine.

I pinch your claws.

39

RUTH and AUGUSTUS GOETZ

1401¼ North Havenhurst Drive
Hollywood, Calif.
c. February, 1942

Dear Ruth & Gus,

We returned to Dixie heavy with constipation and gloom and were met at Pasadena by the usual agent's crimp dressed in Glenurquhart plaid and radiating optimism. We went to the Garden of Allah, where we found Dotty and Alan had been holed in for some time. They are getting along famously, somewhat like the cobra and the mongoose. Alan is working with one Helen Deutsch, and Dotty is on *The Life of Lou Gehrig* with Herman Mankiewicz and Jo Swerling (and you can imagine her account of *that*). Alan keeps getting you aside to tell about Dotty, and vice versa. From what Dotty says, she may go East shortly, but this may be talk.

After a couple of days of inflated living, we took a small flat in one of these beige-colored blocks of apartments which have sprung up a stone's throw from the Garden and got things lined up with our agent. There must have been some high-pressure salesmanship, because very shortly two deals were in the air, one with Gregory Ratoff and the other with Warner's. So as of tomorrow we are starting work over at Columbia to dream up a musical picture Ratoff will produce and direct. Ratoff is something of a loud and forceful screwball and God only knows how long the engagement will last, but we should get some anecdotes out of it and (let's hope) a few rutabagas. For some reason the Warner deal is still warm and we're supposed to confer with a producer there this week, so maybe we'll be able to turn all this activity into a dishonest dollar.

. . .

As for the war, the general attitude (and state of preparation) is just about what it is in New York, with large sections of apathy and laissez-faire visible to the naked eye in the movie colony. I don't think that our relative closeness to the scene of action has jarred the population perceptibly out of its torpor, but it is hard to generalize from the few people we've seen. At a party the other evening, except for ten minutes devoted to the problem of interning the Japs, the principle topic was the $500,000 deal signed by Norman Krasna. You may well imagine how absorbing we found the discussion of the Wunderkind.

We miss you enormously and may say confidentially that at Chicago, Kansas City, and Albuquerque we were on the verge of transferring our baggage to the eastbound train and giving you the surprise of your lives, but as theater-wise old show folk we know the danger of anti-climax (and also we like to eat as well as the next man). The week has been a mess of those cozy little suburban dinners, at three of which we have encountered George Oppenheimer.* He has gained weight but no wisdom. He is as rich as Croesus, as gay as a grig, and as dull as a hoe. He quickly announced in a basso profundo which shook the shutters that he had been sending you royalty checks for *Here Today*. Could be an uneasy conscience?

Laura, as I write, is in the bedroom of our depressing stash arranging her sparse hairs for still another suburban dinner; tonight she's wearing a stunning sheitel which will be the talk of Holmby Hills by morning. I myself am featuring the flannel number whose crotch has spread away revealing a suspicious stain, either semen or Maggi bouillon (just boasting about semen, of course).

Well, dears, here's an end on't, and do write if you can possibly conceive what it would mean to us. The telegram from the gamblers en route moved us to tears. As for the thin mints and Davies book you gave us, it's hard to say which was closer to perfection. Have you tried chewing the Davies book, by the way? It's a delightful new taste sensation—only a few cents at your neighborhood book-dealer's.

If you hear anything from the children or encounter them in the "nite spots," say hello for us. Laura sends you love and kisses (something there in the way of a Hebe joke about love and knishes, but honestly, I have to go and shave).   Ever,

*Drama critic and writer (d. 1977); cofounder, with Harold Guinzberg, of The Viking Press (1925).

AUGUSTUS GOETZ

1401¼ North Havenhurst Drive
Hollywood, Calif.
c. February 27, 1942

Dear Gus,

It's a warm summer's day and we've got about an hour to go before we can decently slip off to our little celotex nest. This is being written in a room about two feet longer and wider than the one I used to have at the Winslow, on the second tier of an inside court filled with offices. The general effect of the courtyard is that of an East Side tenement. The office itself (Ratoff's own, loaned to us while he is shooting a picture over at 20th Century–Fox) is panelled in cheap knotting pine and there is a subdued clicking undoubtedly caused by the dictaphone they have installed to spy on us. Right next to us is a cubby-hole occupied by a corporation sneak, a girl with a toothy smile who searches our desk every night, and immediately next to her, an office housing Ratoff's partner, the dough man. Every few minutes we open our door suddenly, expecting to have one of these worthies fall in; I'm sure one of them is crouched at the keyhole this minute listening.

Laura and I have been cooking up a miasma we are supposed to unload on the firm this coming Tuesday. At this moment, Max Gordon, who is doing something or other on the lot, came hurrying by our window, shouting at the mail-boy.* "Got anything for me, boy?" he was yelling, "Max Gordon!" I told you it was like a tenement. This studio was known at one time as Poverty Row, back in the early days of pictures, and nobody has bothered to repair any of the plaster or repaint. The whole thing looks like one of those billboards you see on the way from New Haven to Westerly, R.I., advertising Gorton's Codfish, No Bones. I just heard the corporation sneak clearing her throat in the next office, she probably knows I'm writing a letter instead of working on the story.

The following Hebe story is going the rounds out here, perhaps it hasn't yet crossed the Mississippi. It concerns the man who went into the Gaiety Delicatessen. "Well, so what'll it be?" inquired the waiter. The man ponders. "Would like a good plate frash chopped chicken liver," he said. "You'll excuse me," said the waiter, "but we are just receiving a consignment the finest quality superb Maatjes harring. Is every one a sheer drimm, try one and you'll certainly be salsified." The customer said okay and the waiter brought a plate containing the herring. The customer was just about to cut into it when he looked down at it and saw the fish winking up at him. He was revolted, got up, and went out. A few days later he was in the neighborhood of the restaurant again and stopped in. "Nu, what's good today?" he asked the waiter. "Am not given to superlatives," said the waiter, "strictly wishing to tip you off to the most sensational item we are stocking here in years, a brand-new shipment Maatjes herring—" The customer tried to order a pastrami sandwich but the waiter wouldn't hear of it. Finally the customer caved in and allowed the waiter to bring him the herring. He was again about to cut into it when the fish winked at him. With an oath the customer dashed out. Some weeks later he found himself near Lindy's. He entered, ordered a combination lachs-and-spiced beef sandwich. The waiter cleared his throat hesitantly. "Begging you poddon," said the waiter, "we're not making a policy of pushing the goods, but today we are featuring a special Maatjes herring which it's pure poetry. One bite and you'll thinking you in heaven." The customer tried to fight off the salesmanship but finally relented, and the waiter brought the herring. Just as the knife was descending the herring looked up reproachfully. "What's the matter, why you don't come in the Gaiety any more?" it asked.

. . . I was sorry as hell to hear that *The New Yorker* had returned your

*Theatrical and film producer (d. 1978); director, NBC.

42

first piece. I always go on the principle that they wouldn't know a master-piece if they fell over it, but go and tell that to Gristede Brothers. Why the hell don't you and I start a rival magazine? We'd get out the first issue just about the time we were both drafted. I take it you registered last weekend, as I did. My man stared at my name for quite a while before he entered it on the card. "Perelman, Perel-Man," he said. "Kind of a Japanese name, isn't it?" Boy, are they winging out here. And boy, have they got a right to be winging.

Laura sends you a bushel of kisses for yourself and Ruthie, and begs you not to falter in your correspondence. Meanwhile, remember our troop motto "*Mens sana in corpore sano*" and take your hand out of your pocket for various reasons.   Love,

L E A H   S A L I S B U R Y *

1401¼ North Havenhurst Drive
Hollywood, Calif.
March 1, 1942

Dear Leah,

Thanks for your note, which finally reached me a couple of days ago. As Swanie† undoubtedly wrote you, our employer is that mad Muscovite Gregory Ratoff and our task is confecting an original musical, which is probably the worst headache in pictures.‡ Ratoff unfortunately hadn't even the germ of an idea to present us with, so it's really starting from the ground up. Nor is it made simpler by Ratoff being involved directing two pictures over at 20th Century-Fox; at present we're involved in a series of night and Sunday conferences charged with good old Russian hysteria. It's pictures, dear.

· · ·

The war situation out here is a strange blending of tension and apathy; as for the purported raid of the other night, we out here don't seem to know any more than you do in the East. I slept right through it and Laura thought it was a windstorm.

Swanie struck us as being tremendously efficient and we were very impressed with the speed and energy he and his staff showed in our behalf. But I know how insistent you were with him regarding us, and we both want to thank you again for your active interest and effort regarding the Perelmans.

Our very best to you and the force.   Sincerely,

*The Perelmans' theatrical agent (d. 1975).
†H. N. Swanson, Salisbury's associate in Hollywood.
‡Gregory Ratoff (d. 1960), Russian-born actor and director (*Intermezzo*, etc.).

43

RUTH and AUGUSTUS GOETZ
1401¼ North Havenhurst Drive
Hollywood, Calif.
March 8, 1942

Dear Ruth & Gus,

The enclosed front page of the *L.A. Times* will give you a faint idea of how the local gazettes handled the purported air raid of last week. Actually I imagine you people know as much about it as we do here. I slept right through it; Laura was awakened by what she thought was the rattling of the Venetian blinds (but which may have been the anti-aircraft fire) and shortly afterward heard a man's voice shout "Put out that light!" Her light wasn't on, but she promptly turned it on, and after a minute or two went back to sleep....Other people, however, did get up and describe the searchlights and orange bursts as "beautiful." Nobody we talked to seems to have seen or heard enemy planes, and the fact that none of our own planes were sent up might indicate that the whole thing was a test.

The past week has been divided between attempting to get somewhere on this wretched musical and carrying olive branches between the warring Campbell factions. Our old friend Dotnick has been in something of a spin — loaded on brandy by eleven in the morning and the like. She clearly resents Alan working with Miss Helen Deutsch, she's fed up with pictures and picture people, and by Thursday of this past week, she had gotten herself into such shape that she had to go off to a sanitarium for three or four days. All through this, Alan was phoning us at the studio and running in to our apartment biting his nails and telling us how unreasonable she was. We visited her at the sanitarium and she said she was going East immediately. We prevailed on Alan eventually to patch it up, and as of last night they were home together again, but it's hardly Paolo and Francesca. I keep telling Laura that it will end by their turning on us, but of course you know how they both love to suck people in on their emotional fireworks, and it's impossible to be honest with either of them.

We fried up a yarn for Ratoff which we told him last Tuesday. His comment was: "It's a mess but it has sensational elements." He then announced that we would hold a series of nightly conferences to straighten out the story, but thus far we have had only one, and this afternoon we're having another. What he's going to end up with, of course, is that good old setup in which the little chorus girl steps into the part and saves the show, but right now he's pretending he must have something entirely new. *You* try to think up a story in which William Gaxton is supposed to play a starring comedy part. We keep trying to hint to Ratoff that Gaxton has been an aging juvenile these twenty years, but some agent undermined him and Ratoff's convinced he's got a great comic under contract. Oh firk.

.   .   .

Well, cuties, need I tell you how we miss you both? I thank you again for your frequent letters, every one of which is an oasis. . . .

Laura sends you a cloud of kisses, and will be writing you shortly. I pinch your claws.   Love,

R U T H and A U G U S T U S   G O E T Z
1401¼ North Havenhurst Drive
Hollywood, Calif.
March 18, 1942

Dear Ruth & Gus,

If there has been a delay in our writing, it's because we've been paddling about heavily in this cesspool of a script with our rather horrible Middle European collaborator hanging onto our back. At night, when we get back to our prefabricated home, we just about have strength to pick up the evening paper, get the latest disaster straight between the eyes, and totter off to bed.

Looking over last Sunday's *Times* a few minutes ago, I ran across an excellent review of Pop Goodman's book by Beatrice Sherman and was very happy for you.* That was a sizable ad Knopf took for it in last week's *Book Review*, and taken with that first-class notice in the *Tribune*, it would seem to me the book should have a good sale. Has there been any movie interest? Those references to the Day family, Thurber, etc. might create some excitement, I'd imagine....I don't know whether Harry Kurnitz wrote you or not, but one evening — completely out of the blue — he began telling us how much he was enjoying a book called *Franklin Street*, advising us to read it, etc. Of course, he did not know you were related to the author, and when we told him, he said he meant to let you know what pleasure it had given him.

As indicated in the lead, we are up to our navels in sheiss. Our employer, Mr. Ratoff, is busy directing a picture at another studio, so that with the exception of an evening conference now and then, we don't see him. However, his business associate and deputy, one Harry Goetz, has been riding herd on us daily. Goetz is one of those vigorous, tanned backers of Max Gordon, the sort of man you see lunching at the Orangerie in the Astor. He's got a cool three million salted away, is rich enough to tell you how much he loathes Hollywood, and likes nothing better than discussing methods of financing a

---

Franklin Street, a book about growing up in Philadelphia, by Philip Goodman, Ruth Goetz's father. It was finished by her after his death in 1940.

45

Broadway show (incidentally, he has large shares of both *Sister Eileen* and *Junior Miss*). He knows absolutely nothing about pictures, which doesn't prevent him in the least from telling you how to write them. To add to our schmerz, the mittel-European sneak referred to above and in previous letters, who was employed on another picture, managed to muscle his way in on ours. It is an involved situation; this rodent is the office stool and intrigant, and as we are anxious to keep working without any layoff, we are compelled to put up with him. It undoubtedly has a humorous aspect; this guy (his name is Kohner) is a Czechoslovakian wolf who is constantly slavering after secretaries and has a breast fetish which may eventually cure me of mine (well, let's not go crazy). He speaks a very patchwork kind of English and we have to stop every couple of minutes and explain the simplest slang expressions, which is great when you're writing a supposedly sparkling musical for Jack Oakie. A couple of times Laura has snatched paper-weights out of my hand just as I was about to shy them at Jocko's noggin, but one of these days I may be too fast for her.

After yentzing around with order and serial numbers and the whole complicated tzimmas of the third draft, I have decided to sit tight and make them come to me; I don't understand it and neither do they. My name hasn't yet appeared in the papers as a draft dodger, so I guess I have done everything expected of me. However, it seems to be a certainty that if I don't wind up holystoning a deck or storming Milan, the government intends to pluck the goose quill out of my fat little fist and put me to work on a turret lathe. Gus, do you recall that conversation we had about learning welding? I was that superior fuck who smiled patronizingly and observed at the time, "Just let those Heinies try to remilitarize the Rhineland. Recent statistics show that the French have the greatest land army in the world."

. . .

Well, kirros, enough of this farrago for the time. Give our best to Lily* and our poker pals, and to Dotty, whom you will be seeing this week. A shower of kisses from Laura, and I enclose a little West Coast journalism.

Love,

*Mrs. Philip Goodman, Ruth Goetz's mother.

RUTH and AUGUSTUS GOETZ
1401¼ North Havenhurst Drive
Hollywood, Calif.
c. March 23, 1942

Dear Ruth & Gus,

We were delighted to learn from Groucho Marx, when he happened to drop into our office at the studio on Friday, all the exciting news about *Franklin Street*. Groucho read us a portion of a letter from Kaufman in which the maestro spoke of the enterprise with high hope and also referred very flatteringly to you both. He told Groucho that you, Ruth, were the unbilled collaborator on *Here Today** and had written the final twenty thousand words of the book, and said that in his one or two interviews with Gus had felt that Gus had a very distinct theater sense. Groucho told us that he thought the enterprise had a great chance and he was very excited about it. In fact, he was already speculating about the heat in Washington on September 28th next, etc. Later that day we ran into Max Gordon, who is also steamed up about it, and altogether the whole thing looks like money in the bank. Now is the time to get Russell Gulden busy on that ornamental fence you always wanted along the road. What are you waiting for?

I think you should get along very well with Arthur Sheekman; he is bright and a hard worker, I am assured by those who know him better than I do.† It is pretty nearly ten years since we worked together, and then under the most unfortunate circumstances, as I have unendingly told you. But since then he has had a good amount of picture experience and should know a lot about dramatic construction, and with George riding herd on things, I don't see how you can miss.

We ourselves are still flailing away at this picture and are about halfway through a treatment which is purest cat-vomit. There is no rhyme or reason to anything in it, the characters behave as in a dream, and what with an increasing shortage of paper, it's practically sabotage. Our middle-European sneak is still with us, riding us like the Old Man of the Sea. From where we stand now, all we can see is a vast expanse of shit stretching away to the horizon. Laura is getting sort of restless and has intimated that before long she may be pulling out. The prospect of remaining here solo is a delightful one, but for all I know Uncle Sam may cut the Gordian knot. If I'm not on a turret lathe by Thanksgiving, I'll be digging latrines at Camp Yamashita.

One of the enclosed clippings will give you the formal report on the robbery of Alan's villa at the Garden of Allah. He was at our apartment during the latter part of it, and when he left here, discovered his place in a turmoil. We haven't seen him since to get any details, but he said over the phone that about seven people seem to have been involved, for nine bottles of liquor were drunk in all. One of the evildoers was apprehended on Hollywood Blvd. staggering along with a case of champagne under his arm. He was clad in a pair of Alan's dress trousers, that strange white fuzzy jacket he used to wear in

---

*A play by Ruth Goetz, George Oppenheimer, and George Kaufman.
†Sheekman, along with Perelman, was a writer on the Marx brothers' picture *Monkey Business* (1931).

47

Pipersville, and had a yellow muffler about his throat. He also had exchanged his own shoes for a pair of Alan's sandals; and later, when he had been put in a cell at the police station, he sent out the sandals with a request that they return his own shoes, as the sandals hurt his feet. Even the criminals are screwballs out here.

Well, kids, enough for the moment — this started out to be a very short note telling you how good we felt about *Franklin Street*. Let's know some of the details, and when are you actually moving down to the country? The house sounds perfect, and I hope we can all be together again this summer. Love to you both and our best to Lily.

L E A H   S A L I S B U R Y

Erwinna, Pa.
May 25, 1942

Dear Leah,

Swanie's script did not reach me until this morning (Monday) despite the fact that it was postmarked Friday 1 p.m. I read it at once and felt it was extremely contrived farce based on a central situation lifted from *You Can't Take It with You*; it deals with a mad family in the South engaged in counterfeiting and despite an occasional smile here and there the general effect was tiresome rather than amusing. Had Laura and I been out on the Coast we might have taken a flyer at it, but it seemed such small pumpkins that I couldn't feel right in journeying 3000 miles to do it.

·   ·   ·

I also enclose the Larry Adler material initialled as you requested.* I got a note from him several days ago saying that he was breaking it in and it was going very nicely. Of course he is making changes to conform to the temper of his audiences, but that is his right and he has enough intelligence to add nothing out of key.   Sincerely,

*The harmonica virtuoso had hired Perelman to write some nightclub patter.

W H I T   B U R N E T T *

Erwinna, Pa.
June 8, 1942

Dear Mr. Burnett,

Thank you for your kind invitation to include a specimen of my work

*Writer and editor (d. 1973); founding editor, with his wife Martha Foley, of *Story Anthology* magazine (1931). Perelman's piece appeared in Burnett's anthology *This Is My Best Humor*.

in your anthology. I enclose herewith a short treatise called "Kitchen Bouquet" which first appeared in *The New Yorker*, and which I think is best suited to represent me.*

In general, I feel that any exegesis of humor is both fatal and dull, but if I show some slight preference for this piece, it is because of its underlying note of desperation. It marks a troubled period when I almost gave up writing to become a charwoman. I'm still not sure I made the more profitable choice. . . .   Sincerely,

*First collected in *Look Who's Talking!* and reprinted in *The Most of S. J. Perelman*.

LEAH SALISBURY

Erwinna, Pa.
July 1, 1942

Dear Leah,

        •   •   •

 . . . To re-state Adler's offer, it was a flat payment of $50 a week on the Paramount and all future theater engagements as long as his salary doesn't exceed $1000 a week; if it does, some provision to be made. He feels that the material as it now stands and as he used it in the Chicago theater is fine. In addition, he wants to pay 10% of all night club earnings, with a guaranteed minimum of $75 a week. He is going into the Savoy Plaza on a percentage and should do better than $750 according to his expectations, which of course would mean over $75 for me if he works out well there. The whole adds up to a minimum of $125 a week, and in your wire you suggested I demand a maximum of $150, which I believe I might get very easily under this arrangement. I told Adler, however, that I didn't know whether we could consent to any outright sale of the material for theaters, if that is what is implied by the flat-price payment for theater use of $50 per week. If we can retain complete control of the material under the above conditions, I am willing to settle on these terms. It means revising the material once in a while as he requires it, but I think I can reduce this to a very occasional chore.

        •   •   •

LEAH SALISBURY

Erwinna, Pa.
c. July 14, 1942

Dear Leah,
 . . . Adler informed me the evening he opened at the Savoy that he wasn't using the material during his second week at the Paramount. Despite

49

his success with it in Chicago before theater audiences, he felt it wasn't getting over here. When I saw him work with it at the Paramount, I could understand why. For one thing, he didn't know it. For another, he was snatching bits from it here and there without any attempt at building to laughs. For a third, he was routined immediately following a noisy slapstick comedian who was making his first appearance at the Paramount and was doing everything but exhibit his pudenda. Adler following directly on this man's heels with my sort of material naturally had no weight. He admitted all these points I've listed but there was no sense in trying to force him to try the material out to its utmost before he abandoned it.

At the Savoy that night, he was stampeded with fright so completely that he just mumbled a couple of lines which even I, who had written them, hardly understood. He played very well, however, and they seemed to like him. I had lunch with him next day and gave him my frankest opinions (also shared by Laura, who was there with me, and Margaret Case Harriman, also a friend of his — her profile of Adler is in this week's *New Yorker*, and you might be interested in reading it, I think it's pretty devastating at bottom). We all three felt that what he needs is the services of a comedy coach, an elocution teacher, or at least someone who can teach him not to declaim lines and will show him a little something about comedy timing and effectiveness. It's really a man's-size job and no part of my bargain. We parted on the understanding that he was to continue using and trying out the material at the Savoy and that he was to write me during this week about how he was doing with it. I in turn would come in sometime this next week and listen and see what it looked like. However, I haven't heard from him. If I should come in, I shall of course phone you and let you know any developments.

Best,

JOHN SANFORD

Erwinna, Pa.
August 2, 1942

Dear Scotty,

Your letter has just caught up with me here in the country, as I've been up in the mountains visiting our kids at camp the past few days. The dates you have for Pep, 1903–1940, are correct, and both Laura and I were moved and pleased that you are dedicating your book to him. I'm writing this looking out of a window at a tulip tree that he and I planted together, and it's good to think that your dedication and this tree will remain to recall him.

I am looking forward to receiving your book from Harcourt and will read it with a lot of interest. By the way, I recently enjoyed Thomas Bell's

Till You Come Back to Me; he has some wonderfully sharp character stuff about Brooklyn people, in particular a grandmother-and-baby theme that made me yell. It's one of those short books Pep always thought Americans should write but don't; I guess Pep himself was one of the few who did, along with James Gould Cozzens, *Great Gatsby*, *Postman Always Rings Twice*, etc.

The very best of luck with *The People from Heaven*, along with our corporate regards. Sincerely,

LEAH SALISBURY

Erwinna, Pa.
August 16, 1942

Dear Leah,

This little man Adler is beginning to get on my nerves. I am returning herewith the letter he just sent you, and also the three letters he sent in the past — one from Cincinnati, one from Chicago, and the most recent which I got about a week ago. Please preserve all these in the dossier relating to the case.

Briefly, it seems apparent to me that having gotten the material and used it to the extent his capabilities permitted, he has now begun to cavil at paying for it. Throughout, his attitude is marked by a remarkable egomania; he reiterates the fact that whenever Adler uses the gay, spontaneous quip he is masterly but whenever the Perelman touch comes in, he falls flat on his face. Considering the passion with which he sought me out and his nagging persistence in persuading me to do the stuff, this financial gooseflesh is tiresome, to say the least. I was perfectly willing to adapt the stuff to his needs, and did so when he came down. I would probably have done some more, but you know perfectly well that it's silly for me to devote time I could employ on profitable writing to massaging a harmonica player's self-esteem.

From the various publicity I saw in connection with his N.Y. engagements, he employed my name wherever possible and for whatever good it would do him, a bit of behavior I had specifically asked him to stop indulging in. Therefore, and in consideration of all the above, would you please do the following.

Please inform him that we *do* expect payment for his use of the material for the week mentioned in the paragraph in your letter I have checked with an "X." He had ample time previously to try out and experiment with it, and our contract with him provides for no free rides. In addition, please inform him that he is to immediately cease and desist from using the material at once, or any material whatsoever I have ever done for him. *This also applies to any extracts from my books or magazine articles*, which he told me he was combing for possible material. In other words, full stop. I have a well-defined suspicion that Mr. Adler is not being altogether truthful with us about when or how much of the material he uses. Miss Ellison heard him at the Stage Door Canteen and reported to me that he used two extracts—this was Sunday, August 9th. In his letter to me dated August 10th, he makes no reference to it. Needless to say, I certainly expect no payment for any benefit he does for our armed forces. I do expect, however, the courtesy of being informed at least that he used it. To what extent he *has* used it in his professional engagements without telling us, I am unable to say. But make it altogether clear that from the receipt of your letter forward, he is not to use anything of mine in any form.

As you see from all this, I am fed up with the lad. We have his own written evidence from Cincinnati, Chicago, etc. to testify that his talking has helped him, that my material has gone over very well indeed in theaters and clubs, and that he's excited about it. This kind of pinch-penny refusal to pay off for it is more worthy of Rivington Street than the Park Avenue entertainer. Go as far as you like.

I'm leaving tomorrow (Monday) morning for a couple of days on the Cape. I expect to be coming back through New York on Friday, and I'll ring you. Laura sends you her love.   Ever,

MALCOLM COWLEY*

14 Washington Square North
New York City
February 16, 1943

Dear Malcolm,

Can you exercise a portion of the compassion which has made your name a household word and forgive me for not acknowledging your letter earlier? I have been caught up in what I believe is called this infernal Amerikanski tempo.

Laura and I were very gratified to read the passage you'd found in *Confluence* about Pep's work. I don't know whether it was made clear in that article, but *Miss Lonelyhearts is* now published in French, or at least should be, as they made arrangements for that purpose about a year ago. We haven't as yet seen a copy, but I guess it ought to be along presently.

It was very good of you, incidentally, to write a blurb for Laughlin's forthcoming reprint of the book at New Directions. Bob Coates showed us the preface he wrote for it and I thought he did a first-rate job. It isn't the usual fulsome, woozy preface most people write under the circumstances; I

*Then associate editor of *The New Republic*.

52

was glad that Bob had tried to maintain a somewhat critical point of view and had honestly assayed Pep's work as though he hadn't known him.

Well, my brave, thank you again for taking the trouble to pass on M. Astruc's words,* and if you get within the orbit of Washington Square, come in and have a ball of malt with us, will you? Laura sends you her very best.

Sincerely,

*Astruc, author of a classic treatise on venereal disease (1738), was quoted as saying that libertines who use condoms claim "that thus mailed and with spears sheathed in this way, they can undergo with impunity the chances of promiscuous intercourse."

GROUCHO MARX

14 Washington Square North
New York City
April 7, 1943

Dear Groucho,

Your initial broadcast reminded me that I was long overdue on a reply; and not to wear out my welcome, thank you for that splendid bit of sewage about Leo (Sunshine) Fon-a-Row and a lot of laughs (spelled "laffs") on the Blue Ribbon show. By now you have probably seen John Hutchens' piece in the radio section of last Sunday's *Times*, which shows that your fans are still legion. I really thought you goaled them and especially loved the business of playing straight to yourself on puns like "aria."

I have been tied up since mid-January on a musical with Ogden Nash and Kurt Weill, which we finished the end of this past week.* Nash and I did the book (based on a short story by F. Anstey, who was the editor of *Punch* back in the Eighties), and Ogden's now finishing up his lyrics for Weill's music. It's the story of a small schnückel of a barber who accidentally brings a statue of Venus to life, and it has turned up a lot of pretty funny and dirty complications. The music and lyrics thus far (about ⅔ finished) are grand, and we're dickering with several leading women currently. Rehearsals start about August 1st...All this happened as I was concluding work on the revue; I have six of the seven sketches finished for that, and the present design is to do it in the fall.†

Otherwise the usual routine; I've been doing a piece every other week for the *Satevepost* and random *New Yorker* things, though the musical crowded out the latter lately. Also, just to make everything really giddy, I've been taking a course in bacteriology in my spare time, and if you need a fast Wassermann any time this spring, mail me the bottle. I'm putting up posters in sub-

*One Touch of Venus.
†Never put on, the revue was to have been produced by Cheryl Crawford, with Adolph Green, Betty Comden, and Judy Holliday.

way washrooms after June 1st: "MEN: why worry? See Dr. Morty Perelman, night or day—no more expensive than any quack."

The theater here is blooming, everything's a hit and the wise guys, who have never been known to be right, claim business will hold up right through the summer. As you probably know, *Franklin Street* is being rewritten as a musical by George Kaufman and Gus Goetz, with prospective tunes by Rogers and Hammerstein. To judge from the reception of *Something for the Boys* and *Oklahoma*, it's a musical year. It's also a Mankiewicz year, to judge from the news we get here.* I saw an issue of the *Journal-American* containing a photo of Mank chained to a harness bull, in which our jolly friend looked like a member of the Kid Dropper arson ring.

Well, cuddles, my best to yourself and all the pretty girls on the bridle path, and let's know the news. Did you, or are you still planning to, make *The Heart of a City*? And are you getting much? In fact, what about a scholarly little monograph on "Muff Memories of an Old Trouper"?

Love,

*The screenwriter Herman Mankiewicz (*Citizen Kane*, etc.) had been the associate producer of *Monkey Business* and *Horse Feathers*.

BETTY   WHITE   JOHNSTON

50 Washington Square South*
New York City
June 1, 1943

Dear Betty,

How are you, you exquisite creature? Don't you ever come up to New York any more? Or are you sitting down there in Norfolk slowly developing a film of unattractive green verdigris?   Yours,

*Perelman's office.

FRANCES and ALBERT HACKETT

14 Washington Square North
New York City
June 25, 1943

Dear Albert and Frances,

Can you find it in your heart to forgive me for not having replied to your letters before? The usual excuses: torpor, work, the heat, the whole ugly parade of excuses, one more shoddy than the other. Though actually so little of any news value has occurred that I think I'm pretty audacious to even start a letter at this point.

Most of the poker group seem to be in good shape; haven't seen the

Keefes for several weeks but can report on the Goetzes and Frances O'Neill. Frances spent a weekend with us in the country just before she left for Hollywood, where she was stopping off en route to Mexico City, with Paul, her boy. The Goetzes have apparently abandoned the musical version of *Franklin Street* they were engaged on, and are deep in an unspecified comedy, which Kaufman is conferring on with them. They appear to be in fighting trim, although Ruth just called up to say that when they went to get their car out of storage this morning to drive down to the country, they found that the gas tank had been ripped out, the gas stolen, a brand new tire stolen, and the clutch ruined. The proprietor of the garage merely snarled, handed them a card reading "Harry Greenberg, Attorney" and said "Don't bodder me." When they called Harry Greenberg, they were told that he was in Attu and anyway never answered the phone. Go sue City Hall.

Ogden and I are currently engaged in a brush-up of the musical, which enters rehearsal August 15th. [Elia] Kazan is directing, Agnes DeMille is doing the dances, and [Howard] Bay the sets. We have signed Kenny Baker and Paula Laurence (for Molly), are negotiating with John Boles for Savory, and within a week should sign our Venus. We have seen a good many gals for the part; we could have taken Leonore Corbett but she didn't prove to be quite right, and that was the case with a lot of them. As a matter of fact, Kurt Weill and Kazan are on the Coast this minute and are seeing Dietrich tonight for a final talk with her. We have two dark horses under consideration, one completely unknown but a likely candidate, the other a tarnished dove who has some things in her favor but isn't really 100%. In other words, the usual headaches. However, there seems to be a generally enthusiastic feeling about the script and music, so if you have any fingers that aren't working, keep them crossed.

The temperature this minute, if you want to believe the thermometer outside our livingroom window, is 119, but of course that's in the sun. In the shade it's only 97. Ogden's moved his family up to a place called Bay Head, N.J., down near Barnegat Bay, and commutes up daily to work. Laura's packing the kiddoes off to camp tomorrow morning, where they'll be until the end of August. They're in what appears to be good shape; Abby had her tonsils plucked out recently and as a result has grown surprisingly; she's about six feet two and is growing all the time. Adam, on the other hand, seems to be shrinking; he was only five inches high the last time I looked at him, but it may be only temporary.

Laura spends a good deal of time working around the Lunch Time Follies* these days, but in between times she is working on a novel called

*Sponsored by the American Theatre Wing for the armed forces.

Remembrance of Things Past, which is all about fairies and things. She has finished fourteen volumes and it doesn't look as if she's finished yet. My, but that girl is wordy.

.   .   .

I read almost daily references to *The Hitler Gang* in the press; when do you start shooting, and more to the point, when are you coming back here? It would be only platitudinous to remind you that we all miss you. Why don't you come back here where the worrying is so much better?

So here is at least a bushel of love from everyone in sight: Laura, Ruth & Gus, Ogden, et al. Why don't you sit down on Y. Frank Freeman's time* and write us a fast letter telling us all about your ideals and ideas, your aspirations, your hopes, your plans, your fears, your dreams, and anything else that occurs to you? We embrace you.   Yours,

*President of Paramount (d. 1940). Studio wags were given to citing him as "Y. Frank Freeman?"

E. B. WHITE*

14 Washington Square North
New York City
July 11, 1943

Dear Andy,

I recall an evening at Joel Sayre's and a discussion of the Dramatists' Guild distinguished by eloquence rather than sense. The enclosed, which has just come to hand, gives a fairly concise picture of the advantages and operation of the Guild. It also makes a nice fan if you spread it open and wave it vigorously back and forth, particularly if you're in an ice-cold bath at the time.

How are you and Katharine, anyway?

Sincerely,

*At the time, contributing editor, *The New Yorker* (d. 1986); married to *New Yorker* fiction editor Katharine S. White (d. 1977).

MALCOLM COWLEY

14 Washington Square North
New York City
November 2, 1943 (?)

Dear Malcolm,

I have here an investigation into the British character through the medium of a magazine called *The Field*. It was written for *The New Yorker*, which confounded me by finding it too tart for present consumption. I disagree completely, and, in fact, was careful not to throw too many punches while writing it. I sent it to you hoping that you will share my opinion to the extent of printing it.

Laura tells me you encountered each other downtown here, and I suggest we get together real soon for ale and kippers. Carry on.

Yours,

VICTOR WOLFSON*

14 Washington Square North
New York City
January 2, 1944

Dear Victor,

Judge of my surprise when I called you some weeks ago and found that you had taken wing for the new Zion, where every prospect pleases and only man is vile. And shortly afterward, your brievel to substantiate the foregoing. I hope that by the time this reaches you your greed will have been quenched and you'll be starting back to these parts.

Everyone locally is on his feet, which is getting to be something of an accomplishment in our family, and outside of chronic sore throats, sinus, and a weekly consumption of forty boxes of Kleenex, we are all in passable shape. The holidays, Gott sei dank, are over. We have a new picture, a Ben Shahn I bought from the eminent farber direct, called *Governor Rolph of California*. It is one of the Mooney series he did and appeared about 10 years ago in *Hound & Horn*, also at the Modern Museum's Twentieth Century Portrait show. I think you will like it; is very funny besides nice painting. Also that Toulouse-Lautrec poster you haven't yet seen.

The show is going along nicely; Six-Toed John Wildberg phoned me this morning to say that our gross this past week was $38,696. Of course this was the week between Xmas and New Year's, but we have been hitting a steady $35,600 since opening, with a full complement of standees every performance. Mary Martin missed four performances last week with flu but is back in, and Sono Osato has been out the past two weeks, returning tomorrow night. However, the show managed to roll right on even with understudies, which makes me hope that we have a road show for the future. As for myself, I go around there once a week or so, brush my hand lightly over any tit that happens to get into my way, and duck out. I have reached the stage with it where the words make me squirm. The only thing that doesn't make me squirm are weekly grosses. On me they look good. I need not add that by the time

*Television documentary writer.

57

I pay off to the Internal Revenue Dep't, I expect to be talking like a member of the National Manufacturers Association.

Otherwise not very much; I am slugging out pieces as doggedly as possible, and trying to build up a reserve at *The New Yorker* as well as the *Post*. I went on an authors' war bond tour for the Treasury Dep't, and am going on another Feb. 9, 10, and 11 up in New England. We've seen some shows: *Voice of the Turtle* (well, I'll tell you); *Carmen Jones* (extremely beautiful, also dull); *Lovers and Friends* (Katharine Cornell, *och und vay*); and Jed Harris' production of *The World's Full of Girls*. The last was a great disappointment, as the novel it was based on, Thomas Bell's *Till I Come Back to You*, was a little gem. . . .

Well, my boy, this is certainly enough for one Sunday's letter-writing; we all send you our best for the new year, and get out of that hell-hole before you start walking on your heels. Before you know it, it'll be time to start putting in onion sets in Tinicum Township. *Zei nicht a nar.*

Yours,

P.S.   Are you getting much?

BETTY WHITE JOHNSTON

50 Washington Square South
New York City
February 25, 1944

Hello, dearie,

Pangs of conscience akin to those of childbirth swept over me when I got your card, recalling that I never answered your last letter. Somewhere right after I got it, I either developed total amnesia or became involved in some furtive enterprise. But the standard principle that there is no bitter without a corresponding sweet was borne out when I learned that you still tend a glowing coal for this shabby correspondent. . . .

Although everybody in Alexandria is undoubtedly wagging her head and saying enviously, "How does Betty Johnston do it? She looks younger every day!," nobody up this way is getting any younger, or, I am afraid, wiser. My coevals flatter me by assuring me that I am still the same springy kid and that I haven't changed a whit. I know better; I am beginning to examine with considerable interest those advertisements of lean, gray-haired fishermen whipping a trout stream with no impaired faculties and a tidy income of $175 a month. I also find that if I bend over rapidly three thousand times, I have to pause to recover my breath. I wonder whether there is anything in the DuBarry Success Course for me?

Otherwise, I'm still plowing the same crooked furrow as ever, writing for a couple of magazines that haven't caught on to me yet and making an occasional foray into the theater, viz., the current *One Touch of Venus*. I'm proud and happy to say, however, that two lovely years have passed since I was in Hollywood last, and God willing, I hope the next thirty pass the same. Do you find, as I do, that the longer you stay away from it, the more loathesome it becomes? I bet that outside of Devil's Island, it's the only place in the world that produces this kind of emotion.

I was in what amounts to your immediate vicinity about a month ago; whipped down to Washington for a day with a theater delegation to brace our representatives about the soldier vote, but it was so hectic and so generally nonsensical that I never did get organized enough to call you. Just think, we might have had a pallid omelet and a glass of inferior Sauterne served by unloving hands at the Gateway restaurant in the Terminal. I think—hell, I know—that you and I could do much better up here; and if you are contemplating that annual spring hat-buying trip, I'll whup you within an inch of your lazy life if you sneak into town without letting me know.

How about an inimitable pen picture of you and yours at this moment— your hopes, your dreams, your ideals, your aspirations? How do you feel about life, not to mention the Administration? How are your shoe tickets holding out? And more important, how are *you*?

Eternally,

I . J . KAPSTEIN

14 Washington Square North
New York City
March 16, 1945

Dear Kap,

Your letter of December 22 has been hanging in the rafters like a haggis and is now of a ripeness to be answered. To drop that tortured metaphor and tell the God's honest truth, it lay for the past three months sandwiched in between an insurance bill from L.H. Goldmark and a piece of sandpaper Adam once used on a toy jeep. I got around only this evening to paying Goldmark (who will certainly drop dead with surprise in the morning), and the shock of receiving a reply may affect you similarly. Though you were always a sturdy *bocher*. (Some say almost a *bolvan*.)

To answer a couple of specific queries you put in your letter, I asked around here and there but nobody seemed to know anything of a reproduction of di Chirico's *Mystery and Melancholy of a Street*. I inquired at the Museum of Modern Art, but a languid graduate of Bennington with rather puny breasts had never heard of it. Well, for that matter, who ever heard of her? I am sick of these god-damned pubescent school-girls who are too busy discussing Martha Graham to give a tumble to a man who knows a possible cash customer up in Providence, R.I. . . . You also asked about the Authors League. It is true I'm on the Council, but apart from having attended one meeting and stared lympathically at Rex Stout's beard for three hours, I know pitifully little about it. I guess it is okay; most of my contact has been with the Dramatists Guild and Screen Writers Guild branches. Both of these, especially the former, are powerful and efficient organizations, and afford their members means of redress, penalties against thieving producers, and the like. The Authors' League gets out a chatty monthly bulletin containing some worthwhile information, and, I'm sorry to say, doesn't appear to do much else. I know they are working intensively to achieve some sort of standard contract between writer and publisher, which would be a wonderful thing for writers young and old. Practically speaking, it seems to me that a good, tough agent is the best protection for you. I don't use a literary agent, but I probably should, because I have been frigged time and again by publishers. There isn't one—and Knopf is no exception—who doesn't insert tricky clauses. Agents know how to smell them out; and it's an axiom that if a publisher wants your book, he'll be willing under pressure to write the contract your way, with stipulations about how much advertising he'll do and what-not. . . .

Hereabouts, the usual end-of-winter fatigue has set in, we are all of us looking ahead to the country. I went down to Erwinna for the day yesterday and it was really gratifying to see the creeks running and the buds charging out on the lilacs. I had a brief affair with a maple, in the manner of Tolstoy, that left us both unsatisfied, but I promised her I'd be back shortly...Currently, I'm putting in the last licks on the first draft of a new musical I hope to get on this fall.* I wrote it with Al Hirschfeld, the theatrical caricaturist of the *Times*, and the draft should be finished in ten days more. Nash will probably do lyrics and we'd like Harold Arlen for the music.† It's been intensive work since January 1st, but it's an idea I've had a long while, and, I hope I hope, a rather striking notion. One thing I'm sure of, with the proper handling it can be one of the most ambitious flops in years.

My *momzerim*, like yours, are shooting up by the minute. Adam's at the stage where he's just launched a three-man secret society whose aims, as I get it, are the extinction of parents and a rollicking career on the Spanish Main. I overheard the members reciting their secret oath this evening and caught the following: "And we shall not rest until Ireland takes its rightful place among the free nations of the world."...Abby is a springy seven and

*Sweet Bye and Bye.
†The score was by Vernon Duke.

has begun preliminary training in ballet. Take it for what it's worth, but Alicia Markova was seen looking pretty green in the Russian Tea Room last Thursday night. Of course, it may only have been a spoiled piroschkeh. On the other hand, Abby is a good deal younger woman than Markova, and in that business, stamina counts. I just hope she doesn't burn herself out.

Well, Morris, I have distracted you long enough from your quill, and I'll let you go back to your lectern. Your letter was fine reading both times, when I received it and tonight, when I reread it. Do tear yourself away from the Oliver long enough to reply, and I again suggest you people should get down here for a few days. Meanwhile, Laura sends her best to you and Stella along with mine, and pinch the little hooligans for me.

Yours,

B E T T Y   W H I T E   J O H N S T O N

50 Washington Square South
New York City
March 26, 1945

Dear Betty,

Reach down deep in that bountiful goodness of yours and forgive me for not acknowledging those Reemstma Sorte cigarettes before this. I've been on the last leg of a new musical I've been working on — if a musical may properly be said to have legs (this one, more accurately, has two heads). Anyhow, the past ten days have been the usual coffee-and-benzedrine period, and now it's on its way to the Broadway judgment seats.

I most certainly will be here around April 19th and I am most certainly not going to any old Coast to do any old motion-picture version of any old *Venus*.* Let them beat their fuzzy brain-pans out whatever way they please. It'll be cinematic genius of the usual sort and I shall view it unmoved at Loew's Sheridan — *after* it concludes its first showing and I can see it for 55 cents.

So there you are; you'll be here and I'll be here and we'll both be here. And I'll cut your throat with a serrated bread-knife if you don't spill a pony of vodka for auld lang syne. As for the heartbreak and disillusion you anticipate, you couldn't be more mistaken. Since you saw me last I have become a whippy, probably homosexual youth reminiscent of Dorian Gray in his early phase but far more handsome. You, unless my informants are deliberately misleading me, have become even more maddening, provocative, and lovely. If anything, our presence under the same roof ought to cause an explosion like a fragmentation bomb. If only in a spirit of scientific inquiry, we must move to arrange a vis-à-vis.

*A Universal film (1948) starring Ava Gardner, with a script by Harry Kurnitz and Frank Tashlin.

61

In any case, I append the phone number of my Turkish corner, where I usually sit wallowing in self-pity and threadbare adjectives. Give me a coup de telephone when you get in, or even better, drop me that penny postal a couple of days prior to your arrival letting me know where you'll be staying and I'll call you. Whichever suits.

For the time being, then, walk softly and speak temperately, always remembering to cultivate your interior garden. We who are about to see you salute you.   Forever,

BETTY WHITE JOHNSTON

50 Washington Square South
New York City
May 1, 1945

Dear Betty,

Just set yourself down as one of the most intuitive dolls in history and myself as one of the least lucky friends of that most intuitive doll. Remember back to your letter when you intimated you might be coming up to NY and would I be out in Hollywood by any chance? Well, I smiled loftily when I read it, muttering some phrase about wild horses dragging me back there, etc. So — for my sins, and on what amounted to 24 hours' notice, I found myself chugging out to that dispiriting and unlovely backwater on April 4th. My collaborator (on this musical I've been belting out this winter) and I decided to whiz out there for a week to talk to several composers and actors. We were certain we'd be back by the 15th at most and uttered statements to that effect to one and all. Well, on April 24th, after nine days of dangling around the Santa Fe and Union Pacific ticket-offices, we finally knuckled under and started back on a tourist train called the Grand Canyon Limited. I'll spare you the horrors of the trip; finally got in night before last looking like a couple of tramp comics at Koster & Beal's Music Hall.

Hence, when I found your 2 billets in my mailbox, the first tantalizing me with the promise of your arrival and the second tinged with delicate rebuke (as well as solicitude for my health), my face registered a swift series of emotions from lust to pathos. I suppose it's just as incredible that you should have come up to NY once in 3 years as that I should catapult out to LA at the same moment. The only thing left to us is to repair separately to the corner saloon and get drunk while imagining the scenes of gaiety and good-fellowship which might have been. I'd gladly come down to Washington and sell you a bond, except that this next bond trip is in Pittsburgh and environs on May 22, 23, 24 and until exhausted. Why don't *you* go out to Pittsburgh and buy a bond there?

As for Hollywood, it's everything you've guessed, except that anybody who ever had the slightest spark has left it. (I don't know who I mean by that exactly—just you and I.) The best comment on it is the fact that the day after the President's death, the *Hollywood Reporter* announced that box-office grosses had fallen off. My partner and I wore a permanent scowl of distaste from the moment the train entered Pasadena until we cleared the Continental Divide heading East. It's a dreadful place to visit, but I should certainly hate to live there.

Well, dearie, it's an unattractive picture you're afther painting of ourselves propped up in wheel-chairs at the Sunnyhill Sanitarium drooling on our bibs, and fifteen years is a long time alanna. All I can suggest is that you suddenly smite your forehead and remember that you forgot to buy a packet of common pins at McCreery's or Wanamaker's. Or maybe some paunchy aide of Morgenthau's will take it into his head to summon me to a drum-head court martial for some crack I've made on the public platform. I'm sitting here with my brow furrowed and a pretty vacant expression. Forgive me in a long compassionate letter.   Yours,

ADA ELLISON*

> Chilmark
> Martha's Vineyard, Mass.
> June 30, 1945

Dear Miss Ellison,

As I write, it is 95 degrees net in the shade. I have just finished pulling half of Hirschfeld's beard out by the roots because he insisted on a scene being written his way, and obviously mine was the only way. During supper he will undoubtedly try to sneak some prussic acid into my borscht, and I have only myself to blame. . . .

I'm coming into town this next Thursday for eight days of work with Hirschfeld, so if Leah wants me, please ask her to phone me at my apartment at 14 Wash. Sq. North after eleven Thursday morning; we'll be working there.

> Best regards,

*Assistant to Leah Salisbury.

BETTY WHITE JOHNSTON

> 50 Washington Square South
> New York City
> November 8, 1945

Dear Betty,

Well, my little cabbage, I had just about decided to send your name to the Missing Persons Bureau and have them send out a nine-state alarm (the cotton states, of course—with your new unreconstructed attitude, I presume you'd rather be caught dead than hiding in a Northern state). However, it was jolly to learn that I still existed around the periphery of your heart, even if we do show scant signs of ever turning this into a flesh-and-blood relationship. All this prose about pink gins in corner pubs is pure literature on your part. I'm sure that if we ever met face to face again, you'd be as thorny as a rambler rose.

Me, I'm not in Hollywood nor much place else, for that matter. Just write or wire me at my cable address, Doldrums, New York. This very fine year has been peed away waiting around for a musical show to be produced; if you ever want a nice case of mental lockjaw, just write yourself a musical comedy and try to get it on in a reasonable length of time. I can't think why it would interest you, but I began work on the god-damned thing last December 1st, rewrote it twice this summer, and (with a break) hope to get it into rehearsal early in January. It loused up the summer nicely; I had five delicious sizzling weeks in sunniest Manhattan tearing into the script with a pneumatic drill, and will probably be doing it all over again shortly...Well, what the hell. Nobody forced me into this craft. I could have stayed in Providence, Rhode Island, and worked in the grocery section of Shepard's. At least in that job you can nibble on those little marshmallow cookies. In this one, they never even give you a little showgirl to nibble on. The producer gets them all.

However, there *were* three or four very fine weeks at Martha's Vineyard wedged in somewhere this summer, during which I fell down into the bilge of a sailboat, was dive-bombed by the Navy, and tried to breathe a clam fritter down my trachea. Incidentally, you needn't be so uppity about your sojourn in Walter Reed, I've just concluded a really dramatic bout of sinus. (Isn't this cunning, two mad glad bad hellions out of the early Thirties trying to top each other's illnesses?)

If by any chance you're sitting around in Alexandria conjuring up visions of all the fun and electricity being generated in New York, it may interest you to know that so far this week I've seen two movies, fallen asleep over the paper twice, and narrowly escaped being taken to a parent-teachers' meeting. My physicians are seriously worried about my blood-pressure. It's so low it doesn't show on the gauge.

Nevertheless, for you I'd climb the highest mountain or swim the deepest ocean, and I expect you to do the same for me. Why don't you come on up here for a couple of days and jog me out of this torpor? Between us we mightn't be able to make great music, but we might sound a noble chord or two. Let's have one of those all-afternoon dialogues over much too much brandy, with nobody giving a damn but the waiter.   I embrace you.

BETTY WHITE JOHNSTON

50 Washington Square South
New York City
December 16, 1945

Dear Pen Pal,

It's downright creepy, your letter coming at this point. Last Saturday afternoon I was in a commercial airplane winging north from Fort Worth, on the last leg of a 4000-mile war bond tour which included such up-country localities as Tucson, Dallas, Waco, and so forth. . . . Modest estimates agree that I had addressed something like forty thousand adult civilians, ten high schools, countless numbers of army and navy personnel, and fifteen million club-ladies. It was getting so that every time I entered a hotel coffee shop and found more than two people, I struck a pose, cleared my throat, and began, "Ladies and gentlemen, Chairman Volney, members of the Arriba County War Finance Committee." Had we connected in Washington, I would have regaled you (on my pocket regaler) with innumerable sidelights on my fellow-travellers, Kathleen Winsor, Louis Bromfield, and Glenway Wescott. I guess these incomparable anecdotes will just have to wait until I can whisper them over a rose-shaded lamp in some infamous roadhouse.

So you see ultimately that your dreaming of me, and the shoe motif, was the simplest kind of thought transference. The imputation that I branded you unattractive, scaly, and elderly is feminine bitchery and you know it. You live, and will continue to, as a rosy-tinted memory, slightly redolent of Bacardi, and no amount of reference on your part to hands roughened with Duz and bunioned feet shall stale your infinite variety (Andrew Marvell).

Turning to me for a moment (and what else have we been doing so far in this unbearably tedious letter?), I continue to be my usual neurotic self. Spent the larger part of the fall tapping out fantasies for *The New Yorker*, etc., and dredging up an idea for a musical show and a comedy, neither of which I've done much with in a constructive way. In between, I alternated in a restless fashion between the country and New York, coddling actors and vacuously contemplating my navel, visiting around at local hospitals and generally lowering myself in a gingerly fashion into embittered middle age. Attractive thought, isn't it? There you recline on your puce-colored chaiselongue with Johnston bearing you old brandy and venison, and I shiver in my one-room-and-bath study overlooking Washington Square...Incidentally, if you did whiz up here for shopping or mischief, the hotel shortage being what it is — and it's plenty — you're welcome to this scabrous eyrie of mine as a shakedown. There's a stout chain and a turn-buckle on the door in case I tried to batter it down in a fit of bull-necked passion.

There. I've answered you pronto, even prontissimo. I suppose you're going to go on being the same delicious will-o'-the-wisp you've been all these years. Consider, however, that all this mutual esteem, bottled up over a decade, may erupt like cordite when we finally get within pinching radius of each other. Don't trifle with nature, girl. Be fair to your glands; they've been fair to you. My Christmas wish to you.   Yours,

I . J . K A P S T E I N

14 Washington Square North
New York City
December 17, 1945

Dear Kap,

Let's dispense with the usual maladroit apologies for not having written each other before. It must be so that really old friends find it difficult to compose a letter; I know in my own case that I always expect I'll be chasing through Providence on some errand or that you might pop into New York for a pailfull of ampersands, and yet we get within jostling distance all too rarely. If your ears glowed about two weeks ago, it was because I ran into an old pupil of yours, a very devoted one indeed, down in Dallas. I was on one of these war bond tours with several other "knights of the pen," and after an evening rally, an extremely thin young lady came at me and introduced herself as a Pembroke graduate who had soaked in the best that has been thought and said at your feet. She was very pleasant and we found nothing to quarrel over in her estimate of you, though I did feel she was a bit fulsome in calling you "the Jewish Erasmus." I had always thought of you as "the Jewish LeSage" or, "The Devil on One Stick."

.   .   .

. . . Then in Fort Worth, a bolvan in a soldier suit pounced on me after I'd finished gasping out my life blood on the rostrum, and turned out to be one Parkman Sayward, a blond beast who I think was president of your class. I managed to keep a relatively even keel, though as you can guess, my joy at encountering one of our brothers in Alpha Delta Phi was unbounded.

You may be interested possibly in one experience I had in Dallas; I was standing in a receiving line at a musicale shaking hands with nine hundred club-ladies, bounded on one side by Kathleen Winsor, the Forever Amber girl, and on the other by Louis Bromfield, the Forever Reactionary boy. All at once, out of the corner of my eye, I saw a plump lady bearing down on me, unmistakably preparing to deliver a prepared lump of goo. She was sort of a Dorothy Vernon of Haddon Hall effect — perky little hat with a scarlet ostrich feather, veil, and long gloves to match. As I braced myself, she caught my hand in both of hers, took a deep breath as though preparing to do the crawl,

66

and whinnied, "THE RAINS CAME*—and so did you!" Everybody was too startled, as well as too polite, to inform her she'd got the wrong boy, and I bet she's still beaming over her epigram.

Otherwise, life creeps along as always; the kids aren't getting any younger and hull down on the horizon I see the great day when they'll be old enough to get their working papers. Adam wants to be a heroin addict when he grows up, and Abby's a mean hand with a luckshen coogle. She's going to make some lucky fellow a nice shrew. They both go to the same school this year and so far have an unblemished record, all zeros.

●   ●   ●

Do give my best to Stella and the brood, and when you can pull away from that smoking Oliver typewriter, pound out about a thousand words of gossip and gentle philosophy as the fragrant clouds of Edgeworth wreathe about your silvering head. Or better still, why don't you run down here for a day or two? You haven't lived until you've tried one of Abby's potato knishes. She's only seven but she can poison you as well as the next man.

Yours,

*A novel by Louis Bromfield.

JAMES THURBER*

14 Washington Square North
New York City
March 5, 1946

Dear Jim,

Many thanks to yourself and Helen for your very kind note, which arrived as I was sitting beside a rainswept window tugging ineffectually at my beard, like Beerbohm's mournful caricature of Lytton Strachey. I was particularly heartened by the theory you relayed about the reservoir of humor we're all supposed to possess. Candidly, mine seems at the moment to have shrunken to a greenish hog-wallow dotted with kerosene cans and old shoes. Every so often, I appear in the sedge bordering this tarn, cup my hands, and shout, "Halloo—are there any side-splitting ideas in there, mate?" A voice from the opposite shore (there must be a Cockney living in there with me) replies, "Coo—not bloody 'arf."

I suppose, however, we should all be refreshed and uplifted by the thought that one person, at least, continues to wear the old cap and bells vivaciously, and that's Bennett Cerf. Among his other exploits this winter, America's Sweetheart got out a Modern Library anthology of humor with a

*The humorist and artist served as a staff writer for *The New Yorker* from 1927 to 1933 (d. 1961).

dust-jacket representing you and me which is going to take some intensive forgetting. One of these days when we're not too busy worrying, what say we sneak over to Random House and clap a commode snugly down over his ears?

I hope, in any case, that you are both bursting with rude health, and let's all toast each other into insensibility some evening with all kinds of malts and grains. Meanwhile, Laura and I send you our very best.

Yours,

GUS LOBRANO*

Martha's Vineyard, Mass.
August 24, 1946

Dear Gus,

Thank you indeed for sending me those reviews of *Keep It Crisp*; I've been marooned up here miles from a newsstand and they were the first I'd seen. By now I'm pretty well inured to critics like Sterling North who review books in what they conceive to be the author's style. Actually, I'm more fortunate than a gent like Nash, who gets 70 or 80 notices all written in hideously tortured metre each time he pokes his nose out of his burrow. As for Time Inc., they have, as you know, hardly any influence on book sales; I don't suppose they influence more than forty or fifty million readers. That leaves me, according to the latest census figures, about ninety million potential readers, which assures me a pretty comfortable living.

Incidentally, in case you decide to forsake editing, you and Jean could work out a pretty comfortable existence up here. With scarcely any effort at all (only eight hours in the broiling sun), I managed to pick a half pint of blueberries yesterday, and the waters are alive with fish; in less than two weeks I've caught three puffers at least four inches long, jam-packed with nourishing little bones. Maybe we all ought to club together in a kind of Brook Farm, free-love community and snap our fingers at Raoul Fleischmann.† Or do you think Sandy and Dotty are too old to begin life anew?

We're pulling out of here Saturday and I expect to be back in town pretty permanently for rehearsals of *Gang Aft Aglee* (that musical I wrote in collaboration with Schlesinger, author of *The Age of Jackson*) by the end of next week. I also have a three-volume life of Mother Cabrini almost completed,

---

*Managing editor of fiction (and Perelman's editor) at *The New Yorker* until his death in 1956. *The Ill-Tempered Clavichord* is dedicated to him.
†Along with Harold Ross, founder of *The New Yorker*, and publisher until his death in 1969.

68

which Sheed & Ward will publish, due to appear on Christmas Day. All in all, it looks like an active winter.

Best from Laura, and I look forward to seeing you soon.

Yours,

DANIEL LONGWELL*

14 Washington Square North
New York City
November 28, 1946

Dear Dan,

Ours is undoubtedly the most torpid correspondence on record. My exquisite Chinese manners reminded me this morning that I had never replied to your letter of August 20, commenting on the piece I'd done for *The New Yorker* on Pequot Sheets. So you're that reader I've heard so much about who likes my work. You may as well know that it puts you in an extremely difficult position; you're a one-man cult. The next time I go into the Jefferson Market in a frenzied attempt to restore my credit, I intend to use your name for all its worth.

You were also kind enough to enclose a White Rock ad out of *The New Yorker* which showed Prince Ali involved in a pretty questionable affair with Miss Psyche. If I haven't done anything about it, it's only because I've been hip deep in that wretched musical show.† Now that I'm clear of it, it turns out that I'm being sent on a round-the-world junket for *Holiday* magazine. But never fear. Probably when I'm sitting in some dubious bodeja in Port Said (the belly dancer, the bead curtains, all that lousy color), I may suddenly get the urge to take off and do the job really required on that ad. . . .

Ever,

*At the time, managing editor of *Life* (d. 1968).
†*Sweet Bye and Bye*.

DONALD KLOPFER

10664 Bellagio Road
Los Angeles, Calif.
February 2, 1947

Dear Donald,

Thank you for your letter of January 2nd regarding our future relations, and you may be sure that I will be happy to sit down with you when I get back from this junket and frame a modus vivendi. Though why I have fallen into that conventional phrase, "sit down," is beyond me. We could just as well frame it standing up, lying down, or under water. Lying down, in fact, and by preference with a couple of Conover models, would suit me best of all.

I feel impelled, however, to raise one point at this juncture. You say that "in the meantime, we are going ahead pushing *Keep It Crisp*." To the best of my information and what I myself have seen since I left New York, no advertisement for *Keep It Crisp* has appeared anywhere since early in December (possibly excepting a *New Yorker* insertion somewhere just before Christmas). Now, Donald, leave us face it. This is not author's vanity; I have no desire whatever to see my name blazoned through the advertising columns, nor would I see it in any case in the remote areas I'll be in the next eight or nine months. It's simply a plain matter of merchandising. Advertising sells books, it has been demonstrated over and over again, and our mutual friend Aaron Sussman has stated to me unequivocally that he has proved it by innumerable keyed tests. I don't know what the present figures on *Keep It Crisp* are (though I should very much like to), but Lou Miller told me before I came West that he fully expected it to have a continuing sale well into the spring. If, however, you people let it die, and don't remind people of its existence, and don't let people who may have missed its publication know that it's out and available in the bookshops, I don't see that you are recommending yourselves very strongly to me as my future and ideal publisher. You were very flattering that day at lunch, and you stated it as your belief that my possibilities in terms of sales were only beginning. *Keep It Crisp* got reviews which were everything I could have desired. What about demonstrating to me in terms of actual promotion and advertising that given these elements, your · house knows what to do with them?

Perhaps there are factors in the picture which I do not appreciate, and perhaps in my absence there has been a thundering advertising campaign; if so, please discount what I have said. If, however, these *are* approximately the facts, I'd appreciate a note before I embark letting me know what's being done to wring as many editions as possible out of this particular book.

·   ·   ·

Yours,

FRANCES and ALBERT HACKETT

San Francisco, Calif.
February 11, 1947

Dear Frances & Albert,

Thank you for sending along that clipping Dave Chandler gave you for

70

me. I ought to get something done about it around the time I get to the Pyramids myself. At the rate this trip is progressing, we ought to be in Honolulu a year from next Tuesday.

However, this is just momentary gloom induced by too much waiting for the trip to start. Actually, we are getting away tomorrow (Wednesday), the ship is due to sail in the early afternoon. We got a chance to inspect our cabin, we're bunking in with somebody named Ferguson attached to the Standard Oil Company and heading for Singapore also. He's probably fifty-five, a pompous bore who has brought along nothing but a beret and a set of Haldeman Julius Blue Books. He will undoubtedly kibitz all our little jars of jam, delicacies, and that beautiful box of chocolates you gave me the night I left.

And there could be no better time than this to register my appreciation of your kindness in every possible way during my stay at the house. Ignoring the fact that I commandeered every facility, dragooned Elsa into the most menial tasks, behaved on all occasions with the insolence of a freebooter, and in general outwore my welcome, I should say that you both were marvels of forbearance, a monument of patience, in short, a duck. I love you both, I bless you both. God keep and preserve the Hacketts.

But at my back I seem to hear / Time's winged footstep hurrying near. I will arise and go now, not only to Innisfree but to the closet and pack my clothes, clean and dirty alike. Adieu, and in the words of Hiler,* goodbye far away, au voir pour Mehico (which is to say rather, pour Casablanca and our rendezvous late next August).   Yours ever,

*Hilaire Hiler, American muralist and designer (d. 1966).

G U S   L O B R A N O

> Bangkok, Siam
> May 2, 1947

Dear Gus,

In order to get the full flavor of the circumstances under which this is being written, you must conjure up a picture of me seated in a room twenty feet square and fifteen feet high into which open five doorways and four windows. The doors are of the type once used in bar-rooms, short swinging ones that goose you whenever you pass through them; the windows have no glass or screens, but remain open to allow birds, bats, and, I suppose, even snakes to pass through freely. There are two overhead fans, a great canopy of mosquito-netting suspended from the ceiling under which are two iron beds, an armoire, and a couple of chairs. Everything wooden in the room is made of teak; in fact, teak is the only wood used anywhere in the house. The time is exactly eight o'clock of a broiling Friday morning; the temperature at the moment is about 90 and will rise before the day is done to 98. Your correspondent is wearing a pair of khaki shorts and a t-shirt. He has a slight case of heat-rash on his insteps, what may be either diarrhea or dysentery in his innards, and a definite sense of remorse at not having written you before this.

To bring you completely up to date on our globe-girdling, Hirschfeld and I sailed the 12th of February from San Francisco, after five weeks in Hollywood, on the *Marine Flier*, an 11-passenger cargo ship of the American President Lines. We were eighteen days crossing the Pacific to Chinwangtao in North China. (As you see, we never did get to Samoa and the Fijis; transportation is still completely dislocated and you have to settle for continents rather than countries.) We sashayed up and down the Chinese coast for the next three weeks, going to Shanghai, back to Chinwangtao, and then back to Shanghai. Some bright boy in the shipping department had bollixed up the cargo completely and the hold resembled a woman's pocketbook as much as anything else. Eventually we reached Hongkong, and, five days later, Singapore. Of all the foregoing places, Hongkong was the only tolerable one, and then only because it's essentially British. Everything else in China is disorganized, corrupt, frenzied, and generally unpleasant to the Western eye. (I brought along a Western eye to view it through.) Singapore, of course, is British also, but it isn't much more attractive; it's all mid-Victorian yellow stucco, stifling hot, expensive, and stuffy, and we lingered as little as possible. We had a couple of interesting passages in both Hongkong and Johore, close by Sinapore; at Hongkong I spent an evening with the deposed Emperor of Annam in Indochina, Bao Dai, and at Johore with the Regent and the Sultan's sister. It's all bad comic opera, and it may well be that the Shuberts were behind it. Their persecution dates back to a musical comedy called *Sweet Bye and Bye*; remind me to tell you about that sometime...I also visited a supposed sinkhole of iniquity called Macao near Hongkong, and remind me not to tell you about that sometime. If you've ever spent a rainy Sunday night in Harrisburg, Pa., you know what Macao is like.

In any case, I flew up here to Bangkok April 10th, followed by Hirschfeld who came by boat. I've spent three weeks here now, living at the residence of Col. Vance, our military attaché, and seeing the sights. Hirschfeld left four days ago on a trip up-country to Chieng Mai (via motor trolley, a strange contraption that runs on the railroad tracks) accompanied by one of the lads in the U.S. Information Service. All this time I've been waiting for my visa to enter Indochina; I had a fine trip all laid out to Pnom Penh, Saigon, Angkor Wat, and an island called Khong in the Mekong River up in Cambodia about which I'd heard very romantic stories. Yesterday, after an interminable hole-and-corner game with the French, I pretty well established the fact that being a writer, my chances of getting into Indochina at this time are pretty slim. Though I carefully explained to them that I was non-political, they don't want any hint of their debacle there publicized. They're in a completely untenable position in Indochina and are sure as hell going to lose it to the Vietnamese eventually for all their 110,000 men and superior weapons. Everyone I've talked to is either overtly or secretly in sympathy with the resistance, but France is muddling ahead in a thoroughly brutal, medieval, and imperialist fashion. The French Foreign Legion, by the way, is described by those who've been to Saigon as largely made up of ex-Nazis who were given a choice of jail or service in the Legion for seven years. Night before last, the Legion held a sort of military review some distance outside Saigon, and a chap who was staying in a hotel there said the Legionnaires roved the streets until the curfew shouting "Sieg heil!" and singing the Horst Wessel song. I also understand that Robert Sherred of *Life* is doing an article plus photographs for his magazine about the Legion, which I'd think would be very interesting reading.

An interval has elapsed between this paragraph and the preceding one; I've been out trying to line up some transportation between here and Penang, down in the Malay States. I have about sixteen days before the S.S. *President Monroe* sails from Singapore for Ceylon and Bombay, and I wanted to spend it in some interesting place nearby. Rangoon, three hours distant by air, has no hotel accommodations, is very badly bombed, inflationary, and hot, so that's out. Penang is only reached by a railroad that takes three to four days and has no Pullmans; you have to change trains frequently, as most of the bridges are bombed out. There is one possibility left, the Siamese Air Company. That doesn't leave until next Thursday, a five-day wait, so here I will sit grinding my teeth impotently at the French for having got me into this box.·

Bangkok, when the sun retreats behind a cloud temporarily, is actually a rather nice place. The vegetation is handsome, the klongs, or canals, which parallel all the streets have a complex and interesting population living on them, and there is more of the well-known Somerset Maugham kind of color here than any place we've seen yet. The European-American colony—about three hundred people in a city of a million—lives pretty fabulously; Colonel Vance, for instance, has twelve servants, the assistant military and naval attachés have about seven each, and the cost of living for anyone paid off in American dollars is trifling. One of the nicer little customs, which I appreciate especially remembering the laundry situation in New York, is the wash amah's gathering all your linen in the morning and returning it completely ironed by four in the afternoon...Americans are well-liked here (one of the two places in the world they are, the other being America) and the Siamese impress one as extraordinarily gentle, polite, and good-looking folk. By the way, while on Bangkok, I've run into a number of old-timers who remember McKelway with affection.* Emily Hahn, of course, is dinner-table gossip everywhere you go.† That girl certainly cut a swath through Asia.

Well, Gus, the heat of noon is on me and all life is suspended from now until four-thirty or five, when my hosts and I form ranks in the sixty-foot livingroom and spend a couple of hours drinking gimlets (gin and lime-juice) or Mekong, a type of palm whiskey. If you can find time to write, I'd appreciate a note at the address below, which will be valid until July 1st. Meanwhile, my best to Jean and the family, and, of course, Ross and everyone at 25 West 43rd. And I do hope you have a much cooler summer than I expect to.

Yours ever,

*St. Clair McKelway Jr., editor of the Fact Department, *The New Yorker* (d. 1954).
†Journalist and author of many books on China (*Chiang Kai-Shek*, etc.).

BETTY WHITE JOHNSTON

50 Washington Square South
New York City
September 30, 1947

Dear Betty,

I got back to the evil-smelling rabbit warren I work at about mid-September and clawed my way through the cobwebs to find your agreeable note awaiting me. The thought that you had deliberately exposed your 14-year-old son to my prose is an insupportable one; a mind already weakened by comics and radio serials may well collapse at this added indignity, but then, you are his mother and must be fully aware what the consequences might be. It is a sad commentary that this promising young fellow spends his time burrowing into Dostoievsky; from there it is only a step to Kafka, and before you can say knife, he will be lounging around one of these Greenwich Village bodegas a stone's throw from here, swilling red wine, plagiarizing Amy Lowell, and generally disqualifying himself for a useful, active bourgeois life. There is still time to avert the disaster; enroll him at V.M.I. or Manlius at once.

I do intend to be in New York this November, much as the impulse moves me to pack up my traps and grab the first plane back to Siam. Perhaps it is only the consequence of living an entirely rootless existence the past eight months, merely worrying whether one's laundry would be ready by the time the next boat sailed, but life hereabouts certainly seems complex and aimless. Does your old man come back from his periodic affairs with the railroads in this woolgathering frame of mind? If it's anything like mine, better watch him like a hawk.

The sole ray of sunshine lighting up my autumn, though, is the possibility you outline that you may again be on the prowl for shoes. No fetishist I, simply a fun-loving, over-sexed paterfamilias who carries the memory of you in his heart untarnished by your cruel neglect. I think it would be matey of you indeed to up-end a convivial glass with me, and I suggest that you let me know when you're coming far enough in advance so we can plan on it. And I think I can guarantee that if you can get a word in edgewise, you'll be lucky. If a trip around the world does nothing else, it very effectively turns people like myself into crashing bores.

I append below the vital statistics incidental to reaching me by either mail or phone, just to bring your files up to date. Jot them down in that well-worn little black book and send up a flare to your ardent pen pal.

Always,

B E T T Y   W H I T E   J O H N S T O N

50 Washington Square South
New York City
February 2, 1948

Dear Betty,

I suppose two months is some kind of world-wide all-time record for tardiness in replying to a letter, but I seem to have hung it up for posterity to shoot at and I couldn't be more remorseful. The interval since receiving yours of November 30th has feen fairly dreamy, what with assembling that *Holiday* nonsense into a book for late spring publication* and revving up the creaky old mechanism to belt out some *New Yorker* pieces and suchlike — "pulling teeth" would be a nice fresh simile to describe what it was like after · being away from it for a year. Anyway, all through it I have kept meaning daily and weekly to write and find out how your grapple with the medicoes turned out — you were on the verge of getting your viscera (polite circumlocution) reupholstered. Are you all hale and hearty again, and was it more gruelling than it should have been? I do hope you breezed through the whole thing without fluttering an eyelid. I seem to recall your swan-like athletic figure whipping off a springboard at the Garden of Allah pool back in the early Thirties with a grace and authority Eleanor Holm might well envy, and I'm sure this recent tick-tack-toe you played with your sawbones will have restored all the verve you ever had.

All of which is introductory to the inquiry, Are you still planning that February trip to New York? At the moment, I *am* here and neither in Hollywood or Afghanistan, as you suggest. . . .

As for your son's penchant for Dostoievsky, that might be written off

Westward Ha!

75

to precocity. His liking for my stuff, however, gets dangerously close to the province of psychiatry, and if you expect any sympathy from me, you are very much mistaken, my girl. I don't let my whelps read it and I don't know why you should. Ever yours,

G R O U C H O   M A R X

Erwinna, Pa.
June 26, 1948

Dear Groucho,

Your letter was a kind deed in a naughty world (a phrase I copped out of *Bartlett's Book of Quotations* years ago and have been trying to work in ever since). It was particularly heartening since it arrived at one of those moments of self-laceration that free-lance writers sometimes experience (never more than 8 hours a day, however). In these rare moods the subject is given to regarding himself through the wrong end of a telescope and inquiring through his teeth, "Too proud to stay in your father's dry-goods business, eh? I told you that you'd rue the day." None of this, of course, would have happened had I actually stayed in my father's business, where my superb acumen would undoubtedly have made me the uncrowned king of the gingham trade.

This is an ideal opportunity, incidentally, to tell you that I enjoyed a considerable social success up and down the China coast after we saw each other last by merely mentioning that I knew you. In fact, in one or two tight spots, I took the liberty of actually pretending to *be* you, so if you are visited by any slant-eyed Celestials from Chefoo or Macao who present IOU's and request that you honor them, I beg your indulgence.

The soothsayers inform me that it's more than likely I may get to the Coast in the next few months and I look forward to sharing a convivial glass with you. Why don't we meet at Jerry Rothschild's barber shop on Beverly Drive, have our hair cut together, and then run over to Armstrong Schroeder's for some little thin hot-cakes? Are you game?

With Laura's tenderest regards, and the sincere assurance that your letter really touched me, Yours,

B E T T Y   W H I T E   J O H N S T O N

50 Washington Square South
New York City
October 3, 1948

Dear Betty,

When we finally do get into the same general area, I rather imagine the excitement will rival the meeting on the Field of the Cloth of Gold. I returned a few days back from Martha's Vineyard and found your Joan Miro postcard in my web; the language was ambiguous and I was uncertain whether the Washington postmark meant you had been in New York at all, but I guess it did. In any case, God in his infinite wisdom realizes that there is enough mischief afoot in atomic energy without coupling us. (And I mean this in its most evil, aphrodisiacal sense, you sultry-eyed jade.)

Here I am, then, taking up in my usual loose-leaf fashion the cares of town life and facing the next couple of months without overweening enthusiasm. Fortunately, it now looks practically definite that I may be shoving off for Hong Kong, the Celebes, and Siam right after January first, so I've got that to sustain me. Yes, another series for *Holiday* and a book. But if you have any sense of obligation whatever, you owe it both to yourself and me to whiz up north and buy me a bumper of champagne to speed me on my way. How about it? For God's sake, cara mia, is there anything wrong with my wanting you to see me before *all* my hair falls out?

But write anyway; surely you can't be so broke that you can't rustle up a few sheets of cream-laid paper and a stamp.

Yours ever,

FRANCES and ALBERT HACKETT
14 Washington Square North
New York City
October 17, 1948

Dear Frances and Albert,

Laura's repeated assurances to me that she had both replied to your letter and that she was about to do so are, I think, characteristic of a mind at bay. I have finally tired of her sneaky, evasive attitude and decided that I am cast, as always, as the town gossip, hence this undignified posture before a creaky Underwood on Sunday afternoon.

We are all reasonably o.k. hereabouts, living off the impetus we got from about seven weeks up on the Vineyard between late July and mid-September. . . . I spent the Vineyard phase deliberately turning a deaf ear to work and succeeded in catching several hundred puffers, skates, and flounders, also played a certain amount of tennis. Albert can, I think, sympathize with the plight of his old opponent who hadn't picked up a racket in seven years. I am told by unprejudiced observers that my breathing was audible as far away as Hingham, Mass., and a few times the final volleys found me face down on the court in a dead faint. But it was fun, and currently I have taken to playing Saturday mornings on the theory that you may as well be hung for a sheep, etc.

We occasionally see returned travellers from beyond the Continental Divide; the Lampells called Laura this morning and we shall be quizzing them within the week, and of course we got a full-dress . . . report on Hollywood from Ruth and Gus. . . . They are mulling a trip to London this fall, as *The Heiress* is probably going to be done there, and I believe that the keel of a special liner is at present being laid at Tyneside to convey them in proper style. The rumor that they are to be met in mid-Ocean by the Queen Mother Alexandra and Lord Linlithgow has as yet been unconfirmed.

Ourselves, we too are on the verge of a bit of sightseeing: right after January 1st, Laura and the kids and I are departing for the Far East, specifically Siam, as guinea pigs for a new series I'll be doing for *Holiday* (to become a book published by Simon & Schuster like the last one). It'll be sort of a Swiss Family Perelman, concerned with what happens to a standard Yankee family transplanted to exotic places, and I hope to include a number of them beside Bangkok, which will be our base. This whole notion is one I've entertained since late last spring and have with some muscular effort grafted onto Laura; however, it's now well along and we're negotiating for an actual sailing date from San Francisco right after New Year's, getting shots, passports, and the like. Its advantages as far as the kids and ourselves go is that it should acquaint them with a lot of places they ought to see and will, I hope, shake us out of the well-known domestic rut.

·   ·   ·

In any event we are looking forward to seeing you before too long, either if you're anticipating a quick trip East or when we wheel through Los Angeles en route. My mother lives there, you may remember, and we'll be stopping off briefly to let her pinch her grandchildren....Laura sends along a nosegay of kisses, and do let us hear the latest harrowing details.

Yours ever,

BETTY WHITE JOHNSTON

50 Washington Square South
New York City
October 18, 1948

Mon ange,

This appears to be the only tint of stationery sufficiently emotional to express the frustration, rage, and ardor resulting from your visit north and the letters we sent each other which went agley. Enclosed you will find the billet-doux I sent you on October 3rd, which, as you see, was returned to me —

why, I still can't figure out. But in any case, I had it propped up on my inlaid secretary (none of your filthy ambiguities) until several days ago, when the spider who is my landlord knocked on the door and handed me your letter of September 8th, in which you wrote me from Birmingham that you were coming up to New York. This high-born type had helpfully plucked it out of my mailbox (I was then up on Martha's Vineyard) and stashed it in his rolltop desk, where it lay cooling all the while. If you are a good enough detective to piece together this farrago, you'll have a general notion of what a hole-and-corner game we have been playing with each other.

Anyway, I now see clearly that some mysterious power above felt it better to keep us apart; and I can only renew the importunities you'll find in conjunction here. Also, in passing, better find out what that postman of yours is about. Some wealthy sheep-herding uncle in Australia may be checking out one of these days and leaving you a packet, and it wouldn't do if his lawyer's notification went begging.   Yours eternally,

BETTY   WHITE   JOHNSTON

50 Washington Square South
New York City
December 13, 1948

Dear Betty,

The delay in replying wasn't caused by pique, though it might well have been; I surely thought that after so many abortive overtures, we were at last going to lock horns like a couple of moose. . . .

.   .   .

Anyhow, the prospect of connecting at the moment is distinctly dim, since the present design is that we take off for Indonesia and Siam January 7th, length of stay being slightly indeterminate. Possibly it will become more concrete after a bout or two of dengue fever; right now, the only definite plan on the tapis is to try to get the young back for next autumn's school term. If we do succeed in covering all the ground I'd like to, it may be a longer stay than that; I don't know. I don't know. . . .

Well, baby doll, there it is, and standing here on the threshold of Christmas, a New Year, and departure, I embrace you as ever, showering you with my kindest and trusting that all will go well with you and yours in '49. When we do see each other again, it's likely that I'll be a small, shrunken, yellow-faced jockey of a man, plagued by the locust and dysentery. Nor will that head of mine, by then doubtless shrunken over many a native fire, arouse much more in your bosom than deep pity. Damn it all, I say. It certainly was my remotest wish that you migrate to the land of the hookworm and you have demonstrated my most pessimistic predictions. Well, you have made your bed. Lie in it and think betimes of your wandering sailor boy, who ever thinks of you.   Love,

BETTY WHITE JOHNSTON

                                        50 Washington Square South
                                        New York City
                                        December 26, 1948

Ma belle,

      •   •   •

    Only the Christmas season and its attendant tolerance prevents me from railing at a destiny which has callously and steadily kept us from fusing. I would hate to think that we are going to sublimate ourselves in heated correspondence and that when we finally do foregather, it will simply be a pair of elderly paralytics whizzing at each other in wheelchairs. Perhaps we'd be better advised to set up a hard-and-fast date at the Kellogg Sanitarium in Battle Creek in 1970. I shall lay in a little stock of psyllium seed at once. Though all heaven crash about our ears, we may as well put our bowels in order.

    Meanwhile, I send you and yours a pinch signifying my hope for a jolly and rewarding year to come, and as I depart into the setting sun, place on your brow a brotherly kiss I hope one day to redeem. May God keep and preserve you so that I may eventually undo his handiwork.

                                        Always,

LEILA HADLEY*

                                        10664 Bellagio Road
                                        Los Angeles, Calif.
                                        January 14, 1949

Dear Leila,

      •   •   •

    The trip across the country was, naturally, a nightmare; the sleeping car my troupe and I were lodged in was hooked to a succession of railroad systems among which I dimly recall the Pennsylvania, Burlington, Denver & Rio Grande, and Western Pacific. On the last-named, we spent a dreamy interlude in something called a Vista Dome car, a double-decked job topped by a large glass blister supposed to be ideal for looking at the scenery. It was filled with mid-Western excursionists who had just eaten the $1.65 table-d'hôte luncheon,

*Hadley was introduced to Perelman by his editor, Jack Goodman, at a publishing party for *Westward Ha!* in 1948.

80

belching softly and discussing the laxatives they preferred to keep themselves "regular." One lady announced in a voice like the Bull of Bashan that the doctors had long since given her up for dead but that psyllium seed had preserved her bowels. When I tell you that throughout this symposium the musical background consisted of a radio program of organ music from the Angelus Temple in Los Angeles, I think you will begin to get a rough idea.

•   •   •

Yesterday was largely devoted to good works, your correspondent having taken his brood to MGM for a gander at the passing scene in motion pictures. The kids shook hands with some kind of a collie dog named Lassie who is reputed to be a sensational breadwinner, and we also watched a somewhat untalented lady by the name of Jennifer Jones impersonating Emma Bovary. I am happy to report to you that the cultural level hereabouts is as lofty as ever. Rouaults and Picassos are being traded like broncos and as you pass the average citizen on Hollywood Boulevard, it is six, two, and even that he is humming a snatch of Stravinsky. The Black Dahlia murder case is occupying the public interest at the moment; the current suspect is a theosophist who was reported in this morning's *Times* as studying to be a midget automobile racer. There was also a stop-press dispatch to the effect that a man out in the San Fernando Valley had invented a thinking machine which lies by his fireside and purrs like a cat. So you see everything is normal.

This present phase in Los Angeles concludes next Tuesday morning, when we emplane for San Francisco to spend three days before sailing for the fabled East. . . .   Yours,

L E I L A H A D L E Y

Hotel Mark Hopkins
San Francisco, Calif.
January 21, 1949

Dear Leila,

To predict that this note will be of the essence of hysteria is approximately as certain as that the dawn will break tomorrow (and I give you the foregoing as a sample of masterly English in the great tradition of Addison and Pope). But you will have to exercise every bit of forebearance of which you're capable, realizing that your devoted admirer is moving in six directions at once, stuffing soiled laundry into bon voyage baskets, jumping up and down on suitcases swollen like gravid women, issuing stentorian commands to people who ignore them completely, and in every way simulating that dreadful woodpecker celebrated in song and story. The steamer is scheduled to leave at 4 this afternoon and other than rushing down Nob Hill to buy a couple of athletic supporters (pure swank, of course), getting duplicates of trunk keys, phoning a bookshop to rush a travelling copy of the *Book of Hours* to the wharfside, paying the bill here, repairing a lighter, tracking down my young, and half a dozen minor errands, I am booted and spurred for Cathay.

I would, however, hate myself in the morning if I didn't register in imperishable type the pleasure your letters gave me. Once I get across that gangplank and the only distraction is that of seagulls croaking outside the porthole (seagulls don't croak, but there's no time for *le mot juste* and Flaubert isn't looking over my shoulder), I hope to take up specific points in your communiques and answer any direct questions. I also plan to make a number of assertions, declarations, and representations of a tender nature which you in your cynical way will probably construe as insincere, but I hope that by sheer persuasiveness and verbal guile to convince you, at least temporarily. I am in the unenviable position of having to win you by mail, to court a lady who almost every hour of the twenty-four is besieged by chaps with the lowest possible motives. May we be pen pals, dear? It's so little to ask, and you have so much to give. And I shall be so far away. God damn it.

If you detect in all this a curious ambivalence about my trip, I ought to explain quickly that you are the unpredictable factor, the thumbprint the criminal did not figure on, so to speak, the element of chance which enters the picture long after the plans are carefully hatched. If you hear the grinding of teeth at a distance of 3000 miles, it should be apparent by now that it's caused by my frustration at not having a *little* more time together. The philosophers would tell me that this is precisely what lends spice to the wooing, as Jimmy Durante puts it, but I am not in any condition for sophistry. I feel as if we had met at a lonely hearts ball, shared a sherbet, and been abruptly plucked from each other. Between us, reading from right to left, are three continents and about fourteen assorted oceans. But I will traverse them, never you fear.

• • •

That, I regret to say, will have to do it for the moment. There are all sorts of innaresting details I'd ought to go into, like the cocktail I had with Mr. W.S. Maugham yesterday when I initiated him into the arcana of pickpocketing, etc., etc., but they'll have to wait. In the meanwhile, don't you think that the very least you could do to reinforce the little I have to go on would be to send me some sort of beat-up snapshot, cabinet photograph, daguerreotype, or (failing these) portrait done in bottle-caps, of yourself? If all else fails, go into the nearest Photomaton and charge it to my royalty account at S&S.

Gosh all hemlock, what happens when two people consider the other party wonderful? Perhaps I'd better pick up a little fast asbestos; by the time

I'll be writing you from southeast Asia, ordinary air mail stationery will never stand the gaff.   Yours as noted,

F R A N C E S and A L B E R T   H A C K E T T

S.S. *President Cleveland*
January 24, 1949

Dear Frances and Albert,

Now that the collective stomach has stopped twitching and the passengers aboard this sleek ocean greyhound have begun emerging from the plastic woodwork with gray, pinched faces, I can again face the typewriter without revulsion. The first thirty hours out of San Francisco can best be ignored. Our average as a family was roughly 75%; Laura managed to stay on her feet (deep down she was just as queasy as Adam, Abby, and myself, but an ingrained stubbornness prevented her from admitting it). The vessel kept executing what its skipper later described to us as a twenty-five degree roll, roughly comparable to what a nautch dancer does with her belly. Our own bellies churned in rhythm to it. Had you asked any one of us at that moment for our honest opinion of this whole jaunt, we would have sold it for ten cents on the dollar.

I don't know that the *President Cleveland* is a ship in any sense that you and I understand it; there is none of that characteristic smell of spilt red wine, greasy oilcloth, garlic, and remote urine we all remember from the prewar French boats. It's all molded rubber, modernique and formalized flowers, splashy murals in the tradition of *Fortune*, monel metal, and catfooted waiters sneaking up behind you with canapés. . . .

Our plans became much more definite in the three days we spent in San Francisco; we are now proceeding directly to Hong Kong instead of debarking at Manila, arriving February 11th and sailing February 17th on the *Tjisadane* of the Royal Interocean Lines for Batavia, Samarang, Sourabaya, and Macassar. At the last-named, we will catch one of the inter-island ships of the K.P.M. and take a trip around the Moluccas endng at Bali, if we can arrange it, for a stay there; and thereafter proceed back to Singapore and up to Bangkok. Though more circuitous than what we'd planned before (which was flying straight from Manila to Macassar), it will allow the folks to see Hong Kong, a city I think is worth seeing, and besides Laura wasn't too keen on the flying where we could avoid it.

I needn't say that both Laura and I feel that after our stay at Hotel Hackett, things are going to seem anti-climactic. The Mark Hopkins, famous from here to there for its service and cuisine, seemed like the Hotel Dixie by contrast with what we had accustomed ourselves to in the week preceding. Nor is it necessary to say that one of the culminating points in my life was reached with the Coupe Alexander that historic night at Chasen's. I get limp in every nerve when I think of it.

Well, one of the catfoots is patrolling the corridors beating a gong for dinner. This is Aloha Night, a festive occasion signalizing our arrival day after tomorrow in Honolulu. There will be music by genuine Hawaiians, paper leis, and guaranteed nausea by midnight. Te morituri salutamus. All our love and gratitude for your kindness, and those redoubtable poker players, Adam and Abby, send you a bevy of sticky kisses. Do write us. . . .

Yours always,

L E I L A   H A D L E Y

S.S. President Cleveland
January 25, 1949

My dear,

•   •   •

This is getting itself written in Cabin 164 aft, a claustrophobic two-berth stateroom without benefit of porthole kindly loaned me by the authorities for the purpose of escaping my dependents and doing some necessary work. Unlike yourself, whose powers of concentration are such that you can write me amid the babble of Capp Enterprises, I am an introvert nail-chewer who has to lock himself into an iron maiden, preferably sound-proofed, to even answer a dunning letter. The American President Lines, which is being too God-damned winsome for words, at the last minute switched the brood and myself out of the perfect two-cabin set-up we had, in which I was assured a quiet place to work, into one of the two deluxe suites. The latter are ideal for pint-sized Filipino diplomats, small and fragile-boned citizens even at their brawniest. For two adults and two energetic kids owning thirteen pieces of baggage, not including four trunks, two inflated Schmoos, and a ¾ size 'cello, they are less ideal. In desperation, after a day or two of trying to marshal my woolly wits in this bedlam, I appealed to the skipper, with whom I had sailed in the past, and the chain of command has passed me down to the lazaret where I now sit. If I move my head sharply to the left, it dents a suspended water carafe; a sudden motion to the right annihilates a mirror. I shall have to be as dainty as a Dresden china statuette to get through the day. . . .

Since I wrote the material dated Sunday, the tropics have moved in abruptly. It's suddenly become extra balmy; last night the Milky Way and all turned out in full dress. . . . This morning all the officers are strutting around in their whites and gold braid, the pool resounds with glad cries, and the *Cleveland* is one big Dole pineapple juice ad. Last night's Aloha Dinner, one of those mechanical galas they put on before touching at these Pacific ports, had all the trappings you'd anticipate—paper hats, noisemakers, melon balls and Beluga caviar. The fat cats I alluded to got nicely oiled and made audible jokes about Harry S. Truman. Later on, in the Marine Veranda (sic), one Carmen Cavallero (who apparently is renowned as a pianist), played what my professional friends refer to as a hotel piano, sticky Kostelanetz interpretations of "When Day Is Done" and "Lover Come Back to Me." Everyone present voted the occasion as the most successful ever. Either I'd had one too many stingers or I am an intolerant son-of-a-bitch who prefers the piano style of Joe Sullivan, Little Brother, and Jess Stacy, but I felt grumpy. . . .

•   •   •

Yours,

L E I L A   H A D L E Y

S.S. President Cleveland
February 2, 1949

My dear,

Now is the horrid hour when the grave yawns and the grisly gaiety of organized fun aboardship takes over. As I sit down to write this, every man jack of the passengers is plummeting around the corridors on a scavenger hunt—which, as a former organizer of parties, will probably curl up your toes with loathing. Retired bank presidents, their jowls flushed with hypertension, sprint by my door searching for unbearably quaint items like a lady's garter on toast, corseted dowagers invade the junior pursers' cabins on the pretext of promoting an Upmann cigar wrapper—jeez, it's a veritable Sodom and Gomorrah, a hell-ship beneath the unwinking Southern Cross. . . .

The one-day stopover in Honolulu was purest Chamber of Commerce, as I anticipated; ruddy-faced boosters in eccentric sports shirts beat me on the back and forced coconut milk down my throat until I bade fair to die, my young were heaped with souvenir ukuleles, paper leis, glossy prints of Mauna Loa in eruption and quiescent, and we ate a Hawaiian meal at Don the Beachcomber's you could not duplicate this side of Hollywood Boulevard. It is a pretty depressing thought that the peculiar two-dimensional, neon civilization of Southern California (William Faulkner has a phrase about "the vicious depthless quality of stamped tin" that sums it up) should have been transplanted so completely to the Pacific Islands. I have no idea what Manila is like except from the descriptions of some of its residents on board, but I hope it's staggering along without a 4-Minute Car Wash and a Skyburger Too Thick for a Straw.

This ship is really pretty droll—a luxury liner (in reality an attack transport capable of being converted within a week into its original purposeful

85

self) which cost $23,000,000 and is now toting 340 first class and 270 Orientals across the drink. Everything is being done (at least in first class) to assure the customers that this is his home away from home. The food is very good, the service obsequious — possibly not as much so as on European vessels, a source of aggravation to some of the plutocrats here — and on the whole all efforts are bent to deceive the wayfarer into forgetting all that nasty old water outside the hull. Personally I prefer the previous way I girdled this ocean, viz., a cargo ship which gave you some sense of accomplishment, and a mite fewer of those elderly ladies with the cast-iron permanents from Shaker Heights and Paoli.

.   .   .

Yours, overwhelmingly,

LEILA HADLEY

Repulse Bay Hotel
Hong Kong
February 16, 1949

Dear Leila,

I seem to be sitting here in what is without doubt one of the loveliest shadow-boxes in the world. Outside the window, if I had the time to look out, I'd see the China Sea (more accurately, Repulse Bay and beyond it the China Sea), studded with small islands and real, honest-to-goodness junks in the grand tradition of those bad parchment lamps you see on Sixth Avenue. *And* a beach as near perfect as any imaginable. It would give me the keenest pleasure to describe, with the small equipment I have at hand, the beauty of this little niche, but I'm afraid it will have to wait. . . . [A] state of dementia prevails — running to the money-changers constantly, hysterical lunches with correspondents and some of the lesser taipans, combing the Thieves' Market (situated on Upper Lascar Row, if that gives your romantic pulses a frisson), and the like.

.   .   .

Manila was dusty, tragic, tense; even after four years of peace, it still looks like what the stories have said, the second worst-bombed city in the world. I think only photographs could begin to convey the horror. We had no inclination to sightsee; most of the passengers went off on junkets to Baguio north of there, Corregidor, and Taygaytay, but we racketed around to a series of heavily alcoholic lunches and dinners. I was, frankly, kind of washed out after two weeks of work aboard the *Cleveland*, and would have preferred to sit on my derriere in the sun after we left Manila, but 36 hours later we were arriving at Hong Kong. I appear to be pursuing this will-o'-the-wisp of snoozing in the sun without any real hope. I'm now pretending to myself that once I get aboard the *Tjisadane* tomorrow, bound for Batavia, that it'll all simmer down — forgetting, of course, that I have to get started on the second piece for *Holiday*, at least two *New Yorker* pieces, and a lot of correction on the ms. of the book S&S is publishing this fall (just a collection of pieces, but it needs some tinkering).*

6 p.m., 6 hours later

Damn and blast this sleazy airmail stationery; when you feed it back into the typewriter, it inevitably rips, ladders, and runs. Might as well try to type on a 51-gauge stocking.

Sister, you must one day fling a few essentials into a bag and take yourself out China side if you would like to see ragged subsistence. I admit that the country of the almond-eyed Celestials has no corner on poverty and that you can find a few noble examples in our West Virginia coal towns and Southern tenantry. But the contrast between the baronial mansions out here at Repulse Bay and the slums on Queens Road Central six miles away is pretty damn abrupt; and after an afternoon of wandering about, as I have today, it may take more than one gimlet to subdue that sickish feeling. So before I manage to communicate my dejection to you, let me get the hell off the subject. . . .

•   •   •

Always yours,

*Listen to the Mocking Bird, illustrated by Hirschfeld.

LEILA HADLEY

S.S. Tjisadane en route Batavia
February 22, 1949

Dear Leila,

Pardon me for feeling somewhat like one of those inept, five-color illustrations in the window of Thomas Cook & Son at 48th St. & Fifth. But for the record, I'm seated at the exact moment under a vast white tarpaulin stretched over the after deck of the *Tjisadane*, dressed in khaki shorts, a faded gingham sports shirt born in Penang two years ago, Chinese slippers, and a pair of Rayban sun-glasses. Out of the left corner of my mouth dangles a 6-inch long Filipino cigarette and the cool, balmy breath of the west monsoon blowing up from the Malacca Passage between Sumatra and Malaya ruffles my scant curls. To my right, less than five miles away, are the headlands of West Borneo. Last night at one o'clock, we crossed the equator; I celebrated this notable experience by expunging with the heel of my slipper a gigantic flying cockroach which zoomed into the cabin, and according to the poor slattern who bears my name, tried to pin her to the bulkhead. Typical feminine hysteria; it merely wanted to cuddle.

In short, we are coming along apace; tomorrow morning at daylight we are due at Batavia after an extremely agreeable run of a little more than five days. The ship, to our taste, and notwithstanding a few minor drawbacks, is much more enjoyable than the *President Cleveland* (perhaps this is my personal opinion, on second thought). There are about 800 souls aboard; about 30 in first class (of whom, besides ourselves, only four are Occidental—a Dutch lawyer and his wife from Batavia, a young Jesuit priest bound for the island of Flores near Bali (Dutch also), and a middle-aged Dutch vrouw in an advanced state of pregnancy and laden with Cadbury's chocolates and fruit drops). In second class, about a hundred Chinese, in third the same, and the balance Chinese deck passengers emigrating from Amoy, Swatow, Foochow, and other south Chinese ports to Indonesia. The latter live in an unenviable, communal confusion on the deck just flush with the water-line, and there cook, launder, gamble, play harmonicas, and generally have a good noisy and odorous time. The officers are, as might be anticipated, Dutch—undistinguishable from Germans, chauvinist, with a sense of humor which may charitably be described as broad (or earthy, if one feels especially tolerant), decent fellows, I suppose you would say. Everyone drinks Bols gin, of course, and tons of Heineken beer; the food isn't particularly good, though plentiful, and the conversation consists partly of good-natured jeers at our American ineptitude as colonists and mostly of disparaging analyses of the Javanese character—their laziness, inefficiency, deviousness, immorality, and aboriginal unawareness all being contrasted constantly to the sturdy, honest, and civilized Dutch character. The Jesuit father, I hasten to add, is not guilty of the foregoing. I like him, just as I liked Father Jim Thornton with whom I crossed to North China two years ago. They both have the highest admiration for the Chinese, a position I share and one that is continually borne in on the traveller. And out of earshot of the other Dutch here, Father Smeets has indicated to me that he doesn't necessarily share our fellow passengers' views.

BULLETIN: We are this instant passing the island of Billiton off the Borneo coast, less than a mile off the port side. Very heavily wooded, full of tin mines and valuable exotic woods like teak and cormoran, says the chief engineer. In case your son needs to be frightened into submission, just tell him that this is the country of the Dyak head-hunters and that there are extensive portions of the interior no white man has ever penetrated. If this fails, go to the nearest men's haberdashery, buy a Hickok belt of heavy-duty pigskin, and apply as needed. I find this treatment as ineffective as any, its only virtue being that it relieves the volcanic pressure of the parent to some degree. . . .

. . .

Oh Lord, deliver us from intemperance and gluttony. . . . [O]n a small tidal wave of three gimlets, I was washed down into the second-class diningroom and made to engulf a nine-course Cantonese dinner presented with the compliments of the line. Birds-nest soup and indescribable variations, sped on by flagons of Heineken and topped off with the largest Corona-Corona in the history of cigar-making. It would have been far more simple to merely hit me over the head with a mallet. Everyone else has now gone aft and is ululating over a game of deck golf, thank Heaven, leaving me to burp undisturbed in the smokingroom. . . .

You ask about W.S. Maugham. . . . Well, we had a thoroughly fine afternoon with the Old Party, who was staying with some people named Alanson to celebrate his 75th birthday. In NY he had told me he was taking *Westward Ha!* along to beguile his plane trip to the Coast, and at SF he plied me with the most effusive compliments, proving what has always been evident, that he has exquisite manners. He also made me promise to visit certain islands in this archipelago he had seen 20 years ago and report to him when I get to France. Where we really got off nicely, though, was in our mutual respect and admiration for con men. I told him about my pal, Doc Maurer (you remember, your New Year's party), and from then on, his eyes were like saucers.* I hope he received the copy of *The Big Con* I asked the Holliday Bookshop to send him; it may change his entire life. . . .

. . .

Yours,

*David W. Maurer (d. 1981), professor of linguistics at the University of Louisville; writer and authority on the underworld and its slang.

LEILA HADLEY

S.S. *Kasimbar*
en route Menado, Celebes
March 7, 1949

Dear Leila,

If memory serves, it is about twelve days since I last wrote you, during which time we have progressed the length of Java, crossed to Celebes, and are now circumnavigating in a leisurely manner. (Forgive my making this section as matter-of-fact and prosy as a report on hoof-and-mouth disease, but I assume you might like some concrete information, if only to controvert rumors that I'm actually holed up in Saugerties, New York.) We got to Batavia about February 23rd; the overnight stay there aboard the *Tjisadane* didn't permit more than a confused impression of a mixture of Dutch medievalism (both architectural and political) and a swarming Indonesian population with which we could have no possible contact, inasmuch as we know only about six words of market Malay. The high spot there was a too rapid tour of the Batavia Museum, whose collections of Hindu-Javanese sculpture, gold jewelry and ornaments from Bali and the Lesser Sunda Islands, and batiks are breathtaking. If we go back there, it will only be to see these at our leisure; the nine-and-a-half-foot mynheers swaggering around and smugly posturing as supermen to their obsequious native servants will be dealt with elsewhere. Fortunately, the couple of gents I had come to see turned out to be good fellows and have been doing their utmost since to make the trip enjoyable. Anyway, we continued on by the same ship to Semarang, where we lay in the bay—there being a 7-o'clock curfew ashore—and watched the sharks circling around below. Sourabaya, two days afterward, was more pleasant, more countrified. Lots of extremely well-favored Javanese from the neighboring island of Madura, the gals especially; practically all very graceful from constant carrying of packages on the head. Very nice sarongs to be bought here, unfortunately we had pitifully small amount of money on our persons, as the customs control is very stringent about the amount you disembark with, and bodily search obtains everywhere. Six Americans here altogether, all employed by a branch of Procter & Gamble Soap Co. The usual enervating lunch with them, conversation as always a wistful recapitulation of the good times they used to have in Sewickley or Oak Park or wherever. . . .

.   .   .

To get on with the hegira, we sailed from Macassar day before yesterday . . . reaching Pare-Pare yesterday. Here we had a cataclysmic, bowel-wrenching ride forty kilometers into the uplands to view a new irrigation project. You know, one of those things they think we gringos are interested in. There is an omnipresent solicitude for our welfare that eventually gets on the nerves; instead of letting you bumble around the native markets or wharves by yourself, some heel-clicker with a shaved head and wolfish blue eyes is always shepherding you somewhere to gape at a turbine. Today was a little better. We arrived at Donggala at noon, a seedy little copra port half-way up the western coast-line of Celebes. Together with a Mevrouw —, the pathetic young wife of a planter, and her 2-year-old child, our quartet was booted ashore and driven out to a fine coral beach. The water was about 75 degrees, the coral growths were pretty close inshore and a menace to the tootsies, and we were warned not to venture over our chests for fear of sharks, but we all had a good time. AND delayed the ship's sailing fifteen minutes, for which the captain will probably have me seized up at the gangway and lashed. However, he seemed to be a jolly and knowledgeable character, very gallant with the ladies and possessed of surprisingly good English, so it all augurs well. Our eventual objective, following our return to Macassar about March 23rd, is Bali, where we hope to attain some slight degree of permanence — at least stay on land several weeks. So much anticipation will have been built up by the time we get there that I'm afraid of the reality. Everyone this side of Singapore drools when he mentions it. . . .

•   •   •

LEILA HADLEY

S.S. *Kasimbar*
en route Batjan, Moluccas
March 16, 1949

Dear old girl,

•   •   •

What's the spring like these days in the temperate zone? Honest Injun, I've lost track completely in all these latitudes and longitudes, and I have a picture of people strolling down Fifth Avenue, in what used to be called their Easter finery, which I must have seen in the pages of *Chatterbox* in 1910. Out here we've been swimming in tepid sea water, about 73 degrees, for the past three weeks or so, and a surfeit of bananas threatens. In that sort of endroit one tends to erase the image of the 20-inch snow we were kicking off our shoes two months back. There is also such a glut of orchids and cockatoos locally that new specimens of both merely induce yawns. It is a rather remarkable sight to see two Yankee children at the breakfast table vacuously stirring their cocoa while a Javanese in a batik turban waits patiently to serve them with mangosteens.

The *Kasimbar* is a very jolly little ship of slightly more than 2000 tons, whose principal cargo is copra and whose skipper is a very amiable and bright chap named Captain Caalen. He has strained every nerve to show us the sights, and in every one of the whistle-stops I listed above, we've toured the countryside in jeeps, pick-ups, trucks, sedans, and minute horse-and-buggies, procured with considerable effort in some cases since transportation hereabouts is pretty scarce. The ship's passenger list contains only 10 in first class, generally Dutch civil servants, Chinese or Indonesian business men, and stray missionaries besides ourselves. The deck passengers we have always with us: coolies bound for the oil fields on New Guinea, assorted families travelling with livestock like chickens and ducks, a whole troupe of 26 actors (Indonesians) which has performed — without noticeable talent — in several of the stops, four Chinese merchants with cases full of needles, hair lotion, thread, baby nipples, and what-not, etc., etc. Until Sorong, the last port, we had as well on the third-class deck a bevy of twenty Balinese cows vaguely descended from carabao, the water buffalo renowned in song and story. All this olla-podrida makes for sound, smell, and lots of activity—*and* no gainful work whatever for your snaggle-toothed admirer, who has been dreaming away the days like crazy. I'm so far behind now on that verdamte *Holiday* series that it'll take me weeks to catch up. Furthermore, I'm doing very little to improve my situation, inasmuch as I'm definitely going ahead with my projected side trip to Banda, the little dot of an island way out in the Banda Sea which I told you a while ago Somerset Maugham had recommended I take a gander at. There is no regular steamer service or airline there, but through the kindness of the Moluccan Naval Training Service, an auxiliary schooner named the *Melbidir* has been placed at my convenience (I am quoting their letter verbatim) and we shall weigh from Ambon three days hence. . . . Reputedly a very charming harbor and volcano, and the chief attraction is a number of old mansions, circa 1615, in which the nutmeg planters used to live. Very probably will regret the whole venture bitterly after a couple of days with the naval cadets, but have now come to the point where I'd reproach myself ever after if I didn't go. The family continues on from Ambon, my point of takeoff, to Macassar, where I plan to rejoin them by plane so that we will then (aboard this same ship) carry on to Bali, a matter of about three days' sail.

All this means, therefore, that with the grace of God we should be arriving at Bali on March 27th, or about ten days distant, and there I hope to unwind for a bit. I really *have* to get some work done, this murtherin' steamship life has unmanned me intirely. I spend all my time gassing with the captain about how a man could buy himself a Macassarese prahu for spit and coupons and drift around the archipelago living off coconuts and little casual pieces for *The New Yorker*. This cannot be classified as anything but woolgathering, nor can the four meals a day, the eleven a.m. tea and the four p.m. ditto, and the frequent sluicing with Bols gin, spotted with hurried trips to the chart room to see whether we should sail the prahu to New York via the Indian Ocean and the Cape of Good Hope or go by way of the Admiralty Islands, the Marquesas, and Acapulco, Mexico.

It's getting on for ten-thirty and our public room, a combination of dining saloon, card room, and bar has emptied completely, leaving a nearsighted journalist pecking away at his portable. Folks hereabouts get into the kip on the early side, since they rise at dawn generally. I'll thank you to keep to yourself the information that for at least a month now I've finished my breakfast by six-thirty a.m. In your feverish metropolitan set, I suppose you're just stumbling in from the Hurricane or the Mocambo at that hour.

.   .   .

Yours always,

LEILA HADLEY

S.S. *Melbidir*
en route from Banda-Neira to Amboina
South Moluccas
March 24, 1949

Carissima,

But at my back I seem to hear / Time's wingèd Diesel hurrying near.
How apt and how adaptable the incomparable Mr. Marvell. I'm sitting at the
moment on the hatch of this forty-foot launch, an ancient contraption bearing no resemblance whatever to the sleek, piratical schooner I'd expected from
the advance build-up, and scarcely six feet off, down a Stygian companion-
way, a ferocious old Diesel sputters, coughs, and belches forth enough smoke
for Etna, propelling this hoary tub a scant five m.p.h. back to where we started
four days ago. This is Thursday morning; last Sunday night, we cleared from
Amboina and made the 120-mile run to the Banda Group in about 22 hours.
If, in the following lines, I pause to proffer my snuffbox, adjust my ruff, or
emit a rolling Netherlands oath of the period of William of Orange, I ask you
to excuse me, for I've spent the past forty-eight hours in the 17th and 18th
centuries. Honestly one of the weirdest experiences of my life. I don't feel quite
real.

Banda, which I suppose you'd call the matrix of the Spice Islands, was
settled by the Dutch in 1604, and in its time (now long since passed) was the
Beverly Hills of the Indies. The perkeniers, the Dutch planters who amassed
incredible fortunes from nutmeg and mace out here, built themselves mansions in serried rows on Banda Neira so lavish that only a color camera would
begin to convey their opulence to you. (And, of course, I had with me exactly
one roll of Kodak film and none procurable thereafter.) I don't know just
how to describe the place to you. Scenically it's utterly beautiful; first a sharp
cone-shaped volcano rising steeply out of the sea; you round this into a lovely
placid bay which makes a left angle, the mansions lying on your left shaded
by huge kenari trees each one the size of the Charter Oak. Several boat land-
ings with music pavilions where the mynheers and mevrouws used to listen
to Handel. Today, in 1949

(damned wind just caught this
sleazy paper and shook it like
an O-Cedar mop)

the nutmeg trade is about as thriving as the traffic in ruching and diavolos.
The ninety tons they take out of Banda in a year pretty well supply the world
demand, from what my informants locally say, and the perkeniers have gone
to that bourne from which the traveller returneth not. I stood among their
graves yesterday morning in a fashionable Shelleyesque pose, and as the smoke

of a mildewed Chesterfield curled around my head in the still heat, reflected on the folly and impermanence of your life. . . .

Altogether, Banda is what you might get if you took forty or fifty Southern mansions, pillars and all, and popped them down on a pin-point in the Pacific. About half are untenanted, roofs fallen in and tropical mold staining the walls. The other half shelter vast families of indolent, apathetic natives and half-castes who can barely summon up enough steam to grate the large white sweet potatoes and catch the fish swarming around on which they subsist. There hasn't been a vitamin on Banda since Constantinople fell to the Turks. All the kids are spindly-legged, their mothers are hags at thirty, and the diseases, from the terrifying one called framboisia, through elephantiasis, trachoma, and leprosy, are as luxuriant as the foliage. Nobody there can be persuaded to eat a vegetable; the one vacuous medical officer and the venal Eurasian controleur who represents government have no interest in bettering the lot of the population. It's a pretty dispiriting picture. If ever Nature smiled on any corner of the earth, it's Banda; there's every conceivable fruit and flower at your elbow, bananas, mangoes, coconuts, cotton, what-not. And amid it all these indescribably lovely houses, all floored with Dutch tiles worth fortunes, some of them still containing bits of their original furniture, rotting away.

·　　　·　　　·

. . . Tomorrow morning I propose to swim at Soeli Beach (superb fine white coral sand, big shade trees over-arching the beach, water ranging in color from emerald green to royal blue) and in the afternoon pay a courtesy call to Mr. Pelaupessy, the Resident, whom I shall certainly call Pelaupessary in my blubber-mouthed fashion. In the evening I hope to dine with Mr. Lim, the most prominent Chinese merchant in Ambon, straight out of Sax Rohmer. His bah mee is said to be outstanding and if he thinks he can make a mill or two, he will extend himself. From Macassar, the day after arrival, I fly to Bali to meet the arriving *Kasimbar* with my brood. . . .

Yours only,

LEILA HADLEY

Oriental Hotel
Thung Mahemek, Bangkok
April 20, 1949

Dear Leila,

·　　　·　　　·

If you were at all surprised by the absence in my letters, while I was careering around Indonesia, of any political references or allusions to the Dutch

94

and whatever, I can at last enlighten you. I won't launch into a full-dress narrative; I expect to get all that happened into easily-digestible type for the family trade consumption in *Holiday*, but I can in any case tell you that I'm pretty sure all my mail was being censored, shadowgraphed, X-rayed, and read carefully. Without going dramatic, we emerged from the Indies with the sensation that we had been confined for approximately two months in a gigantic concentration camp. Every move we made was watched and reported on, and up to the very last moment when we left Dallang Airport in Singapore, we were never permitted to communicate with any American press service people, embassy staffs, or the like. In addition, every step of the way was punctuated with the most outspoken hatred of the Yankee on the part of the Dutch (never from the Indonesians) and a state of mind verging on the psychotic. The Dutch see their most valuable territory vanishing inevitably (it's only a matter of time now) and they visualize their empire shrunk to the dimensions of Poughkeepsie — rightly so. I have come away with the most vitriolic loathing of these cheese-headed bastards I've entertained for anybody since the Germans, and I intend to fry them in the deepest literary fat I can render. Although they were fully cognizant of the fact that I might well be a forerunner of lots of American tourists and although they were straining to be polite and helpful out of a mixture of greed and anxiety for their future, these demented imperialist tinpot bureaucrats, smug with 350 years of straddling seventy million people, couldn't contain their bile at our interfering in their affairs through the United Nations. I picked up enough in furtive contacts with the Javanese and eastern Indonesians, as well as in scanty encounters with the few Americans in the area, to convince me that the Dutch are sitting on a volcano that would make Krakatoa look like a pimple. And brother, when that erupts, there will be reverberations. It's useless to continue in this strain, I could go on for quite some time. But I do know that everyone who has gone in has felt exactly this way, just as those who know Indo-China regard the French rule there as intolerable and the British capers in Malaya as fantastic.

In any case, we've been here in Bangkok as of last Thursday night, or almost a week, and . . . I expect to be on my way soon. I believe my wire said we were dusting out for Europe May 2nd; I've since extended it a week so as to get in a trip to Angkor Wat — and perhaps a day trip to Ayudyha and Lopburi, the old capitals of Siam up-country. We're lodged in an extremely comfortable pension run by the Oriental Hotel; not in the center of town, which is shrill and shabby, but out near the embassy quarter. In the 2 years since I was here, goods and cars have become very plentiful, sometimes almost to the point of absurdity. Everyone rolls around here in those little British, Italian, and French sports cars like the MG and the Jaguar, which are very cheap here. I am dickering to try to buy one of them for using in touring around France and Scandinavia, if the financial details can be arranged. (Excuse those participles, we all converse in a weird mixture of pidgin and mangled English.) I've been doing some exploration in the matter of archaic Buddhist sculpture with special reference to Buddhas; the situation, similar to 2 years back, is not glorious, inasmuch as lots of Americans have been through here meantime, but there are still things to be had. . . .

Well, this is now 11:10 a.m. The room-boy has finished dusting up, folding back the mosquito bar for the day, and is now withdrawing with our laundry, which will be returned in three days with all the greasespots and betel expectorations neatly pressed in. I should tell you before dropping the curtain that I'm angling for a house at St. Jean Cap Ferrat beyond Nice, a block or two from Maugham's, where we would hole in on arriving in Europe so that I can get some work done. I'm way the hell behind and must get off at least two pieces for *Holiday* soon. We'll head out of here, as I said, May 9th, break our trip at Istanbul two days, and land at Rome. Our heavy baggage has gone on to Genoa, and if the house I speak of becomes a certainty, we'll scoot down there for six weeks or so, maybe two months. Then we'd like to get into that sleek little sports model, work up toward Siena, Florence, Bologna, and the Abruzzi, [then?] drive up into Sweden and Denmark. From there, I'd probably [?] home, cross into England and maybe Ireland for a brief look, and get home about the end of September or very early October. . . .

My love,

L E I L A H A D L E Y

Ambassador Hotel
Rome
May 19, 1949

Dear Leila,

•   •   •

The Bangkok phase, in retrospect, was one of the less successful periods in the trip. I knew it was going to be hot, having been there at precisely the same time two years before, but you forget heat just as you do pain. Well, Peaches, it was a jim dandy. For 3½ weeks of the kind of weather one gets in late August in New York, we panted and staggered through the days and cursed feebly through the nights. Nobody I ever read on the subject has quite conveyed the absolutely murderous intensity of the sun. You walk half a block in it and you're so dizzy and exhausted that every ganglion dries out to the consistency of kelp. The only extensive reader I know there confessed to me that after three years in Siam, it takes him four or five days to get through the Miscellany column in *Time* and a good six months to read a novel. Of course I sneered at all the warnings and ran around like a decapitated chicken, buying up objets d'art and trivia like a half-ton Cambodian deity with a teakwood base slightly smaller than Cleopatra's Needle and such. It's God's mercy I'm here to tell the tale. I also thought the circumstances propitious for acquiring an English sports car, an MG one-and-one quarter litre tourer which I'll pick up in England at the end of June and use for touring Scandinavia. It's a cunning little thing, and will present an interesting problem when the four of us, together with luggage and our new mynah bird, prepare to go wayfaring. Oh yes, I haven't described Tong Cha, the latest addition to the group. He's an Indo-Chinese grackle (mistakenly called a mynah) whom I bought from a Chinese firecracker shop. I don't know what experience you've had with mynahs; you may know that they are perhaps the most accomplished talkers in the bird world. Tong Cha says (without prompting) "So what?" (actually "so wah di," the standard Siamese greeting), "Hello HELLO!," calls himself by name, viz., "tong cha"—the breed is known as "koon tong cha" in Siamese, and has a repertory of various piercing shrieks, grunts, and gargles that scares the femmes-de-chambres and sommeliers in this hotel out of their skins. Naturally, I have spent practically 23 hours of every day cleaning his cage, feeding him (he lives on a fantastic diet of rice, bananas, minuscule chili peppers, and bananas), and worrying about his health, to the complete exclusion of all profitable work.

The trip from Bangkok west, as you have guessed in your intuitive way, was slightly involved; we took off the evening of May 9th with 20 pieces of baggage and the bird aboard a PAA Constellation and reached Calcutta five hours later. There we were allowed to sit up until dawn in a dirty airport lounge amid snoring Indian sweepers and then transfer our goods to an Indian Airways plane. It took all day to cross India, stopping at Delhi to change to still another old Dakota crate (no smoking for six hours aboard this one) which bumped us painfully into Karachi. Here, after a handful of sleep, we again switched to a PAA plane and flew via Basrah (Iraq) and Damascus (Syria) to Istanbul. Interesting fact: at Jodhpur, in India, it was 114 on the runway; we like to died. None of this gives you any indication of the fantastic, nightmarish complications with the health authorities, immigration, and customs at every stop, the cheeseparing bureaucracy and arrogance you encounter. Matters were not helped by the fact that I had 67 cartons of Chesterfields in our baggage which we'd been toting ever since Hong Kong. Well, we finally made Istanbul and stayed there five days to catch our breath. It was a good experience, fortunately; we were delighted and very pleased with the Turks, who were completely different from anything we expected. Spent lots of time rummaging around the mosques and the Grand Bazaar (where Constantine stabled 40,000 horses during his tenancy), also took a day's sail into the Sea of Marmora to the island of Prinkipo, to which Trotsky was exiled. The Bosphorus is everything you've heard, but I didn't see any discarded wives being flung into it inside burlap bags as advertised...And so on to Rome, which at the moment is very springy and fine. Our exhilaration at being shut of the heat, dirt, and bloodshed of the East is indescribable. Siam is something not commonly encountered, a military police dictatorship, chock-full of road blocks, sudden unexplained murders, and a brooding sense of impending catastrophe. Coming on top of the Indies and the horrors there, we're awful glad to be back in what passes for normal in the West.

•   •   •

Yours always,

LEILA HADLEY

Hotel Metropole
Beaulieu-sur-Mer
Alpes-Maritimes, France
June 17, 1949

Leila dear,

•   •   •

... It was sweet of you to send along the clipping about us Nihilists who are proscribed by the American Legion; nobody else bothered to, figuring that if my pelvis was bleaching on a coral reef, it wouldn't make any difference. It is an illustrious catalogue of saboteurs, and, as you no doubt noticed, was incomplete, omitting any mention of Dorothy Parker, Lillian Hellman, and a few more of those names that always monotonously show up in that sort of dispatch...By the way, did you read a column of Billy Rose's which appeared in the Paris edition of the *Herald Trib* last week? It was his usual fulsome garbage about the white sun-god, General MacArthur, and his wife's Olympic swimming, but it wound up with a statement that he had, concealed in his safe deposit vault, his *own* list of dangerous subversives in the theater which he'd be glad to furnish. That little man really is beginning to develop serious sconce trouble. He always had megalomania, even back when I did some work for his then wife Fannie Brice,* but now it's exhibiting complications Dr. Gregory Zilboorg† can better define than myself. What the hell happens to these song-pluggers and cabaret operators like Winchell and Rose? Instead of rolling up a snug manure-ball of moola and sitting in Lindy's,

---

The Royal Gelatin Hour in 1933.
†A Russian-born psychiatrist with a fashionable left-wing clientele that included Lillian Hellman, Ralph Ingersoll, and Marshall Field (whom Zilboorg convinced to put up the money for Ingersoll's paper, *PM*).

spitting cherry cheese-cake over each other and slowly festering with paresis, they gotta be philosophers and statesmen. In Rose's case, he also sees himself as an art connoisseur which is doubly emetic. Please remind me one day to describe to you how I acted as accoucheur to George Gershwin, another celebrated art collector, back in 1929. It's a dolorous tale.

.   .   .

. . . Tong Cha is perfect. Friend, in that mynah bird's he rt I see no guile; he loves me and I love him. When I feed him his morning h lf a banana and stroke his breast, we both achieve a type of Karma. His eyes roll backward in his head and he gives forth a series of shuddering little sighs only Pierre Loti knew how to describe. This procedure is also extremely soothing to my vanity, since I'm the only one he allows to handle him. Maybe I ought to give up threading literary beads for a livelihood and become a wild animal trainer like Mr. Court of the Ringling show. He undoubtedly looks better than I would in a tunic and jackboots, but I bet you those black panthers would be niggling up to me in jig time.

.   .   .

Yours always,

FRANCES and ALBERT HACKETT

Shelbourne Hotel
Dublin
August 14, 1949

Dear Frances and Albert,

Dublin on a Sunday afternoon in mid-August is so close to being buried alive that I had better not chill your blood with any further description. There are 4,238 churches within one mile of where I'm sitting (sorry, where I'm *after* sitting), and that part of the population which isn't macerating itself inside them is closeted in the pubs. This morning the children and I walked miles through the slums — and O'Casey was being photographic in *Juno and the Paycock* — to find something called the Bird Market, which turned out to be a dozen louse-ridden canaries. That constitutes the total amusement facilities of this place. They don't even have the opportunity as they once did of sitting around and slandering the English, now that they have achieved their independence.

I believe that Laura wrote you way back there in Bali sometime around early April, since which time, as you see, we have crawled a considerable distance across the intervening continents. About the middle of April or thereabouts, we took off for Bangkok. The trip around Celebes and the Moluccas had been wonderful, and Bali itself even more so. I managed to squeeze in an all-too-short excursion into the Banda Sea on a 30-foot motor schooner to the island of Banda Neira, which used to be the center of the Dutch nutmeg trade in the 17th Century. It was a remarkable experience from every angle, including the fact that I probably got malaria there, but anyway, to get on with the narrative, we landed up in Bangkok plumb in the middle of their summer heat and had ourselves a month of really gruelling weather. Our original plan, to spend a while there, soon got itself amended for a whole lot of reasons — political instability, the kids' schooling, and changes in the scheme for the *Holiday* series. We flew out in mid-May, crossing India and the Middle East and stopping off at Istanbul, which we all thought was an extremely colorful and agreeable place. (Incidentally, such furniture, general antiques, jewelry, and curios in the Grand Bazaars there as to drive you out of your senses.) From there, on to Rome — a week's stay and a most fantastic reaming, inasmuch as the Romans are killing off the golden American goose with complete contempt for the eggs. And then to Beaulieu, twenty minutes' drive from Nice, where we sat down for six weeks of work and recuperation. This was a thoroughly first-rate part of the trip. It was not cheap by any manner of means; I don't think there is such a thing as a moderate, and at the same time good, hotel to be found in Europe any longer, but the Hotel Metropole there was situated smack on the Mediterranean, the food was good, and the staff by and large was cordial. They were nice not only to us but to Tong Cha, which prejudiced us in their favor. Tong Cha, I should explain quickly, is a mynah bird I bought in Bangkok. I always wanted to own one and now (if the pension I left him at in Paris is doing right by him) I hope to import him into the States when we return at the end of September. He is an extremely well-favored specimen — formerly the property of a Chinese fire-cracker store in Siam — with glossy, purple-and-black iridescent plumage, primrose-yellow wattles, a beak like a candy corn, and an extensive repertory of Chinese and Siamese words. . . . *Gracula javanensis* is his technical classification, if Albert wishes to look him up in that pocket manual. Although commonly regarded as savage and unapproachable, this one is Trilby to my Svengali, and one of the more nauseating sights is to see me stroking his wings and muttering little heartbroken cries of affection.

By the time we got ready to leave Beaulieu, our various tropical ailments had vanished. These, incidentally, were fairly extensive; Abby had had a lingering case of jungle boils, I'd had the possibly-malaria and something called Singapore ear, a spectacular fungoid malady, and Adam drew a particularly tenacious case of tropical ulcer of the leg, which demanded protracted and complex treatments at Nice. We moved out of Beaulieu with twenty pieces of hand luggage and first went to Marseilles to intercept six trunks which had come by water from Singapore. We repacked all this and shipped it on to Paris, flew up there and spent five days, and flew on to London. Here we picked up a British sports car I bought, and after two weeks started a tour of southern England. We've spent the larger part of the time since at a truly dreary spot called Sidmouth in Devon, advertised to us as a delightful seaside resort and as stuffy as they come. Since I worked most of the time there, I didn't take the punishment the rest of the troupe did, but it was bad enough. England is very depressing these days, there is hardly any food and less liquor and no sweets and no fun and the future looks grimmer than ever. Meat is unheard-of, eggs rare, butter very strictly rationed, sugar scarce, etc., etc. Our progress after Sidmouth, therefore, was chiefly a matter of whizzing through handsome scenery — Herefordshire, Shropshire, and up to Liverpool, from which we flew over here to do some eating. Fortunately, the latter is available without any trouble. We have been ramming protein into our gullets three times a day; steaks of the most handsome proportions are very cheap, bacon and butter plentiful, and lots of candy, even if it isn't up to our standards at home. We expect to leave here this coming Wednesday, that is, in three days, flying back to Liverpool, where we'll pick up the car and drive down through Derbyshire to Oxford for two days, then spend a day or two in Surrey, and leave England from the east-coast port of Harwich by a Danish steamer across the North Sea to Esbjerg. Thence by road to Copenhagen for about a month and driving down through the western zone of Germany, Holland, Belgium, and to Paris for a final week before embarking on the *De Grasse* September 29th.

I haven't forgotten that when we parted, I promised to give you the dope on what our trip through the East Indies was like, whether it was feasible for yourselves and the like. As to whether it was enjoyable or not, it was easily, far and away, the high spot of either of the trips I've made. I recommend it unreservedly, and Laura agrees with me without qualification. You must understand that we were something of a curiosity there; we were the first tourists who'd come through since the war and I don't believe any have come through since. . . . I think, to belabor the point, that it is an absolutely unique experience, and I honestly believe that we all got more out of it than we anticipated in our rosiest dreams. You will forgive me for sounding ecstatic, but I am only echoing Al Hirschfeld's estimate of Bali when I say that it's the closest thing to Paradise on earth. And, far from being spoiled by tourism, it hasn't been touched in the slightest degree.

Well, girls, I'd better cease this panegyric before the saliva spoils my only remaining clean shirt. The kiddies are off seeing *Sorrowful Jones*, a Bob Hope epic, in some theater on O'Connell Street and if I stop now, Laura and I just have time to sneak down for afternoon tea in the lobby. That means bread-and-butter sandwiches, frosted cakes, and Irish county families muttering "Divil a bit." We think of you all the time and wish you'd write. Considering how long it's taken us to do so, you'd be justified in waiting six months before replying, but it would be very nice to get the gossip from Sepulveda and Westwood. . . . Love and kisses from us all, and up the rebels.

Yours ever,

E . B . W H I T E

14 Washington Square North
New York City
November 17, 1949

Dear Andy,

As I understand the theory and technique of the fan letter, it always begins with a pompous statement to the effect that the writer is not commonly given to writing fan letters, so that the reader is supposed to experience a grateful glow for being singled out on this particular occasion. The writer then goes into his bootlicking for a paragraph or so, abruptly breaks off to warn the reader that he had better toe the mark and not fall below his standard if he wants to keep the fan's devotion, and finally asks the object of same for all his out-of-print works, his autograph, and maybe the loan of fifty dollars until Easter.

So you can see how refreshing this letter is going to be, completely devoid of all this snide and fulsome nonsense. In fact, I shall end it right here and subscribe myself   Yours always,

P.S. However, just to hold the franchise, I'd like to add the final thought that your appraisal of New York was all that I had heard abroad and much more.* I read it twice—once for sheer enjoyment, and more slowly a second time to find out how you did it. Laura says you have some kind of magic ink or a feather pen or something. That's what Laura said. I see where I'll have to read it out loud to her a third time.

*Here Is New York.

G U S L O B R A N O

S.S. *President Cleveland*
January 22, 1950

Dear Gus,

This is getting itself written somewhere in the gray uncharted wastes three days out of San Francisco, at a point when our collective stomachs are just recovering from 36 hours of buffeting by the groundswell off the California

102

coast. . . . Waves easily seven and eight hundred feet high lashed our frail vessel, and torrential rains streaming from skies especially designed by El Greco beat on her decks. This morning, however, a flashy, Woolworth-type rainbow (undoubtedly arranged by the Honolulu Chamber of Commerce) appeared on the right-hand side as you go toward Pearl Harbor, and some degree of well-being has returned. Laura and I this minute returned from the first tenable lunch since we sailed. We have that peculiar purplish, off-register look you see in color photographs in *Collier's*. This whole deal bears no more resemblance to a ship, as you and I know it, than the present-day comic strip does to the funnies of our youth. . . .

You may be receiving shortly from a gent named Gordon Kahn in Hollywood a piece which might repay your attention. I don't know whether we ever discussed Gordon, but he is an old friend of mine, a one-time newspaperman around New York who's been a scenario writer these past fifteen years. I think he has a real comic gift. Three or four years ago, Charles Morton on *The Atlantic* wanted a series of inside Hollywood pieces; I suggested Kahn for the job and he turned in ten or fifteen, many of which were very funny. He also did a long one on Mexico last year for *Holiday*. You may know him as the editor of the book of testimony on the Hollywood Ten who were hauled up before the Thomas committee. Gordon himself is one of the nineteen individuals who were combed over in that investigation and it's doubtful that he'll ever work again in pictures. That's all by way of biography; the piece itself as he showed it to me had a lot of merit, I thought, and I promised I would direct your attention to it.

>   •   •   •

. . . Meanwhile, love to all the boys and girls, and if you can find an idle half-hour in between battling those queries springing up like thistles in the margins, your pen pal will sure appreciate a chatty note. Best to Jean and the family.   Yours ever,

FRANCES and ALBERT HACKETT
Erwinna, Pa.
August 2, 1950

Dear Frances and Albert,

Excuse this blush-pink stationery, a souvenir of the time I bought out a job printer at Oak Bluffs, but my usual cream-laid stock has dwindled. The unconscionable delay in our replying to your letter was caused by one of those domestic misunderstandings; Laura thought I'd written and I imagined she had, the result being that you probably have started to think we are somewhere in Asia again. Not so; we have been perched on our roost here in Pennsylvania since about June 5th or so, leading ineffably dull lives and slowly turning into vegetables except for those galvanic interludes when we turn on the radio and absorb fresh disasters. Everybody up to this writing has been in decent enough health, the kids included; they are growing in size if not in sweetness of disposition. Adam is at the stage now where he gets up in the middle of the night and wolfs a whole can of tuna, thereafter concealing the tin on an out-of-the-way shelf until the ants lead us to it. Every so often, by dint of shouting, we manage to get him to sickle a few weeds or bike down to the post-office for the mail, but these superhuman efforts exhaust him so that he has to spend a week resting up, the radio turned up full force and his mouth agape over *Fear Comics*. Abby is more malleable in the sense that it takes only a small-size baseball bat to persuade her to dry a dish or hang out the towels. Next Tuesday we are off to the Vineyard for our annual four or five weeks of exposure to sunburn; at least the two little charges can occupy themselves to some degree in the surf instead of frazzling their parents' nerves.

Life hereabouts goes on with its customary torpor; I have been tapping away at pieces for *The New Yorker* since early spring when I finished up that last *Holiday* assignment (appearing in book form sometime in November).* Laura and I got the rights to adapt a book of George Orwell's called *Burmese Days* as a play, but so far have done nothing but talk it over intermittently. Al Hirschfeld and family were down here last weekend, an occasion our cesspool had been eagerly awaiting and celebrated by backing up the first day of their stay. Fortunately, we managed to stave off disaster and yesterday secured the services of three gnarled dwarfs who did the necessary first aid measures for ailing septic tanks. . . .

I suppose you heard the interesting news that Dotty Parker and Alan were remarrying, we heard it from Louella Parsons' saccharine harelips. I have a sneaking feeling that the whole process of their buying a house in Pennsylvania and remodelling it, with its attendant hysteria, may be repeated. . . .

Always,

The Swiss Family Perelman.

LAURA PERELMAN

in flight between Tampa
and New Orleans
November 11, 1950

Dear Laura,

The cold front and bad weather blanketing Key West refused to lift sufficiently to let me get another day's fishing in the Gulf Stream on Thursday, and when Friday dawned dreary again, I decided to pull out on the afternoon plane. . . .

I'm moving from here to New Orleans by Delta Airlines, from there to Dallas by National, from Dallas to Phoenix by American, and Phoenix to Las Vegas by Bonanza. On the last-named line, the planes don't have fuselages; the passengers ride on the wings.

I phoned Wylie as he'd asked me to but found he had gone to the Coast meanwhile; his wife said he was due back today. Well, I guess I'll have to go another fifteen years without knowing what those scientists at Caltech are doing about the cyclotron. By the way, he said in his letter and his wife mentioned over the phone that he's a very VIP civilian adviser to the government, I presume on interplanetary copulation. From Siegel's Restaurant to Stratospheric Sex in one generation, etc.

.   .   .

Love,

MEL ELLIOTT

19 Washington Square North
New York City
April 24, 1951

Dear Mr. Elliott,

God, whom you doubtless remember as that quaint old subordinate of General Douglas MacArthur, works in mysterious ways his wonders to perform. You may have forgotten that in June of last year, you were kind enough to send me a slightly daffy excerpt from *Science Magazine* on the use of music in Chicago surgical clinics as a complement to anesthesia. After steeping for almost a year in my giant underground vats, it has finally eventuated into a piece which *The New Yorker* will be publishing sometime in the next couple of months.* Needless to say, I am beholden to you for planting the initial seed. Lest you think this acknowledgment is tardy, I may add that in the same mail I'm getting off a letter to a maternal uncle for the gold watch he gave me when I was confirmed. This calm, measured behavior is my retort to the pressure of metropolitan life.

With many thanks, and hoping you won't be too severely disappointed, I am,   Sincerely,

*"Swing Out, Sweet Opiate," collected in *The Ill-Tempered Clavichord* (1952).

I . J . K A P S T E I N

19 Washington Square North
New York City
May 28, 1951

Dear Kap,

Your "screed" to hand and I hasten to reply ahead of my own arrival, the mails being slowed down to a walk these days. I also wonder how the hell I ever consented to spread my gederma out for the greater glory of the [Brown] Alumni Association, and I can only suppose that some obscure form of paresis I must have contracted years ago while wrapping men's suits in the basement of the Outlet has paralyzed my will. Bigelow (or Bigeleisen, if his capacity of flattening opposition is any indication) bought me a watery business men's lunch, fed me a couple of martinis, and the next thing I knew an illiterate was addressing me on the stationery of a butcher store in Pawtucket with the news that S.J.P. — "Humorist" — would speak at 8:40 sharp. I can already envision some of those Judenfressers we went to school with, buoyed up with — , seated there with arms akimbo and saying, "Humorist, eh? Well, let him show *me!*" *How*ever, persons taken in raids on brothels are peculiarly vulnerable, and it's my own God-damned fault if I surrendered to Bigeleisen. I suppose I thought June 1 would never come, way back there in April.

I'm booked into a single at the Biltmore for Friday night, but I'm much obliged that you would consider bedding Laura and myself down. The fact is that Laura hasn't been able to get down to the country much these past four or five weeks, due to Abby's social activities weekends prior to her graduation from school here: SO-O-O, she's going down to Pennsylvania with her in-laws and Abby instead of coming up with me. She has stated categorically, indeed, that her only charge in coming up would be to see you and Stella, otherwise she isn't carried away by the thought of seeing her spavined old schoolfellows, and I believe that she is on the whole sagacious. So you'll have to endure my company solo.

I may tell you privately that a major portion of the remarks I intend to deliver was tested last Tuesday in Cleveland at the American Booksellers' Association convention, where I addressed first 1100 junior high school children in the afternoon and then 2200 booksellers. Between them these guinea pigs represent the nadir of perceptivity, so do not be afeard that I'll be over the heads of our old associates. Just the same, I'll take out that word "dichotomy" on page 2.

As for Curtis of the Brown News Bureau, sorry, but no advance copy of the speech. I've been using it, and variants of it, since Pearl Harbor, and

106

I intend to go on using it. Of course, I can't prevent anyone from taking short-hand notes, but why pee in my own elixir? . . .

With all best, and looking ahead to seeing you,

Yours,

FRANCES and ALBERT HACKETT
Erwinna, Pa.
June 24, 1951

Dear Frances and Albert,

With your native intuition and flair for detecting deceit, chicanery, and wool-pulling, you will immediately spot this for a begging letter, and in some measure you'll be right. Not to delay the subterfuge unnecessarily, herewith the pitch. After considerable hauling and haggling, the project I submitted to *Holiday* whereby I'd be sent to Europe this summer to interview certain notable literary personalities, viz., Maugham, Eliot, Beerbohm, and Norman Douglas, for a series, has been transformed into a series wherein I'm to revisit the great comedians of my youth. The mortality rate on the foregoing being extensive—Fields, Howard, and others are obviously only to be reached across the Jordan—I'm now definitely coming to the Coast by plane July 6th to see Groucho, Jessel, Durante, Chaplin, and Bob Hope. It's anybody's guess how Hope got in there—I'm older than he is, but they want it, so that's that. Anyway, I expect to spend between two and three weeks exposing myself to these charming personalities, and I thought that you might let me occupy my old cot on the second floor facing the golf links for a couple of nights after arrival until I figured out what the best plan of attack was. If you have any leeches (any *other* leeches) fastened on you at the moment or pencilled in to fasten at that period, just recoil and I'll shake down at one of the hotels. Needless to say, I get so much pleasure out of seeing you that if you could stand me for a couple of days, I'd prefer to park on you until I set up the machinery for the interviews. Actually, if I can so persuade the people involved, it may be most productive of copy for me to stay with each one of them for two or three days and see them in their native habitat.

.   .   .

In any case and whatever, I am looking forward to seeing you, and I am herewith nailing you down to have dinner with me at Chasen's your first free night so that I can have Coupe Alexander for dessert. The thought of that ambrosial sweetmeat has sustained me for two years in some very trying periods.

With love and regards from us all,   Yours,

107

GUS LOBRANO

Hollywood, Calif.
August 6, 1951

Dear Gus,

. . . I've been in a lather of interviewing, social complications, and general foolishness, with a few pleasant intervals of tennis. Most of the time's been spent on Groucho, Durante, Jessel, and Chaplin, and I needn't add that Chaplin has been the most enjoyable. I guess he comes closer to being a genius than anyone around here, though he has his detractors, you may be sure. I put in most of Friday listening to him and a 50-piece orchestra record the ballet music for his forthcoming picture, and yesterday had three hours alone with him just talking generally. I must say that he makes magnificent good sense.

I've also spent considerable time with Corinne Griffith, Doris Kenyon, and Billie Dove on that project I mentioned, and plan to do the same with Nita Naldi, Carmel Myers, and Louise Brooks in the East. The three out here, you'll be glad to know, are still capable of wrenching our middle-aged hearts. Jean and Laura are in for an uphill fight from here in. You can expect that when we lunch again I will furnish minute anatomical details.

Enclosed are a couple of clips that may help to adumbrate the line in that last piece of mine about movie shorts in which chimpanzees enact human roles. To judge from them, it practically amounts to an industry hereabouts.

I'm taking off tonight for Las Vegas, and Wednesday night flying on to New York, where I hope to pause a couple of days before going on to the Vineyard. I'll give you a bell when I get into town, with the thought of capturing you for either lunch or a drink. Best to everyone.

Yours,

BETSY DRAKE*

Chilmark
Martha's Vineyard, Mass.
August 17, 1951

Dear Betsy,

It goes without saying (*ça va sans dire* to bilinguals like yourself) that I'd have replied to your graceful thank-you note long before this if I'd had half a chance. I got away to Las Vegas, finally, on the Monday evening plane after we saw each other last, and spent a hysterical forty-eight hours trying to distil the essence of that improbable community: an exploit that netted me

*Actress, married at the time to Cary Grant.

three hours of sleep and a conviction that any anthropologist who pretends he understands our dollar civilization lies in his teeth unless he has seen Las Vegas. I also discovered that I'll have to return there before I'll ever be able to write anything about it, both to assure myself that what I saw really existed and to spend a little longer looking at it. It's really fantasy with ribbons.

．　　　　　　．　　　　　　．

I was both horrified and immeasurably flattered by your confession that you had in the past quoted from my work: horrified because unbeknownst to yourself, you ran the risk of verbal infection (the kind of words I use are liable to become imbedded and fester, like the steel wool housewives use); and flattered for obvious reasons. However, your statement that by so doing, you were able to appear rather witty is pure gallantry, and only confirms my suspicion that you possess the exquisite manners of a Chinese mandarin. Despite my seeming torpor around the Gershwin tennis court and the Brooks' livingroom, I was at all times aware that you handled the epee and the foils like a master. A Mary Wortley Montagu? A Madame de Montespan? Perhaps not, but a redoubtable opponent. After all, it is only given to one or two women in a generation to be really dazzling, and Louella Parsons, Hedda Hopper, and Sheila Graham have reached a stature in our time which their sisters can only behold enviously.

．　　　　　　．　　　　　　．

I hope, therefore, that nothing interferes with my present design to call in at the City of Our Lady the Queen of the Angels sometime in October and that the four of us may resume those rewarding doubles. Be advised that your sly references to my sneaky serves and odious gamesmanship haven't escaped me. Anybody who deliberately affects a basketball helmet and smoked glasses to conceal her charm from her male opponents is in no position to bandy questions of sportsmanship. Double fie on you.

Yours,

BETSY DRAKE

513-A Sixth Avenue*
New York City
September 24, 1951

Dear Betsy,

Ordinarily wild horses couldn't have prevented me from answering your very nice letter of August 20th (mailed, as you recall, on August 26th). It

*Perelman's office until 1966.

arrived, however, just as some delayed-action *dolce far niente* caught up with me, not to speak of Homeric packing to leave Martha's Vineyard for New York. Once back here, I promptly became mired in a piece I had to do to meet a deadline. I have met the deadline and it is mine, to paraphrase some obscure quotation of consummate unimportance.

From the emphasis you place on water in your letter, the references to showers and the fact that you think best under water, I probably should be typing this on Vinylite or some other repellent substance; I have a mental picture of all this disintegrating and clogging the drains as you skim through it. (How did I ever get into this unattractive subject?) You also refer to a scary dream about being stung by a centipede. My knowledge of the unconscious is a little less than encyclopedic, but I can tell you readily that yours is preoccupied with multiple legs. What commonly-met-with creature possesses multiple legs? The spider, of course — and who do you know who most closely resembles a spider? Jessel, of course. It's your old Jessel fixation bubbling around in your subconscious mind. I'm very much afraid, my dear, that you are going to have to undergo a jesselectomy. Better get over to Magnin's real quick and pick out something becoming in a bed-jacket.

Tennis, which brought us together, produced an incident not without drama just before I left Martha's Vineyard. I was playing doubles against a pair of people, one of them a New York dermatologist, one very hot afternoon. My partner was a 62-year-old grain broker from Chicago, an excellent player but inclined to overdo. He'd already played three sets that afternoon, but as there was a gallery of attractive ladies, he wouldn't quit. (Yes, you're anticipating, and you're partly right.) Well, our opponents, sensing my inadequacy at the net, kept lobbing to my partner in the rear court, and after some exhausting footwork, he caved in with a thrombosis. (He's since recovered, so it had a happy ending.) The ironic part of the thing, though, was that the dermatologist didn't want to get involved. No doctor likes to be confronted with a dead patient, and he kept saying that somebody ought to call a doctor, meaning a general practitioner. While all the excitement was going on, the next team of players arrived, one of them a fancy surgeon. He was appealed to, took a quick look at the victim, and said, "Get a doctor, somebody! Forty love!" Well, we were just braiding our arms to carry the sufferer into a hotel room nearby, so that he wouldn't spoil everybody's fun by dying in the middle of the set, when another doc pulled up in a car. This one was a pediatrician, and we fully expected him to shear off and say he treated only measles. Luckily, a bystander managed to get hold of an ordinary three-dollar medico, and my partner will be back in the wheat pit gouging his associates before the snow flies. I guess the moral is never drop dead around a specialist.

New York has been purgatory ever since Labor Day, soupy temperatures

110

in the lower eighties, dust, hypertension, squealing brakes, stuttering compressed-air hammers, and everyone you know in the hands of psychiatrists and allied headshrinkers. The farm in Pennsylvania, 64 miles away, is possible for escape about every other weekend, but the Sunday night pile-up of traffic at the city's approaches pretty well destroys the total pleasure. I wish I were an eagle soaring over the Himalayas. (This is a point of view also shared by my family. They'd even be willing to have me be a centipede.)

· · ·

Yours,

FRANCES and ALBERT HACKETT
513-A Sixth Avenue
New York City
October 6, 1951

Dear Frances & Albert,

. . . I suppose I should have sent you . . . the news story about Little Brown & Co. being singled out by *Counter-Attack* as a nest of Reds, their discharging Angus Cameron, their editor in chief, and the mention of my name as one of the Red authors on their list (they once published the script of *One Touch of Venus*). Here we go, fellas.

We are all well here and having the delayed hot spell that hit you when you last wrote us. I hope you had a fine time in Coronado and made sure to revisit the Zoo in San Diego; the thought of it makes me emotional. . . .

· · ·

I'd like to ask one favor of you, and don't hesitate to ignore the whole thing if it complicates life in any way. Leila Hadley, whose name is not unknown to you both as the target of some of those phone calls and the gal who returned them, is arriving in Hollywood next Tuesday evening, the 9th, with her young son, Kippy. She'll be staying with Carol Saroyan for the ensuing nine days or so prior to sailing about Oct. 20 on the *President Madison*, a freighter of the American President Lines, for Hong Kong. (She intends to spend about ten months in India, Siam, and Indonesia, collecting material for pieces and a book.) I think you will agree with me that she is very attractive; the three years I've known her have done nothing to alter this view. I'd appreciate it if you asked her to dinner, since I believe you'd like each other. I've told her about your pictures (which is to say paintings, she knows your work in movies better than Allenberg), and be sure to point out my favorite Bombois with the shadows of the trees on the river bank...Laura and I threw a farewell party for her this past Tuesday, to which Marc Connelly* and George

*Playwright (*The Green Pastures*, etc.), director, and actor (d. 1981).

Oppenheimer and some others came; she is a friend of Marc's and George's, so it won't be too difficult making conversation. It never has for me, but then, it's more or less necessary to see her before understanding why.

•   •   •

Yours ever,

LEILA HADLEY

Hotel Roosevelt
Jacksonville, Fla.
October 19, 1951

Leila darling,

It's 11:05 p.m. and the air is like kapok twice-breathed and I'm half-dead after sightseeing miles of the World's Largest Alligator Farms, swamps, and scrub from early this morning until a couple of hours ago. I flew into this God-forsaken place late last night from New York and fly out again to Miami tomorrow morning. In between I have managed to put in as arduous a day as any mortal man ever did, and if I never again see the interior of a Greyhound bus, it's okay with me. The point was that I had to get to St. Augustine and take a hinge at the Fountain of Youth for the first piece in that *Redbook* series, and the only way to reach it is by bus. I also decided, what with one thing and another, to extend it to Marineland, which was really worthwhile. St. Augustine, however, was real horror, the whole depressing busload being bundled off every ten minutes and reamed into paying to see the Oldest Wooden House in America, the Dingiest Monastery, the Smelliest Fortifications, God knows what-all. This is really loathsome country, the land of lynch—the special windows in the bus terminals where colored people have to buy their tickets, the seats in the back of all public vehicles they must confine themselves to, the mean, ignorant faces of their white superiors, the fake good cheer beamed at the tourists, and the appalling ugliness of everything. I'm checking into the Roney Plaza for a mandatory 24-hour look at the gilded levels, and apart from a brief whirl up the line to Dania to see Leila Roosevelt's Anthropoid Ape Research Farm, am heading straight for Key West to get to work. It's obvious to me I'll have to invent the whole God-damned thing anyway, so I may as well face up to it and get it over with.

•   •   •

. . . I have been reading with enormous pleasure a book I mentioned to you before you left, *A Dragon Apparent* by Norman Lewis, just brought out in England by Jonathan Cape. It's his travels in Indo-China, and one of the best things of the sort I've read in years. It gives a very up-to-date, extremely graphic and penetrating, and often very funny picture of conditions

112

there, and although I very much doubt that you'll get there—it sounds damned dangerous, by the way—I wish there were time for you to read it.

There wasn't much news of note around New York in the ten days after you left. I finished up the Hollywood piece and it was received with ringing plaudits by *Redbook*, Hanna,* and Hirschfeld, the three sources principally concerned. I had dinner with Mark one evening at Dinty Moore's and then returned to his apartment to talk business for some hours. He's a weird blend of a very amusing companion and an (at times) utterly absurd, old-maidish, posturing bachelor. All those fussy ashtrays and gilt clocks and guff about how he talks over the intercom by his bed, when he wakes up in the morning, to his cook and tells her how many slices of bacon, etc. I wish to God he'd realize that there are times when the sound of his voice becomes a little overpowering...

                    •   •   •

... I altered my own travel schedule to just Florida and Las Vegas at this time because it would have removed me for too long a time from actual productive writing to continue the trip to Sun Valley, Arizona dude ranch, and Mexico. I'll take another trip beginning about January 5th which will include the three latter. The piece in the current *New Yorker* in the Cloudland series is the last one of mine they had on the bank, and I must lay off working for anyone else long enough to belt some stuff out for them...

                                        Always yours only,

*Mark Hanna, Perelman's literary and theatrical agent (d. 1958).

PHILIP   WYLIE

                                        Southwind Motel
                                        Key West, Fla.
                                        October 24, 1951

Dear Phil,

If you felt any peculiar glandular tremors this past weekend, I was in Miami from Saturday to Monday afternoon in a state of frustration comparable to that of a man whose lingam is laid up for repairs only to have Ava Gardner, Jane Russell, and Marilyn Monroe prancing around him in the nude. In dashing down here for some fast background for a piece in a series I'm doing for *Redbook*, I stupidly forgot to call Harold Ober or whoever your current thief is and extract your address. My subsequent detective efforts in trying to gouge it out of the Miami city desks would have made Raymond Chandler drool with envy. Unluckily, they didn't have it; the gent on the *News* said you'd been in recently and I saw your mingy phiz (hangdog, rather) in a group of Miami authors on Sunday, but I was up against a stone wall. I hung around the Roney chewing my nails and by Sunday evening I had it figured out. The next a.m. I braced the Doubleday bookshop on Lincoln Road, and after suitable self-identification (though the manageress is still convinced I'm Moe Pearlman, a handicapper for *The Running Horse*), succeeded in getting your street address. She's probably stalling and this letter will come right back to me.

Anyway, I'm sorry I couldn't have connected with you two charmers for at least a quick gin sling and a chin. You and I have now reached the age where we're type cast to sit around dipping snuff and cackling over old days at Siegel's restaurant opposite the Jefferson Market Court. On the other hand, perhaps you've had yourself rejuvenated like Gertrude Atherton and would unexpectedly deadpan me.

I'm breezing back through Miami for Las Vegas about November 9th or 10th when I finish work here. Drop me a chit with your phone number and maybe we can work it out then. My kindest regards to the mem.

Yours,

RAYMOND CHANDLER *

Key West, Fla.
October 24, 1951

Dear Ray,

I'm seated in an all-plastic motel overlooking another all-plastic motel which in turn overlooks the Gulf Stream, but there is no man in America (or for that matter the world) but yourself who could convey the grisly charm of the establishment. It's roughly three in the afternoon, sun beating down in a fury, and no sound but the occasional flapping of the laundry on the line outside and the occasional flush of the toilet in the next cubicle as the obviously clandestine lovers who sneaked in an hour ago punctuate their ecstasies. Hurray for progress and a cheap, hygienic rassle.

My contrition at not having acknowledged your letter of September 4th is profound; it has been in my hands a dozen times, and I've gotten as far as the salutation and what we used to call "the body of the letter" in school. However, a rush of work has had me on the ropes since just about six weeks ago, and as of day before yesterday, I holed in here to belt out an article in a series *Redbook*'s starting in midwinter. I'd spent the four or five days prior rubbering at Miami Beach and points immediately north, and a depressing

*Novelist and screenwriter (d. 1959). He was a fan of Perelman's parody "Farewell, My Lovely Appetizer" (based on Chandler's *Farewell, My Lovely*), collected in *Keep It Crisp* and reprinted in *The Most of S. J. Perelman*.

114

sight it is, too. There are 97 blocks of skyscraper hotels fringing Miami Beach, all with piss-elegant names like the Lord Tarleton and the Sherry-Frontenac. I actually had a cocktail (you see what I have to subject myself to for copy) in the Peekaboo Room of the Broadripole Hotel, a conjunction of syllables I wouldn't have believed had I been told about it. When you reflect that within the past two months I have been in Las Vegas, Miami Beach, and am returning to Las Vegas for another treatment when I leave here, I think you will admit that I earn a hard dollar.

It was kind of you to fill me in on Rancho Sante Fe, the school situation, and the Audograph and I appreciate it. Regarding our possible migration to the Coast, my wife appears to be frozen with irresolution at the moment. As you know, I managed by sheer pushing to steer them around the world, but a little sleeper jump to California has the family deadlocked. Obviously my son, aged 15, would like nothing better than to tool around in a hot-rod, grow nine feet tall, and wind up as relief manager of the Canyon Cleaners on La Cienega, but I guess my penchant for tropical animals didn't go over as I'd hoped with the matriarch. She takes the position that it's all a ruse to get her back to Hollywood, which she abominates with good cause, and counters with the suggestion — not an unreasonable one — that inasmuch as we have 83 acres of farm in Pennsylvania and a practical house, maybe we ought to stick to that. The only thing, I never heard of anyone carrying a Leadbeater's Cockatoo or a Humboldt's Woolly Monkey through a Pennsylvania winter. You can barely live through it yourself with five sweaters and oilstoves per man.

I certainly intend to invest in an Audograph when I can scratch together the price, but I am starting the other way around and am saving up for a lush secretary, something about 5'7" with a capacious bosom who'd be willing to sit on my lap and keep my mind off sex. It's very much on that theme at the moment, since this room I'm in has one large double bed, one single, and one folding cot in the closet. It seems pitiful to me that all this potential trysting space should go begging. And begging it will go if the missies I've seen around here the last two days are any sample. They all wear pince-nez, speak with the Florida drawl commonly recognized as only second to the New Jersey accent for pure horror, and simper. It's a melancholy prospect, and I'll thank you to feel some compassion.

Well, the afternoon mail pickup will be along most any time and after these weeks of delay in answering you, every day adds to my burden of guilt. I trust you are meeting each adjective as it comes and giving no ground. Half a league onward and never say die. I hope to get out to the Los Angeles area not in November as I'd previously thought but in early January. I hope we can get to see each other again then — even if I have to drive down the coast again. But this time I plan to slip an economy-size gibbon under my coat when I touch at the San Diego zoo.

.   .   .

L E I L A   H A D L E Y

Southwind Motel
Key West, Fla.
October 26, 1951

Darling,

.   .   .

There couldn't be anything more diametrically opposed to everything you're about to experience than the place I'm living in (that is, the Southwind Motel), so you'd better know about it for purposes of comparison. It's one of 7 or 8 motels grouped here on the Atlantic side of Key West; the ocean's a block away at the foot of the street, but my room overlooks (a) a laundry-line and the rear of another motel, and (b) still another motel. I'm seated at 11:20 p.m. in a room exactly 17 feet square containing a very large double bed, a single twin bed, and (in the closet) a folding cot. . . . The beds have headboards of pink tufted plastic simulating leather and orange-and-red plaid spreads. The tile underfoot is grey veined with white and doesn't appear to be real tile: it has a soapy, slick feel as though milk and soy-bean had gone into its making. The toilet seat is made of celluloid; there was a frilled bib on it when I checked in, informing me that it had been sanitized for my protection. My experience is that this is the only type from which I have consistently contracted crabs. There are so fucking many grilles, slots, steel Venetian blinds, portholes, louvred shutters, slats, and roll-up casements in this one room that whenever I strip, it takes half an hour to veil me from the public eye. The water tumblers, ice-pitcher, and tooth-glass are all made of foam and have a way of bouncing out of the hand and levitating; so I now scoop up water in my palms rather than touch them. Altogether, it makes one feel something like that girl who is constantly under the impression she went shopping in her Maidenform Bra.

If I weren't working here, of course, I wouldn't remain in Key West ten minutes, because it's a generally depressing place, and despite some surface changes, much as I remember it in 1934 before the big hurricane that blew away the Florida East Coast Railway. It's weedy, poverty-stricken, a tropical version of a New Jersey small town on a much lower economic level. It has a large Cuban population who must be involved in the shrimp fleet and commercial fishing of some sort, as there's no agriculture or industrial set-up on

116

this key. One main street lined with bars, cheap haberdashery shops catering to navy personnel, six or seven dreary restaurants, a lot of very debilitated Floridians (natives) locally called Conchs, and droves of lonely sailors staring into souvenir shops or sitting mournfully in the bars drinking cans of beer. What the Thielens or their friends can find tolerable except the comparative cheapness of living here, I don't know; personally, I think it would drive me starkers, as they say. . . . [T]he only demoiselles I've seen are pallid filing clerks with dramatic varicose veins peering listlessly out of the other motels, or moving heavily toward the community beach club where we all eat. (As it's too far from the center of town to walk and I have no car.) The only pleasure I've had here in five days is to retreat nightly to the end of the jetty that extends from the beach club into the water, get a fix on Orion, and think of you. Well, don't get unduly depressed by all this, as I'm not, really. If the verbiage doesn't dry up, another ten days or so should see me on my way. Right now, I'll suspend for the time being and resume eventually when there's something to write. Some old windbag with an ear-trumpet who writes the society column for the local paper is coming out here tomorrow noon to interview me. I must get into condition to be quicksilvery...

Wednesday night, Oct. 31

I see that my social life has broadened as I reread the above; I've had dinner several times with the — , which was pleasant, but they're unfortunately mixed up with a pair of people who are strenuous, making-crazy types who "just laugh and laugh," as Mrs. Make-Crazy puts it. This is a hyperthyroid dame who fastens on you like a succubus to the 74th power and shreds you to pieces, I really may have to kill her. She is one of that all-too-common breed that idolizes *The New Yorker* and is constantly reminding you of cartoons that appeared in it years ago, which she then proceeds to describe in detail (guffawing) and then "Oh, dear, if I could remember the caption!" She also remembers everything I ever wrote, and quotes passages from it written by Max Shulman and Geoffrey Hellmann...

Beavers—Stakhanovite beavers yet—would resemble sloths compared to the way I've been working here; I have better than two thirds of this Florida piece done, and would probably finish it by the end of the week, ahead of schedule, except that I'm now taking a couple of days out. I've wangled the Coast Guard into carrying me over to the Dry Tortugas and Loggerhead Key on their cutter visiting those places every two weeks with supplies. You may remember that Tortugas is the site of Fort Jefferson, the grim old Federal penitentiary where Dr. Mudd, who treated John Wilkes Booth, was confined. It's sixty miles out at sea and was declared a national park by FDR back in the '40's. I'm going out there for overnight leaving early tomorrow morning

117

and carrying bedding—could I be going to sleep in the prison itself? I'll find out soon enough. It's also the nesting grounds of several million sooty and noddy terns. Sounds like babytalk, but not, I'm sure, to an old ornithologist like you…Saturday, I've lined up a charter boat and am taking the Thielens fishing in the Gulf Stream. Did this only once, back in 1934, but it was real enjoyable, and maybe may add some copy for this current piece.

The only news of moment—and should be kept under your cloche, not to be mentioned in any dispatches you send back until the ink dries on the contract—is that I've switched publishers and am going with Doubleday. I've been fed up with S. and S. for lo, these many, many months—all the way back to that dreadful job they did on *Listen to the Mocking Bird* when I was in Europe two years ago. Their listless handling of *Swiss Family P.* really began to tout me off them, and then, all this year, they've betrayed such complete uninterest—to the extent of never even asking whether any of these series I'm doing were book possibilities, etc.—that I finally decided to give them the heave-ho. Mark handled it, and did, I'm glad to report, a very canny job. The storm broke right after I reached here; the Doubleday people let it leak out and Messrs. Goodman & Leventhal* evidently put on a manic performance, nickering and keening and ululating and rending their clothing in sorrow. It turns out that despite their reserve, they'd secretly worshipped me all this time, etc., etc. Of course, the plain and dismal fact is that they are really wretched business men, for they needn't have lost me as an author if they'd shown a particle of concern. So it hardly mends matters that Leventhal's been trying nightly to phone me down here. But I've erected a cheval-de-frise of mystery around myself; one day I've gone to the Everglades, another I'm in Nassau, etc. It's delicious; I can just see that little roach storming on his executive levels.

•   •   •

*Jack Goodman (d. 1957), editor in chief and advertising director of Simon and Schuster; Albert Leventhal (d. 1976), executive vice-president and chief operating officer.

LEILA HADLEY

Erwinna, Pa.
November 23, 1951

Darling,

•   •   •

The eight days in Las Vegas were as hectic as I'd anticipated. I spent the first three at the Last Frontier Hotel and then a Nero-like individual named Belden Kathleman, who owns El Rancho Vegas, arbitrarily had me moved over to his hotel and installed in a whore's dream of a villa, all yellow satin and stall showers. I suddenly found myself seated in breakfast conclave with a man named Harry Cohn, who presides over Columbia Pictures, a monsignor of the Roman Catholic Church so drunk he couldn't speak intelligibly, a 300-lb. gambler named Bones Remmer currently on the lam from the Treasury Department, his bodyguard, and a daffy ne'er-do-well named Levy who owns a thing called the Blum Candy Corporation. This kind of weird existence, interspersed with a somnambulistic progress through the casinos of all the hotels and attending the floorshows they all feature, managed to cut down my sleep to a mere nubbin. In the interests of copy I also interviewed a couple of strip teasers attached to a Minsky unit appearing at the Desert Inn, did a little sightseeing out at Hoover Dam, and altogether managed (I hope) to scrape together enough factual miscellany to justify the piece I'll do on the town next month. . . .

.   .   .

Much more news than this I ain't got, principally because I spent the entire 48 hours after returning to NY in the arms of — — of *Redbook*, throwing out changes he'd made in the mss. of my first two pieces of the series there. As an earnest and token of what awaits you in your new career of penwoman, they'd made *103 changes* in the opening pieces of the series, the one on Florida: a piece, incidentally, on which I had worked harder and into which I'd put more ganglion-grinding thought than any I've done for years. The bulk of the changes was an effort to dumb the piece down for the *Redbook* reader; the balance were arbitrary re-paragraphings and duller methods of saying what I'd said. On the whole as tiresome an experience as I've undergone, and the phrase "Fuck you, big boy" trembled on my lips every three minutes. I've really never been angrier in my life, but there is far too much at stake — considering that the series may well run to twelve articles — to blow my top. If it was any consolation, they behaved the same way with Al's drawings, forcing him to alter, change, and generally muddy everything he did. I shall return to writing pieces for *The New Yorker*, generally held to be a very finicking outfit, with a song on my lips.

.   .   .

Yours alone,

LEILA HADLEY

513-A Sixth Avenue
New York City
December 1, 1951

My dear,

A fine, fat letter from you this morning, full of the color and excitement of Hong Kong. I feel the same pride in the pleasure you're deriving that a midwife must enjoy. You know now how impossible it is to describe to

119

anyone who hasn't been in the East what it's like. Last night I flung aside a dreadful book recently published by Doubleday called *Seven Leagues to Paradise* by Richard Tregaskis. Mark, who's his agent, gave it to me with the warning that it was puerile, but Mark, who usually overstates everything, was guilty this time of the reverse. Tregaskis spends all his time restating the obvious and quivering over the prospect of finding bare-bosomed Balinese girls and such Republic-picture, teen-age aphrodisiacs. Really lamentable that anyone should dignify such *scheiss* by wasting a Mergenthaler linotype on it. And while on the subject, the same for Michener too. This latter, . . . pitch-forked into success by the accident of a Broadway hit musical, is now turning out book after book on the Orient, each greeted by the press as authentic observation. I wish someone (and I'd do it if I had the time) would come out with a blast, pointing out that the book I spoke to you about some time ago, Norman Lewis' *A Dragon Apparent*, is a model of what travel writing should be. It's superb — funny, packed with real observation, and written out of true experience in areas of Indochina almost nobody has penetrated for years.

.   .   .

. . . My switch-over from S&S to Doubleday was attended, as you may imagine, with high drama. The former had begged and beseeched me not to sign the Doubleday contract without letting them plead their case. Mark, myself, Jack [Goodman], and Leventhal had a sweaty conference last Tuesday morning at which the last two grovelled. . . . Shouts of "mea culpa" filled the air; it appeared that Jack thought Albert was looking after my literary welfare and needs while Albert thought Jack was, etc. Oh, the greasing, the blarney, the lubrication. Everyone, it emerged, adored me in the firm, from Bob Bernstein to the man who changes the rolls of toilet paper in M. Lincoln Schuster's private lavabo. I was a combination, I was assured, of Mark Twain, E.M. Forster, and Voltaire. Well, to paraphrase what Lord Chesterfield said about coitus, the position was uncomfortable, the expense untenable, and the pleasure momentary. We guaranteed that we would give the matter every consideration and took our leave. Inasmuch as I'd already given my word to Doubleday and the contract was being rewritten there to include a few necessaries, the whole discussion with the boys was academic. . . .*

Otherwise, not a great deal; I've been steaming myself up to get a *New Yorker* piece started, always an effort after concentrating on other work. I have about 3 weeks clear before I start on my 3rd *Redbook* piece on Las Vegas, and somewhere I've got to fit in a piece on Durante for *Holiday*. In about 15 minutes, the painter's arriving at my office to repaint the inner sanctum;

*In the end, Perelman did not sign with Doubleday.

did I tell you that he did it in my absence in a loathsome shade of apple-green instead of the bitter-green I'd picked out? It's beginning to look pretty tasty, though; I plan to send down to Jacksonville for a plant called a Monstera Philodendron I saw there, and my favorite Buddha head goes up on a wall-bracket over the psychiatric couch to brood upon its owner's figure hunched over the typewriter. . . .

.   .   .

LEILA HADLEY

10664 Bellagio Road
Los Angeles, Calif.
February 3, 1952

Leila darling,

The emblem on the cover of the pad this sheet of stationery came from reads "Hytone — Zephyr Laid" and it is peculiarly applicable, since I feel both hytoned and as though I had been recently laid not only by a zephyr but a whole typhoon. I've been in L.A. since a week ago Friday, having come here from a ranch on the Mexican border in Arizona and to *that* from Sun Valley. . . .

.   .   .

. . . My pals the Hacketts flew to NY for a 6 or 8 month stay; they are turning the Pagnol trilogy of *Marius*, *Fanny*, and *César* into a musical. This means I have been alone in this chateau except for Daisy, the maid, and her elderly dachshund, but the two of them have been cooking and sweeping for me devotedly. The usual round of dull parties at the Gershwins, etc.; it's as though I never had been away.

.   .   .

. . . I'm now trying to figure out whether to seesaw down the Coast to San Diego, which would give me a chance to stop off and lunch with Raymond Chandler at La Jolla, revisit the San Diego Zoo and tickle my favorite gibbons and birds there, take the Mexican airline out of Tijuana and stop off for a day's fishing in Guaymas, and thus arrive at Acapulco. . . . Laura is scheduled to meet me in Acapulco on the 13th; she has been caged up in NY during all these sorties of mine and is really deserving of a breather away from the domestic treadmill. . . .

.   .   .

Longingly,

GUS LOBRANO

Hotel Reforma Casablanca
Acapulco
February 11, 1952

Dear Gus,

•   •   •

As you see from the piss-elegant letterhead, I am in Acapulco, Gro., whatever Gro. means. The Reforma Casablanca is one of those vast cement booby-traps that must have been built in between breakfast and lunch by the most dishonest of Mexican contractors; everything is peeling or crumbling, the chrome nickel shower-taps come away in your hand, the modernique neon lights around the medicine cabinet don't work, and there is a pervasive smell of chicken fried rice and open drains in the halls. The architects apparently weren't told about the catastrophic heat here and designed mingy little windows which hardly admit a spoonful of air, and, of course, there isn't an electric fan in the joint. Right now (early afternoon) it's like an August dog-day, without any air-cooled bars to escape to. "Ah, yes," one says here, "but after all, it cools off at night." Well, last night — my first here — it must have cooled off to at least ninety. I slept in a shower of perspiration, awakening from time to time to bang on the wall in a vain effort to persuade the señoritas next door to stop playing their gramophone....At this stage of my travels, I would ordinarily be suicidal were it not for the fact that Laura is joining me here day after tomorrow, and four days after that, we will return to Mexico City for a week before coming back to New York. I have a snootful of vacation spots for the moment, what with Sun Valley, an Arizona ranch, and a couple of weeks in Los Angeles piled on top of those junkets in November to Key West and Las Vegas. In fact, I may very well settle down in some industrial center like Carteret, N.J., to get the taste of the tourism out of my mouth.

The six days at Sun Valley were marred by a continuous snowfall that broke all records, and as you no doubt read, climaxed in avalanches that killed at least three skiers. I put in only one day on what we skiers call "the hickories," and offers started pouring in immediately from all the resorts like the Laurentians, North Conway, and Aspen, begging me to resume my amateur status. I thereupon took off for Rancho de la Osa, a dude ranch 70 miles south of Tucson on the Mexican border. This was a place recommended by Erskine Caldwell, who, needless to say, had never been there, and by all indications should have been grisly, but it turned out to be very pleasant. Spent all my time in the saddle, which meant nightly soaking in a bathtub full of epsom salts, inasmuch as I had never been in a saddle before. The finale was an all-day ride into Sonora state in Mexico that included a descent down a rocky gorge: an interlude that can be pigeon-holed under "N" for nightmares. Following this, I flew on to L.A., caught a hell of a cold that effectively deafened my right ear, and continued here. Obviously I am a man who will subject himself to anything rather than be static.

I was bowled off my pins to learn of Bill's ascension to the wheelhouse* and I learned it from . . . Max Shulman (you remember the chap, he writes funny). I encountered him at some Hollywood party and he was achieving some small celebrity by virtue of having seen the story in *Time* before anybody else. I hastened to get myself a copy, and frankly, the news gave me quite a turn. I suppose I had taken it for granted that if anyone were chosen for the post, it would be you, and I am still trying to puzzle it out. I of course know nothing whatever of the subterranean currents at the office, but at this distance it occurs to me there must have been an unexpected upheaval. What, if you care to speak under the seal of confidence, gives?

•   •   •

Yours,

*William Shawn was named editor of *The New Yorker* after the death of Harold Ross. At Lobrano's death, William Maxwell temporarily handled Perelman until Shawn became his permanent editor. *Chicken Inspector No. 23* is dedicated to Shawn.

LEILA HADLEY

513-A Sixth Avenue
New York City
March 31, 1952

Leila darling,

•   •   •

. . . What a lovely time you're having, and how pleased I am that I could have been instrumental in mid-wifing it. I was particularly touched by your letter of February 10th mailed from Penang just before you sailed for the Nicobars, containing the peacock feather. It breathed such a feeling of contentment, of having shed so many bothersome and ridiculous complications with which you'd managed to fuck up your life here. I assure you that everyone you know is just as bemired, befuddled, and crazed as when you left — more so, no doubt. Myself, I am going along in a kind of meaningless vacuum, weeks of hard work relieved by stretches that have absolutely no significance or pattern. Not that I'm actively unhappy, outside of missing you very keenly — just a kind of vegetable existence and seeing people who don't affect me one way or the other. I last wrote you in Los Angeles February 3rd, where I was doggedly belting out a piece on Jimmy Durante and combatting a vile cold. I licked both, and flew to Acapulco on February 10th. It's a dreadful place, the epitome of touristic enterprise: gouging, arrogant mid-Western trippers, diarrhea, heat, and poverty and filth peeping out behind a Miami Beach façade. I spent a week there; Laura joined me half-way through, promptly contracted all the local malaises, and we flew back to Mexico City. This was more tolerable; we spent another week there with a side trip to Cuernavaca, and flew back to New York on February 25th. Since then, I did a piece on Acapulco for the *Redbook* series, another for *Holiday* on George Jessel in *that* series, and spent the better part of a week in bed with the virus which has had everyone on his back here this winter. Now, with a few weeks clear until I have to dish out another instalment for *Redbook*, I'm trying to do something for *The New Yorker* which I've been neglecting all winter.

⋅ ⋅ ⋅

Started going to the country this past weekend, where we are installing an oil heating plant after 19 years, also building on a bedroom sorely needed. This venture, together with remodelling the kitchen and re-financing the mortgage which has overhung the place these past two decades, is going to bind me up like the celebrated trussed fowl for the next ten years. An attractive prospect.

⋅ ⋅ ⋅

Enduringly yours,

BETSY DRAKE

513-A Sixth Avenue
New York City
April 5, 1952

Dear Betsy,

⋅ ⋅ ⋅

I have thought of you repeatedly, most recently during this past month when I was engaged in the back-breaking task of spawning a piece for *Holiday* on George Jessel. The job of cleansing the Augean stables was child's play by comparison. The few paltry notes I took last summer on his witticisms had turned to ashes, and about all I was able to remember were your snappish comments about his boorishness and general lack of loveliness — with all of which, I hasten to add, I agreed then and now. However, that didn't absolve me from the obligation I'd undertaken of delivering a nostalgic, funny article about the man. Whether I did or not, posterity will have to judge. At least I was paid, thank God.

⋅ ⋅ ⋅

. . . How are *you* — psychically, professionally, physically? I see your name and Cary Grant's everywhere I roam on marquees, billboards, and in fan magazines, and I shouldn't wonder that you two are carrying on some sort of affair, or living together, or something dubious. Are you still taking those showers with the same fierce, unrelenting ardor, and still brooding about your career? And more important, are you at all considering coming East this spring? I'll buy you the best lunch our Manhattan Brillat-Savarins can contrive, you can wear your most eccentric hat, and we can annihilate Jessel till the cows come home. Write me in any case, and keep your backhand supple.

Yours,

B E T S Y   D R A K E

513-A Sixth Avenue
New York City
May 12, 1952

Dear Betsy,

Contrition, Remorse, & Heartburn—it sounds like one of those untalented trios in vaudeville consisting of two men and a girl who pretend to parody society ballroom dancers simply because they can't dance very well themselves—you know, the types who simulate adagio and then drop each other. Well, actually I'm full of all three, seeing that it's taken me the better part of five weeks to acknowledge your nice letters of early April. . . .

I was floored by your decision to exchange the grease-pencil and the mummer's mask for the quill. Convinced, like everyone, that anybody else's profession is better than his own, my stomach turned over twice at the thought of you sitting in a hot little office in South Beverly Hills scratching verbs. Or adjectives. They are the least responsive, most ornery little critters in the world to work with, and I needn't tell you how exasperating, befuddling, and dismaying a full day of struggling with them can be. I take it you are hacking out some sort of treatment which by now, undoubtedly, has burst its cocoon and become a beautiful screenplay. Well, kid, take a tip from a bruised refugee from the medium. The agony of creation is as nothing compared to what you will endure when (unless you yourself propose to speak all the parts) the actors get at it. And the producer. And the director. . . . In short, you are batting a sticky wicket. You are, as W.S. Gilbert said, playing billiards on a twisted cloth with elliptical billiard balls. (He said it more felicitously—I can't remember the exact words.) The aces, to put it still another way, are all tucked up your opponent's sleeves. In spite of all of which pessimism, don't lose heart. After you've succumbed to impulse and flung the portable against the wall and gone out and got drunk and bought a new hat and sobbed yourself to sleep and awakened with a hangover, sit down again and look at what you wrote yesterday. It isn't that bad; in fact, it's acquired a strange kind of validity from just lying there overnight. At least, it's a beginning. This is what I always tell myself. And I am capable of as much self-deception as any man of my weight and age in existence.

Your suggestion for that piece on Jessel, that I call it "There is less under this toupee than you might think would meet the eye," was inspired, but unluckily, that prose gem had sped off to the foundry by then.* I am not sure what Georgie-Porgie will think when he reads it. It may be that he will engage a couple of George Raft's stand-ins to call on me and muss up my features; on the other hand, capricious and lovable chap that he is, he may revel in the publicity. All I know is that it was a chore and a migraine, and I was never so glad to get any incubus off my back. As of this writing, I am waist deep in another one in that series, on Fred Allen, who is quite another cup of tea and a much nicer person, but the labor is no easier. Gee, wouldn't it be nice if they paid people to lie around in an old negligee and read stuff they'd always wanted to and go out to lunch for three hours?

I wouldn't be true to my obligation to relate the whole truth, nothing but the truth, and so forth if I concealed the fact that this has been (and in fact, is now) the loveliest spring in memory. Maybe the fact that the world generally is in such a mess and that the boys in the smoke-filled rooms are considering Taft and MacArthur to remedy the situation makes one more responsive to buds and flowers, but it's surely been a delight out this way. . . .

I'd probably better stop before I begin giving you little travelogues about Washington in cherry-blossom time, the witchery of girls in their summer dresses on Fifth Avenue, and roguish-eyed cops flirting with nursemaids. I shall be lunching on Friday with an editor who has it in his power to dispatch me to the Coast on some trumped-up mission this summer, like measuring the size of Dore Schary's hindquarters for the Smithsonian, so keep your fingers crossed. . . .   Love,

*"The Swirling Cape and the Low Bow," collected in *The Road to Miltown* (1957).

LEILA HADLEY

513-A Sixth Avenue
New York City
May 27, 1952

Leila darling,

•   •   •

There came through the lines of your letter very unmistakably a sense of peace; the peace you have been making with yourself through all these past months, and if not a complete cessation, a distinct lessening of the turbulence

126

that had made you miserable the past few years. This is the wonderful thing that one can't explain to people who've never travelled in the East. It has nothing to do with words like mysticism, I believe it springs purely from being able to leave behind the whole complex of anxieties and pressures of metropolitan life in the States and move as a bystander among a wholly different set of civilizations. You must feel at all times that whatever the trip has cost you materially, even if it has in any way meant pledging your future, is inconsequential; you were extremely lucky that at this very disturbed time in history, you had the opportunity to see the more important part of the world, and to use your experiences to bring yourself into focus. . . .

.   .   .

This is a rather busy period for me. The *Redbook* series is now formally finished. It was a bad experience, and has taught me a lesson I thought I'd learned a long time ago, that you can't please everybody. I gave them the best I was capable of, and I put a great deal of time and labor into it. I can't write down to any special audience; like any writer with self-respect, I've spent a good many years perfecting my tools and evolving a point of view and a manner that is characteristic. The survey of reader opinion on the first piece in the series disheartened them, they lost their editorial nerve (which had impelled them to engage me to do this series — *their* editorial idea, not mine), and they wanted out. So the piece on my experiences at the dude ranch in Arizona, "Give a Man Enough Latigo," concludes the show — that is, five pieces in all. Needless to say, this doesn't mean I am abandoning *Springtime for Sidney* as a book. I did research Sun Valley (for which they gracelessly refused me even expenses), I have three *Holiday* pieces out of the past which I hope I can convert into chapters for the book, and that will leave me with the necessity of doing three further pieces of locales I haven't decided on yet...The current *Holiday* series, on the comics, now stands at Groucho and Jimmy Durante (the latter in the current issue), and Jessel and Fred Allen, both in their shop. Four all told; they would like one on Ed Wynn, but he's unfortunately moved to the Coast and they don't want to pay my expenses just to go out there for one piece. Hence, I consider that series pretty well washed up. Actually, I am relieved as hell, as I haven't had a decent chance to get back to anything for *The New Yorker*, which I'm now starting. I'm resuming the Cloudland Revisited series* but this time on some of the old movies — Erich von Stroheim's *Foolish Wives*, Griffith's *Intolerance*, one of Wallace Reid's 1921 automobile-racing epics, a 1916 version of *20,000 Leagues under the Sea*, all that sort of thing. The Museum of Modern Art has proved to be a tip-top outfit; through Monroe Wheeler and several other friends up there I'm being given a projec-

*An umbrella title Perelman had given to a series of takeouts on popular novels of his youth.

tion room and the right to inspect 57 films I selected from their catalogue, which really contains some treasures the public knows nothing of. I'm starting a projection schedule Monday which will bury me like a mole up there for a while, but I hope it will be productive of an extensive body of material for future pieces.

T.S. Eliot's in town fleetingly before departing for England, I had lunch yesterday with him and Ted Kauffer at the latter's apartment and it was a good meeting. The shabby old eagle and I get along well, he is as sharp and dry as can be, loves to hoist his bourbon, and vitally interested in everything. I told him about Doc Maurer, *The Big Con*, and all that fabulous life of the underworld based on the con men and pickpockets and he's going back to Britain in a transport of excitement about the subject...

• • •

... People here are buzzing about Lillian Ross's current *New Yorker* piece, the first in her series on Hollywood: from my standpoint and that of people whose judgment I value, a snide and completely unfair searchlight trained on John Huston and a couple of others. There are amusing bits, conference scenes with L.B. Mayer and such, but it's a ratty job, vicious in a professional sense, and will cause a lot of totally unnecessary talk and hard feeling. I yield to nobody in my distaste for a lot of Hollywood, but I don't like the way Miss Ross presents it any more than I did Evelyn Waugh's *The Loved One*.

• • •

Yours always,

LEILA HADLEY

513-A Sixth Avenue
New York City
June 14, 1952

Darling Leila,

• • •

I've spent almost all the past two weeks at the Museum of Modern Art projecting ten films I plan to write about in the Cloudland Revisited series in *The New Yorker*, things I saw between 1915 and 1925 — *Foolish Wives* (von Stroheim), *20,000 Leagues under the Sea*, *Way Down East*, *Male and Female*, *Excuse My Dust*, *Stella Dallas*, etc. The Museum's film division was extremely co-operative; I'd been trying to set up this scheme for about two years and had been at some pains to figure out where I could uncover the particular films I wanted, as they've largely disappeared. MGM finally tipped me off that the Museum has an enormous library of 14 million feet which it shares with the Eastman Foundation in Rochester, and through Monroe Wheeler, who's an old friend, its facilities were extended to aid this work. I worked with a tape recorder while the films were being shown, talking into it and describing the contents of each scene and the subtitles. I now have the secretary in the adjoining office transcribing the tape, and thus am accumulating a sizable bale of information from which I can draw quotes and descriptions of the action. A somewhat bulky method, but the only feasible one and I'm hopeful that it may result in some good material.

. . . I may or may not have mentioned [T.S.] Eliot's being in town briefly; it was good to see him again, and he wrote a very sweet inscription in my copy of *The Waste Land*. Both the Democratic and Republican conventions are looming, and the press is full of interminable horseshit about the candidates. Out of it, and using a three-tined pitchfork, I extract two items to give you a dispiriting idea of what our lawmakers are busying themselves with. The witch-hunt continues, people are daily puking up their past to the Congressional sub-committees, and you can be fairly sure that anyone who ever contributed a dollar or signed a statement for any liberal cause whatsoever will be pilloried in due time. Out in Hollywood the thousand per center Americanos have formed a glamor committee for Taft, which lists people like John Dos Passos, Jimmy Stewart, Morrie Ryskind, Charles Coburn, and the like. It's all depressingly evil and snide and it's increasingly apparent that a process of brain-washing and thought control has stifled almost every bit of independent thinking. I myself read nothing but *The New Statesman* and books, preferably about travel and ornithology.

.   .   .

Yours always,

GUS LOBRANO

Erwinna, Pa.
July 16, 1952

Dear Gus,

.   .   .

. . . I haven't as yet read enough of Patrick Campbell to form any judgment, but if you're still looking for bright young humorists, you might like to investigate the pair mentioned in the enclosed clipping.* I think that the adventures of two modern young Nuns (for example, how they come to be kidnapped by a white slave ring in Marseilles, their introduction into a Buenos

*An ad for a book *Convent Belles* — "Gay! Dashing! Funny! . . . but thoroughly reverent."

Aires brothel under the impression that they're entering an Argentinian finishing school, and all kinds of laughable mistakes in identity growing out of such a background) might make a lush series for *The New Yorker*. All you'd have to figure out would be what to tell your Catholic readers.

Yours, gaily, dashingly, funnily,...but always reverently,

LEILA HADLEY

Erwinna, Pa.
July 20, 1952

Darling,

This is about the tenth consecutive day of a stretch of Lizzie Borden heat which has been deranging the Atlantic seaboard ever since the spring: one of those damnable summers when the humidity never falls below 60% and everyone's in a real murder mood. I've been down in steamy Bucks just a couple of days over a month and have only gone into New York for two quick visits, largely to pick up your letters. . . . I think I know how much you must have revelled in Beirut when you first arrived there after the heat and squalor of the Middle East. I felt the same way when Hirschfeld and I arrived in Alexandria after our Cairo stay and the previous journey across the Arabian Ocean. For my money, the whole area between Istanbul and Burma could be flushed down a great cosmic toilet. . . .

A fearful absence of interesting or provocative news here; I've been seated on my Pennsylvania slipware ass for the past four weeks doing nothing but working, as the exchequer's in a sorry state, the breach in the financial dike is widening, the balance in the bank is dwindling, and any other colorful image you can supply. Hysteria, playing on her jangled lyre, has been furnishing an obbligato meanwhile, inasmuch as we've had four carpenters whacking away at the small extension being added to the house here. How so much cement, plaster, wire lath, slate, and crumbling brick can mount up in the course of constructing one bedroom, bath, and closets is beyond me. It hasn't been made more stable by the presence of a plumber and electrician, both of whom are the most exasperating feebs I've ever met in two decades of dealing with Jukes and Kallikaks. The kind of gentry who invade my workroom at ten-minute intervals to report disaster and who get a fiendish pleasure out of discovering reasons why whatever you want done will not work. And who make rapid little decisions to mount electric light switches behind sideboards or seal plumbing fixtures under flagstones where it needs a pneumatic hammer to rectify the damage. Most of the time I sit up here in my den with my face a subdued fuschia and a nimbus of steam around my head, so palsied with rage that I can't hit the typewriter keys accurately.

. . .

. . . The Republican convention and its absurdities is past, thank God, and now the Democratic one's getting revved up. Everyone with any conscience hopes Stevenson will consent to run; the prospect of Eisenhower and that fearful s.o.b. Nixon as a possible pair in the White House is appalling.

Me myself, I've been working, as I said earlier, have done and sold the first two pieces on the old movies in that Cloudland Revisited series for *The New Yorker*, and am well into a third. In so far as any writing can be said to be enjoyable — I categorically deny that it can — I find this new stuff of some slight absorbing interest while working on it. . . .

While on this tedious subject of writing, let me drop a fast bit of unsought-for advice. . . . I hope you aren't wasting a lot of energy worrying about what *kind* of a book you're eventually going to write about your experiences, that is to say, the exact form or the over-all significance or whatever. I submit (and forgive my possible harping on the subject) that one has to beat out a first draft — good, bad, or indifferent — no matter what the emotional effort. Once he's got that, the rest is mechanical. In other words, there are plenty of experts around, whether disguised as editors or friends, who'll be able to assist you later on in molding the stuff, or switching it about, or suggesting ways of conquering what may seem to you to be obstacles, and who'll have a perspective you may not agree with but which will have some value. . . . I'm reading Gerald Brenan's *The Face of Spain* at the moment — not bad, but a Catholic's view of Spain, no matter if fairly liberal, has shortcomings. By the way, there's a fairly interesting natural-history number called *King Solomon's Ring* by Konrad Lorenz which you might try to pick up if you find an English bookshop in the Mediterranean area. Some startling revelations about jackdaws though the book's written in a generally irritating Germanic style.

. . .

L E I L A   H A D L E Y

West Tisbury
Martha's Vineyard, Mass.
August 4, 1952

Darling,

. . .

We got up here this past Friday night, the first, in one concentrated day's

131

driving from Pennsylvania, laden with baggage and animals (the kids had preceded us by two weeks) to find a pleasant enough little house set up on a hill overlooking the ocean, in a terrain straight out of Charlotte Brontë. Moors and stone walls and only a couple of other cottages in the distance. The place is smaller than the house you stayed at with us and a lot dinkier; rock maple furniture, a suicidally small bathroom, and every wall covered with the excruciating paintings of the landlord, a hideously untalented academic artist. But there are plenty of windows and inasmuch as the place is only a year old, it doesn't have that depressing, moldy atmosphere so many houses here do. . . .

Myself, I expect to spend most of August indoors working; I have done and sold three Cloudland Revisited pieces on those old movies . . . and want to do a couple more if I can before Labor Day. . . . Thank you for your nice words about the Mexican instalment of "Springtime for Sidney," and even more for purging yourself about *Redbook*. Of course you are so right about what a dreadful and dispiriting magazine it is. Some day I'll describe at length what contempt its editors have for their readers, which is really the sin against the Holy Ghost and the same thing I saw at first hand in my eleven years in Hollywood. The producer mentality works on the assumption that people are incapable of understanding or appreciating anything above the comic strip level, and goes on forever farting out this miasma of detergent fiction and home-making claptrap, justifying it with dishonest, lying surveys and opinion samplings whose only raison d'être is to support a hierarchy of advertising moguls and their fuglemen. I alternate between periods of violence and despair when I consider what faces anybody who wants to really write as well as he can. There is literally no market whatever outside *The New Yorker*: almost every sortie I have made away from it has had some element of heartburn. *Holiday* gave promise five years ago, when Al and I made our trip together, of possibly becoming a magazine of principle, but that quickly faded. Today it's a flatulent, shiny, and indescribably dull sheet with interminable photo-articles on "Hartford, the Insurance Mecca," "Fun in the Gaspé Peninsula," and "The Mesabe Range—Canada's Iron Treasure Trove," interlarded with advertisements for Jantzen Swim-suits and Hickok Belts. Every time I've approached my old compadre Ted Patrick, its editor, with a project that was a tiny bit off the beam, I've gotten smothered, and now I don't much care whether they send me to Africa or not. . . .

· · ·

. . . The thought of becoming embroiled with these mean little suburbanites up here gives me a sinking sensation in the pit of the stomach. If they can only read the distaste in my face, I'm sure they'll let me alone, but inevitably I get drawn into a round of dinners and cocktail parties at which I behave morosely and totally without charm. It's so idiotic to waste money, that could be spent to some purpose, in exposing oneself to their mingy personalities. I really must make a point of not leaving the house here. . . .

Yours,

LEILA HADLEY

19 Washington Square North
New York City
September 29, 1952

My darling Leila,

•   •   •

. . . If you plan to exist in this Moloch when you return — as you must — you owe it to yourself to work out some kind of life independent of the pressures that operate on all the people we know. The world of the columnists, publicity, the Wheeldex, all that hideous, clanging, empty, nerve-destroying, and utterly futile life that washes people out at forty — darling, go out to the stern of the *California*, spit into the wake, and vow that you're through with it.* It is not only possible, it is perfectly reasonable, to evolve a living by free-lance writing. I have been doing it for twenty-seven years and I can tell you that while it is no joke, it has its rewards in terms of independence and self-respect. Equipped with what you've seen of the earth and some of the people on it, and a very lively intelligence, humor, worldliness, and *determination*, you can cut yourself free from the horrible phantoms you've lived with in the past. Forgive me for all this awful canting type of advice — it's beginning to assume a pattern, I'm afraid; but Jack's mention of that publicity job with Walt Kelly . . . somehow has lingered in my mind, and I urge you to stick to your resolution to begin a fresh chapter.

•   •   •

*Hadley was sailing around the world on a three-masted schooner with a crew of four.

LEILA HADLEY

19 Washington Square North
New York City
c. October 1, 1952

•   •   •

There seems to be a spurt of activity involving the African safari plans, although I am not at all convinced it will materialize into anything. The East African Travel Ass'n has vouchsafed considerable interest in bringing such

133

a junket into reach of yrs. truly, whose reach is paralyzed with pauperdom at the moment. Also Mark has stirred up some enthusiasm in the higher councils at CBS in the notion of my making a pilot film for a possible TV series out there. S&S would presumably give me the advance they offered in the past for a book on it. This all sounds like action, except that it can only be done if I have an outlet for some pieces, namely, *Holiday*, which faltered on the idea about a year ago as being too expensive. Well, as of this moment, they are making up their dawdling minds about how many articles they could absorb, and when all the pieces of the puzzle are fitted together, I'll be able to see whether it's feasible. . . .

[continued on] October 7

. . . [W]hat a week, all the hysteria of moving out of our apartment at 19 Washington Square North, total disorganization, barrels and boxes and crates and cartons, arguments with Venetian-blind fabricators, painters, landlords, movers — in any case, we're finally settled again across Washington Square, at 39½ Washington Square South in a rather decrepit old Victorian apartment house but a cheerful and sunny arrangement far superior to that grim, barred cavern of the last year and a half. Went down to the farm for three days while the painters sloshed their typical one-coat-covers-everything over the premises — even painting over an aspirin tablet left in the medicine chest by the previous tenant. The apartment commands a noble five-window view of the southwest end of Washington Square, where the chess and checker players sit: somewhat noisy but, I guess, colorful. The noise all Saturday night was apocalyptic; all those Catholic secretaries in gray gabardine suits with boutonnieres of ferns, who come to the Village with their boy-friends to rubber at the Bohemians, were squealing like rats, the fairies in form-fitting dungarees who lounge along Washington Square West exhibiting themselves in the barracoon brawled and giggled, and the biennial open-air art show did a land-office business. Fortunately, Saturday seems to be the only bad night.

The African project described above washed out at *Holiday*; after interminable flirting and a maddening series of postponements on their decision, they decided against it for a lot of silly reasons too tedious to relate. Money is probably the chief one, though as I pointed out to them at some length, the trip could be done economically. I broached the thing to Lobrano, the editor I work with at *The New Yorker*, today at lunch, and he was quite obviously taken with it, though he, too, wanted some concrete figures. He's taking it up with Bill Shawn (who, as you probably know, succeeded Harold Ross) on Thursday. I don't have too much faith that they'll go for it, but they do keep telling me how much they want more articles that it's worth a try. Mark (who has been practically incommunicado the past week because of the

World Series — he takes his lunch to Ebbets Field) also wants to approach two other likely markets, *True* magazine and *Collier's*. The last showed a good deal of enthusiasm for the notion a year ago all the way up the editorial staff to the man who controls the dough, and he, of course, smothered it.

. . . *The Ill-Tempered Clavichord* is off the presses, I have my gratis copies right here in the office, and it looks good. McKnight Kauffer's jacket is a very effective one and the book is pleasing without being over-fancy. . . .

•   •   •

LEILA HADLEY

39½ Washington Square South
New York City
October 30, 1952

Darling,

It's all balls here, everyone's worked himself up into the usual election fever with Stevenson as the plumed knight (and I have no doubt that it could be very dismal days if he isn't elected, what with the utterly reactionary and morally bankrupt opposition), but it's amazing how sensible people forget the Democratic machine, the ward-heelers, the gravy-dispensers, the patronage, and the filthy, venal political manoeuvering. There isn't a shadow of a doubt that Stevenson is a literate, cultivated man with as sharp a sense of humor as any politician in American history has ever displayed, but he is most certainly not the Abraham Lincoln many have persuaded themselves he is. I've had a stout conviction for months now that he's a cinch to be elected, and it should be amusing for you to open this letter and see whether I'm right. In any case, believe me that you're lucky not to have had to endure all the attendant claptrap, the loudspeakers blasting at street-corners and the bunting, the denials and counter-charges and hosannas and flatulence in the press. The enclosed picture of Nixon gorging himself on bagels isn't a-typical. Plenty of shots of Stevenson in ten-gallon hats slobbering over babies.

•   •   •

LEILA HADLEY

39½ Washington Square South
New York City
November 12, 1952

Darling,

Nothing at all eventful has occurred here much except that the trip to

135

East Africa has become very concrete. *The New Yorker* has placed what Mark *loves* to call its imprimatur on it, and to such an extent that I was (up until four or five days ago) tentatively set to take off from here about January 2nd for Nairobi. Two considerations, of which the lesser is the Mau-Mau uprising in Kenya, have decided me to postpone leavetaking until — it looks now — the latter part of May. . . . The deal, as consummated, involves going to East Africa by either ship or plane, as I prefer, and covering as much or little as I find needful for copy. The East African Travel Ass'n has signified after checking with Nairobi that Safariland Ltd. will furnish me with a free safari (white hunter, black help, supplies, tents, etc. included) and BOAC says it will give me a free ride on its Comet, in addition to all kinds of offers of lagniappe from hotels, etc. In short, what with Mark's megalomaniac plans for tie-ups with CBS, the Ford Foundation, and the ghost of Sir Rider Haggard, it should at least get me within recoiling distance of a rhinoceros spoor. I have a bunch of rather disjointed notions at present about places I probably ought to see as well as peoples, with which I'll bore you later on in the year. . . . I break off here to attend a Chinese dinner up in Harlem with Fred Allen. Back in a jiffy...

Monday, November 17

The jiffy, as you see, became five days with the addition of a little of that usual old New York turmoil. The Chinese dinner was a wearing affair; Allen had invited along a couple of highly-benzedrined TV writers of his acquaintance, who punched jokes over the crash of dishes. The following evening, I invited him back to a symposium at the P.E.N. Club where Arthur Kober, Russel Crouse, H. Allen Smith, and the editor of *Punch* discoursed on "Humor Today" under the grandmotherly aegis of Louis Kronenberger. Like all discussions of humor, it only achieved being ridiculous. . . .

•   •   •

Yours always,

FRANCES and ALBERT HACKETT

39½ Washington Square South
New York City
April 2, 1953

Dear Frances & Albert,

Many thanks for all the clippings and curiosa you sent along, particularly that charming bulletin on transvestism — the man who loved to slip into something comfy like a girdle after the day's work was done. I have just had passed on to me a lovely story in the same general department as related by

Ethel Merman to Mark Hanna at a dinner party. Seems a U.S. government census taker was ticking off the residents of an apartment house over in the East Fifties near First Avenue. Knocked at one door and a young man answered; census taker asked his occupation. "I'm a cork-soaker," he replied. "You see, in bottling wine, we have to first soak the corks so that they'll fit into the bottles." Census taker thanked him, moved on to the next apartment. Young chap there, in response to the question, said he was a sock-tucker, explaining that he worked for the Interwoven people, folding three socks into each box for retail sale. Census taker continued to next flat, fellow there said "I'm a coke-stacker. You see, working for the Coca-Cola people, we have to stack the cokes in even rows so they'll move efficiently into the carrying cases." The census taker knocked at the next door and a willowy young person answered. "I'm the real McCoy, sweetness," he said. "Come right in."

We are all of us O.K. here, with one vestige of news at least, which is that we've managed to get out of our lease in Washington Square and are moving down to the country for good, worse, or whatever, but permanent. Laura and I are delighted to be yielding our franchise as city-dwellers; as we probably have indicated for a long time now, we're fed up on the discomfort, the expense, and the generally pedestrian existence hereabouts, and we hope that by emigrating to Erwinna, we can not only get a pleasanter taste in our mouths in the morning, but so gear our economics that we may scrape together a little travelling money. The house down there is certainly adequate for our needs now, and if we can relieve the inescapable tedium by occasional trips by freighter to all those places one should see, we don't care who writes the nation's songs. . . .

This is Abby's week of spring vacation from Putney School; she and several girl friends have seen as many as three, and in some cases as many as five, movies a day, and their faces have that stunned, undone look you get from being in a dark auditorium with Kirk Douglas all day. At this age, there is almost no communication with the adolescent female child; they incline to snarl at almost anything you say to them, and if you suggest that they (for Christ's sake) disentangle the wet bath-towels before they jam them on the towel-rack, you got to run out of the house to escape the consequent yowls.

.   .   .

Leila Smitter—good *God*, what a name (no matter how much of a charmer her Yvor is)—was here briefly over a weekend to inter her father, which probably was made easier by the fact that he was dead. Burying a live man is not so easy. We didn't get to see her, as it turned out, but it seems to be fairly well-established, both by rumor and, in fact, her actual declaration over the phone, that she is already in an interesting condition. I am not certain just when the papoose is due, but I'm sure that a baby is just what the young couple needs as Yvor studies away in the evening for his doctorate and Leila bustles about the kitchen making salmon croquettes out of the left-overs.

Well, this is the situation as of here, and we are both hoping that nausea with 3-D and your natural restlessness will combine to fetch you East again real soon. We miss you, and this piece of paper constitutes a license to come stay with us in the country forever. Honest to God and no kidding, we'd really be pleased if you would, for as long as you could. We hope to be moved down there by May 1, and we're dying to show you all the improvements. In any case, do write, and love from us all.

Yours,

HEYWOOD HALE BROUN*

Erwinna, Pa.
June 23, 1953

Dear Woodie,

If you think you're bug-ridden up there in Woodstock, move over. Several days ago, as I was teetering on my heels in front of the barn, making my usual morning survey of the bank's property, a swarm of locusts with satchels bearing postmarks of such outlandish places as Birobidjan, Libya, and the Hindu Kush shot by me, picked up a black walnut tree well over three years old, and disappeared in the direction of Allentown. That's how bug-ridden we are. And I could go on like that for hours. I mean, that isn't just an isolated instance.

Your recital of the session with Colston Leigh's staff chilled the marrow.† I told you, I think, that this muzzler has been working on me to play the perspiration circuit. My self-styled agent, Mark Hanna, constantly says to me, "Sid, why don't you put your imprimatur on the deal?" This is one of Mark's favorite words. He doesn't want me to do anything of the kind, as he knows god-damned well he'll have to split commissions. He just wants a chance to use the word "imprimatur" so he can mispronounce it...I must admit that ever since my appearance June 10th at the Brandeis Festival, where Fred Allen and I were co-conferenciers of the evening known as "The Comic Performer," Colston Leigh has been as mum as the grave. Don't know whether you heard this atrocity on its broadcast several times recently over WNBC, but it sure was a daisy. The program, besides ourselves, was Arthur Kober reading one of the Bella stories very nervous and fast, Jack Gilford (fairly good), a 35-minute commedia dell'arte with harpsichord accompaniment given

*Sportswriter, columnist, stage and TV actor.
†Broun had auditioned as a lecturer.

138

by three students, Alice Pearce (passable), and Erwin Corey (hilarious). What this has to do with the comic performer, only time will tell. Leonard Bernstein got us into it, and, of course, has fled like a rat. . . .

Had dinner the other night in town with Harvey Orkin and Jizzeleh, after which we ran into Andy Duggan and girl (Betty Something) and wound up at a movie called *Man on a Tightrope*. Unquestionably one of the worst pictures in the history of Hollywood, though you wouldn't know it from reading Dr. Bosley Crowther, the noted cinema critic. Remind me not to speak to Dr. Crowther when, as I usually do, I meet him on Martha's Vineyard later this year. . . .

Haven't read anything extra sportif lately, but the title essay of George Orwell's book, *Such, Such Were the Joys*, is a humdinger. . . .

Best to Jane and yourself from Laura and me, and anytime you could steal away from rehearsals, we'd love to have you come down and case the joint. When you call, I'll give you directions for the train, or possibly, one or the other of us may be coming in and could drive you out. In any case, you're officially invited and lemon pie has already been ordered to place in your bed.   Yours,

BETTY WHITE JOHNSTON
                                                        Erwinna, Pa.
                                                        June 28, 1953

Dear Betty,

Like the famous grain of wheat supposedly sealed in one of the pyramids which sent forth a green shoot after a couple of thousand years, I respond leafily to your very *doux* billet of several days ago. *How* good to hear from you, and especially on such a vibrant artistic level. Who (besides me) would have dreamed that the Betty White with whom I used to sneak clandestine cigarettes on the second floor of the Paramount administration building back in the early Thirties would have had wrapped in her silky little cocoon a Renoir and/or Rodin? . . . Of course, in keeping your emergence as a graphic artist from me all this time, you've been rather sneaky, in a way, and I don't know whether I like this trait; I remember you as a straightforward, black-and-white, sort of go-to-hell girl (awful good-looking, too, while I'm up on my feet). But pooh on these snippy little recriminations. I was truly delighted to get your letter—pleased as Punch, damn my eyes. . . . This new incarnation, while more costly in terms of supplies like Canson & Montgolfier watercolor paper and Wolff crayon—you remember I put in a few years at the graphic arts myself—is one that should give you far more genuine catharsis. It always did me.

139

Your assumption that I might be belly-whopping down Everest is just as inaccurate as your canard that I might be too old and rickety to consummate that lunch date we've had for at least two decades. As to the former, I've been static up at this general corner of the map for well over a year; haven't done any travelling to speak of since a swing I took for a magazine called *Redbook* (forgive me, I had to feed my dependents) about 16 months ago to places like Key West, Sun Valley, Arizona, and Mexico. However, I've been trying to get started for East Africa and an interesting safari I've got lined up for *The New Yorker*, but the Mau Mau trouble there and general confusion have delayed me. I keep telling myself I'll really take off around November. The reason for the dateline above is that we gave up city life this past April and are based on the farm we've had all these years, though this is actually getting itself written in New York at a cubicle I keep to brood in. I get into town here every week or ten days to comb the hayseeds out of my hair and whimper to the overdraft clerk at the bank...On our long-range lunch project, of course, you're up to your old tactics of being a Lorelei. You wouldn't come up here even if you got your fare paid and a platinum-washed suite at Pierre's to boot. Wouldn't it be *gemütlich* of me to offer them to you? Unfortunately, dear, the only thing that prevents me from doing so is the money. Besides, from the cozy picture you draw of yourself in your air-conditioned studio, I doubt whether you could be budged.

I look the same but for a martial red cavalry moustache that everyone says is what I've needed all these years (is that what I've needed all these years?) and a somewhat more peppery expression. And my instinct tells me that the only change Time has wrought in you is to square your drooping shoulders and enhance your magnetism. Stop telling me that you *buy* my books; I buy them myself to reinforce my ego. As for your offer to trade my next one even Stephen for a sculpture by you, done and done. Got any ideas for a book?

I *do* love you, you *are* a lovable person, and let's consolidate plans to demonstrate it; the choice of weapons is yours. Do let's try to think of something more enticing than typewriters, but failing, let's not abandon those.

Yours always,

LEILA HADLEY

Erwinna, Pa.
July 23, 1953

Dear Leila,

I probably would have written before but for the weather; everyone's energy locally has gone into just existing through the heat, which has been formidable. It broke today with torrential rain, falling on desolate, burned-out lawns and dry creeks. Really like India here. . . .

· · ·

You asked about Africa, and when did I think I was going. I really don't know yet; much depends on the family situation, and primarily on economics. Contrary to what you deduced from my last letter, about the things we did to the house here, I'm dead broke, more so than I've been in years. These remodelling changes I described were effected on a big chunk borrowed from the bank, and though I guess I hit *The New Yorker* as steadily as anybody on it, that brings in barely enough to support the five people involved. Try supporting five people sometime by freelancing. Nice graying work.

Well, what *is* new? I have a magnificent, bronze-red cavalry moustache that I've been cultivating for, let's see, just six months now, and that general opinion regards as very successful. It swoops. I had one once before, years ago, but never allowed it to get much beyond the rag-bag stage. This, however, is something you'd see in the Muthaiga Club in Nairobi, and, in a way, I grew it with that in mind. It'll certainly give me some form of protective coloration with any Blimps I encounter if and when. . . .

· · ·

Yours ever,

LEILA HADLEY

Erwinna, Pa.
September 6, 1953

Leila darling,

Your very good letter of July 26 (prior to starting for the banana republics), and your bombshell of August 30 regarding the toucan, both illuminated and enchanted (bombshells don't enchant, but frig it). I was full of good resolutions to reply briskly to the first; however, early August was dramatically hot, and on the 14th of same, we took off for Martha's Vineyard and after that, the mere proximity of a typewriter brought on hives. (I did send you a grudging little postcard of Gay Head, though.) As always, the Vineyard was idyllic . . . just about as perfect a dot in the ocean as one can find north of Loggerhead Key. Its most considerable drawback is the people we always become complicated with there, most of whom you met on the occasion of your visit — a mean-spirited, backbiting, pharisaical bunch of suburbanites, carrying little morsels of gossip around in their stingers and flying into waspish little rages if you don't turn up at their merdelike little cocktail parties...ugh. I really got a bellyful this time — the busy little bastards battened on us so during the two weeks of our stay. At last the only solution, which

I put into practice letting the umbrages fall where they might, was to hustle down to South Beach — you remember that vast expanse of sand and cliffs and Atlantic Ocean — early in the morning and disappear when the ladies arrived with their knitting. . . .

Your description of Central America sort of endorses what I've always supposed it must be like. I've always felt that there must be something lacking in me that has made me anaesthetic to both Central and South America; hate tango, samba, all that gurry (though I adored Spain and wish it were possible to go back there). Incidentally, I got a card from Sinnie Lang the other morning, she's living in Madrid and urges that I come over. For Sinnie I would do much, like laying down my life, going to the ends of the earth, and whatnot, but it will have to await the eradication of the Phalange and General Francisco Franco to get me back there. One of the minor things that appalls me nowadays is the easy sophistry with which people allow themselves to travel in that country, I mean to say people who should know better. . . .

•　　　•　　　•

Finally getting around to Mr. Toucan (I suppose he has a name of some sort, or hasn't he?), in the light of the upcoming junket to Africa, it's the extreme of irrationality to consider taking him, since I haven't the wildest notion of what's going to become of Tong Cha, Kootzie, and Tartuffe, but if I'm ever going to have the aviary I've dreamed of, I'll have to figure all that out later. Hence, I'm writing in this self-same mail to Mr. Roberts in Managua directing him to ship the creature and I'll pick him up at La Guardia and worry subsequently what to do with him. I am, of course, flabbergasted by the efficiency with which you've figured out all the angles like shipping him in a carton, taking care of the export papers, and such. I do have a cage, that beautiful red wire one I'd been grooming for an eventual Leadbeater's Cockatoo — and I'll get that too, by God, some day. . . .

•　　　•　　　•

With love,

LEILA HADLEY

Erwinna, Pa.
October 23, 1953

Leila darling,

•　　　•　　　•

There's no great news locally; I haven't set up any concrete date as yet for departure for East Africa, though I'm trying through several avenues to arrange a sea passage there. . . . I really have no desire whatever to fly, just want to sit still aboard a cargo ship for a month, get some very necessary work done, and dissolve the mush that has silted up in my head. I've had about half the requisite shots, the bothersome ones, that is, and with a little more medical and dental stuff, will be pretty ready to leave. Do you detect a strange absence of enthusiasm in all this? Most likely; I've thought about, and talked about, the venture so long, and it's been through so many variations since Al Hirschfeld and I originally planned it as part of our trip in 1947, that a lot of the fizz has evaporated. I suppose, of course, that once I get going, much of the excitement should return. However, it demands such readjustments here—Laura getting a sub-lease apartment in NY, all kinds of moving and shaking with the animals, closing the house here, etc.—that I get daily qualms, and I'm in the very strange position of having to assure myself that it's something I want to do, should do—a great deal different from the runaway verve that distinguished the two preceding trips.

This is one of those end-of-autumn Indian summer afternoons in the country, sunny, warm, and no intrusive sounds, and as complete a contrast to the three days I spent in NY earlier in the week as can be. In case you pine for Manhattan—and I know the full horror of LA—you should be reminded again and again of the filth, the tension, the noise, and the general unloveliness of New York. All of midtown seems to be in a state of reconstruction, there are at least five huge buildings going up in the 'Forties and 'Fifties; traffic is fantastic, people's tempers worse, all one's friends are in turmoil, living on the barbiturates and alcohol, everyone mismated—God. Really, it's unspeakable, and while you may feel that you're in a wasteland, that the vitality of New York *does* occasionally infuse one, and that LA is sheer barbarism, don't repine unduly. I get back out here after each trip to the city and luxuriate in the quiet—just the fact that there aren't any bodies pressing up against me, doors closing on my feet, riveters dinning in my ears. The individual in NY has no dignity, no identity, nothing; he's just something to be shovelled through openings, pressed into conveyances, fed, gouged, insulted.

•   •   •

With all my love,

LEILA HADLEY

513-A Sixth Avenue
New York City
November 18, 1953

Leila darling,

•   •   •

There's remarkably little news. We've been more or less hermetically sealed in the country, which, at this time of year, is a procession of gray days

143

and waspish tempers. We *have* come up to town for overnight every so often, but I haven't seen much of anybody. Mark H[anna] was tendered a 55th birthday surprise party by a whole lot of people he esteems, at which toasts were delivered and funny hats donned. Also sportive presents. I knew nothing about all this but happened to walk into his office the next day just in time to be presented with a two-hour recital of the details. He pretended to be bored with the whole event, at the same time licking his chops at the social and artistic eminence of the people present — you know, Quentin Reynolds, Helen Hayes, Dick and Dorothy Kollmar, Dick and Dorothy Rodgers, and Dick and Dorothy Asshole. . . . Laura and I plan to drive up to Putney School in Vermont to see Abby on Thanksgiving, as I probably won't get a chance to see her before I go otherwise. We have a date to meet Jerry Salinger and have dinner with him up there, entailing a 50-mile drive for him from his mountain retreat at Windsor. He has been holed in there all this time presumably forging verbs and gerundives. Personally I'd go crazy all alone on a crag, and I fully expect him to break into wild laughter during the meal and goose waitresses.

.   .   .

Always,

T .   S .   E L I O T

513-A Sixth Avenue
New York City
November 22, 1953

Dear Tom,

Merely an epistolary splinter to let you know that I'll be in London from December 11th to 22nd on my inexplicable way through to East Africa and that it would give me great pleasure to feel that we might spend an hour or as much time as you can spare together. You may recall that you generously gave me lunch at the Garrick Club back in 1949, a piece of high-spirited altruism I've never forgiven you, and I'm determined to repay you in kind. I shall be staying at Brown's Hotel in Dover Street, and if you leave a message there advising me where to reach you, we can speedily work out the sordid details.

I have just seen our old compadre, Ted Kauffer, who also asks me to bear you his personal assurances.* If by any chance you're en route to the States and we don't meet in London, I urge you to see him in New York. . . . He is very bleak indeed, and I think you are one of the very few people whose friendship has meaning for him.

I hope, though, that you will be in England when I course through, and

*E. McKnight Kauffer (d. 1954), poster artist and designer, to whom *The Road to Miltown* and *Listen to the Mocking Bird* are dedicated.

144

that we may discuss this and much more over a spoonful of Falernian.

Yours always,

LAURA PERELMAN

Brown's Hotel
London
December 13, 1953

Dear Laura,

I sincerely hope your feet are warmer and your social schedule fuller than mine, and they couldn't help but be. London is in the grip of a smog attack that makes anything we've ever seen look trifling; it's a wonder to me that everyone here isn't hospitalized with some kind of pulmonary illness, because breathing is like burying your head in a smokestack. The temperature, as the experts predicted, is cold, intensely raw, and I must say right off that I bless you for insisting that I take my overcoat. Even *with* it, you just about survive the damp chill—and, mind you, this morning's paper referred to this as a continuation of the abnormally mild weather. It's hard to say why, in the face of this, everybody here has a pinched, gray look, but it's probably a combination of weather and the grisly food. In short, the situation is not exactly ideal, complicated by the fact that thus far I've seen nobody I know and have conversed only with waiters (and very few of those). Evidently I must be more gregarious than I'd supposed, or maybe I've become so late in life, because it's well over three days since I got here and I'm beginning to talk to myself in the room for lack of anything better.

The flight over was simple enough . . . and eventually I was deposited at Brown's Hotel. Unluckily, my room wasn't ready to be occupied, and it was almost two in the afternoon before I could get into a hot bath and get sorted out. I was somewhat appalled when I first saw the room, which is the size of a hall bedroom in a brownstone, and I squawked. I was told that (a) this was the usual single bedroom size, and (b) the only room open. At the equivalent of seven dollars a day, it's no bargain, although as it's worked out, the service is very good, it's very clean, and the water's boiling hot. The hotel *is* very old-fashioned (but rigidly kept up), full of brass trim and mahogany and decrepit wealth. On the lobby floor, there's the usual series of depressing public rooms, dimly lit and dotted about with corpses breathing gently. Gentility hangs over the place like a pall, also servility. If you can remember the Knowle Hotel in Sidmouth, you'll get the picture, except that this is far fancier.

Arriving as I did on a Friday, I was just in time for the weekend, and that wasn't good planning. The whole city shut down with a snap Friday night; yesterday (Saturday) the place looked as if it were stricken with pestilence,

145

all the shops closed and many of the restaurants, and today absolutely nothing was open. As for people I wanted to see, apart from Norman Lewis (who must be a nice guy, as he wrote me a note regretting he wasn't in London and confirming our appointment next Wednesday), I received no tumble from Eliot or Leigh Ashton, to whom I'd written. . . . This morning I sent off a batch of notes to some people on *Punch* I've met, to C. Day Lewis, Angus Wilson, etc., and I'm sure that business will pick up shortly. Actually, nobody is to blame; I did my best to line up some engagements in advance, but the English social mill grinds slowly, it's all done with correspondence, and you can't find out people's phone numbers.

The most parlous aspect, as always here, is the feeding arrangements. The whole god-damned city seems to be made up of nothing but snack bars and bottle clubs; I'm so hollow with hunger that I catch myself staggering on the street. It's all tea-shops, with dainty little sandwiches of Spam, cream gateaux, and savories — nothing to put your teeth into. (Not because of rationing, either; plenty of food, apparently, but I suspect the English have got out of the habit of eating after all the years of austerity.) The only half-way decent meal I had was night before last in a dickty Italian place, all rose boudoir lamps and waiters in tails, in Wardour Street. I was the only occupant in a room about seventy feet long, and I had four waiters hovering about me. Antipasto and ravioli and ice-cream, if you can call that a meal; the roasts were so forbidding that I passed them up. Fortunately, there is no danger of my getting scurvy, as I have to consume at least two gin-and-limes every evening to keep the cold out.

•   •   •

Love,

LAURA PERELMAN

Hotel Lutétia
Paris
December 23, 1953

Dear Laura,

•   •   •

. . . London got real busy right after I wrote you that first letter. . . . Leigh Ashton called up Monday morning when he returned from the country and that night cooked an omelet . . . for me at his flat in Albany, where you remember we had dinner. . . . [H]e bore me off to Sadler's Wells Theater in a chauffeur-driven limousine to see a performance of an opera called *Don Pasquale* that he stated was an 1826 equivalent of *Oklahoma*. Leigh is one of the directors of Sadler's Wells and I must say that although opera is not

146

my dish, this was handsomely done and beautifully sung; really nothing to do with all those flyblown old garlic buds at the Met. Next day I lunched with Dwye Evans of Heinemann's at the Ivy. He takes some knowing but by the time I left the city, we were on pleasant terms. I paid a visit to his office; none of your Simon & Schuster chromium stuff, but a wonderful 17th-century building near the British Museum where we had tea and talked about Beerbohm, another author published by the firm. . . . Then began a series of lunches, drinks, and dinners at an absolutely headlong clip, and I literally was flailing away invitations from around my head as if they were mosquitoes. I had dinner three times with Norman Lewis, who, as we suspected, turned out to be a delightful and most interesting guy. We have become fast friends and have great schemes for the future. He is 45, a product of Cambridge (I think; the British are frequently reticent about admitting this sort of thing), Welsh by derivation, slightly taller than I am, feverish black eyes, hair, and mustache, pallid face, and reminds me more of Hilaire Hiler than anybody else. He was at one time a professional motorcycle racer . . . *and* turns out to be as bewitched with exotic birds as I am. His library on the subject is a beauty. He has a weird kind of flat in a very commercial district of London, with some marvellous Burmese paintings. . . . He drives a German car called a Porsche at a nervewracking rate around London and I thought my hour had come the last night I was there when he picked me up at the theater and we drove to Soho for supper. In short, he's a wack, extremely good company (and very funny, as his books suggest), and a man I know you'd take to.

. . . Eric and Louise Ambler I had two meetings with, and expect to meet again about the beginning of next week here in Paris. . . . Ambler is a very youthful-looking character with white hair, sort of whippy, who vaguely resembles the ex-Prince of Wales. Very bright and quick on the uptake, blue pop eyes that stare off into the infinite when he talks. . . .

I also saw Richard Burton, Harvey Orkin's friend whose Hamlet is said to be the best since Barrymore's (I didn't have time to go to the Old Vic and see him act, we just got loaded together); had drinks with Eliot and . . . John Hayward, at their flat in Cheyne Walk ("Tom," as I never would want to be quoted as calling him, but he calls me Sid and is altogether comradely on his part, was very nice; he's sailing for South Africa this week on a cruise, and Mr. Hayward also very matey); Angus Wilson, who asked me to drinks at his flat (he's a fragile, dried autumn-leaf of a man, bright as a diamond . . . white-haired at forty, in touch with everything that is being written everywhere), is in charge of the Reading Room of the British Musuem; Emily Hahn, who works at the Reading Room quite often getting biographical data for her books, and who heard from Wilson that I was around town; your heart throb C. Day Lewis, who asked me to lunch at the Savile Club, brought along his 20-odd-year old son, and on the whole proved to be a rather difficult host (he's aged considerably, I'm sorry to inform you, and is inclined to be somewhat pompous, I thought); and a whole host of people from *Punch*. The nicest of these are an article named Russell Brockbank and a writer named Boothroyd, who asked me to lunch at *their* club, the Savage. The most trying of these various encounters was the evening that Malcolm Muggeridge, the new editor of *Punch*, asked me over for drinks. He too lives in Albany; he and Madame had as guests also one of Britain's press lords, a pursy individual whose name I never got who's something very high-echelon on the *News Chronicle*. Muggeridge is . . . a chatterbox all smile and prussic acid, bristling with insincerity. The press lord and his lady, on hearing I was bound for Kenya, began giving me unsolicited advice on people to see in London who could square me away on the political situation there. All this, and it lasted aeons, was delivered in that staccato and utterly incomprehensible way that certain English have of talking and that gives you the most fearful headache trying to grasp. What happens is that they eventually give you a patronizing, frosty smile indicating they think you're a slow-witted Yankee peasant and carry on their own conversation teeming with local allusions. Eventually, we all went off to a party at Ronald Searle's, the artist's.* Oddly enough, this was practically a counterpart of an evening at the Hirschfelds', made even more uncanny by Searle's having a beard. They live in a four-floor modernische house in Bayswater, top floor of which is his studio, like Al's. It was one of those progressive parties, where waves of people had been piling up since five o'clock and it was now ten-thirty . . . a real bedlam. Finally, though, Searle and I got a few minutes alone in his studio, inscribed books to each other, and had a short interval of sense. He's an extremely talented man, as you know, and among other things I learned that he first learned to draw when he was a prisoner on the Burma-Siam frontier in a Japanese camp, being the only man in his company who ever got out alive. . . .

Other than the above, I saw very few people during my visit to London, and often got as much as four hours' sleep of a night. The inevitable, of course, happened about three days before I left. I was in a stationery store buying the air-mail envelope this is sealed in when a woman lifted my hat-brim and said uncertainly, "Isn't this—this Sid Perelman?" — —, and brimming with friendship. My cavalry moustache had failed me. As we were next door to my hotel, I had to ask her in for tea, and that resulted in her trapping me into dinner one night after the theater. It wasn't too grisly, however, as by then I had become so fluent socially that I could take anything, and luckily they didn't ask any of the other outcasts. They have a very snazzy flat . . .

*Searle was also a frequent illustrator of Perelman's pieces in *The Sunday Times* of London.

and they've brought to it a feeling of Beverly Hills. I expected Arthur Kober to plummet in at any moment, execute a spirited tango, and fall asleep on the divan. . . .

•   •   •

I guess this will have to be the story—no, a quick report on Philippe and Muriel, who have already outdone themselves to be nice to me and I haven't been here 24 hours yet.* I found a note from Philippe when I checked in. . . . Ph. and Muriel came around to fetch me for dinner at the hotel—were *enchanted* with the presents and beg me to embrace you. Philippe has been saying over and over how he regrets you couldn't come, asking about the kids, etc. They rushed me at Philippe's usual tempo to a boite in Blvd. St. Germain, then to a very good little restaurant down near the Seine where we had a capital time. Philippe looks fine; has put on some weight and it's becoming, actually. Not portly, of course, but filled out. He's still a very handsome man and I shouldn't say has aged measurably. Muriel seems much thinner to me but says I think so because of her false chignon, which she then removed *en plein air* in the restaurant and handed to Philippe. They seem very devoted, and she told me they're part of a co-operative group building a new apartment out in Passy. I get the impression that Philippe's much better fixed than he was in our day, and Muriel herself works on the staff of a magazine called *Réalités* that's the hot magazine here now. Before we broke up last night, Ph. forced me to promise to come to lunch at his apartment today, which I did, and the three of us had an excellent meal and much laughter. . . .

Other than this, let me say that last Sunday I spent two hours in the bird house at Regent's Park Zoo in London and had what was for me the second best experience of the stay (the first being my several evenings with Norman Lewis). The place was quite empty, and they have about eight various types of mynah from all over the East, one or two of them wonderful talkers. Well, I got into conversation with the man in charge and he spent practically the whole time giving me dope on the varieties of birds I was interested in, etc., etc. Then we got onto the white mynah, and out of that it developed that he is a friend of Frost, that elderly English collector you met in Macassar.

*Philippe Soupault, poet and novelist, was a leading figure in the surrealist movement. "It was on a ship, when I was returning from the United States, that I met Perelman. We began to laugh together immediately. He was very observant of the other passengers, kept staring at them. He was always adjusting his spectacles and smiling to himself—inward smiles, if I may put it that way. Sometimes he gave silent little laughs. The stories he told were always funny and unexpected. I helped him discover Paris: the cheese counters at the Halles, the Quai de la Mégisserie, where he bought a superb toucan one day—its cries terrified the guests in his hotel. As he told me, he was always on the watch for things to happen—'looking for trouble,' as he put it. In order to write stories about it all. He was melancholy at times, never *triste*, never nasty or cruel" (*Vingt Mille et Un Jours*, Paris: P. Belfont, 1980; trans. Francis Steegmuller).

149

Frost has just left on another collecting expedition to Indonesia at the age of eighty, specifically to acquire some white mynahs, and he has taken for the purpose one of three such white mynahs, the only ones in England, owned by a man named Mr. Ezra in Surrey. Seems that this variety is so shy that they can only be lured by what's called a call bird. The principle of the call house. *And*, said the keeper, he believes that when Frost returns in the spring he'd have five or six of them, one of which he'd ask him to save for me. Please don't show this paragraph to Tong Cha. If he steams open the letter, though, tell him I only want a white one to show him off to better advantage.

Love,

ABBY PERELMAN

Hotel Lutétia
Paris
December 25, 1953

Abby darling,

I sent Laura a long letter yesterday which will fill you in on the activities I was involved in around London and which prevented my writing until now. I wanted, had I had any time at all, to drop you a line up at Putney or in New York with my Christmas wishes, but once I got caught in the hysterical social round in London, I was doomed and never had a minute. Paris is proving to be a much more sensible experience; I'm seeing a few people, the fewer the better, and sorting myself out after a fashion. Strangely enough, I find that Paris takes a bit of accustoming oneself to, much more so than London; I think it's due primarily to getting used to speaking French again, and I'd forgotten practically all of mine. I'm only now beginning to be able again to make myself understood, and regretting that I didn't keep up my knowledge of the tongue over the past four years, difficult as it is when you're speaking only English in America.

. . . [L]ast night—that is, the night before Christmas—[Philippe Soupault and his girlfriend, Muriel] had me invited to a dinner they were going to, given by a well-known Swedish journalist whose name I can't spell. The other guests were an assortment of English people connected with the BBC, a couple of correspondents for the American newspaper *The Christian Science Monitor*, and so on. It was a good dull party, made all the duller for me by the tendency of everyone to converse in staccato French full of idiom. Half the time I didn't know whether I was coming or going, and mouthing what I am sure were the most fearful absurdities. I spent the whole time finally discussing English public-school life (a subject of which I have no knowledge whatever) with a suet pudding of an Englishwoman who thought I was too,

too quaint, and then was pitchforked to the side of an English spinster named Miss — who was under the impression that she was a fascinator. *She* explained to me — at length — the work of the British military mail censorship during the war, but I don't remember that I had asked her to. Altogether, I put in as tedious a four hours as I can recall in the past twenty years. You might tell Laura as a footnote to all this that Philippe was on his best behavior, popping about pouring coffee for everyone and generally conducting himself like a suburbanite from New Rochelle. I think that the years have considerably tamed Philippe, who in his younger days wouldn't have spat on the best of the dinner guests last night. However, I suppose this is what happens to all the wild characters as they age, whether they derive from Greenwich Village, Chelsea, or Montparnasse.

I also put in a pretty tedious dinner night before last with —. She resigned her job last summer to come over here and live, and has been travelling around Europe a lot since, also doing some work in Paris. The French language has gone to her head; she is studying four or five nights a week at the Alliance Française and has cultivated an accent that's more French than the French. I'd been told to look her up over here, so I called her and we had dinner at an expensive and lousy restaurant (her choice) called Drouant's near the Opera. She took the position that this was my first trip to Paris and I was an awkward rustic to boot, though I politely implied that I'd started coming over here before she was weaned. Whatever I said to the waiter, she translated into her own tutti-frutti accent. Then, just as I was perishing with fatigue, she insisted on dragging me over to a café called the Select opposite the Dome (Laura will tell you where all this is, in a section we know better than we do Erwinna) to see the artistic life. The artistic life consisted of some unshaven loafers sitting around on a freezing cold café terrace and eyeing you speculatively to see whether they could cadge a drink. My female companion, throughout this interval, kept up a bright patter about various German boys who are also studying at the Alliance Française and who (she says) take her out constantly and have convinced her that Hitler was just a horrible error and not typical of Germany. Inasmuch as I happen to detest Germany and all Germans, and was at that moment sliding off the chair with my yawning, you can get some idea of what an absorbing evening it turned into.

Fortunately, and although this may sound as if I were having the most grisly time, I'm not. I had a leisurely walk this afternoon over a good deal of the Montparnasse quarter, which is where your mother and I spent our honeymoon and a lot of successive visits, and it's still very rich in associations and a charming part of Paris, which is a wonderful city. We must contrive some way of your spending a while in Paris and in France — and, for that matter, in England, which I really enjoyed more than I ever have before. The

French are an *impossible* people—erratic, unreliable, feverish, tricky at times—and yet they have tremendous taste, they're witty, never dull, and they know what constitute the important things in life. They've had such a great history and have been through so much that they're somewhat overcivilized now and have become too cynical about everything, to the point where they no longer care about much. But I do think that nobody's education or taste can be considered even half-formed unless he has spent some time with them. As for the English, they're such a decent, considerate, and really courageous people—also with a tremendous cultural tradition out of which our own has grown—that I'd like you to absorb some of it for yourself. Their theater right now is the most active and dynamic in Europe, and as for writing, they're producing so many worthwhile and interesting books that you want to buy out half the contents of every bookshop you look into.

Well, dear, I hadn't meant to get off into such generalities, which I'm sure have encrusted you with boredom, but perhaps you'll be able before too long to absorb the essence of these two great cities and their people and I truly hope so, because you'd find it an exciting experience. Meanwhile, how are you enjoying the mid-year vac? Are you doing the ballet or what as your project? Have you been to the theater? (I guess you've already seen Hermione Gingold, and I'd love a report on it.) Get Laura to take you to *The Seven Year Itch*, it's funny. Whom are you seeing? Any boys? How do you like the apartment? These and any other details would be pleasurable to hear about. . . . Love and kisses to you and everyone, and have a wonderful vac.

Yours always—

P.S. What are you especially interested in as presents? Let me know, as I'll be in lots of places and want to know what to keep watching out for...

FRANCES and ALBERT HACKETT

New Stanley Hotel
Nairobi
January 8, 1954

Dear Frances & Albert,

At length, and after boring my friends ceaselessly for several years with the subject, I seem to have bestirred myself and finally coupled with Africa, and I think both of you deserve a special award for having loyally stood by me during the labor pangs. I arrived here six days ago from Addis Ababa, having departed from NY on Dec. 10th and in the interim spent 11 feverish days in London and 9 gentler ones in Paris. London was very stimulating and

I saw a lot of friends old and new. . . . In Paris I hung around mainly with my old friend Philippe Soupault, but I saw Janet Flanner* four or five times to my very great enjoyment & instruction, and that is why I now enclose the card you find. Janet is leaving Paris this week or next for a stay of a couple of months in the States. As I remember her itinerary, she will be out on the Coast sometime after Jan. 15th visiting her sister, the poet Hildegarde Flanner (Monhoff), who lives, if you can decipher Janet's handwriting on the card, at 530 East Mangold St., Altadena. We talked about you, and Janet remembers that she met you that time she was out there when Laura and I were. In any case, I did want to suggest that you offer her a drink or dinner or something because I know you'll find her enormously knowledgeable and wonderful company. Her grasp of conditions in France, and Europe generally, and her refreshing & courageous political thinking will — I know — impress you. She is expecting you to get in touch with her, and I'll feel happy at the thought that you may meet each other again.

·   ·   ·

Since returning Tuesday night, I've been making arrangements to join a couple of safaris, one of them into the Northern Frontier fringing Ethiopia and the other down in Tanganyika. I also expect to go down to Mombasa possibly this coming Monday and take a voyage on an Arab dhow from there to Zanzibar or up the coast to a place called Lamu. (All this, as with everything else, in the hope of getting some workable copy for *The New Yorker*.) Hence, I've been through the usual routine (usual here) of getting the requisite clothes & footwear — all of it depressingly like what Robert Ruark persists in getting himself photographed in — and bracing a lot of people for local information & introductions. This afternoon, the all-girl safari you may have seen publicized & which I understand will have its trip televised in the States gets into town, and I have previously arranged to join *les girls* for a four-or-five-day junket while they're here. This is a kind of Phil Spitalny-cum-Ina Rae Hutton notion born in the fertile brain of a girl who writes publicity for Scandinavian Airlines, and it has snowballed into incredible proportions.† Fifteen dames plus Bunny Allen, the most beautiful white hunter in Africa (who handled the *Mogambo* hunting stuff). Incidentally, and for your private ear, — — . . . gave out with sulphurous curses at MGM, stating that they still owe him 800 pounds from that venture and generally behaved like bastards. Thought you might like this exotic sidelight on Alma Mater.

Well, this started out to be just a note & now look; so I'll pull in my horns & stop trading on your patience. . . . I send you my love, and should

*Wrote the "Letter from Paris" as Genêt for *The New Yorker*, 1925–75 (d. 1978).
†Spitalny and Hutton were both leaders of all-girl orchestras in the thirties and forties.

you get a free minute, I would adore to hear from you. . . . So, with affection, and the same to anyone who in your estimation I'd want it bestowed on,

Yours always,

LAURA PERELMAN

Manor Hotel
Mombasa, Kenya
January 11, 1954

Dear Laura,

I arrived here at 9:00 a.m. this morning after a quick and easy transit by East African Airways of 2 hours from Nairobi; I am in first-class shape, having a perfectly wonderful time, and have just risen from a refreshing nap following a somewhat liquid lunch with a couple of chaps here and a visit to a potent official called the Liwali of the Coast. The Liwali, a joint administrator of British and Zanzibari power along the extensive coastline of Kenya, has fixed me up to cross from Mombasa to Zanzibar aboard an Arab dhow sailing at dawn Wednesday, so I'm all set. He has also kindly given me a personal note to someone I construe to be very close to the Sultan of Zanzibar, so tomorrow a.m. I shall provide myself with some sleeping kit, some tinned food and biscuits, a thermos of coffee, a box of Keating's powder to drive off vermin, and obvious necessities like sunburn lotion and dramamine, and embark my effects. Everything is going exactly as I planned it.

· · ·

. . . [The trip to Treetops] was a great experience and I was very glad I went.* There were nine of us in the party plus the retired white hunter in charge, and, for part of the time, the manager of the Outspan. Of the eleven of us, eight were armed, two with Sten guns (these were members of the Devon Regiment), two with rifles, and the rest with pistols. The three unarmed people were a Canadian couple and myself — we weren't allowed to carry weapons because we were visitors to Kenya. The reason for the arms, as I have told you in my earlier letter from out here, was the Mau Mau business, and Nyeri is in the very thick of it. We drove in a safari car from the Outspan Hotel a matter of ten miles to within ⅓ of a mile of Treetops, and then walked in single file through heavy brush until we got to the tree. At intervals along the path there were ladders on the trees placed there so we could spring up if a rhino or forest hog or something suddenly charged. Nothing did — especially,

*" . . . that weird hotel in a giant fig-tree where Princess Elizabeth learned of her father's death and her accession" (Perelman in a letter to Abby). His party was the last to visit before the Mau Mau burned it down.

154

thank God, an adherent of Mau Mau. (This may sound a bit melodramatic to you, but I believe you will see from the attendant clippings that it's no tea-party here. However, the Mau Mau have abandoned their attacks on whites as of some months, so there is no reason for anxiety for my personal safety.) Anyhow, we stayed in the tree lodge all night and beheld a marvelous variety of animals as they appeared at the salt-lick and waterhole 40 feet below us. This was the tally, more or less as they followed each other:

15 baboons	7 rhinos, adult and small
2 families of wart-hogs	7 Cape buffalo (most dangerous)
4 waterbuck	2 elephant
4 bushbuck	2 hyenas
15 giant forest hogs (adults	1 hare
are 4 feet high)	assorted cranes, egrets, etc.

The elephants were terrific; nobody has ever pointed out to me that a wild elephant is as different from what we know as can be. He really looks like the monarch of all creation, and when the first one appeared and drove off a buffalo (as they are mortal enemies), we were faint with excitement. Conditions (i.e., the wind and the fact that the heavy bombing in the area has disturbed the herds of elephant) prevented our seeing as many of them as are frequently observed — sometimes 125 at a time — but we didn't boggle. Accommodations and food were both ample; in fact, we had a piping hot chicken pie that really was the best food I've had in Kenya. It was brought up and re-heated by the servants.

On the way back to Nairobi, the Dunfords (with whom I'd gone up there) and I detoured into an even more lively portion of the countryside, from the standpoint of Mau Mau activity, and visited an animal trapper named Carr Hartley at his farm in Rumuruti (recommended by Ylla*). Saw some indescribably beautiful animals there, including two tame white rhino, a tame leopard, beautiful quartet of cheetahs, etc. Also a pair of 6-week-old baby cheetahs which I photographed and which I will send pictures of if they turn out. They were just recovering from being poisoned by one of Hartley's servants — a Mau Mau activity and apparently typical of the kind of brutal and senseless things they do. Hartley and his four sons, ranging in age from about 9 to 15 — and his wife — weren't there when we arrived but showed up fresh from a skirmish with the gangsters — all armed, of course, even the kids. It's really incredible what's going on. From their farmhouse, at night, they can see the torches of the gangs in the meadow bottoms about a mile-and-a-half away. But of course people always work out some scheme of living under

*Pseudonym for Camilla Koffler, Austrian-born wildlife photographer (d. 1955).

the most violent circumstances, and the Hartleys weren't really very different from any middleclass English family out in these parts.

We got back to Nairobi on Tuesday evening, having been gone almost three days, and thereafter I stayed put at the New Stanley until this morning — a matter of five days. I had a lot of arrangements to make with Safariland *re* which safaris I might join; also the all-girl troupe was arriving; and finally I wanted to set this Coast junket. . . .

During the five-day stay in Nairobi I naturally got to meet a lot of local people — settlers (as the farmers are called here), etc. I was taken to the South African Consulate for drinks, to a coffee plantation about 40 miles out, to a settlers' cocktail party ditto, and most recently, on Sunday, had dinner at the American Consulate General's. This last was, on the whole, tedious but necessary. I also lunched with various and sundry, moseyed around the shops in my customary fashion, and got a general glimpse of Nairobi, which is sort of a dynamic frontier town crossed with the typical British colonial outpost. The worst aspect of the place is its food, which is as grisly as what I had to contend with in Penang — you know, fried plaice and caramel custard. Everyone eats at home, & the only place they go to is something called The Lobster Pot which is pretty fierce grub for the money. As for the shops, there's absolutely nothing to buy here. The tourist schlock is typical Far Eastern — filigree silver as on Eighth Street, mass production negro sculpture, & unending Indian stores filled with sleazy remnants and plastic. All I bought was a bush jacket, two pairs of khaki pants, two shirts and a pair of desert boots, all these for the future safari interludes.

•   •   •

Well, this will have to be the burden of the song as of now; somewhere in the middle of this letter yesterday, I let it lie fallow until today (Tuesday) and resumed it. I've completed my preparations for the trip on the dhow, and this afternoon after two o'clock have to take my gear over and check it through the Registrar of Dhows, as he's actually called (this is customs formality). Sometime tonight I'll slip aboard, rearrange the roaches and fleas so I can lie down among them, and we're presumably weighing anchor at daylight. I have purchased 1 box of Bent's Water Crackers, 2 tins of Brislings, 1 can of salmon, 1 bar of chocolate, and my sponsor locally has loaned me his thermos. When these supplies evaporate, I'll have to live on dates, which I am told is the staple food aboard the dhows...I'll whip off a fast postcard to you from Zanzibar letting you know I arrived, or if I can find a cable office, will wire. Meantime, love to all, and continue writing me at Nairobi as always. And, of course, pinch all the four-footed friends. The consul at Nairobi has two standard poodles, but neither holds a candle to Tuffy. How is he right now? Is he all over the enteritis?   With love,

156

LAURA PERELMAN

New Stanley Hotel
Nairobi
January 23, 1954

Dear Laura,

I flew back here from Mombasa last night and was gratified to find six air letters from you dated from Jan. 8th to Jan. 16th that had accumulated here during my absence. (Or I should say five letters and one letter and postcard from Abby.) Anyway, I was very glad indeed to get all this recent mail, as I'd been away from here about twelve days and hadn't had anything forwarded. . . .

I'll recapitulate as quickly as I can the events since I wrote last, just before the dhow trip, from Mombasa. The morning of January 13th, I repaired at daylight to the old port of Mombasa, accompanied by a nice young American couple who were staying at the hotel and wanted to see me off. I was rowed off to the dhow *Amantulla*, 90 tons and crew of 29 Arabs, which had sailed about November 1st from Basra on the Persian Gulf with a cargo of sharks' fins and dates and had taken some 10 weeks to get to Mombasa. The only other passenger for Zanzibar with me was a dejected Arab who kept fingering his prayer beads all through the trip and mumbling obscure wisdom from the Koran. The nakhoda, or captain (nobody on the craft had one word of English), immediately spread a Persian carpet for us passengers up on the poop-deck, and a breakfast of dates (rancid) and coffee was brought us by one of five ragged urchins who served as maids of all work (and much more, I shouldn't be surprised). The ship's longboat was then put over the side, and twelve men, aided by complex tom-tom music and handclapping, rowed out to raise the anchor. All the work done on the voyage, by the way — the raising of the sail, furling of same, hauling of ropes, and so forth — were all attended by chants, drumming, and off-beat hand-clapping. By the time the customs squad had made a thorough search of the dhow for contraband arms and dope and the sailing papers were in order, it was 8 in the morning, and then we were away with a spanking breeze. The dhow in motion had sort of a corkscrew action, a roll and pitch combined, that was somewhat on the nauseating side, though at no point during the 28½ hour trip did I become more than vaguely queasy.

I never got to eat the provisions I'd laid in on the advice of the Liwali of the Coast, the functionary who arranged the trip; I distributed the Bent's Water Crackers and milk chocolate to my shipmates, and they in turn pressed on me their own food prepared in transit. They'd let out lines and, in trolling, hooked two very sizable fish. Up in the bow of the vessel, a remarkably hazardous wood fire was burning, on which the fish were roasted, and with it

157

appeared a vast plate of rice with some kind of curry sauce. Dates provided the dessert at each meal, followed by small china cups of coffee and later by very hot tea flavored with cinnamon. It was obvious, and I'd been told beforehand, that they'd be offended deeply if I spurned their food, and anyway, the fish was quite succulent, even if the rice was not seasoned to my taste. As there were only two of these little china cups on board, they circulated from lip to lip among the whole 31 of us, so we exchanged whatever bacteria we owned generously. Before it got dark — we were now exchanging signs of amity, smiles, etc., and they were offering me rather hard, filthy pillows to prop up my back — I got out my camera and took a lot of pictures of everybody. This proved to be a great icebreaker. Each man insisted on posing for a separate picture of himself; then the captain and his four aides, or associates, or mates or whatever they were — I couldn't quite fathom the relationship — produced their silver-mounted daggers and swords, strapped them on, and posed dramatically for me. I conveyed the fact that I'd send them prints after they were developed, and they've come out very well. . . .

As the wind increased in intensity and we put further to sea, the problem of sleeping on the poop-deck became more difficult, something like reclining in the inside rim of a large soup-plate, and I was constantly sliding toward the waist of the ship or rolling down against the steersman at the wheel. By the time it got dark, I began wondering what they were going to do for riding lights, i.e., the usual red and green lights to warn any other ships of our approach. Nobody ever did anything; we ran on in the dark and I suppose it was only the mercy of Allah that prevented some steamer from slicing us in half. The only dim light on the dhow was a flickering oil lamp by which the steersman watched the compass. Well, it wasn't by any means the most restful night I put in, though actually it was nowhere as bad as my trip to Banda four years ago on the *Melbidir*. The Arabs seemed to be very expert, noisy as the operations were. About four the next morning, I awoke to find that our sail had been hauled down — in the nautical phrase we were hove to — and that we were bobbing about on the waves. The wind had become quite strong, and I believe they were waiting for it to abate somewhat. After a half hour or so, we got under way again, and by nine a.m. began nearing the island of Zanzibar. It's a pretty sizable island, and took about three hours sailing down its coastline to arrive at the actual port of Zanzibar. Well, these are the high-lights of the trip, except to say that the sanitary arrangements consisted of two small platforms about 2½ feet square *on the outside rim* of the dhow; in other words, you stepped over the side (they had a low canvas fence about 2 feet high running around them) and presumably squatted down there. This was all very well for the Arabs, who wore those white nightgown effects called khanzus, but in my European garb and with the crew of 29 watching me attentively, it was something else. I finally decided to wait for cover of nightfall, and my scramble over the side, I imagine, was something for the comic books. At Zanzibar, the immigration launch took its sweet time coming off to clear us, as after all we were presumably just a pack of Arabs. The authorities' eyes really bugged out when they saw me, as nobody'd alerted them. After a period of finger printing the crew to check their prints against their passports, the launch took me ashore, before which the Arabs and I took affectionate leave of each other. They actually did everything in their power to make me as comfortable as they could. They are poor men and work hard for very meager profits, and when, a day or two later, I ran into several of them in the bazaars, they showed great emotion and apparent happiness. I was able to get hold of someone who translated for us then and there, and got from them the address to which I'll forward the photographs of them all. It was a great experience, and I'm certain will work out as a piece when I put in the trimmings.

Zanzibar is a very pleasant place, tiny crooked alleys, beautiful trees and foliage, and a very polyglot population of Indians, Arabs, whites, Portuguese hybrids, etc. The place teems with Indian shops selling cheap and tasteless silver filigree and ivory, all made in India and worthless. The only hotel has but 24 rooms, and unfortunately is smack in the middle of the town away from the ocean breezes so that it's stifling hot. . . . I stayed in Zanzibar three days, hired a car and toured about some interesting clove plantations and agricultural experiment stations in the interior. Also there were some interesting folk at the hotel among the British colonials; one young couple who are coffee planters up near Mount Kilimanjaro and insisted that I come to visit them later, and particularly a weird Bessarabian Jew named Mischa Fainzilber, an all-rightnick who's in the building-materials business at a place called Arusha in Tanganyika. I can't go into details of his story other than to say that he worked at Frank Buck's exhibit in the World's Fair when he was 19 years old, has had vast experience with animals, and owns a cheetah, several pet ostriches, and some other curiosities. We had a quite immediate rapport, were exchanging Yiddish in no time at all, and he is very insistent that I come to visit him in Arusha, which I'll probably do when I fly down there to join my three Mexicans on their safari...After a whole lot of bargaining and comparison shopping, I bought you a very large Arab silver bracelet, an old one and quite extraordinary in shape, which I think you'll find worthy of inclusion in your collection. It's even more massive than the Burmese one and certainly than the Chinese one, and I think will attract some notice.

On Sunday of last week, then, I flew back to Mombasa, and after a day's breather, started up the coast toward a place called Lamu, a very old port that has been successively Arab, Portuguese, and Lord knows what. I

had heard that among other oddities, this place—numbering a white population of four old remittance men—had two bordellos, one of which is called
The Eskimo Pie and which weekly parades its girls through the town square
to discomfit its rival, whose name is something equally improbable. Well, the
transport to this place is pretty difficult, a rattletrap truck owned by the Mamu-
jee Royal Mail and Service Corp., an Indian firm, and the passengers are black
Geriama tribesmen and Arabs. The trip is supposed to take some fourteen
hours, and the intermediate point is a seaside resort much patronized by local
settlers called Malindi. After an agonizing 4½ hour ride over a road like we
used to have in Erwinna, strangling in dust and heat, we reached Malindi and
I found that the only bus for Lamu leaving for that period had left that morning. I thought I'd spend a day seeing what I could work out, so repaired to
one of the 3 local hotels, the Sindbad. They were full up, but sent me to the
one next door, a place called the Eden Roc, and this was the one stroke of
fortune that one gets in a lifetime. A spacious and beautifully designed place
right smack on the Indian Ocean, with the breakers pounding away on the
limitless beach in front, and opening out from the hotel at one side, an enormous fresh-water pool. I was installed in what amounted to a suite directly
facing the ocean, a large twin-bedded room, bath, exterior sleeping porch,
and outside porch running the length of the suite. The food was the best imaginable and prepared with skill, the service was irreproachable, the management completely cordial, and whiskey & soda or Collinses were twenty-four
cents apiece. And when I tell you that room and board came to 25 shillings
a day, or precisely $3.55 a day, you'll see why I was somewhat enraptured.
(I should have said earlier that at the Zanzibar Hotel, their rate for room and
board was also $3.50, but of course it didn't compare with what you get at
the Eden Roc.) The place was quiet and very restful, and inasmuch as there
was a full moon, you may imagine how perfect it was. So I stayed there 3
days, during which I found that there would be no bus to Lamu until this
weekend, and consequently decided not to go on there. I also made the acquaintance of the local Liwali of Malindi, an Arab gentleman who invited
me to his house for lunch, and a Professor Kirkman, who is excavating some
important ruins at nearby Gedi, dating back to the 12th century. This past
Thursday morning, I returned by the same bus to Mombasa, lunched with
various and sundry notables over the next 24 hours, and last night flew back
here to Nairobi.

The reason for this tripping about at this time on the Coast was to fill
in the time before the safaris coming up. . . . Meanwhile, the all-girl safari
has just returned from Tanganyika, and just this evening, I arranged with
Beverly Putnam, their chief Girl Guide, to travel with the party on an over-

night excursion on Lake Victoria to Murchison Falls. . . . Hence, by present arrangement, I'll do this Murchison Falls deal about February 10th with them. As you see, it is taking a certain amount of wangling and rearrangement to straighten out all these trips, the Mexican safari included, because the all-girl group is now altering its schedule daily and I don't want to miss the possible article I'd get by stringing along with them. Incidentally, dissension is already rife in their ranks, the girls are spitting and scratching and tussling over the white hunters, and two have already flounced off in a huff on their own tack. Miss Putnam told me earlier today that their actual 2-week safari that concluded today was sheer murder, one vast orgy of temperament and stabbing with bobbie pins. (Cataclysmic tears, too, when the first animals were slain.) Inasmuch as there were only 3 white hunters for the fifteen women, there was considerable competition — I gather — to see who could get into the hay each night with the boys, and Putnam observed that everyone's personal body fleas were liberally exchanged. . . .

•   •   •

MICHAEL DUNFORD*

513-A Sixth Avenue
New York City
March 28, 1954

Dear Michael,

•   •   •

The homeward passage after we said adieu at Entebbe went off smoothly enough, even though it was gruelling to fly that much distance in so short a time. . . . We got into London about 9:30 the next morning and I went out that evening on the 9:00 p.m. TWA flight to New York. I had one trifling experience that day in London, though, that might amuse you. Happening to be in the vicinity of Simpson's in Piccadilly, I remembered your suggestion that I look over their slacks and odd jackets. I went in, snatched the opportunity to get shaved, and proceeded up to the third floor. A salesman with a long, cold, codfish countenance detached himself from two others with whom he was chatting and languidly approached me. I said I was interested in seeing a casual jacket in some shade of lovat green if he had one. He pulled from the rack a fearful-looking thing of a gunpowder blue shade and said, "Try this on for size." Well, the fit wasn't too far off, but it had fantastically-padded

*At the time, general manager of the East Africa Tourist Travel Association. He was asked to look after, and provide assistance to, Perelman on the African trip. He and his wife, Cleo, a conference interpreter, are the "Mothersills" in "This Is the Forest Primeval?" — one of a series of pieces titled "Small Bore in Africa, or, Dr. Perelman, I Presume" in *The Rising Gorge*.

shoulders, great wings that stood out at right angles to the Perelman frame. I explained that I wear as little padding as I possibly can get, which objection he ignored. He then yanked out another, in some shade of mauve and covered with globular leather buttons. I permitted him to slap this on me and then repeated that it seemed far too dramatically padded. At this, his full waspishness burst its bonds. "Well, then, we can't suit you," he snapped, returning the jacket to the rack. I said I was sorry and would have to look elsewhere. He allowed me to crawl back into my own jacket unaided. As I was doing so, I showed him that my jacket had practically no padding whatever, and added that it was a custom suit that had been tailored in New York. "Yes," he said spitefully, "and if you ask me, it looks pretty awful." I had too many errands to attend to at that point to either dress him down or — which I should have done — hunt up the managing director and explain that Simpson's had that day forever lost a potential customer. However, during the night flight to New York I composed some pretty brilliant vituperative letters I was going to send Simpson's on my return, none of which, naturally, will ever get themselves written. . . .

Even a fairly short trip, and mine was just under three months, succeeds in scrambling one's existence measurably, and since getting back, I've been busy picking up the threads of routine. I've been engaged mostly in setting a style for narrating my East African adventures for *The New Yorker*, which hasn't been easy, because — as you don't have to be told — the canvas out your way is gigantic, colorful, and confused. In writing about it, I find I have to leave out more than I put in, and those jobs of selection are not simple. However, I believe I'm well on my way now, and with the usual inhuman perspiration, should soon have the first article in hand.

I skim through the papers daily for news of Kenya and the M.M. situation, but there has been surprisingly little. For a while, I did see reports that General China was winning over some of his associates, but that died away, and since then, nothing. Of course, our papers are so jammed with the idiocies of Senator McCarthy and his precious aides, Cohn and Schine, that you wouldn't know anything else was going on in the world. I think that nationally we've managed to besprinkle ourselves more successfully with merde than almost anyone — and I don't under-estimate the good work done in that sphere by the all-girl safari...Incidentally, did you ever learn whether — — climbed Kilimanjaro (or vice versa, for that matter)? And did Hemingway clear off on the 10th from Mombasa as scheduled? . . .

Well, I think I've run off at the mouth sufficiently for this occasion and have managed to convey less in more language than any white man of comparable age and weight. My love to you both, as well as to anyone you feel should have it. May I say in closing that when showing people those photographs of Treetops, you both get honor marks from the viewers? Everyone has exclaimed over Cleo's comeliness, and more than a few ladies have exhibited a marked inclination to tiptoe barefoot through your beard. Maybe I could earn a sizable East African shilling by showing the pair of you about at country fairs. The three of us would be sensational.

Yours ever,

ABBY PERELMAN

39½ Washington Square South
New York City
April 15, 1954

Dear Abby,

Sorry I haven't had a chance to write before this, but I've been knocking my brains out on the African stuff for the magazine, and what with interruptions, only just completed the first in the series. Trying to get the complex picture there on paper is just no fun, especially in a piece that begins a series.

Your postcard about *Crime and Punishment* didn't surprise either Laura or myself; it's a most depressing book no matter how young or old, how high or low, one is, and that goes for all of Dostoievsky. I wouldn't have let you read it if I could have prevented it. Of course, it's a great book, but you must realize life isn't necessarily that bleak. For all the woe implied in the lives of those characters, you only have to look about you to see that people can enjoy themselves and laugh and rise above their adversities. Dostoievsky was writing about a group of people in a period of history when there wasn't too much to laugh about — and yet, in another remarkable book called *Dead Souls*, another Russian writer named Nicolay Gogol wrote some very funny pages indeed about the gloomy Slav soul. (Not, by the way, that I'd advise you to read that either, at this point. Even their comic writers are fairly gloomy people.) The Russians have produced some wonderful writers, and when you're next in the country, you could profitably read a little of Turgenev's *Sportsman's Sketches* and bits of Maxim Gorky. However, I repeat, all these men and Tolstoy too were writing about a historical period full of tyranny and oppression in a country full of people who take themselves very seriously. I think that if you'll switch over to Booth Tarkington (be sure and reread *Seventeen*, will you?) and Mark Twain, you will agree with me that life needn't be as heavy-hearted an affair as *C. & P.* suggests. You say in your postcard "What's wrong with me? It deeply affected me." The answer is that nothing is wrong with you because it deeply affects everyone. I told you once, I think, about how people start betraying all the symptoms of T.B. after they read Thomas Mann's *The Magic Mountain*, and I think I also told you that our friend Kurt Wiese, who'd once had a touch of the disease, even took to bed with a temperature after reading it. This should illustrate the power of suggestion that words have when they're used by experts. But there are all kinds of experts, and when George Ade is at his best, or Don Marquis, or any really good comic writer, you can be as deeply moved by laughter as you can by misery. Take the advice of an old broody type — namely, the undersigned — who has learned the hard way, and put aside this sort of literature for the time being. It's all right in small doses, but it's only one side of the picture and should be taken at long intervals.

Laura and I returned to the country after you took off, as you remember, and had a good week there. The weather was everything one could have hoped for, and the afternoon we walked up to the woods was just what both of us needed. Perhaps Laura mentioned it when she wrote you, but we found masses of daffodils and grape hyacinth in bloom around the tumbledown foundation of the old Charity Sumpstone house. Somehow this touched us both, and I think it has a significance for all of us. Seventy-five years ago or more somebody planted a few clumps of daffodil and hyacinth around that house. Except for a few stones balanced on end, which another winter or two will topple over, there is no sign that man ever went that way, but every spring nature produces a brief and lovely memorial. The only other memorials that are in any way eternal are great works of art — the really first-rate music, painting, sculpture, writing — and they give us the same sense of gratification. And the reason, the paramount reason, for education such as you're getting is merely to enable you to know where to find and to appreciate these first-rate things in life. Whenever you tend to feel low, darling, and to wonder about the meaning and the direction of life, remember that there *are* compensations, and great ones, for the difficult times. I think about the sunrises we saw together off Celebes aboard the *Kasimbar*, the terraced rice fields in Bali, the temples in Bangkok, the harbor of Hong Kong with the coolies dressed in those shaggy straw cones dripping with rain, the Taj Mahal at dawn as Al and I saw it for the first time, the island of Prinkipo off Istanbul and the wisteria blooming over those Turkish cafés along the Bosphorus, the rhinos and elephant moving in on the salt-lick at Treetops, the great gorge at Murchison Falls, the papyrus reeds along the Albert Nile with the hippo peering out at our launch — these are some of the things we've been lucky enough to be part of. And, just as important, all the witty and diverting and eccentric and charming people like Benchley and Al Hirschfeld and Dorothy Parker and Somerset Maugham and so on endlessly. Nobody can possibly regard life as futile or depressing when he has experienced the things and known the individuals — not only celebrities, but all kinds of people — who crisscross the daily existence. . . .

Love,

"an Aquarian born
on the cusp of Snafu"
(*Eastward Ha!*)

Portrait of a dandy, age six

Sid and Laura Perelman, France (?)
1929

Sid and Laura, Arthur Kober
Seville, 1934

Top: Al Hirschfeld, Perelman. Bottom: Laura, Laura, Adam, and Abby, c. 1948
Boris Aronson. Coney Island, autumn, 1946

Aboard SS *Marine Flier*, en route to China, 1947

At 513-A Sixth Avenue—"a cubicle I keep to brood in." David Niven's hat from *Around the World in 80 Days* sits above the "balloon smugglers." c. 1957

"The outbuilding where I worry"— the summer kitchen, Erwinna, 1961

"When I returned to the soil, I had a ten-cent screwdriver and the mechanical skill of a turtle" (*Acres and Pains*)

" . . . one of those people of whom Thoreau says that they would find fault with Heaven" (p. 273)

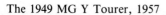

"Button-cute, rapier-keen . . . "

With Michael Dunford at Treetops in Kenya. They were among the last visitors to Treetops before the Mau Mau burned it down.

The 1949 MG Y Tourer, 1957

On the rue Royale in Paris, June, 1975

At home, the Gramercy Park Hotel, 1977

Peking, 1978

JOSEPH BRYAN III

Erwinna, Pa.
August 28, 1954

Dear Joe,

I see your point in fearing that "Bangkok spelt backward is Kokgnab" might mantle someone's alabaster cheek with flushes, and it raises all kinds of entrancing possibilities. It wouldn't be beyond the bounds of credibility, for instance, that there might be a Siberian town—maybe only a post-chaise stop—called Tsaredep—and you'd really have to struggle to keep from reversing that.

I don't know how you'd change the one I sent you to work with Zanzibar, other than to have the message read "Zanzibar spelled backward is Rabiznaz. There's no biznaz like Rabiznaz." This is what you get for even consulting me.

Dark Continent footnote: When I was in Nairobi, I went into Shaw & Hunter, said I was a friend of yours, and was thus enabled to purchase a 3/6 jar of Dalhousie's Human Marmalade (made from freshly-potted Kikuyu babies) for 3/4. Joe, it was delicious. Bless you, boy.

Wish I could revel with you in the Corso, but my purse is leaner than it's been since Lena was the queen of Palestina. If I can get *Breezy Jugoslav Stories* to underwrite a continental swing, I'll meet you in Split at blossom time. I hear the Slivovitz there is *ausgezeichnit*, not to say *épouvantable*. In any case, a fine Roman holiday to you from Laura and me, and if we can get over there, let's all plash around in some convenient piazza and justify the title Three Groins in the Fountain.   Yours,

LEILA HADLEY

513-A Sixth Avenue
New York City
December 30, 1954

Leila darling,

.   .   .

As you see from the superscription, I'm back at my office; we moved into town about October 15th and spent a month at a vile hotel called the Brittany on East 10th Street and then removed to a sub-let right around the corner from your former apartment, at 120 West 58th St., where we now are and will continue to be until May 1st. It's diagonally across the street from the Barbizon-Plaza, a little coop of a place very artsy-craftsy in décor on the 9th floor overlooking Steinway Hall. It's claustrophobic in the extreme, altogether too small for our needs and those of three animals, and we loathe

165

it, but it was all we could find at the time. . . . It's strange living uptown as we are; the tailors, grocers, liquor dealers, and so on are damn suspicious in that neighborhood and looked upon us for a good while as fly-by-night characters: couldn't get a check cashed or even get merchandise with a check for weeks, until Fred Allen, who dwells upon the corner of 58th and Seventh, put in a good word locally. He wouldn't have, I'm sure, if he could have had a glimpse of our bank account.

•   •   •

. . . My friend McKnight Kauffer, I am sad to have to relate, died several months ago after a lingering illness. It was a real tragedy that he never succeeded in getting people here to appreciate his work as they should have, and it would have been much better if he'd never left England....Your button-cute friend Truman Capote had a premiere last night, a musical show called *House of Flowers* (for which he wrote libretto and lyrics and Harold Arlen the music); Atkinson panned everything this morning and said (I thought significantly) that Capote's plot revolving around a bordello lacked relish, or maybe he said gusto. That's understandable.

•   •   •

Yours always,

L E I L A   H A D L E Y

513-A Sixth Avenue
New York City
February 22, 1955

Darling Leila,

. . . Today, as you'll recall, is Washington's Birthday, which is to say that I got to the web here 2 hours earlier than usual. This fetched me smack up against the porter, who was enjoying a leisurely inspection of my mail and had, I suspect, just compensated for the nip he'd taken out of my bottle of Scotch by filling it up with water. I overlooked the peccadillo, however, and seized the opportunity to re-inspect the office opposite (i.e., the one formerly occupied by the Harold Shapiron Cable Co. and vacant these many months). I'd toyed with the notion of acquiring it as a pied-à-terre, inasmuch as it has (glory be) wall-to-wall carpeting, a wood-burning fireplace, a splendid large room, and one smaller one. Unfortunately, I've since learned that it's available *only* as an office, due to some technicality about fire laws, and though it has gas laid on and could accommodate a peachy small medical icebox and could be turned into an ideal set-up, my landlord won't rent it as living quarters.

166

(Forgot to add that the rent is cheap, I think I could get it for $75 or a shade less.) In any case, there's no way to work it out that I can see, and it would be a distinct indulgence to take it in addition to my own flytrap, because that would hike my rent to approximately $135, and what I have is perfectly adequate. . . .

. . . The theatrical season [other than *The Boyfriend*] smells. The only other thing I've enjoyed was Harry Kurnitz's *Reclining Figure* (title changed from *Reclining Nude* because some pussy-foot decided it was too blue for the old bags with purple hair). That show lasted 13 weeks and closed for the very obvious reason that after the first couple of weeks, the audiences — geared to Maxfield Parrish — didn't understand who Renoir was. But it was very funny on the whole.

Always and always,

LEILA HADLEY

513-A Sixth Avenue
New York City
March 16, 1955

Darling,

Thank you for your tuneful remarks about my work; I have the conceit of a diva, as you well know, and despite any pretense of being blasé, it is good to know that one has achieved a calculated effect. . . .

. . . At longest last, I yesterday got hold of — via phone. . . . She was — as usual — breathless. The moment she heard my voice, she squealed joyfully, then begged me to hold on because someone was at the door and she was stark naked. I'm sure she was wearing a raccoon coat, ear-muffs, and galoshes, and only said it to inflame me, but she dashed off phone, returned to give me a lurid account of how she had faced up to a messenger with only a Martex towel between them, and then quieted down. I expect we'll get together, with or without the Martex, within the next several days. . . . Our three-minute phone conversation, perforce hurried because her "father" was calling for her in twenty minutes, pleasantly recalled the hysteria of old times . . . which I'd trade for all your putative diamond mines down Johannesburg way.

. . . [T]he only travel I expect to indulge in (apart from not having the thousand dollars) is a free trip courtesy of the Air Force to the North Pole

167

shortly. . . . Was supposed to have left two days ago, but a mysterious silence has descended from the direction of Washington, so maybe the Defense Dep't didn't clear me. This is only to get material for a *Holiday* piece, and I have no appetite for it, and really hope it falls through. The prospect of 40 below and a week with a pack of sex-starved birdmen encased in plastic bubbles holds no charm. For a few minutes about 10 days ago, I thought I might be able to work in a 3-week flight to London and Paris next month, but then more bills came in and snowed under the wherewithal.

. . . April 1st we've moving into a new apartment at 134 West 11th Street, midway between Sixth and Seventh Avenues. It's a windfall of sorts, a floor through — *with terrace* — in a very good-looking remodelled brownstone belonging to one — —. . . . (He himself, on short acquaintance, strikes me as all crud and a yard wide.) It's the floor over the parlor floor, whichever they call that; I never know in these remodelled effects. Anyway, it's to be redecorated in those various shades of mustard and lime green we like starting next week, and we'll move up some furniture we have stored in the country. There's an extra bedroom there for Abby, who'll be either at Smith or Pembroke this next year and will be home only for occasional weekends and vacations. Fine large kitchen with breakfast area, large livingroom and master bedroom each with open fireplace, full bath and a powder room thing besides and, as I say, a dandy large terrace with southern exposure and lots of open space beyond. Cost: $260 a mo. We're taking a 2½ year lease on it, and of course I'm continuing on at my 513-A web as always. . . .

What else? I spent an indescribable lunch and afternoon one day last week with a willowy chap named — — . . . , who was detailed to guide me through the intricacies of the new Gourielli Men's Salon. This is a high-class barber shop and haberdashery, ads for which you may have seen in *The New Yorker*, etc., and I figured might be workable material for me. It still may be, though my day with — gave me enough data on the genus queen to write a volume the size of *La Terre*. Your wee friend Truman Capote, by the way, is a devoted customer of the barber shop; both he and Tennessee Williams make a practice of dropping in to luxuriate under the strictly unionized fingers of the operatives...We spent last weekend in the country and I returned with a crippling charley-horse from washing and waxing the MG. After all, it would have cost me nearly $2.00 to get it done in a garage...Next Wednesday I shall drive it up to Providence to rendezvous (as they say) with Abby, who'll be interviewed that day at Pembroke, and I'll have some old home week talk with faculty friends at Brown. That sort of thing always sends me back to my workbench with a sigh of relief.

·　　　　·　　　　·

LEILA HADLEY

513-A Sixth Avenue
New York City
April 19, 1955

Darling,

. . . We're finally moved into the apartment of 134 West 11th . . . and think it's great. A whole floor through as I think I wrote you plus a nice large terrace looking smack into a huge flowering cherry now in full bloom and other trees beyond. Pursuant to the usual color scheme of a subdued mustard color for livingroom, I picked out an odd shade up at the Plaza Paint Co. on 3rd Ave. and discovered when it was finally on the wall that it's the exact color of those robes worn by Buddhist monks in Siam. However, don't flinch—actually it's very effective and a peach of a background for the big Cambodian statue. The bedrooms are in some color called desert green, most soothing for les nerfs and the nerves need soothing. . . . The mention of the Cambodian statue reminds me: Allen Saalburg, the painter who lives near us in the country and whom I think you met when you were there, tall nice-looking guy, has been doing a series of wonderful silk-screen prints of which I have several samples. He recently asked to borrow the Tang head you brought me from Hong Kong, to do a silk screen of that, and I'm sure he'll do a great job. . . .

I'm at a loss to account for my activities since writing you last; I've been working in a desultory sort of way and just finished a piece today on the British peerage based on some news snippet or other. . . . My exchequer's in dismal shape what with the income tax payment of four days ago (the balance of 1954), the cost of moving, and all types of subterranean bills, and if I had any strength of character, I'd spend 24 hours a day working. . . .

. . . On Mickey Hahn, I'm sure she was everything complimentary you said in your letter, and I always have a hell of a stimulating time with her. Nevertheless, I'm not at all sure I like her politics, or shall I say her ethics and/or her sense of journalistic morality. You know she has just published here a biography of Chiang Kai-shek. Max Lerner's review of it in the *Post* made it sound like a real venal job of whitewashing this bastard who may yet cause us all to be radioactively dissolved if the Quemoy-Matsu business goes through. I can't humanly understand how anybody with the slightest pretensions to decency can write about the General as a Christian gentleman, as Mickey has, or has gone on to even greater apologies for him. Henry Lieberman's review in the *Times Book Review* was less condemnatory than Lerner's, but you could read between the lines that he thought little of the book. It's pretty much as if anyone had brought out a book whitewashing Bao Dai at the time we were tickling that distinguished Asiatic's pussy during the Indo-China affair. . . .

•   •   •

LEILA HADLEY

513-A Sixth Avenue
New York City
June 17, 1955

My love,

•   •   •

I defy anybody, particularly myself, to narrate with any exactness what I've been doing since I wrote last. The last month, in terms of work, has been utterly unfruitful; for some reason, my brain has felt like a tureen of cold pork fat, and everything I've touched has instantly turned to dreck. Added to which, the financial aridity has been gruesome; the move down to 11th Street proved to be expensive beyond all prediction, what with reupholstering, carpets, and things one shouldn't have to buy like kitchen cabinets, and then up popped unexpected Federal income taxes, doctors' bills, what-not, totalling thousands. How in Christ's sweet name I shall ever see light again, I have no idea, and we constantly resolve to sell the farm, only to back out at the last moment whenever we are about to go ahead and list it with real-estate agents. However, why particularize? From your own letter, I get the picture of what you yourself face. On the positive side, there's (in the far distant future) the musical comedy Ogden Nash and I are nibbling away at whenever we get a free day,* and one fairly new feature, a lecture tour I'm committed to go out on the next two seasons. Have signed up with W. Colston Leigh—largely at Nash's instigation, he contends that it sells books and stimulates one, even if it doesn't produce any great revenue—and as of October or so, I shall be nipping off around the country on scattered dates. I did some of this sort of thing for the government during the war and wasn't too unhappy with it, though this future stint will have to embrace a much more organized and extensive job of speaking. . . .

•   •   •

. . . Tonight, I'm scheduled to have dinner with Harvey Orkin, whom you may recall,† and Cary Grant, whom I'm sure you do, to discuss a project for involving the latter in a TV production of *Westward Ha!* There isn't even the proverbial Chinaman's chance of its going through, but wild-eyed agents

---

*Never finished, the show was to have been called *White Rhino*, based on Perelman's East African adventures.

†Talent agent, TV writer, and wit who later became a television personality in London (d. 1975).

have set it up and I've gone too far into it to back out. I will, therefore, break off here and continue when I next get back to these unlovely precincts.

. . . [Cary Grant] turned out to be a very agreeable surprise, in that he was not only full of charm — which we expected — but was most receptive to the idea advanced by my companions. Nothing immediate, to be sure; it'll be two years before he could possibly do it, but he did tell them that if they'd show him three scripts based on *Westward Ha!*, satisfactory to himself, he'd throw in his lot with us. It appears he has been a loyal reader of mine for quite a while, and was as complimentary as anyone could have asked. All this is balmy for the ego but unfortunately of no emollient value to the pocket.

    •   •   •

P.S.   Extract from an interview of Robert Ruark* . . . in *N.Y. Times Book Review*, apropos of your question about what I thought of former's success with his novel (I quit reading same after 70 pages; man's preoccupation with viscera threw me): "I did the best book I could with the tools I had. It wasn't a story about Peter Pan and my name ain't Mary. Look, I ain't humble and I ain't played Uriah Heep lately. This is the way I think: I have been a highly successful guy in whatever I was doing. I did a column and I think it got to be one of the best. When I was on top I quit. I been married to the same wife for eighteen years. During the two years I was writing the book I did sixty-five magazine pieces and sold them. I managed to shoot a couple of tigers. I fished in New Zealand. I don't wind up a beachcomber and I come back with a best-seller. This is not to be tolerated. This does not make you friends in the Third Avenue bars."

Oh, Hemingway, what crimes are committed in thy name. . . . When you've finished your present book, why not a scarifying novel about this bloated pipsqueak and his rise to eminence? Lord knows it wouldn't be easy (the extract above so infuriates me that I've been unable to do a piece on it), but it's certainly something that needs doing.

*Best-selling author whose novels included *Uhuru* and *Something of Value*, the book in question (d. 1965).

LAURA PERELMAN

Hollywood, Calif.
July 16, 1955

Dear Laura,

    This probably won't be much more than a note, inasmuch as the pressure has already started ("We got to have all the club sequences by Monday, don't worry about the scene in the employment agency right away, that can go till

Tuesday, but before you do anything, we must have the scene at Suez and maybe the balloon sequence if you possibly can").* It's all pretty much what I anticipated, hysteria and money being spent like water, ten-million-dollar deals, Todd talking into three phones at once and flying to Mexico and returning from Mexico and Christ-all knows what. It has a vaguely old-fashioned flavor, I find; the Hollywood of *Once in a Lifetime* and *Boy Meets Girl*. Todd's busy living up to his legend, standing off from himself and admiring this Napoleonic figure he's created who's consummating ten-million-dollar stock issues, producing *War and Peace* and *The Life of Toscanini* at the same time he's releasing *Oklahoma* and preparing *Around the World in 80 Days* and sleeping with sixteen dames alternately and flying back from Las Vegas and leaving for Paris tomorrow and returning from London yesterday. With all the meshuggahis, the fact remains that he does have an extraordinary development in movie technique, this Todd-AO process, and that *Oklahoma* is going to really create a sensation this fall.

This little number I'm doing also may come out right side up, but as of this moment, I wouldn't care to make any predictions. It's going to have any number of gimmicks—Noel Coward, Gary Cooper, Bogart, and people like that appearing briefly throughout, Eddie Fisher warbling on the sound track, etc.—but as usual, nobody has bothered about the script right up till now. There was one which had been done by somebody called Richard Sale several years ago in England; Todd owned it, sold it to [Alexander] Korda, bought it back, and has now thrown it into the ash-can. A couple of months ago, John Farrow, who's directing (remember him? Pattie Paramore's father), went back to Jules Verne's book and simply set it up into movie script form using Verne's own dialogue, and this is pretty much what I'm basing my rewrite on. The leads are David Niven, Cantinflas, and Peter Ustinov, as Phileas Fogg, Passepartout, and Mr. Fix, the detective. Cantinflas, who is the idol of the Spanish-speaking countries, can't speak English much, if at all, so you can imagine what kind of dialogue I'll have to fashion for him. It will all undoubtedly wind up as some sort of gigantic spectacle, with Cantinflas doing pratfalls and thousands of naked dames. However, I needn't underline the obvious, which is that the longer I stick with it, the bigger the take. If I can cling on after the 3-week guarantee of ten G's and last the ensuing four weeks—all of which would total twenty-one thousand in salary—we could be out of the woods financially, and that's what I'm bending every sinew to accomplish.

· · ·

Love,

*Perelman had begun his work on *Around the World in 80 Days* for Mike Todd.

LEILA HADLEY

Darling,

The postmark and the imprinted envelope will undoubtedly give you the story in a flash, and any explanations I add can only be tedious. However, here it is, just to get through it. I'm out here doing a stint for Mike Todd, furbishing up the dialogue for *Around the World in 80 Days*, and have been since July 9th. It began with an urgent phone call from here the afternoon before, demanding that I whisk out for a showing next day of *Oklahoma*, which he's produced in this new Todd-AO process of his, and would I be available, etc. Considering the Kanchanjunga of unpaid bills I have, the appalling heat of N.Y., and the even more appalling sparsity of subjects for *New Yorker* pieces, I was aboard the plane and practicing yesmanship before he'd hardly finished talking. The job seems to fall into two halves: a 3-week rough brush-up of the script ending about August 2nd or 3rd, and thereafter I'm to fly to London for the two weeks of shooting they've scheduled there – in other words, seven weeks' engagement over all, but it could be longer. It could also be shorter, since Todd's a capricious homuncule who lives between half a dozen phones and changes his mind hourly. If Mark Hanna can collect my salary weekly from his hatchet men, however (unpredictable), and he doesn't welch on his contract, I'll be assured of the first three weeks, and that, faute de mieux, should stand off the creditors somewhat. And if, God grant, the London trip they're all assuring me is set comes through, I ought to get a brief European visit on the juiciest possible basis, namely free gratis. . . .

.   .   .

This place is what it always was – *plus ça change*. The usual interminable dinner parties, the same conversation about the same banalities. The other night the Hacketts took me to a particularly ghastly one at Malibu, 135 people all eating in a rented marquee, at –'s place. He's . . . been assiduous in the vicinity of Darryl Zanuck's anus, and it's paid off. Here they were, the survivors of my epoch out here, gray and twitching, as fatuous as they ever were, all of them heavy with annuities and real estate and Jaguars, and dreary beyond description. The Hacketts remain the phenomenons they were – incredibly kind and gracious people who do their work conscientiously, who take just as dim a view as I do of this insane place but simulate good cheer, and who continue to act with consideration and modesty. They themselves are leaving here August 1st for N.Y., as their play – a dramatization of Anne Frank's *Diary of a Young Girl* – goes into rehearsal later in the month. They've spent almost two years of work on it, and if [God] isn't too busy . . . I'd like him to ensure the success of their show.

. . . I have just finished *Bonjour Tristesse*, Françoise Sagan's short novel; I thought there was some effective writing in it, and yet the preoccupation with love eventually tired me. It's obviously a best-seller because everyone in it is laying somebody or being laid, but a 17-year-old's palpitations about venery can pall. . . .

Well, here it is five o'clock, blazing hot, and the Hacketts dragging through the door after nine hours of productive screenwriting, so I'll cease and terminate. . . .   Always and always,

GUS LOBRANO

Los Angeles, Calif.
July 27, 1955

Dear Gus,

It was even more demented than I anticipated. Nobody's spoken to me in less than a shout and I've been riding in nothing but Cadillacs and Thunderbirds. Fortunately, I am a level-headed, thoughtful sort of chap, incapable of being swayed by this sort of gaudy nonsense. Marilyn Monroe and I are just going to go ahead with our plans and get married, then settle down on her 12,000-acre citrus ranch, and make our own little world. This we basically feel is how the real we can best fulfil ourselves, deep down.

I'm returning East tomorrow night, i.e., Thursday, and if Mike Todd's devotion doesn't sour — which has been known to happen in the twinkling of an eye — I'll be going to London for a couple of weeks of shooting there about mid-August. That should give me plenty of time to describe to you what has been happening locally. Meanwhile, I enclose a snippet from Hedda Hopper about one of our favorite boys.* With love and kisses,

Yours,

*"Leo Rosten and I dined at Chasen's, and had a cocktail in Dave's private quarters. Standing before a portrait of the late Harold Ross of *The New Yorker*, Leo said, 'There was the greatest editor of them all' " — *Los Angeles Times*, July 27, 1955.

LEILA HADLEY

Brown's Hotel
London
August 21, 1955

Darling,

The past five weeks have been so chaotic that I seem to have lost all sense of time, place, and identity, and if this letter appears slightly deranged, just chalk it up to the hysteria that envelops everything concerned with Mike Todd plus exhaustion, a second-hand Olivetti, and the remains of a dramatic head-cold. . . . As it worked out, I was in New York about eight days, just time enough to work like a navvy in 96-degree temperatures. Then Todd, who meanwhile had flown to Spain to supervise a bull-ring sequence being prepared at a town called Chinchón 40 miles from Madrid, decided that I ought to fly over to be on hand for it; he thereupon flew back to New York, pulverized a series of directors' meetings set up for him, and collecting me, his lawyer, and a couple of other appendages, flew back. This — as near as I can recall — was on August 9th. The journey over was a trancelike experience, divided up between Mike's puttering with the dialogue I'd hastily written for our London scenes (manfully trying to make it as illiterate as possible) and his playing gin rummy with the rest of the party. By skilful arranging, we succeeded in missing our Madrid connection by ten minutes. This gave him a splendid opportunity to rush us all to the Dorchester, where a suite had been emptied of the King of Trans-Jordan or somebody so that Mike could place five or six international phone calls and dispatch thirty or forty cables to all parts of the world. In between, he chartered a small eight-passenger aircraft called a Dove, into which we were all piled together with quantities of roast chicken and box lunches, and we took off on as bumpy a 3-hour trip to Bordeaux as ever recorded in the annals of aviation. After a Gargantuan lunch absorbed at top speed, we zoomed forward again over the Pyrenees and got in late at night, disrupting the entire Spanish customs. The next four or five days consisted of frequent visits to Chinchón, dramatic conferences and arguments with his director, John Farrow — who has since quit the picture, taking most of his technical staff with him — dinner-parties with potent Spanish types, matadors, and French film tycoons, and such a mélange of intrigue, gossip, and back-stairs knifing as you can't imagine. The actual bullfight stuff at Chinchón was very colorful; Luis Miguel Dominguín, the matador whose pants have often been perilously ripped by Ava Gardner, dispatched three undersized bulls with considerable élan, and one of our three leads, Cantinflas, did what seemed to be an effective comic bullfight. Inasmuch as my sympathies were at all times on the side of the bewildered and brutalized bulls — I'm afraid that my brief stay in East Africa cured me of any neo-Hemingway notions about the beauty of bullfighting and that I take a rigid, pro-animal position — I didn't toss my beret quite as high in the air as my confreres. Anyhow, by Sunday the shooting was completed, Farrow and Todd had dissolved their union, and Todd, loading another half-dozen of us into the Dove, whipped off to Biarritz so that he could subdue the baccarat tables. I left the casino at 1:45 when he was 3 million francs ahead, but thanks to the unvarying law of percentages favoring the house, he was even again by 5:00 a.m. At 9:00, four hours later,

175

we continued on to London, where — by main force — I resisted importunate demands that I hole in at the Dorchester and sneaked off to this fairly quiet roost. It was quiet for almost eighteen hours, and then the London press came scuffling in. I enclose a couple of the dubious end products. Mike's adoration of publicity is such that I have to hold still for a certain amount of this kind of merde. The only consolation is that thanks to Mark Hanna's relentless maneuverings behind the scenes, I am extorting a weekly fee that would cause a brigand to blush, and also there is the negative satisfaction that I haven't yet been asked to pose in my underdrawers.

•　　　•　　　•

LEILA HADLEY

513-A Sixth Avenue
New York City
September 16, 1955

Darling,

•　　　•　　　•

. . . The whole *schmier* of five weeks — from Madrid through Paris up to this past Sunday night when we took off for home — was just about as brutal, unnerving, and distasteful as possible, and it gives me great pleasure to report that as of 48 hours ago, I've managed to disentangle myself from Todd's slimy tentacles and return to private life.

Just to get him out of the way, all I need say is that as the days drew on, the psychopathic little bastard reached an absolutely indescribable pitch of dementia, enraging everyone about him and treating the entire organization to such outbursts of temper and petulance as have rarely been seen outside children's playgrounds and mental hospitals. He became increasingly fixed on the idea that I had to be at his bidding every hour of the twenty-four, made scenes whenever I tried to get away for lunch — even press luncheons concerned with publicity for himself — rang up Joe Liebling one morning at 1:30 (though he didn't know Liebling) to trace me because I'd been missing for several hours, and altogether qualified himself for admission to a looney bin. He was unable to find any evidence that I wasn't working as contracted, and I suppose that galled him in some twisted way. But there were some lovely high-spots — as, for instance, when he ordered me to run to the wardrobe to fetch a hat-pin for Hermione Gingold prior to a scene we were shooting, etc. — and perhaps one day, when I've cooled off sufficiently, I can use a portion of all this as copy. Anyhow, and only to round off the recital, he at last got around to financial mayhem in the final two weeks and that broke the spell. As soon as I was able to complete my moral obligation of not abandoning the picture on location, I got Mark Hanna to function, and Mark gave it to him in the pit of the stomach, or rather the pit of the pocketbook, and that dissolved our ill-starred union. Previous to that, of course, Todd had been painting a rosy future in which I was cast as a coach-dog running at his heels and fulfilling myself as his major-domo in charge of purchasing his cigars. . . .

. . . Over here, the summer's dying hard — it's school time, your sex is beginning to break out in basic black, and various shows are beginning their out-of-town try-outs. The Hacketts opened last night in Philadelphia — *The Diary of Anne Frank*, upon which they've been laboring these past two years, produced by Kermit Bloomgarden and directed by Garson Kanin. Haven't yet heard reports, but am hoping with every fiber it's the success the Hacketts deserve.

. . . I expect to be going down to the farm tomorrow for the first time since early July. . . . I'll be in the city pretty constantly hereafter until — God help us all — my lecture tour's scheduled to start sometime after January 1st. I also want to resume working on the musical I started with Nash et al., and — most important of all — get back to doing some *New Yorker* pieces.

. . . Spoke to Jack G[oodman] this morning but only to say hello; my new book, *Perelman's Home Companion*, is due for publication October 31st and he says the advance sale is very encouraging. . . .

Yours only,

BETSY DRAKE

513-A Sixth Avenue
New York City
September 28, 1955

Dear Betsy,

. . . Let me advise you at once that you'd better throw away George Jessel as your standard of all that's most revolting in human behavior. This sinister dwarf who consumed nine weeks of my life has no peer in his chosen profession, which — stated very simply — is to humiliate and cheapen his fellow man, fracture one's self-esteem, convert everybody around him into lackeys, hypocrites, and toadies, and thoroughly debase every relationship, no matter how casual. His enormity grows on you like some obscene fungus; you go to bed in the belief that nothing that happened all day possibly could have, and then, the next morning, it intensifies. Honey, you don't *know*.

177

. . . I thought that between Irving Thalberg, Hunt Stromberg, and a number of other megalomaniacs — God help me, I almost forgot Zanuck! — I'd worked for, I had seen everything, but this boy is the all-time winner... Anyway, to give you some halfway coherent notion of our junket, we spent about five days in Spain . . . a month or so in London, making exteriors and indoor stuff out at Elstree, and a few days in Paris disrupting the French. In addition to usurping his directors' prerogatives — as you may know, John Farrow quit and Todd's now using a young English chap recommended by Noel Coward — Todd interfered in every conceivable department of the production, not excluding my own; indeed, so far as I know, he is now rewriting the picture as he goes along, grinding the crank, building the sets, unnerving the actors, and generally qualifying as an up-to-date Leonardo da Vinci. It's inaccurate to describe his cyclonic conduct as energy or vitality — it's much more a violent frenzy I'm sure the head-shrinkers could classify. His background as a carnival barker, however, aided him in convincing an impressive bunch of actors to string along with his project, and if you ever go to see the picture — or should I say, if it's ever finished this side of ten million dollars — you'll catch glimpses of Noel Coward, Gielgud, Robert Morley, Trevor Howard, A.E. Matthews, Bea Lillie, Hermione Gingold, Glynis Johns, John Mills, Fernandel, Martine Carol, and probably God Almighty himself. . . .

•   •   •

. . . Please give my very best to Cary, together with a message that if I can assemble string, paper, and cardboard, I'll ship him a weird little memento I picked up in London. Meanwhile, and with love,

Yours,

T . S . E L I O T

134 West 11th Street
New York City
September 29, 1955

Dear Tom,

This is the most belated of responses to your note of 6th September. At the moment you were writing it, I was in — of all places — London, and I hope you will not judge me too harshly for failing to call you. I was then at the tag end of a thoroughly exhausting experience, involved in working on a movie called *Around the World in 80 Days*; we had been in Spain for a week shooting a sequence outside Madrid, then spent a hideous three weeks filming exteriors in Kensington and Knightsbridge and interiors at the MGM Studio in Elstree; and finally crossed over to Paris for a final weekend of shooting there. I was at all times hag-ridden by an indescribable megalomaniac named

178

Mike Todd, a combination of Quasimodo and P.T. Barnum, who never let me out of his sight for more than five minutes, and I can honestly say that (apart from the loot I succeeded in extracting from him) I've never had a less rewarding visit to Europe. Even after almost a month's rest, I still feel like a sand-hog who has been projected at jet speed from the river-bed into mid-air, and when anyone addresses me unexpectedly, I still double over with the bends.

I was very sorry to miss you at the Poetry Center that night, and was indeed impressed with the way you manipulated all of us out front. As one who has unwisely committed himself to a lecture tour this winter, I can tell you that I was overcome by your aplomb and very envious of your pear-shaped tones and dégagé manner. I half expected you to flick an infinitesimal speck of ash from your lapel at one point, but thank God, there were no lapels on your suit – or perhaps I was too overcome by your magnetism to notice them.

It especially grieves me that I shan't be in England this autumn to see the exhibition of Ted [Kauffer]'s posters you speak of. I'm hoping that someone conceives the idea of importing it...Do you think there is any likelihood of your returning here this winter? If so, please do let me know so that we can broach a bottle of Jack Daniels Sour Mash. If I should get back to London, you may be sure I'll bring along a bottle so that we can snap our fingers at the licensing laws. Meanwhile, and with all my best,

Yours ever,

LEILA HADLEY

Los Angeles, Calif.*
c. October, 1955

.   .   .

. . . [A]n old acquaintance of mine, James Agee, many years the movie reviewer on *Time* and latterly engaged in doing a script for John Huston on *The African Queen*, is also on the beach and occupying a room in Dotty's house (no romantic connection; he spends his time drooling over some unseen dame Dotty calls The Pink Worm). Parker says Agee consumed three bottles of Scotch unaided last Friday. I didn't get Agee's closing quotations on Parker's consumption. They both exist in a fog of crapulous laundry, stale cigarette smoke, and dirty dishes, sans furniture or cleanliness; one suspects they wet their beds. All this, added to an absolutely manic pitch of fear out here on everyone's part that he's about to be jugged by the FBI – and people *are* being so jugged and blacklisted – makes for a Hollywood that is nothing

*Perelman was doing a series of interviews with comedians for *Holiday* magazine.

179

like any I ever knew, a combination of boom town gone bust and Germany in 1935. By Monday I was in such a dreary frame of mind I was strongly tempted to cry frig to my various assignments [and] jump the eastbound plane. . . .

I put in most of Monday with Groucho on the set at RKO. He's nicer than I've ever known him and was excessively flattering about my work. To the point of being fulsome. Naturally, it cast me into an extreme of anger. He's finishing the picture early next week and so we've postponed serious interviewing until he's rested. . . .

•   •   •

LEILA HADLEY

Hollywood Knickerbocker Hotel
Hollywood, Calif.
November 20, 1955

Darling Leila,

This is a letter that has defied writing these past three weeks, which is the length of time I've been in this abysmal hole, but now that I'm poised to depart—tonight, thank God—the chain is riven asunder and I regain the power of speech. . . . [S]hortly after I got your letter telling me about your sojourn on the Zambesi . . . Mike Todd started cajoling me to return here for some added work on the script of *Around the World*, etc. I resisted until he acceded to the salary I demanded, and when, churlishly, he did, had no excuse not to come. I've put in the three weeks doing some added bits for personalities like Dietrich, Red Skelton (God help us all), Geo. Raft, Sinatra, and Ronald Colman, whom he's cramming into the picture along with 87 other luminaries, and most latterly have been compiling a complete script for the use of the cutter in editing the thing. Several days ago, one of the Paramount producers tried to tag me to remain out here and work on several pictures he's doing, and if I were at all career-minded and sensible and cared to face the fact that I could use the money handsomely, I should stay; but the place and the people are so God-awful that I prefer to go back to my rickety existence back East, with all its drawbacks.

My stay here's been so arid that it's difficult to freeze your blood with any especially grisly details. . . . I've been in close contact with Hollywood Boulevard, on which the tin Christmas trees are presently being erected. Next week it formally becomes Santa Claus Lane and the Christmas parade, headed by (I believe) Lex Barker and Vulva Greyhound, will be held. Someone a good deal more articulate than me will have to chronicle the miles of cheap shoe-stores, costume jewelry booths, delicatessens featuring crazyburgers and

180

mile-high malteds, and vitamin shops — not to mention the tide of raddled faces that undulates past, staring emptily before them. This really is the sump-hole of the universe.

.   .   .

In the five weeks or so between my return from England and my departure for L.A., I did a couple of pieces for *The New Yorker* which haven't appeared as yet but should momentarily; I want to get busy on a couple more very soon. I've also indentured myself to a god-damned lecture tour, the first appearance being in Dayton in early February, and this requires some intensive preparation; and also, I've got to resume work with O. Nash on our musical, which isn't much past the early outline stage. Forgive me for boring you with these inconsequentialities, but after one's been dipped in this atmosphere of smog and barbecue sauce, there's an overpowering necessity to re-establish one's identity. I have to remind myself that people *do* live otherwise than they do here.

.   .   .

Yours always and ever,

L E I L A   H A D L E Y

513-A Sixth Avenue
New York City
December 15, 1955

Leila darling,

. . . The Hollywood stint lasted 3 weeks to the day; I got back here just before Thanksgiving, which wasn't a second too soon. My stay out there (as must have been self-evident from my letter) was notably bleak, and I began to get plenty of signals before too long that whatever Mike Todd was using for money was running low, so that if he'd kept me on any longer, I'd never have been paid. As it was, it took a hammerlock and snuffling on my part to disgorge the final week's salary. His general manager kept trying to get me to agree to have it sent on to me in the East, but I clouded over and protested that would get me in trouble with my agent and similar idiocies, and I finally all but siphoned it out of his veins. As for the picture itself, I hear it got itself finished, and come next May or whenever, I can disappear when the reviews come out...

I hardly know what to offer in the way of news, but if you'll project yourself halfway across the world and remember how insipid Christmas usually is hereabouts, with everyone scuffling around the stores buying junk and the newspapers littered with Yuletide feature stories and the din of "Buy — buy — buy" echoing from radio and TV, possibly you'll recall what it was like when you saw it last. Just ahead is the prospect of several parties which I view with stolidity—the first of them one that we ourselves are giving tomorrow night, more or less because it seemed like a good idea way back there but now, on the eve, looms up as a nuisance. A whole bagful of odd and unrelated people . . . and their wifey wives down through some of our country neighbors . . . whom I exchange dry grins with, are descending on us to the number of 25 *after* dinner—which means they will stay for hours, hating each other, breaking our glassware, and becoming embroiled in loud, senseless arguments...On New Year's, it seems we are pledged to turn up at Lilly Hellman's,* and I can't tell you how exciting is the prospect of again seeing that roll of toilet paper — — uses as a face. Lilly, by the way, is enjoying a hit; her play *The Lark*, an adaptation of Anouilh's play about Joan of Arc, is a success that nobody begrudges her, because she's barred from working in pictures and TV by her political taint...Endeavoring to think of people you know whom I've run into, almost the only one is George Oppenheimer; I came across him at an art show-cum-cocktail staged for Allen Saalburg up at the Illustrators' Club. George is filling out nicely and looks like the vice-president of some solvent chain of haberdasheries, say Rogers-Peet. We exchanged tense, unfunny salutations and caromed off each other. I gather that his and Arthur Kober's play, a collaboration decorated by Claudette Colbert, tried out unsuccessfully somewhere up on the Cape last summer, but is scheduled to go on again this winter with Katharine Cornell, I think it is. . . .

·   ·   ·

Otherwise, "paucity" pretty well sums up what's been happening in these latitudes, especially insofar as work's concerned; I've been dithering about with a succession of snerd-like little ideas, trying to convert them into pieces for *The New Yorker* and achieving nothing more than daily frustration. Incidentally, a week or so ago, I finally cut the Gordian knot that bound me to my proposed lecture tour and backed out. Months of worrying about it at last convinced me of something I've always known—that I'm not a public or platform personality and that the obligation to prepare at least sixty pages of boffs had become a nightmare. The thing had been so arranged that I wasn't supposed to read from my past work, as so many lecturers do, but converse in a chatty, informal manner that would leave audiences helpless with laughter. In addition to which, the quid-pro-quo was very meager indeed. For better or worse, then, I'll leave that area of endeavor in the hands of Bennett Cerf and George Jessel...

·   ·   ·

*Perelman met the playwright Lillian Hellman in the early thirties, when she worked as a reader for Horace Liveright and lived in the Sutton Club Hotel with her husband, Arthur Kober. The hotel was managed by Nathanael West, and the Perelmans lived there as well.

LEILA HADLEY

513-A Sixth Avenue
New York City
February 22, 1956

Darling,

•   •   •

. . . Al and Dolly are back from a couple of weeks' trip to Florida; Al
had done a mural for a new megalomaniac hotel in Miami called the Eden
Roc, and was cuffed in there for a few days. His reports on the spectacular
vulgarity of the hotel make it tops in the field. Most of the rooms average
about $125 to $200 a day, and there are two 5-room suites on the roof costing
$1250 *a day* apiece. The manager told Al that these have a waiting list into
July. Out at the pool, says Al, the cabanas rent at an extra $100 a day, and
are occupied by garment-center types the color of cordovan boots wearing
jock-straps and eyeshades, arguing over gin rummy. By the way, it costs $5.00
for non-residents merely to enter the lobby, and the lobby's so churned up
with them that you risk life and limb to get through it. . . .

•   •   •

. . . [We saw] a fairly new play by Paddy Chayevsky, author of *Marty*
and much-touted successor or lineal descendant of Clifford Odets, called *The
Middle of the Night* and starring Edward G. Robinson. The play was thin,
amusing in spots, and Robinson was excellent. There's been an unconscionable
amount of publicity about Chayevsky locally — you know these annual Wunder-
kinds in New York — and it's now at the point where you wouldn't mind if
you never heard his name again. We also saw a quite pleasant production of
Uncle Vanya with Franchot Tone and Signe Hasso, well-acted but unfortunately put on in what looked like a cold-water flat down in East 4th Street — one
of those theaters-in-the-round where half the audience is facing the other half
and you have to remember to keep your fly buttoned. These off-Broadway
productions are getting an increasingly large play; used to be just Restoration
revivals at the Cherry Lane and Ibsen at the Provincetown, but they're
mushrooming all over the city.

•   •   •

KATHARINE WHITE

134 West 11th Street
New York City
March 16, 1956

Dear Katharine,
I can't possibly convey my gratitude for your letter; I was inexpressibly

183

touched that in the midst of your grief, you should have been concerned about me. This has been a very sad period for us all, and I still find it difficult to realize that Gus is no longer here.* We were, indeed, very close to each other and I couldn't begin to describe how sympathetic and appreciative he was to me and what a source of strength and guidance in my work. I speak of my own sorrow with reluctance, knowing that your and Andy's relationship with him was so long and intimate, and I have thought of your desolation again and again these past weeks and grieved for you.

Believe me also that I am very moved by your reassurance about my work, past and future, and your anxiety to help me continue it. It sustains me to feel I can call on you for counsel and friendship, and I shall do so unhesitatingly. Laura and I send you our love. I look forward to seeing you both very soon. As always,

*Lobrano died on March 1.

LEILA HADLEY

513-A Sixth Avenue
New York City
May 10, 1956

Leila darling,

. . . As you describe the daily round of life in Johannesburg, it sounds even more tepid and meaningless than I previously imagined, and that was plenty....Between this last sentence and this one—an interval of half an hour—two television repairmen arrived and pulled the innards out of the set reposing here beside my green couch. Quell your surprise at the thought of me having a TV set in the office; it's merely one I've been renting in the vain hope I could get some material out of the soap operas. After a couple of days of watching them, I was so sickened that I gave it up. . . .

. . .

I've been working recently—and only recently—and put in some long hard hours the past ten days or more on a piece for *The New Yorker* that I turned in yesterday. It's been such a barren winter that I certainly won't look back at it with nostalgia. I keep my fingers crossed now and hope that I can continue to be productive. The financial picture's very murky at the moment, and there are going to be an awful lot of bailiffs nipping at my heels unless I can rustle up some of the long green. Believe me, I'm nobody to consult these days on the advisability of pursuing a writing career, and specifically one as a humorist. I think it would be far less hazardous to join the circus and ascend one of those 75-foot diagonal wires balancing yourself with a parasol. At least, the suspense in that job lasts only a few moments.

.   .   .

Always and always,

JAMES THURBER

Erwinna, Pa.
June 28, 1956

Dear Jim,

This is a hell of a belated note inasmuch as I firmly resolved to write it at the time you were in Bermuda; procured your address there from Katharine White; got as far as typing an envelope and then mislaid it; and finally kept procrastinating right up until this moment.

However, if you can forgive such really unpardonable conduct, I can file my message, which is simply that I've been deriving tremendous enjoyment from *Further Fables*. They're witty and wonderful in every way, and I can't remember when I've had such acute pleasure from the printed word. Bless you.

With all best from us to you and Helen,

Yours,

LEILA HADLEY

Erwinna, Pa.
July 16, 1956

Darling,

.   .   .

Your vignette of — — and the arty-tarty set with their "dear old sausage" talk, etc., made my blood run cold — I know exactly how stultifying it must be and the glassy grins you must have to assume to get through such *emmerdant* gatherings. Nadine [Gordimer], I'm certain from everything of hers I've read and what I've heard about her through our mutual editorial connection and you, must be a friend precious beyond rubies. I'm sorry we missed meeting each other when she was in New York last. I remember Gus Lobrano telling me at lunch one day about having seen her the day before, and how much he thought of her and her work — an admission he reserved for a very small handful of people. But getting back to the horrors of social intercourse and the goons you describe, I do hope you're managing to keep a journal or even scattered notes now and then on what you're living through because (I again needn't bother to belabor the obvious) it may be fruitful material for the future. Every passing day makes me regret that I never developed this most useful,

185

and, in fact mandatory, habit of recording the daily trivia. I used to preen myself in an especially objectionable fashion about my memory, but I can tell you that it's become a most unreliable instrument of late as I develop into a wrinkled figure out of a valentine.

Scattered bits: . . . Latterly I've been toying with the thought of moving from [my office] at the end of September when my lease runs out, for several reasons. (1) It's so long since I've worked in real daylight, (2) Memories of frustration and inability to work there over long periods, and (3) a new and noisy set of neighbors across the hall called Poetry Inc. or The Poetry Society of London or some such ghastly title. There are three or four bemoustached Sarah Lawrence dikes in blue denim pants, swirling around an Indian aesthete named Tambimuttu who runs up-and-downstairs in a flapping jibbah. They made such an unconscionable racket the last month I was there that I was on the phone all day complaining to the landlord, until I forced them, by sheer unpleasantness, to install air-conditioning and keep their door closed so I could hear myself think. However, I'll probably maunder along there (having found out that I can't discover anything in the neighborhood as convenient or reasonable in price). . . .

• • •

Only yours,

LEILA HADLEY

Erwinna, Pa.
August 25, 1956

Darling Leila,

• • •

. . . I'm back here as of yesterday, preparing to take up our prairie-dog existence for an indeterminate period and faced with getting some saleable prose on paper. The Vineyard trip was an indulgence, our exchequer being what it is, but it *was* enjoyable; we stayed at the — don't flinch — Stony Squaw Inn in Gay Head, a small and very pleasant hostelry way out at the very tip of the Island. I can't recall whether we drove up there when you came up; anyway, it's a dramatic combination of Scottish moorland and precipitous, vari-colored cliffs, sparsely settled by the few remaining members of the Gay Head Indian tribe and their hybrid descendants. Laura, Abby, and I were the only guests for four of our seven days, and during the balance of the time, a self-composed British lady who read Alan Paton's novels while she ate and a pair of young honeymooners were the only other people in view. The place is run by an extremely nice young unfrocked rabbi named Weissberg who's married to an Indian girl; he teaches English in a Cuban high-school in the winter, and spends the summer at the Stony Squaw discouraging potential customers.

We saw a good deal of the Thielens—who, as you know, I like very much—also saw Lilly Hellman a couple of times, and not much of anyone else. Lilly's bought a house in Vineyard Haven, where she's putting the final touches on a musical version of *Candide*, score by Leonard Bernstein, that goes into rehearsal next month. We had a picnic lunch at her beach that was diverting, just the four of us, and were joined later by the young man who's writing the lyrics for her show, a poet named Richard Wilbur whose things have occasionally appeared in *The New Yorker* and who teaches English at Wellesley. . . . A night or two later we again encountered her at a mass beach picnic full of revoltingly smug people. . . . On this occasion Arthur Kober, Lil's ex-husband, was in evidence—fatter, more complacent, and less appealing than ever, and I had ample opportunity to ask myself how on earth I could have borne him in all those houses we shared in Hollywood during the Thirties, and how I could have put up with his ponderous cutie-pie antics. He was busily engaged in pawing La Hellman around the embers, a pursuit it was evident she wasn't deliriously happy about, but there. . . .

. . . Myself, I'm in the initial stages of a possible second job for Mike Todd, necessitated by the pinching financial situation. *Around the World in 80 Days* (which, according to Todd, is the most stupefyingly great colossal superb movie in history) opens October 17th at the Rivoli, and a month later in Moscow, the first picture from here to be shown in Russia since the start of the Cold War. Mike's flying over a planeload of 40 American newspaper publishers for that premiere, and the domestic opening is going to be preceded by such a barrage of publicity in *Life*, *Look*, etc. as you can't imagine. The picture now has a prologue delivered by Ed Murrow, an epilogue laden with gimmicks, and indescribable riches within (quoting Mike, of course— I've seen nothing but the rushes I saw all through last fall). In any case, Todd's made a deal with the Russians to co-produce six pictures, and it's one of the first two on the schedule he's talking to me about. It'll be an English dialogue job, transferring the Russian soundtrack into English I mean to say, to fit the picture, which he wants to retain in its entirety. This is as much as I know at present, and not having seen the film, I can't tell you more other than that he says it's a superb comedy about a travelling theatrical troupe in Russia. I'm due to hear more sometime late next week, if I can catch him between plane jumps. . . .

I haven't said anything thus far about your proposed book title, *Give Me the World** —I like it very much, and like the quotation you drew it from.

*Published by Simon and Schuster in 1958.

So does Herman E,* to whom I told it. It has a good, and commercially promising, ring. From your labors of typing 220,000 words let all kinds of blessings flow. . . .

•   •   •

Always,

*Herman Elkon, friend and diamond dealer from Belgium, living in New York (d. 1984).

LEILA HADLEY

Erwinna, Pa.
September 30, 1956

Darling Leila,

•   •   •

. . . — appears to be happy, if that's the word; privately, and I guess I've hinted at this, her new husband reminds one of an egg. I don't think there's a mean bone in his body, but of course, I've seen only the ones that show. . . .

•   •

3 p.m. next day

The cocktail gathering was what I expected, the same faces grinning like Cheshire cats, the women furtively sneering at each other's clothes and the husbands standing lumpishly about anaesthetizing themselves. Thanks to smoking twice as much as ordinarily, I feel like the old soldiers' home today and wince when a sunbeam strikes me. Luckily, few do between the house and the retiring chamber up here on the brow of the hill...

. . . [Mike Todd]'s assured me with his customary fervor that I'm to resume in his employ on the 29th of this month (October) but shows characteristic reluctance to put anything on paper. *Around the World in 80 Days* is advertised to open on the 17th at the Rivoli, and currently, in Hollywood, there's a battle going on about the writing credit, Todd demanding that I be given sole credit against the assertion by two anonymities that they really wrote the whole thing but will consent to my receiving third credit. I remain dignifiedly apart, wrapped in the old miasmal mist; since I haven't seen the picture, sole credit for the notices it may attract might be hazardous... I've been plugging along on things for *The New Yorker* as usual; one appeared in the Sept. 15th issue and another's scheduled for October 20th or 23rd or thereabouts, and I'm turning one in tomorrow, with the usual crossed fingers. . . .

•   •   •

Always —

ABBY PERELMAN

513-A Sixth Avenue
New York City
October 5, 1956

Dear Abby,

I'm writing to you from New York, a city between two rivers where we've been the past couple of days getting that dirty old country air out of our lungs and making a few totally unnecessary phone calls. The one card we've received from you seems to convey a pleasant satisfaction at your surroundings;* I guess this first week's a process of shakedown and adjustment, of digging your toes into the stirrups, and I may say that if you think you're missing anything here, you're mistaken. The trucks are clattering up Sixth Avenue splitting one's eardrums with their insane racket, the inhabitants are scurrying about like the proverbial ants (the proverbial ants complicate things by scurrying around like people), the new school on 11th Street is going up with the greatest tumult possible, and altogether, there appears to be little reason for anyone's dwelling here.

　　　　　·　　　　　·　　　　　·

There isn't much arresting news: Mr. Williams, postmaster of Erwinna for at least 35 years, has finally yielded to a Mrs. Lutz, and the postoffice is now located in Erwinna's one side street (which leads diagonally from Hager's chicken-house to Mrs. Eichlin's palazzo) in the former barber-shop. . . . Among the minor items of interest is the fact that a week from today, on the 12th, I'm making my debut on television — on a program called *Stand Up and Be Counted*, which, if you're near a set, you'll find on Channel 2, CBS, at 1:10 p.m. (early afternoon, not midnight). As I don't know who else is going to be on this, other than about two hundred mid-Western curiosity-seekers in the audience, I can't tell you any more, but if you're looking for kicks, tune in.

Last night, Laura and I had dinner with Herman Elkon at the Mexican place on 46th St., and afterwards proceeded to Costello's saloon, where we fell afoul of an old college acquaintance of mine — drunk, insufferable, and a nudnick of purest ray serene. By the time we managed to shake him, it was two o'clock in the morning and we were limp-wise rag-wise, i.e., as limp as rags. I wish I were in your shoes, curled up with a good hundred best books.

Well, doll, if you think I'm going to race on like this endlessly, giving all and taking nothing, you are not nearly half so intelligent as I have been advertising you to friends. So I'll call it quits right here and now, enclosing

*Abby had entered St. John's College in Annapolis, Maryland.

your devoted family's rapturous love and hoping you have plenty of everything needful, and if you don't please holler. Anyway, if there's a spare minute in which to jot down a line or two home, let us know how things are marching.

With all love,

P.S.   What are the banking arrangements there, and when will you need some booty? Let us know, and don't let yourself get to the brink.

E . B . W H I T E

Erwinna, Pa.
October 8, 1956 (?)

Dear Andy,

My thanks to you, shamefully belated, for *The Wonderful World of Cooking* by Edward Harris Heth, also the author of *My Life on Earth*, *Some We Loved*, *Told with a Drum*, *Light over Ruby Street*, *Any Number Can Play*, *We Are the Robbers*, and *If You Lived Here*. To say that I have read it all would be to draw the long bow; I am currently between "Veal and Shaw Sandwiches" (two parts milk-fed veal, one part G.B.S.) and "Aunt Dell's Breaded Pork Loin Roast." Aunt Dell, you recall, took London society by storm last winter and was much loinized.

Anyhow, I can assure you that I haven't got out of my wrapper since the book arrived, and the house is a perfect mess. But you *are* a sweet to send Mr. Heth's latest, and one of these evenings, you and Kay must come up for beer soup and Slippery Slims. 'Bye now.   Yours,

A B B Y   P E R E L M A N

513-A Sixth Avenue
New York City
October 19, 1956

Abby dear,

As you will gather from the enclosed, the picture's a smash and a wild success. Hy Gardner's prediction that it could play Madison Square Garden for years is especially encouraging to our future. By using plenty of influence, maybe I can get myself a job as an usher there. There certainly haven't been any hysterical demands for my services yet from any other quarter.

Why don't you take a half hour off from declining irregular Greek verbs — after all, you can't keep declining verbs *forever*, one must eventually suit you — and let your tired old parents know how it's marching at St. John's?

Or are you frisking around in your teddy with some couth midshipman?

Ever with love,

ABBY PERELMAN

513-A Sixth Avenue
New York City
October 22, 1956

Dear Abby,

A couple of today's catch, sparkling and flashing like Arctic bonita. Miss Kilgallen's estimate of 50 million is regarded as conservative hereabouts. Leo Shull, publisher of *Show Business* (and 9 other show-business sheets, says his mast-head), reports that at the post-premiere party, various film executives stated that Todd would gross between 80 and 100 million on the picture eventually.

In all this pandemonium, I sit untouched, scratching away at my Royal Noiseless and trying to outwit Gristede's. Other than a lunch date on Thursday with Todd from which I hope to emerge with another job, I haven't received any bids for my slipper from champagne-drinkers.

It was very good to hear your voice Saturday night and the intelligence that you're liking St. John's. Onward and upward with the arts!

Always,

P.S. A late bulletin: a pair of tickets for *A.T.W.I. 80 D.* were traded in the black market for $75.00. Where's my opium pipe?

LEILA HADLEY

513-A Sixth Avenue
New York City
October 24, 1956

Leila dearest,

. . . *Around the World* etc. opened last Wednesday night and is a sensational hit — columnists raving, tickets reportedly selling in the black market for $75 and $100 apiece, all that dreck. About all I can say is that it appears to have justified Todd's predictions, which everybody regarded as maniacal but which have in actuality been surpassed. I went to the opening (though I hadn't intended to but was cozened into it by Todd) and I must shamefacedly admit that it was very soothing to the ego. Dick Rodgers, Moss Hart, Max Gordon, and assorted ilksters were all over me like a swarm of gnats at the

191

party following the premiere, unleashing superlatives, and the press next morning, as these samples indicate, caught up the view halloa. The current *Life* carries a color section on it, along with letter-press ad infinitum on Todd, and all the other magazines will be popping off hereafter. In short and not to abuse your patience, the thing's a smash — and speaking realistically and personally, has done nothing but discombobulate me, disrupt my working schedule, and prevent me from concentrating for a whole blessed week. I wouldn't mind if I had a wee percentage, even an eighth of one per cent, of the take, but as you're aware, I was a journeyman employee and was paid off at the time — all of it now unhappily vanished. So what I now look forward to is the possibility that it will get me some immediate and rewarding assignment, whether with Todd or in Hollywood. The maestro and I have a verbal understanding that I'm to work on his next effort, and we were to have lunched tomorrow to seal the bargain, but I've just learned that he's flying to the Coast tonight — ostensibly to do some minor cutting and buffing, but I suspect rather to swell around Romanoff's — and our lunch date's off. As I'm somewhat sick of tagging after him like a coach-dog and having him put me off with promises, and as, furthermore, I need to make some dough fast, I'll keep my Hollywood kimono very available if any attractive offers develop from there.

· · ·

LEILA HADLEY

513-A Sixth Avenue
New York City
November 22, 1956

Darling, darling Leila,

· · ·

. . . [Publishers are] all alike, and the only rule of thumb I know is, get the biggest advance you can (which in turn forces them to try to recoup their investment) and be as demanding of advertising, publicity, etc. as is consonant with your own sense of decency. Publishers regard writers as vain, petty, juvenile, and thoroughly impossible (just as movie producers do — I think I may have once told you Irving Thalberg's classic: "The writer? The writer is a necessary evil"). So there's no use in attempting to be reasonable with them, or trying to prove that you, as a writer, are a person with a sense of dignity who's merely interested in their merchandising your work, a job they very frequently aren't equipped to do by any business standards. Fred Allen* told me

*Radio comedian and author of two books of autobiography, *Treadmill to Oblivion* and *Much Ado about Me* (d. 1956).

192

last year before his death—obviously before, it would have been pretty arresting afterward—that, having long been convinced that book publishing was infantile in its business approach, he contributed the money to support his first book's advertising campaign, his argument being that in show business, you behave like a rooster on a dung-heap and crow endlessly about your wares until the customers take notice. (The publishers contend that you only advertise a book to any extent *after* it's beginning to sell, which is certainly Alice-in-Wonderland thinking.) As a consequence, his book—aided by newspaper advertising, radio appearances, TV plugs, anything he could force the publishers into by a personal and day-to-day harassment—started selling and got into the mild best-seller class. I urge you, when your book appears, to be on the ground and participate in all the Martha Dean, Tex and Jinx, and TV panel merde you can evolve. . . .

> .   .   .

Your description of the Matterhorn of bills and the general difficulty of Making Ends Meet could subject you to some of the most tedious language you've ever read, and out of regard for you, I'll automatically censor myself. It *is* a murderous process getting by, and I don't know how I do it. And just wait till your chickadees get older and start attending private schools, college, etc. Incidentally and *re* your question "How do you manage two establishments?" kindly recall that it isn't two but *three*—the farm, the apartment, and this office. Three sets of utilities and rents and cleanings and all. Hence, the unimportant fact that all my insurance is borrowed on to the hilt, that we consume every last penny, that there's a respectable Alp of bills, and that I haven't a notion in the world where my tax obligation's coming from at the end of the year, all these parenthetical worries bumble around in the background of my mind waiting to fasten on me just as I'm falling asleep or trying to bestir myself in the morning. It would be nice to report that as a consequence of *Around the World*, these considerations have become academic, but thus far all I have are rosy prospects as yet. The ineffable Irving P. Lazar, who has arisen as the Hollywood end of Mark Hanna, assures me that various deals of mammoth advantage should be consummated soon, and ostensibly Todd still plans to have me work on his next venture. But these—along with a scheme I'm supposed to discuss with John Huston in the next fortnight and a couple of other chimeras—are only vaporous thus far. . . .

Well, I guess I'll have to conclude, Abby having just called to urge me to go up to the Museum of Natural History with her this fine, cold, and sunny afternoon. . . .

With all my heart,

LEILA HADLEY

513-A Sixth Avenue
New York City
January 5, 1957

Darling Leila,

.   .   .

The holiday season's just ended here with the usual wreckage bobbing in its wake—forgive the churning metaphors, but all the past wassail and the pressure of events have left me thoroughly unscrambled along with the other nine million victims. Most of December was—as you'll remember—the customary stampede to assemble all the depressing little gifts, cards, and nerds that people exchange; interspersed, in my case, by laggard attempts to work, the increasing hysteria surrounding Todd's picture, agents' yacketing from Mark Hanna and (a somewhat recent acquisition) Irving P. Lazar, who's supposedly handling my Hollywood destiny, occasional conferences about my forthcoming book at S&S, and excursions to the country. In between all this, I somehow finished a *New Yorker* piece that's appearing shortly—one did appear about Dec. 6 which I guess you saw, "Pulse Rapid, Respiration Lean, No Mustard"—and a day or two back, I consummated a new deal with *The New Yorker* that allows me much more freedom to work elsewhere, while still retaining the first-reading agreement I've had for years with them. So much for that. The screenwriting award from the film critics, coupled with their choice of *Around the World* as the best picture of '56, was, of course, satisfying, and impressed a lot of people too horrible to name. If the Academy follows suit, Todd's triumph will be complete, though he has attained a pitch of megalomania so lofty that I'm seriously concerned lest they go after him with butterfly nets. At the moment he's in the middle of a 6-day whirl around Europe starting at London and finishing at Belgrade, setting up theaters to show the film; within the past fortnight, he bought 4 paintings to the tune of $275,000 including a Frans Hals for a hundred grand, and put down option money on a 175-foot ocean-going yacht; and has been buying theaters in Chicago, Boston, and elsewhere in between holding hands with Liz Taylor at the Harkness Pavilion, where she lies ill with a crushed disc (needless to say, all meals being sent up from the Colony and Pavillon). I've seen him once since the picture opened about ten days ago, up at his apartment, and had an indescribable afternoon. He's now toying with my suggestion that we make *Don Quixote* with David Niven and Cantinflas, which I feel is a just and logical follow-up on *Around*, etc. The consistency with which he avoided me from the opening on, for no conceivable reason, occasioned me a touch of passing anguish, relieved, fortunately, by a stir of activity the past few days in other quarters.

194

At the moment, I'm just starting work on a high-pressure 2-week job for *Omnibus*, a takeout on the early days of burlesque to be called *The Big Wheel*, starring Bert Lahr. . . . January 19th, after the gruesome exercises incidental to being handed this film award, I am supposed to streak out to Hollywood for five days of conferring with David Niven on a television series in which I'd be cast as a sort of editorial consultant—no TV writing, ça va sans dire. I'm submitting to this junket, as you can guess, merely in the hope that something in the way of a small continuing weekly check may result. And, of course, while in Hollywood, it's not beyond possibility that a picture job could become actual, since Todd's opera has opened there and nationally to great success. The most recent, and very heartening, development here is that there may very well be a critical fuss over my new book, *The Road to Miltown*. Dotty Parker has reviewed it for the *Times Book Review* (the unofficial word is that it's to be the front page review) with superlatives, and if the other papers and magazines take their cue as they generally do from the *Times*, it could sell and pay back a bit of those heavy advances Jack [Goodman] has given me. I pinken with embarrassment at the awful way I've gone on above, but I'm endeavoring to convince myself at the same time I do you that out of all this *emmerdant* business, I can derive enough loot to experience a better year than this past one. Which was lean and filled with anxieties. . . .

. . . Edmund Wilson's new book, *A Piece of My Mind: Reflections at Sixty*, is very well worth reading. . . . It's the exact antithesis of the phoney High-Bohemia posturing you describe in Johannesburg literary circles, an accomplished and sensitive man with unquenchable curiosity writing about real things. The piece at the end of the book on his father is absorbing. . . .

Always,

L E I L A   H A D L E Y

Hibiscus Motel
Key West, Fla.
February 11, 1957

Dearest,

. . . The Hollywood session, foreseeably, got out of hand, the usual rushing around to lunches and the social entanglements the Hacketts created for me in their mistaken altruism; and I sped back to throw myself into the last stages of rehearsal of the television program covered in the enclosed newsprint. Anyway, what with assorted repercussions of this, the publication of *The Road to Miltown*, negotiations with Todd for the future, another TV venture, some hysterical radio appearances, and similar gurry, I was mired down right up to a couple of days ago when Laura and I entrained for Key West. We're staying until next Sunday, the 17th, to enable our emotional tuning-forks to quit vibrating, and judging from the analgesic effect of the sun and brine thus far, the interval ought to be beneficial.

I air-mailed a copy of *Miltown* to you six or seven days ago, which I trust has reached you by now. I think S&S did a fair job with it physically, all but the flaps; the lifeless and constipated photo of me on the rear jacket flap is one they chose from a welter I handed them, and in case it revolts you, I don't resemble it (in my own egotistical judgment) in the slightest. My mustache, since it was taken, is now as luxuriant and swooping as a subaltern's in the 11th Hussars. . . . The book got what I'd suppose anybody will admit was a practically perfect reception, and Dotty Parker's review—from which, I understand, further superlatives were excised—made some very gratifying points. I was in Hollywood on publication day, and while I hate to sound gleeful, I derived a certain twisted pleasure from being fawned on by some Yahoos I had detested for years. Their smarmy plaudits, of course, weren't induced solely by the book: chiefly by the success of Todd's picture and the screenwriting award, but it was all cumulative and delicious, and the fact that I was merely in town for a fast visit and oblivious to offers of jobs secured me an eminence attained only by Marilyn Monroe's bust in recent times...It seems unnecessary to note that Mark Hanna, who's on the beach-head gouging the ultimate drop of blood from parties interested in my unique and special services, is in a state of almost manic excitement. The pleasant success of the *Omnibus* show, coming on top of the picture and the book, excited the TV networks and has put Mark in a juicy bargaining position where he can treat their moguls with such contempt that they writhe in masochistic agony. Throughout the week preceding our departure for here, he was phoning me a dozen times a day to recount the jobs he was turning down, the megalomaniacal demands he was making, etc., etc. I quickly add . . . that neither of us lost sight of our enlightened self-interest, and that we've managed to garner a couple of showy financial blooms that may make life easier this year and next. Chief among these are Todd's next picture—on which I'm presumably pondering down here—and a TV spectacular to be done later this year for CBS. The latter was announced in this morning's papers in New York, according to a phone call from Mark an hour ago; he also says that *Miltown*'s made its appearance on the *Times* and *Trib* best-seller lists in yesterday's (Sunday) papers. So these, together with a project or two for later on still in the haggling stage, should give us all some assurance of short ribs on the table by Thanksgiving, if not a downright Strasbourg goose.

I know—or rather hope—that you'll overlook all the preceding vainglory,

196

understanding that it's somewhat heightened by twelve or fifteen months of very lean times, of continually swallowing my resentment as I labored away for *The New Yorker* and tried to conform to their mercurial — and parochial — whims. It was a rough year, and all through it, when I shook with anger at their august editorial decisions, their fussy little changes and pipsqueak variations on my copy, I used to sustain myself with the thought that one day I might achieve some independence: some status whereby their acceptance or rejection of a piece wouldn't be a life-and-death matter. I'm not at all sure that the present situation warrants my belief that I've attained it, and I'm superstitious enough to keep my fingers, loins, and toes crossed. But the plain fact is that all through last year, the realization became more positive that I'd fallen, virtually, into a state of servitude, and that somehow I'd have to escape from it. Soon after January 2nd, when my reading agreement with them expired, I laid my cards squarely on the table and told them I couldn't continue on the old basis. They gave all the signs of agitation they're capable of, enough to convince me that they *are* very anxious for me to go on contributing my zircons, and as a result, we worked out a much more flexible arrangement that will permit me to write elsewhere at the same time enjoying the advantages of their bonus-and-cost-of-living system. Hence, with what I should ostensibly be able to reap on the outside from movies and/or TV, and a general free-lance deal with *The New Yorker*, *This Week*, etc., it may not be beyond the bounds of possibility that I can make ends meet more easily.

•   •   •

Yours always, always,

PHILIP   WYLIE

513-A Sixth Avenue
New York City
April 12, 1957

Dear Phil,

•   •   •

I was very touched by your letter about Pep, and Roger Straus kindly sent me a photostat of the copy he received from you.* You recall as I do those nights at Siegel's unromantic palais de blintz opposite Jefferson Market Court, and the many bizarre companions of our youth, the Pussy Johanns, the Marcus Goodriches, etc., etc. (I don't mean to imply that there was more than *one* Pussy Johann or *one* Marcus Goodrich, because such a possibility is enough to unhinge a man.) But in any case, it is real nice to see Pep's work

*Farrar Straus & Cudahy had brought out *The Complete Works of Nathanael West.*

finally assembled in one handy vol, and to think how flattered and pleased he would be to see his work achieving solid recognition. I feel as positive as you do that had he lived, he would have been one of the truly important novelists of our time.

Yours,

L E I L A   H A D L E Y

513-A Sixth Avenue
New York City
May 20, 1957

Darling,

. . . [A]ll the merde that has been flying since the beginning of the year has been subsiding slowly, all the nightmarish phoning and offers and deals and schemes and tie-ups and publicity and truly sickening, time-wasting, ridiculous, and degrading activity that you could possibly imagine has (I devoutly hope) died down, and within the past few weeks, I've been able to return to some normal kind of program. I've just finished the first piece I've written this year for *The New Yorker*, and now plan to get in a few licks on a second before undertaking one of the two television projects I'm committed to, a thing called "The Changing Ways of Love" for a series starting this fall named *The Seven Lively Arts*. To scotch a highly mistaken notion contained in your last note, I am not only *not* ENORMOUSLY rich, as you suggest, but only just solvent, inasmuch as these past five months have been so hysterical with abortive schemes and trips to the Coast and putative deals that no real work got itself done. I don't doubt that when Todd gets back from Europe next month, he'll again begin badgering me to work on *Don Quixote*, which, as I've already made it more than clear, I have no earthly intention of doing. There were a couple of other grandiose deals as well, one to do the next Cinerama picture and another to do the screenplay of *Auntie Mame* that I've also had to eschew, so, in short, I'm back on the customary treadmill. I'm afraid the sobering conclusion out of all this is that I have no place in or affection for . . . all the sparkling people who inhabit Leonard Lyons' pantheon. . . .

I tried to get a line on what's become of —, and gathered she has sunk into that comfy social world of Pasadena where every prospect pleases and only Marx is vile.

In the department of useless activity of which I spoke earlier, I made

198

a couple of inglorious appearances, one at a book & author dinner in Richmond, Va. sponsored by their Junior League a couple of weeks ago, and another at a grand conclave of authors lasting three days here recently at the Biltmore. The first was a two-day ordeal replete with luncheons at country clubs, cocktail parties in historic old gardens, visits to celebrated old mansions on the James River, and unending exposure to that horrifying Southern cracker accent, which outdoes T. Williams at his most vinegary. My fellow-victims were Phil Wylie, Catherine Drinker Bowen, one of the writing Chute sisters, Charles van Doren, and Edward Weeks of *The At. Monthly*. The only concrete result of this keelhauling is a Smithfield ham which arrived this morning, perhaps a mute comment on my temerity in exposing myself...The authors' assembly thing took the form of a panel I was sucked into on (sic) "Emotional Problems of Writers"; our distinguished quartet there was composed of Dr. Lawrence S. Kubie, the w.k. psychiatrist, Elizabeth Janeway, Lilly Hellman, and me-ums. Kubie ran off at his facile mouth for thirty minutes with lantern-slides of weird diagrams showing Neuroticism on one side and Creativity on the other; Janeway burbled on about faith in one's deep wellsprings; Hellman made good sense with a blast at the artistic and political conservatism of young writers; and I spawned a blistering attack on Robert Ruark's boasts about his unquenchable speed as a writer and his general genius (which have been appearing with some regularity in the press locally in connection with the movie version of his drecky novel, *Something of Value*). So as you see I manage to keep myself away from any profitable endeavor with great success...

·   ·   ·

Always,

LEILA   HADLEY

Erwinna, Pa.
June 16, 1957

Leila darling,

This is a sweltering night in the opinion of one who has spent many of them in a lot of distant corners; when Pennsylvania sets its mind to it, Bangkok and Washington, D.C., seem almost like spas. It's Sunday night about 10:30 p.m., and other than a few trillion bugs and rodents, snakes and rabbits, I'm alone in the middle of these eighty-three acres, having elected to remain down here for four or five days and work while the kin swelters in town. . . .

·   ·   ·

I've been occupied, the past 2 weeks, with the TV script on "The Changing Ways of Love" for this *Seven Lively Arts* program starting in mid-autumn; a cumbersome, arduous, on the whole rather boring assignment, as it now

199

shapes up, and one that I suspect will prove a headache before I'm finished with it. John Houseman, who's producing it, is an old acquaintance of mine dating back to my Village days circa 1926; he's bright, much more so than most of the TV lordlings, and knows about words but may very well be tricky and devoid of humor, which in this case can lead to a mess. I undertook the job only on the understanding that it was to deal with fucking and that I proposed to show everything short of the actual grapple on the screen: in other words, a really bold and saucy take-out on the loosening up of inhibitions and conduct from 1918 until the present. Well, in the ritualistic fashion that all these things follow, I was then presented with a trio of Houseman's aids, who'd been busy amassing a hillock of research material—books, magazines, records, films, still pictures and what-not. In addition, they'd prepared a kind of syllabus as well, a formidable 70-page document tracing all the socio-anthropological aspects of the subject, a dead serious and indigestible kitchen-midden that I'm beginning to get the uncomfortable notion is expected to become part of my script. If it does, the whole business will deteriorate into a somber and humorless Ph.D. treatise that'll be deadly, so that's what I'm currently trying to circumvent...Meanwhile, the man who's planning to do "Aladdin" is phoning me feverishly every day, in an agony of anxiety, demanding when I'm going to whip out a treatment to show his superiors, and Mark Hanna, who got me into all these difficulties, is cooking and bubbling like a cracked earthenware tea-pot.* Oh, well, just the exigencies of earning a living...As for a certain 20-cent magazine called *The New Yorker*, I had another volcanic run-in with them which has effectively convinced me that by and large, that chapter of my life is closed. I really don't think that it is any longer possible for me to function there as I have done for almost twenty-five years. . . . Its whole character has changed; none of the vivacity, the gaiety it used to have is apparent any more. . . . I just won't take it any longer: i.e., if I can possibly make a living any other way, and people tell me I can.

Last Wednesday night, Laura and I allowed our better judgment to be prevailed on, and pretending we were led on by curiosity, went to dinner at Billy Rose's. Perhaps you've heard about this fantastic new house of his on East 93rd Street, but if not, it has 47 rooms, more or less, and used to belong to George Baker, the railroad magnate, and after his death to his daughter, Mrs. William Goadby Loew. Rose paid half a million for it, and has spent between two and three more in furnishing it. Items like the wall-to-wall carpeting—cost, $44,000—will give you an idea of the scale of the operation. The pictures are mainly Raeburns, Romneys, and portraits of that sort, massed up in front of which are Hebraic silver candelabras, ikons, and other religious

*With a score by Cole Porter and an all-star cast, "Aladdin" aired on February 21, 1958, and had a brief run in London a year later. Neither production was well received.

totems reflecting Billy's deep devotional preoccupations. In his bedroom, fully authenticated, is the massive writing desk on which Swift composed *Gulliver's Travels*, and facing it, a French military officer's brass travelling bed, in which Tom Thumb Rose sleeps. Also strewn around the premises are the forty or fifty Maillols, Rodins, Nadelmans, and assorted pieces of modern sculpture Billy has been acquiring the past few years and which weren't consumed in the fire at his Mount Kisco estate. I can't begin to describe the dinner party, but it may spring into high relief if I tell you who was there. The guest of honor was − −, accompanied by that indescribable harridan, his wife. . . . Then a real Miami-Beach pair named −, she a red-haired toots beset with those hyper-globes spilling out of the strapless sheath. We sat down at a table easily 75 feet long excised from a castle in Wales; Billy, at the head of the table, was barely discernible over the edge, and at that was, I believe, seated on a pillow. He and Joyce, his wife—who was seated at the other end— exchanged dialogue in a shout, cupping their hands around their mouths. This dialogue, and that of all the rest of the guests with the exception of Al and ourselves, dealt with boasts about worldly possessions, opinions on arts and letters delivered as certainties, and corresponding *bêtiseries*. There wasn't a single moment of the evening when one's cheeks weren't aflame with em- barrassment at the spectacle of how gauche and full of effrontery people can be. . . .

At this juncture, I pause and discover to my consternation that it has somehow become 1:10 a.m., and so I'm afraid I'll have to knock off. I find I haven't mentioned a number of things—the wonderful notices Nathanael West's omnibus has been getting, some of which you've perhaps seen . . . Kingsley Amis's *Lucky Jim*, which I've only just got around to reading but which I thought was very, very funny indeed (and could make such a funny film if Alec Guinness were starred in it); and a hilarious movie called *The Green Man* with Alastair Sim—and especially a sensationally comical man named Terry-Thomas. . . .

·　　　　　·　　　　　·

Only yours,

LEILA HADLEY

Erwinna, Pa.
July 27, 1957

Darling,

·　　　　　·　　　　　·

My own existence has been as uneventful as can be—work on my two TV projects, trips to the country most weekends, slow stultification. "The

201

Changing Ways of Love," the first draft of which I turned in to CBS, drew very pleasing reactions; I'll have possibly a week's rewrite sometime next month and then that'll be complete. Currently, I've just finished a treatment of "Aladdin," a boring experience to write and equally, I'm sure, to read; when that's approved — and as soon as a composer's been hired — I'll start grinding out the actual text. I can only describe my feeling about the project as one of immense lassitude, which I suppose is terribly naughty of me considering how important an undertaking some folks think it is. (What folks? Agents? TV executives?) Anyhow, as must be apparent, this is a caper I was cajoled into for no reasons other than financial, and I have to indulge in strenuous moral setting-up exercises every morning to keep from wrapping it around a paving-block and heaving it into 485 Madison Avenue. . . .*

I recently read *Close to Colette* by Maurice Goudeket, her last husband (it was reviewed not long ago by Maxwell in *The New Yorker*), and became interested in trying to read Colette again, after failing to some years ago. So I've just finished *Chéri*, and liked it quite well, though *The Last of Chéri* bogged me down. Oh, incidentally, I haven't thanked you for sending *Justine*, Lawrence Durrell's book. Do you want brutal truth or tactful evasions based on my gratitude for the trouble you went to? The book reminded me in many ways of Paul Morand's *Open All Night*; it had a sort of smart-alecky, desire-to-shock, Bohemian-snob overlay, attitudinizing at times to an almost insufferable degree, and the sex on occasion was practically laughable. By the time I finished I was convinced that its author was one of those Englishmen whose eye is especially made for spitting into, and that if I ever had the misfortune to meet him, that was exactly what I'd wind up doing. All this (while not blunt) will serve to indicate how I liked *Justine*. But mind you, it was very sweet of you, etc. . . .

> > > .   .   .

Yours, always yours,

*CBS headquarters.

JOSEPH BRYAN III

Erwinna, Pa.
August 6, 1957

Dear Joe,

Four Cohens in the fountain indeed. I don't suppose you're aware that I'm currently involved in writing a pro-Semitic musical starring Menasha Skulnick, the title of which is to be *The Rape of the Lox*...Well, you're aware of it now.

202

Except for a hurried trip in mid-June to collect Abby down in Annapolis, we haven't been south of the Amboys in donkey's years. However, as all the astrologers loxally (sorry, *loc*ally) are referring to 1958 as the Year of the Donkey, it's highly possible we may be down that way later on: in which case we'll certainly give you the soft word.

Love from Laura.   Yours,

ABBY   PERELMAN

Erwinna, Pa.
July 4, 1958

Dear Abby,

Laura and I, Gordon Kahn, and Marge & Alex King went to see *Ulysses in Nighttown* a couple of weeks ago, off-Broadway down near Lupowitz & Moscowitz. Zero Mostel was very good as Leopold Bloom, the rest of it — except for the language, which shouldn't have left the printed page — was pretty blah. Molly Bloom and Blazes Boylan, to mention only two characters, were hideously miscast, the latter by a leaping fagot, and in a part the whole essence of which is masculinity. . . . [T]he stage at all times was knee-deep in *feigels* — or *feigelich*, to give the correct Yiddish plural. And whatever else can be said about this great scene, Joyce certainly did not intend it as a ballet. I hope that it's open — undoubtedly it will be, as it's drenched with sex — when you return to NY, you should see it in any case...We also saw, quite recently, a TV dramatization of *The Great Gatsby* on Playhouse 90 or something, which was probably one of the most offensive perversions of a worthwhile book that has ever been projected. This nonesuch was . . . introduced, live, at four intervals during the production by a crop-eared chromosexual named Rod Serling, who bears a great reputation in TV circles as a Maupassant of the outer boulevards.

·   ·   ·

. . . Laura and I are figuring on staying here for approximately five weeks or so, then making a small tour by auto out to Long Island, then via Boston to Gay Head for a short sojourn. So we'll undoubtedly get to spend a day with you — and of course, will arrange it to fit in with your free time.

Everything else is under control; I've just packed up a small parcel which is going off to you in an Abercrombie & Fitch cardboard carton that will secure your social standing at your lodgings. Write me sometime when you're seated soaking your feet after the day's work, and meanwhile, all love from Laura and

Sid

ABBY PERELMAN

134 West 11th Street
New York City
November 12, 1958

Dear Abby,

Whether it causes a cynical smile to wreathe your lips or not, I may say that both your parents were disappointed that you weren't able to get up here last weekend. We haven't seen you in so long that I've almost begun to doubt your existence, and it's therefore heartening to know that the Washington junket is set. Our hotel reservations are confirmed at the Willard for Wednesday and Thursday, the 26th and the 27th. So (except for having to submit myself to at least one newspaper interview and a visit to a couple of bookstores in behalf of book sales) we can look forward to some pleasant eating, reminiscence, and viewing of beasts and masterpieces.

Locally, our apartment is now eighty or ninety percent refurbished — very grudgingly on the part of Landlord —, who is a madman to end 'em all. He has bombarded your mamma with a series of communiqués that are so insulting and unprovoked that we were left breathless, but not for long. I'll save them for your inspection. Perhaps his enforced connubial relationship with Mrs. —, who has frequently been compared with the eagle who pecked at Prometheus's liver, has addled his wits. Whatever the case, he certainly behaved like the fat little creep he is...When you again see the flat, you will be greeted as you gaze out from the terrace by something resembling the hollow socket of an ex-wisdom tooth. They've almost finished eradicating P.S. 41, so that you now have an uninterrupted view of a china shop on Greenwich Avenue, . . . defecating dogs, and tourists from Jersey, ecstatic at the prospect of Angus steaks at the Steak Joint.

· · ·

Another surprise that will greet you on your return is a Ouija board, presented to me by somebody at S&S because of my weird experiences with one on the occasion of my interview several weeks ago with Maurice Dolbier of the *Herald Trib.** Laura is more than suspicious of the fact that I have gone soft in the head because I was unwise enough to describe the uncanny messages I received, from outer space and from such worthies as George Ade, Ring Lardner, Bob Benchley, and Scott Fitzgerald. I believe, however, that she is merely jealous because she wasn't there.

You would have been diverted to the point of enchantment the other night had you seen the Siamese gibbon who was capering about in the pet

*Dolbier was the *Herald Tribune*'s book reviewer and a Ouija board devotee. Perelman's accounts notwithstanding, the messages received had a distinctly Perelmanesque ring to them (Dorothy Herrmann, *S. J. Perelman: A Life*, New York: Putnam, 1986, p. 224).

shop below my office. I happened to drop in there for some seed for Cha just as the proprietress was exercising this 13-month female gibbon, named Ginger. Her fur was a reddish brown, whitish face and tan palms, and she was twirling over and over, holding onto the woman's hand, like a Fourth-of-July sparkler. Then she'd leap up on the cages, tease the cats inside (who seemed to enjoy boxing with her), spin back to the ground, somersault, and bound up and down like a pogo stick. You've never seen such vitality and playfulness, interspersed with amorous bites at whomever she could reach.

•   •   •

It's now 6:30 p.m. and since I have to rush home, get into my Alexander Shields pleated-bosom shirt and pipestem trousers, flick cologne on my earlobes, and accompany your dejected mother to the play, I'd better stop here. There has been no time to comment on the content of your most recent letter, or rather, the generally fatigued tone of same, but I trust it was only temporary. In any case, and looking forward to seeing you in Washington....

Always with love,

W I L L I A M   Z I N S S E R *

513-A Sixth Avenue
New York City
November 24, 1958

Dear Bill,

Many thanks for the copy of your new book, which I can tell from a lightning perusal is going to make enjoyable reading.† Your refusal (which rhymes with perusal and differs from it only in one letter, a weird circumstance I intend to confront this magazine's editors with at my earliest opportunity)— your refusal, I say, to wrap yourself in Bosley Crowtherian pomp and pontificate about the movies endears you to everyone. I should tell you that I was right there before the TV machine on the occasion of your recent symposium with Susskind, Schary, et al., and that you were the only person in view who looked human or spoke with the slightest degree of sense. Which was a superhuman achievement, considering that you had nobody—apart from Justin Gilbert intermittently—with any measure of bite. Schary, who already back in 1936 was the most rabbinical of B picture writers at the writers' table we shared at MGM, has by now become so constipated with his own importance that

---

*Author (*On Writing Well*, etc.), editor, and, at the time, film critic for the *New York Herald Tribune*. Of all the journalism concerning Perelman generated during his lifetime, Zinsser's long article "That Perelman of Great Price is 65" (*New York Times Magazine*, January 26, 1969) is the most thorough and satisfying.
†*Seen Any Good Movies Lately?*

205

his smallest pronouncement sounds like Pitt the Elder. Susskind is a combination of detached retina-and-arsehole who is plainly destined to inherit the earth, a braying ass whose motto is "No matter what happens, no dead air — Keep talking." He told me on the occasion of our one meeting that he was a deck officer somewhere in the Pacific campaign (told it to me repeatedly, I should make clear), and his egregious, flatulent personality was displayed to fullest on your show. As for that v-p in charge of advertising at Columbia, he really was Mr. Prototype. I like to split my drawers when he burped out that complaint about John McCarten liking nothing. I had wondered prior to it what was holding it up.

Well, I hadn't meant to bombinate away at such length, and so I'll try to recover my poise by congratulating you and Caroline on the arrival of the new tenant. With your comeliness and Caroline's brains, it's obvious who will be class president at Vassar in 1979. Blessings on all of you, and let's see you soon. Yours ever,

EDMUND WILSON

134 West 11th Street
New York City
December 15, 1958

Dear Edmund,

Thank you for your kind note accompanied by the Bodley Book Shop catalogue . . . a veritable trove of priapic goodies — flagellation elbowing female impersonation (I swear I never knew that about Clyde Fitch), aphrodisiacal recipes nuzzling posthumous bawdy tales by Woollcott. And for the truly dedicated collector, who so blasé that he could resist Emma Calvé's Spanish shawl or the ivory-and-pure-silver opium pipe circa 1850 — not to mention Twain's celebrated essay on flatulence?

The references of mine in *The Most* [*of S. J. Perelman*] you speak of — tag-ends like Elbert Hubbard, Climmie Fadden, and Hashimura Togo — are simply the residue of a Providence boyhood. *The Sage of East Aurora*, in limp green leather, was a fixture on the calfskin throw of every mission table there from 1904 onward, and as a passionate reader of *Chatterbox*, the Mark Tidd saga in *The American Boy*, Montague Glass and the Wolfville stories of Alfred Henry Lewis in Hearst's *International*, Kirk Munroe, Frank Castlemon, Emile Gaboriau, and similar masters, I managed to acquire a lot of miscellaneous culture. As to how many readers dig references of this sort, the mere mention of a Globe-Wernicke sectional bookcase or Poslam Ointment seems to evoke as many memories in them as that celebrated cookie did in Proust. Since they can't recall even the slightest particulars of the Sakuntala or X's Anabasis,

206

I guess this phenomenon will have to be known hereafter as Zilboorg's variant on Gresham's Law.

I hope you and Ileana are planning to bestir yourselves shortly and hop down here for some high life. I'd love to show you the notes of some bewildering conversations I had recently via the Ouija board with Lardner, Bob Benchley, and Scott Fitzgerald.   Yours ever,

JAMES LEE*

> Grand Hotel
> Rome
> February 23, 1959

Dear Jim,

  •   •   •

. . . Let me say that your letter of 13th Feb. was one bright spot indeed, it's the only time since I've been here that I really have laughed out loud. Plenty of them awestricken sighs at the historic sights and satisfied belches at the guinea fodder, but no bellies. Your account of the lunch at Tim's with Laura and the ensuing levee you and Harve[y Orkin] held with Pepper Powell was a delight. I can only hope that your general account of Coal-Oil Laura's spending is hyperbole. The man at the Bankers Trust Company, as I was concluding my hurried last-minute preparations for departure, scratched his grizzled chin thoughtfully, and said, "I know you'll understand the spirit in which I say this, Mr. Pebblestein, but do you feel that you should continue this joint checking account with Mrs. Pebblestein whilst overseas?" I smote him across his fisk with a flounder I carry for the purpose and exited in high dudgeon. Surely it never occurred to me that this scrawny termagant whom I liberated from a life of shame in Buenos Aires would start buying blue mink at Revillon Frères the moment I was airborne. In the words of a dismayed child to Shoeless Joe Jackson in 1921 at the time of the Black Sox scandal, "Say it isn't true, Joe."

  •   •   •

To imbed a few pedestrian facts in this soufflé, a thing I'm always urging our friend Harvey to do, I'm enjoying this Rome bit very much; I have a very snug bivouac here at the Grand — which is certainly a hell of a fine hotel even if it does remind you of Saul Steinberg crossed with Mary Petty.† The

---

*Theatrical and television playwright and director, married to the actress Neva Patterson; with Michael Dreyfus, directed Perelman's "Malice in Wonderland — Three Hollywood Cameos" for *Omnibus* (1959); directed the first production, at the Bucks County Playhouse, of *The Beauty Part* (1961). At the time, Lee was renting Perelman's office at 513-A Sixth Avenue.
†A *New Yorker* cover artist whose work amusingly and meticulously chronicled the vestigial life of the Upper East Side, Edwardian dowager, with special attention to interiors and clothing (d. 1976).

small suite in which I find myself has, by virtue of my throwing out half the ginzo embellishments, emerged as a tasteful drop, and the service is only great. (As we used to say way back there during "Malice.") As for the town, I could foresee a situation where it might take a hell of a lot of prying to get me out of here. It's a great city to walk in, as I used to say about London, and I'm often to be seen, hands clasped behind my back, peering into all those anticas and libreros along the Via Babuino and the Via della Due Machelli. Many people mistake me for Anatole France, but his prose is fuzzier, and his pecker longer...The job itself is going along O.K. I regurgitated a little story thread-ed with ambergris that Mr. Lombardo, the head shamus of Titanus, slapped his thigh over, and as of tomorrow—as soon as I select the least attractive of four secretaries submitted for my approval—start dictating a treatment.* The girls they have chosen, as I understand it, are not actually typists; it seems that they are the runners-up in a competition held at a small town called Mam-malia in the north of Italy to see who could support a fiaschi of red wine on her bosom with hands interlaced behind her. None of these contestants won out, but our casting director—who, interestingly enough, has goat's feet, like Pan—tells me that they all sport knockers that would put Messalina to shame.

Well, friend, I have to go downstairs into the Palm Lounge and have a cup of tea instanter with − and −, as frightening a pair as ever stepped off a Gothic church, so I'll bid you adieu. . . . Meanwhile, a moist and sensual kiss to Neves and all the best to the rest of the midshipmen and Wrens. Please write soon again when you can. With all best,

Yours ever,

*The film, which was to have starred Harry Belafonte, was never made.

CHAIM RAPHAEL*

Grand Hotel
Rome
March 2, 1959

Dear Rab,

I wouldn't in the least blame you for cutting me dead in Rotten Row the next time we meet, considering how delinquent I've been in acknowledg-ing your note. However, these Eyetalians have had me bound hand and foot, which is a hell of a way for a man to try to write a movie, but like the great Harry Houdini, I am out to show them that you can't down a Hebrew. We

*Then an official of the British Treasury, writing books on Jewish history and mysteries under the name Jocelyn Davey. Perelman described him in an interview with Mary Shenker as "the Marcel Proust of British Jewry."

proved it with Disraeli and Sholem Aleichem, and by the eternal, we'll do it again.

I am of course overcome with delight at the prospect of insinuating myself into the Reform [Club] for however brief a period, just so I can write an offensive letter on its stationery to Bennett Cerf (or maybe even post a letter on its bulletin board worded somewhat as Queensberry did to Wilde). The only trouble at the moment is that I can't look forward to any definite date when I know I shall be in London. I have to complete the first stage of the phantasm I'm spawning by March 23rd and immediately return to New York for three weeks, after which—approx April 15th—I must return here to work further on the thing. This being the case, I don't think it will be much before summer that I'll get into London. So may I have a rain check marked when, as, and if?

Should you, on the other hand, be coming down to Rome to displace a few fettuccini or should you be planning to weave some maidenhair fern into your locks and run naked in the Forum Romanum, I shall be at this address (with the exception of the above-noted 3 weeks) and will be enchanted to buy you the best dinner in Rome. Which, if you know us Hebe gourmets, means only one thing—the best in the world. So long, and do let me in on the gen when, as, and if.   Yours ever,

JAMES LEE

Grand Hotel
Rome
June 18, 1959

Dear Jim,

Hail from the catacombs. The temperature is rising, the tourists are pouring in like locusts, and none of us is getting any younger. . . .

.   .   .

Abby got caught in the Italian Lines ship strike last week and didn't sail aboard the *Giulio Cesare*; instead she flew over by KLM, reaching here safe and sound. We are currently installed in what amounts to the entire second floor of the Grand Hotel and are entitled to use the diplomatic side entrance, fly a flag over the hotel like Grace Kelly, and issue our own stamps. The sightseeing (from what I hear Laura and Abby saying as I sit here and work) is terrific. Next Thursday, the 25th, we move down to Sorrento for approximately five weeks, where I continue work and they continue loafing. Do drop us a line at the Hotel Carlton, via Correale, Sorrento, if you find strength. Our love to Neva and yourself; leave us know all about the adoption, Huck Finn, and sex, in that order.   Yours ever,

N E V A   P A T T E R S O N   and   J A M E S   L E E
                                                            Grand Hotel
                                                            Rome
                                                            August 1, 1959
Dear Neves and James,

To begin with the excessively mundane and then progress to flatulence, let me say that our business relationship is just corking. Neva, if I were the head of a great soul-less corporation, I'd certainly retain you as my head book-keeper: not so much because I respect your math, but I think you'd look simply yummy in one of those crisp white shirtwaists with sleeve-guards, all kind of cinched in at the waist and with your hair in a high forward roll. God, it makes me horny just to think of it...Anyhow, your statement of telephone biz at the Sixth Avenue shop was dead accurate, and many thanks for rent deposits to Bankers Trust.

Well, friends, if you were strolling down the old Via Barberini and were confronted with a fat greaseball in an ill-fitting suit of white tussore, his hair roached across his forehead and agleam with bear's grease and his arms en-circling a couple of quiffs, you'd have a pretty good approximation of yrs. truly, except that I'm just throwing in the detail about the quiffs to build myself up. The zook dep't is just parlous hereabouts, and anyone who in future tries to expatiate on glorious Italian womanhood is going to have a scrap on his hands. Call me Philistine if you will, but in my so-to-speak lay estimation, they are a pathetic lot. Many is the evening when Laura, Abby, and I have sat on the Via Veneto examining what passes for femininity, and the verdict is strongly negative. "If," as Laura has frequently pointed out, "I or any woman of my acquaintance in America were to unsheathe the girdle from our but-tocks and strut along like that, tossing first the one flange and then the other as these coozies do, we would be run in by the Watch and Ward Society, strung up at the forward gangway, and given six dozen with the cat." And as if all this were not enough, their taste in clothes is enough to make one's blood run cold. Cabbage roses are the big number here this year and those large coif-fures which knowledgeable friends assure us derive from squirting white of egg into the waveset. Look, Jim—you think I'm being picky, don't you? Well, I admire as much as you do what a certain genius named Robert Herrick has aptly called that brave vibration each way free, but it just doesn't send you here. I mean, on Madison Avenue you can get so worked up that you have

210

to duck into Chock Full O'Nuts for a cooling chocolate frosted and a chance to assemble your scattered wits, but in the Eternal City, it's just rotating fat. Of course, one must make allowances for the fact that Laura and Abby are right there at all times, commenting on it and pointing out the little imperfections that I might otherwise be tempted to ignore...

The trip South took an even three weeks, all of which we spent at Positano, a perpendicular little town some 37 miles from Naples. It was an attractive hotel, was the Sirenuse, but the fodder proved monotonous, and Positano's too small to shop around for other places to eat. L. & A. got in a certain amount of bathing (very pebbly beach, and lots of jelly-fish on certain days), and I stayed indoors dictating verbal fantasies to my idiot secretary. The girls also did some sightseeing at Pompeii, Paestum, and Herculaneum that they stated was rewarding, and the three of us spent an aesthetically satisfying but otherwise depressing weekend in Naples. Heat, filth, hordes of beggars, etc. On the drive back to Rome, we found by sheer luck two very worthwhile bits of antiquity, the excavations at Baiae and the cave of the Cumaean Sibyl. L. & A. have done a lot of looking at antiquities in Rome, and as of three days ago, departed on a 3-week swing around Perugia, Florence, Assisi, Bologna, Venice, Verona, and Ravenna. They're due back here August 21st, and on the 25th, leave for a final ten days in Paris before sailing Sept. 3rd for home on the *United States*.

I meanwhile have been beating the tar out of that old screenplay, and have just finished the first draft. This means six more weeks to the tape, and I'm planning to shove off from here for London on Sept. 17th. With the usual dilatory tactics that seem to apply here, I'm sure they'll try to muscle me into remaining longer, but I've been away from what I really want to do too long, and I have to get back to England to do some legwork on those English pieces I've promised *The New Yorker*. Also, it's been kind of a lonely experience working here in a vacuum, nobody to gas with or laugh with, and the only people you encounter are horrors out of your past you thought you'd finished with years ago. . . .

Well, dears, this is a hot Saturday afternoon in Roma, and for want of anything better to do, I'm going down to a shoe shop I spotted in the Galleria Due Machelli this morning after my lunch at Babington's Tea Rooms and order myself a pair of light canvas shoes to wear in Erwinna when I'm standing picturesquely in front of the barn showing the hired boy where to dump the manure. I couldn't squinch up close enough to the window to make out whether the shoes cost 180 lire or 180,000, but if it's the latter, then I'll be the only man in Bucks County with canvas shoes costing two hundred and eighty-eight dollars. Fuck it, I say; easy come, easy go.

I know how easy it is to forget your old friends, the ones who really matter to you, when you're caught up in that film-colony set at Friedkin's, but if you get a minute, do write. You can't know how impressed those hall-porters become here at the Grand when they see that Malibu postmark.

Love from us all, and Neva, I'll get you into that shirtwaist yet —

I. J. KAPSTEIN

134 West 11th Street
New York City
October 15, 1959

Dear Kap,

Delighted we're going to have a bit of *gelechter* next week. Laura's coming along; some deep masochistic instinct, I suppose.

This is just a note to ask whether it'll be necessary to wear a dinner jacket for the Friday evening caper; at my back I seem to hear / Time's wingèd mothball hurrying near. Could you drop me a fast word on this?

All best, and see you presently. Yours,

KARL FORTESS *

513-A Sixth Avenue
New York City
December 5, 1959

Dear Karl,

A *macchayia* to receive your letter (first time I've ever tried writing the word "delight" in Yiddish, in English). Which, of course, is a subtle cue into saying that I also read the note you did in the *New York Times* about the story of Ruth, the midrash, etc. I am half inclined to agree with e. e. cummings, who voiced the thought to me about a year ago, that Edmund Wilson is at the bottom of all this heavy Jewish preoccupation in films, Broadway, and the like. The current success kid in this division, as you undoubtedly know, is Padraic Chayevsky. Wild horses wouldn't drag me, and I trust you also, to *The Tenth Man*. In his review of same in the *Village Voice* recently, Gilbert Seldes compared it unfavorably with *Abie's Irish Rose*, which he said was a far better piece of dramaturgy. (Or should I say "dramaturgid" and then have Bennett Cerf take credit for it?)

• • •

Yours,

*Painter.

212

JACK LEVINE *

513-A Sixth Avenue
New York City
December 30, 1959

Dear Jack,

I suppose that since no guest book was in evidence when I visited your show yesterday, I should have scrawled my name on Charles Alan's collar, but you know how hard it is to write on glazed surfaces with a ball-point pen. At any rate, I do want to signify what tremendous regard I have always had for your work and what deep satisfaction these latest paintings gave me. Your ability to maintain the standard of achievement you do strikes me as nothing short of extraordinary. I wish you long life.

Sincerely,

*Painter.

JOSEPH BRYAN III

513-A Sixth Avenue
New York City
January 7, 1960

Dear Joe,

Many thanks for sending along the *Punch* review of *The Most of*. English publishers being what they are (i.e., chary about wasting stamps), I never get to find out what the press says about any book of mine until years later, and then only in red ink on the publisher's statement. Did I, incidentally, tell you . . . what I saw in a bookshop in Nice last April? I was walking along the rue de Malfésance or whatever the hell it was, and there in a display case was some book like *Crazy like a F[ox]*, I don't remember which, sandwiched in between Sacher-Masoch's *Venus in Furs* and the standard work on flagellation, *A History of the Rod* by Dr. Pleasureably Birchley. Some critic once wrote that I give pleasure to a small coterie. Now I understand what he meant.

•   •   •

Yours,

I . J . KAPSTEIN

Erwinna, Pa.
June 20, 1960

Dear Kap,

As president and board of directors of the Vicarious Boot Company,

213

I invariably get a vicarious boot when any friend of mine goes west of the International Date Line; and I can't tell you how your impending hitch in Saigon has set my saliva to flowing. You must already have realized that you're one hell of a lucky son-of-a-bitch to get a free trip to Southeast Asia. Myself, I never got to Indo-China (Siam, Malaya, Burma, Indonesia, and, of course, Hong Kong I am reasonably familiar with, but the situation was so disturbed in I-C on the two occasions I tried that it was no dice.) In particular I envy you the possibility of getting to see Angkor Wat, which ça va sans dire — you see I'm already adopting one of the mandatory tongues you'll employ — is one of the great sights of the world. Anyhow, it was great news, and it's unnecessary to add that you and Stella are in for a tremendous experience. If at all possible, you should get to Hong Kong, which is all the well-known romance of the East — Conrad, Maugham, everybody rolled up into a ball and then some. Also try to get over to Bangkok. Am told it's gotten much more Amerikansky-tempo than when I was there last, but it will take a lot of spoiling. You can pass up all of Malaya, and especially Singapore, which is Jersey mosquito country and strictly for goyim. Indonesia is a different matter, and if the chance permits, break your ass to get to Bali — really the Garden of Eden. . . .

Re your friend Jack Hawkes and his interest in Pep. I am as you know so tired of these inquiries; half my mail nowadays comes from young folks working for Ph.D.'s and so forth who admire his work and implore me to allow them to ask a few details etc., etc. I don't want to sound like a curmudgeon, but you can believe me that if I were to answer all their questionnaires, inquiries, and catechisms, or to open the files they suppose I have containing unpublished treasures and revealing letters, I could fill up a 56-hour week. In any case, and for your own information, I am myself working on a project which will involve certain material on Pep, reminiscences, und zo weiter. You will appreciate, hence, that it would be soft in the head if I were to disgorge anything that might be of personal use. We are all of us duly delighted and touched that this posthumous fuss has gone on about Pep; but at the risk of sounding callous, I'll just have to return a categorical "nein" to Mr. Hawkes' request.

Everybody here is O.K. and we're just after seeing Abby graduated from St. John's very creditably. Her plans now are indeterminate, as undistinguished from ours. I look forward to a hot summer of work here, and maybe a week on the Vineyard. However, I'll sustain myself with rosy pictures of the two of you in the Far East — and for Christ's sake, snap up all the sculpture, especially Khmer, you can lay yours hands on. My love to you both, and if you don't get the chance to write before taking off, please do so from there. Remember, after a short exposure to the Lord Buddha, you may need a contact back here to send you whitefish and bagels. One gets pretty homesick for the old *meicholim*, down there where the dawn comes up like thunder over China 'cross the bay.

  Go with God —   Yours,

CHAIM RAPHAEL

Erwinna, Pa.
July 13, 1961

Dear Rab,

  I know that a long-standing Joyce scholar like yourself will have been familiar from boyhood with the term "agenbite of inwit," which Lord Jim uses throughout *Ulysses* to signify the very deepest kind of remorse. And I am reduced (or elevated) to using it in order to convey a smidgen of what I feel at not having written you before this. But it is all true, my ululations when you were last here about how hard I was working on this play, the report you latterly saw in *Time*, and your own suspicions that I was bent over a smoking typewriter. All the weeks since your departure blend into a gray furk (amalgam of fuzz, murk, and fusc) of grinding labor. I am now, Gott sei dank, somewhere in sight of the finish line, and indeed, hope to have the first draft complete within the next week. Since rehearsals start exactly five weeks from now, it's none too soon. Mike Ellis, the deus ex machina at the Bucks County Playhouse, is still in a state of utter ignorance about the subject of the play, the cast of characters, and the whole damn venture, which I consider a major triumph of bulldozing and doubletalk on my part. . . .

  First of all, let me quickly say that I'm more than ever keen, determined, and in fact, psychologically prepared for a remove to London this autumn; and that I'm inexpressibly cheered by any advance preparations you'd be kind enough to make to facilitate it.

•   •   •

  . . . In whatever case, I trust that through the above, there has slowly been forming over your tonsure a fleecy cloud in which you and I are visible, each equipped with young ladies whose measurements are roughly 37-22-31, tooling down the Loire Valley, lolling at Beaulieu, participating in orgies at Fregene, roistering at the Osteria dell' Orso in Rome, and generally behaving like high-class Jewish wastrels. *Sérieusement* (seriously, that means, because I am now totally oriented to a life of extreme pleasure come the fall) I think we might have some high times if we start planning right now.

  . . . Broadly speaking, I feel I should not settle too far out of London, as I do want every opportunity to absorb as much of the metropolitan life

215

as I can. Incidentally, and though it may not be necessary to add, all the foregoing plans apply to me on a solo basis, as it's unlikely that Laura will be coming over with me. She's vaguely contemplating a trip to India at some time
during the winter, but as yet has not developed it much beyond the wishful
stage. Hence, in outlining my needs for digs to anyone, you can indicate that
I shan't require too much space, and I therefore think that anything in the
nature of a house that arises (as opposed to a flat, which would be far more
sensible) should be definitely snug. . . .

All this egomaniacal concentration has obviously prevented my saying
how glad I am to hear that your book was indeed accepted for publication
by Little Brown. They are a first-rate firm, as I know from various friends
like Ogden Nash who speak very highly of them. Also — necessary to say
even? — I will be more than ready to help publicize, furnish blurbs, and read
advance galleys (preferably bound), so don't hesitate to tell L-B to get in touch
with me. I very likely may know or be able to suggest influential persons to
help the book along the road, and don't be shy about enlisting me.

•   •   •

Writing you reminds me that I promised to let Patty Englund know when
activity starts in this show of mine, since, of course, I want her among the
pals I'd like to sail with me on this perilous passage. Let's just hope it won't
duplicate the celebrated affair of the *Marie Celeste*, and that *The Beauty Part*
won't be sighted listlessly drifting off the Azores, its crew missing and every
indication that some horrid tragedy overtook it. On which grisly note, I
pinch your claws, wish you all possible success in your chosen career (woman-
izing and refined peculation of Her Majesty's inland taxes), and beg your
return favor.   Ever yours,

P.S.   Have you happened across a curious volume called *The Best of
S.J. Perelman*, recently issued by the Reprint Society via Heinemann? It says
on the jacket "Special edition for World Book Club members only," and contains what is perhaps the most glowing encomium I've ever received in the
form of an introduction by A.P. Herbert.* While I'm enormously indebted
to Sir Alan (whom I had the pleasure of also introducing, but to Benny Goodman), this volume will be the straw-that-broke-the-camel's-back in my relations with Heinemann for about five separate and distinct reasons, all too
tedious to burden you with now. But the minute this show's off my back, I
will move like the terrible swift sword in the celebrated hymn. Goodby William
Heinemann, hello Hamish Hamilton (or whoever).

*British humorist (*Misleading Cases in the Common Law*) and member of parliament (d. 1971).

216

WILLIAM ZINSSER

Erwinna, Pa.
August 29, 1961

Dear Bill,

. . . I've been mired in a slough of write and rewrite of my forthcoming show, *The Beauty Part*. . . . [W]e open a 2-week stand here at the Bucks County Playhouse on Sept. 18th. I dare offer no predictions other than that the ticket stubs will most certainly be incorporated at some future date in the pulp used at the Riegel Paper Corp. up the river. As cast, we have Bert Lahr starring, supported by a cast containing many pals and co-workers from "Malice in Wonderland." . . . Anyway, I'm hoping that besides being a swift kick in the ass to a number of pretensions, it emerges with some commercial appeal. The gods usually reward such modest aspirations by bloodying an author's nose, so I'd better dummy up.

As one who's spent the entire spring and summer indoors, I'm a fine authority on anything, but I guess it has been a traditional one here in Bucks County. Laura vacationed on the Coast for a couple of weeks, during which time I up and bought a fearsome machine called a Bush Hog that gobbles up weeds and honeysuckle in an alarming way. It weighs ¾ of a ton and can be operated only by a man driving a Russian-style tractor fifteen feet high, but it makes a pretty picture as I peer out at it through my besmogged windowpane. From time to time, I teeter on my heels uttering a choice bit of dialogue out of Trollope, and then, refreshed, resume my place behind the Royal portable.

Anyhow, this is chiefly to say that we're still vertical, if not sassy, and hope that all the Z.'s are likewise. Both Laura and I send all best to you and Caroline, and one of these days, when the smell of greasepaint evaporates, I hope we can have one of our infrequent parleys at the Blue Ribbon or the restaurant of your choice. It's too seldom.

As always,

FELICIA GEFFEN *

Erwinna, Pa.
October 24, 1961

Dear Felicia,

.   .   .

I don't want to seem to crow, but did you see this morning's review of *Catch-22*, the Joseph Heller novel I tried vainly to sponsor at our last Grants

---

*At the time, assistant secretary-treasurer of the National Institute of Arts and Letters, to which Perelman was elected in 1958.

Committee meeting, . . . in the *Times*? If a pantywaist like — was that impressed (and Maurice Dolbier several weeks ago in the *Trib* was even more impressed, but with sense) I can't make out why I was the only affirmative voice on the committee. I still think *Catch* is an extraordinary piece of work and hope my colleagues can reconsider it.*

Yours,

*Heller finally received a grant in 1963, for which Perelman wrote the citation.

CHAIM RAPHAEL

134 West 11th Street
New York City
January 23–March 9, 1962

Dear Rab,

.   .   .

If this letter takes as long to complete as it has thus far, it may be kind of a history of our times, embracing the entire decade of the Sixties. I forget what happened when I reached the bottom of the previous page; it was either a blonde or a phone call or both, and I'd like you to feel, Rab, old man, that the only reason I hung you up for six weeks was pneumatic bliss. In point of fact, I did have to go out to Los Angeles for a couple of weeks due to the illness of my mother, who lives there, and subsequent nursing-home complications chillingly akin to Muriel Spark's *Memento Mori*. I was once more oppressed with the uncanny way that Los Angeles becomes uglier each time I revisit it. They've reached what can only be described as the nadir, except that I'm sure it'll be worse next time I see it. Incidentally, while dining with a couple out there, I was privileged to hear one of those Hollywood remarks you always think satirists confect but which happen all too often. I chanced to mention the name of a producer out there at Twentieth Century-Fox whom we'll call Charlie Brackett, though that is his real name. "Charlie BRACKETT?" my host exploded. "Why, he's the stingiest man in Hollywood, Sid! Do you know something?" he asked earnestly. "Do you know that Brackett is still driving the same Jaguar he bought fifteen years ago?"

It gives me pleasure to add further that I'm feeling a hell of a lot better in general than I was when I wrote the previous page. I'd spent most of the winter in a state of what I believe Cyril Connolly referred to as accidie, a combination of despair and sloth. Had been unable to write anything, immersed in the gloomiest possible thoughts, etc., etc. — I hope you're familiar with the condition without ever having succumbed to it. Anyway, I like to think I've emerged from it; at least I've recently sold *The New Yorker* a couple of pieces, done some more rewrite on the play, and have stopped playing a Yiddish Hamlet, a part I really have very little talent for...

It's hardly likely that I'm going to be able to get over to Europe this spring, my exchequer resembling as it does an aged scrotum at the moment, so I wonder whether you have any travel plans involving America. I fervently hope so; perhaps you could be lured back to Bucks County to see what it looks like in the spring? . . . Bucks County reminds me that throughout this past winter also, prejudiced parties have assembled a TV pilot film based on that country series of mine called *Acres and Pains*.* This is now being shown to unwary advertising agencies and prospective sponsors, and if sold, would result in a TV series that might earn me a few groschen. Need I say with what alacrity I'd spring to spend them in the U.K.?

Well, I'm clinging to the Reform Club application in the hope that despite my shortcomings as a correspondent, you still love me and will intercede with Mr. Bell *next* autumn. But apart from such minor considerations, range yourself beside the carpenter of Galilee as a model of toleration and forgive this long period of seeming neglect. I think of you very often and my lips move in a silent prayer for your welfare and prosperity. I hope you're up to your groin in beautiful women, yellow doublones, and critics' encomiums. And if all your faculties aren't too abstracted with the foregoing, do write.

Yours ever,

*Reynal and Hitchcock, 1947.

KATHARINE and E. B. WHITE

Erwinna, Penn.
August 10, 1962

Dear Katharine and Andy,

Laura and I were desolated that our brief trek to seaboard Maine coincided with your New York trip, but Bill Shawn's word that you're both as healthy as Four-H winners helped assuage our disappointment. At one point, heading north on Maine 6 (?) we saw a marker indicating Blue Hill off to the right, and dallied with the notion of just driving in to mess up your ash-trays and sneer at your hand-towels, but there was some motel reservation ahead beckoning to us. Incidentally, and I speak with the franchise of a Rhode Islander, the best blueberry pie (maybe huckleberry) Laura and I ever ate is to be had at Moody's diner, an unprepossessing structure somewhat south of Lincolnville on Maine 6, as I recall. After my second helping, I groaned weakly, buttonholed the wonderful lady who'd baked it, and offered her an annual stipend of $11,500 to take over the job of pastry chef here at Erwinna. George

Ade's description of this toothsome dish in *Subtreasury* would, of course, be embroidered on her apron, I specified.* But she felt she didn't want to emigrate to any tropical climate like Pennsylvania.

We were enchanted with the houses we saw in the towns we passed through, and a couple (Saco and Thomaston) were really jewels. Subsequently we bivouacked at Hanover and spent some time with Jerry and Claire Salinger. Jerry's in fine shape (though looking a little hunted because of those acolytes who steal up his mountain in their bare feet to get The Word) and is just about to build a small garage with a workroom above it. This appears to be his only concession to notoriety.

I'm faltering through what I hope to God is the final rewrite of my play, now set for rehearsal in late October. The cast is almost entirely set . . . and we open in New Haven Nov. 24, do a week there and three in Philadelphia, and open in N.Y. December 26. Since eighteen months have gone into this venture, it'd be nice to have it stick around for a while, but it's a medium as fickle as they come. . . .

We think of you both very often and send you our love.

Ever,

*"It is the *Pièce de Résistance*, the *Dénouement*, the Dramatic Climax, the Grand Transformation, Little Eva ascending to Paradise. Nothing comes after it except the Pepsin Tablet and the Hot-Water Bag" ("The Waist-Band That Was Taut up to the Moment It Gave Way," reprinted in the Whites' classic anthology, *A Subtreasury of American Humor*).

E D M U N D   W I L S O N

134 West 11th Street
New York City
December 24, 1963

Dear Edmund,

Your Tutankhamen bat enclosure succeeded beyond your most fiendish expectations, inducing a fright just this side of a coronary seizure. It arrived this morning, forwarded by *The New Yorker*. It just happens that I was out on the town last night, and as a result of being a bit over-convivial, had a quaking hangover when I opened your letter. As the bat fluttered out at me, I struck out much in the fashion of W.C. Fields in *The Bank Dick* lashing at the small boy with the cowboy pistol when the latter enters the bank with his mother. Since you obviously meant me to perpetrate this horrid trick on others, I thereupon carefully rewound the bat, replaced it in the letter, and when daughter Abby came in, handed it to her. The effect was convulsive. I've never seen quite that color of violet in a young lady's face.

I have been thinking of you also, being about two-thirds of the way through *The Cold War and the Income Tax*, which I am enjoying immensely. This book, as they say, needed to be written, and every writer you know will be obliged to you for stating the financial position of writers, the discriminatory taxation imposed on them, and, of course, the disheartening uses that our taxes are put to. I don't know why it is, and I have often wondered, that short polemic tracts have gone out of favor as a means of expression. (I'm ignoring the kind of drivel that Norman Mailer prints in *The Village Voice*, etc.) I suppose it's the economic factor of publishers being unwilling to invest their money in such ventures, and the fact that neighborhood printers no longer are acting as publishers, as they used to.

I should tell you also that during this past year I reread *Classics and Commercials* as well as several other collections of your pieces, and was again struck by the soundness and prophetic quality of so many of them. (As for instance, your introduction to Hemingway's *In Our Time*.) But the one I never tire of rereading is the tri-partite piece on Southern California in *The American Jitters*, in which you really ticked off the place so long ago. At the time I first read the part about the Coronado Beach Hotel, I hadn't seen it, and when I came to do so, I realized what a beautiful piece of social comment and observation it was. I remember talking to Raymond Chandler about all this the last time I ever saw him. He was a great admirer of yours, and himself a man whose knowledge of everything dealing with Los Angeles has probably never been equalled. Have you read the collection of his letters called *Raymond Chandler Speaking*? I think that the essay therein on screenwriting is perhaps the definitive piece on the subject.

Well, this was really meant to be merely an acknowledgment of your good wishes (however diabolically transmitted), and Laura, Abby, and I hope 1964 will be a healthy and wealthy one for all the Wilsons. Laura and I are hoping to come over to France and England for five or six months beginning about April first, and we trust our trails and yours will cross. With all our love,

Yours,

CLEO DUNFORD*

134 West 11th Street
New York City
January 31, 1964

Dear Cleo,

. . . I had a long and vexing spell of acute inertia after returning to the

*See note, p. 161.

States from Nairobi, interrupted by six grisly weeks in London where I labored over a wretched TV spectacular about London for Elizabeth Taylor.* Elizabeth as it developed gave it all the histrionic fever of a broom handle and managed to effectivly louse up the air waves. However, 90 million more or less viewers saw it, and I managed to get off with no bruises from the critics, who concentrated on pinning *her* ears back. Anyhow, somewhere in mid-autumn I recovered my desire to write again, and have been energetic ever since. I suppose that this attack of accedia was a hangover of the aborted run of the play; in any case, it certainly cooled my theatrical ardor for years to come. . . .

I don't know what the conventional attitude is that one adopts on learning that his married friends are planning to separate, but I guess I've seen it on my own friends' faces when I've announced my plans to ricochet around the world without Laura. I'd analyze it as a combination of timid disapproval tinged with pity and glozed over with infinite Christian sweetness; the total effect is as though the listener had swallowed a prune pit the wrong way. So your news that you and Michael were planning to take a breather produced something of the sort in me. I suppose I incline to feel that monogamy is at best a very shaky and provisional arrangement invented by some rather smelly monks for the purpose of preventing the extinction of the race. On the other hand, and although it would have been pleasurable to see you in the States, I expect to be in Europe from about mid-April to mid-September. Laura and I are currently trying to get aboard an Italian liner sailing April 3rd for Cannes, where we'd pick up a car and do some eating and viewing in France, Spain, and Italy. We'll end up eventually in Paris, I should think; so it would be great to encounter you somewhere during the course of the summer. Let's keep tabs on each other's movements, yes?

All the trouble in Zanzibar and Kenya, Tanganyika, and Uganda have had extensive coverage in our local papers, where it's now felt that Burning Spear's political future looks unenviable since he had to call in Britain to bolster his regime. Parallel with the political tohu-bohu, I read in the movie columns that all kinds of loathsome people are flocking to Kenya as a kind of holiday resort; it begins to take on the dubious quality of Miami Beach, which I sincerely hope isn't true. Because these movie characters could really ruin the place beyond anything the Mau Mau could accomplish.

In giving Michael my love, Cleo, you must tell him that if he wants to read one of the most monstrous documents ever penned, let him get hold of David Ogilvy's *Confessions of an Advertising Man*. It's of a surpassing ar-

---

The Beauty Part opened on Broadway in December 1962, shortly after the printer's union struck New York City papers. In February, with the strike still on, Perelman went to Nairobi on his way to Seychelles. In spite of favorable word-of-mouth publicity, the play soon closed, and he abandoned the trip.

rogance, and as dishonest as a small-town roulette wheel. He particularly singles out *The New Yorker* as a target for his spleen, and I (though he doesn't name me) am probably responsible for more than a share of his bile, as I've kidded him in pieces on several occasions. But I believe that to Michael it'd be interesting as a portrait of managerial pomposity in the great Dickensian tradition. . . .   Ever,

LEILA HADLEY

Hotel des Trois Couronnes
Vevey, Switzerland
c. June, 1964

.   .   .

. . . [W]e unfortunately struck [the Loire valley] square on the Pentecost weekend, and it out-Coneyed Coney Island. There were all of fourteen million trippers at Amboise, Blois, and Chenonceau, and a mad scramble for over-priced accommodations and bum food. However, we reached Paris on 21 May, found a kennel for Misty, the poodle, after plenty of to-and-fro activity, and saw a marvelous show of Thailand art most of whose pieces came from the Nat'l Museum in Bangkok. Paris, though still a wonderful city, is fast going down the drain because of the combustion engine. There are, for instance, six rows of cars parked along the Boulevard Raspail, and two rows of vehicles rushing between. The noise and the carbon monoxide are infernal, to say nothing of French motoring manners, which are execrable. Like the Italians, the French believe they can prove that they have big, stiff cocks by beating you to a light, cutting ahead of you from either side, and speeding onto sidewalks if the roadway's crowded, gunning their fucking motors and beep-ing their horns like Judgment Day.

At any rate, we then flew over to London for two weeks, staying at Brown's Hotel and having a generally over-stimulated time. I had to deliver a speech at the British Society of Authors' 80th anniversary dinner, a solemn affair at Stationers' Hall attended by wowsers like Compton Mackenzie and (of all people) Jean Paul Getty, now an author since he's written his memoirs. Luckily, Thos. Stearns Eliot sat next to me and proved a true friend by ap-plauding loudly. It was just as well, inasmuch as I later learned I had spoken into a dead mike and was audible to exactly eight people. I *thought* I saw many puzzled faces in the audiences; I guess the poor bastards weren't lip-readers...Also spent a very nice weekend with some folk up at Northampton and an extremely pleasant Sunday down in Kent. Groucho was in town for some TV stint, and I collared him for dinner at the American Embassy, which proved a pleasant evening also. Laura and I also had dinner with the Eliots at their flat, which was hardly an evening with the Beatles for excitement, but I wanted to do it because (I fear to say) he looks very poorly...And so back we flew to Paris, spent three days there, and drove on here to Vevey, where we've been for about 12 days now. It's dull as ditchwater but useful for work purposes; I hope to finish a *S.E. Post* piece tomorrow before we move on to Italy. We had dinner with Oona and Charlie Chaplin the other night, they're both in fine shape seemingly and he as always was a memorable experience. What a great man...Should mention as well an incredibly wonderful art show now in Lausanne, the chefs-d'oeuvre of the Swiss collections. It's the high point of the big Lausanne Fair, which otherwise isn't anything to melt a cheese fondue over.

Here enclosed an *Observer* interview you mightn't have seen; [Kenneth] Tynan overstresses the Jewish angle (which we really didn't discuss to that length) and wrongly attributes a gag to Harry Kurnitz which was really Lardner-Kaufman's in their play *June Moon*, but otherwise it's not badly written. . . .   All my love as always,

OGDEN NASH

Erwinna, Pa.
June 21, 1965

Dear Ogden,

Thank you 1000 times for sending along the *Boston Herald* editorial. The anointment as Litt D took place on what was possibly the hottest a.m. in Providence history, and the anointees had to walk at least two miles from the Brown campus to the 1st Baptist church & back.* I certainly would have perished on this Bataan march had it not been for Tommy Corcoran, the legal eagle of the Roosevelt administration, who was also getting capped & who sustained me with Irish-Pawtucket witticisms of his youth. The very next morning I had to fly to Washington to a reception for Presidential scholars at which J. Cheever was a great help. Also present at this was that éminence gris, J. O'Hara, and that somewhat younger eminence & literatus, J. Updike. The latter read extracts from three works of his to the assembled scholars, which I didn't personally hear as I was overtaken by the characteristic nausea that attacks me when this youth performs on the printed page. But Cheever brought me tidings that all three extracts dealt with masturbation, a favorite theme of Updike's. When I asked Cheever whether Lady Bird was present, he informed me that she was seated smack in the middle of the first row. What are we coming to?

*Perelman received an honorary doctorate of letters.

224

There is some kind of sudden, and I suspect phony, activity regarding a production of *The Beauty Part* in London, which may take me over to London for a week shortly, but other than that, we're here until we go up to Martha's Vineyard on 19 July for 2 weeks. If we get anywhere within hailing distance, we'd love to stop by and say hello to you and Frances...Albert & Frances Hackett are on the Vineyard already & we're looking forward to hearing details of their global dash. . . .

At the annual fish fry of the Nat'l Institute last month, I was imprisoned in the platform chair immediately next to our Hibernian Sappho, Phyllis McGinley, who gave me such a headache with her non-stop chatter that I like to died. This past issue of *Time* carried on my ennui. I suppose that the reason for her cover story is that she's beloved of Clare Luce, her sister Catholic; I couldn't discern any other excuse for it.

Laura and I send you both our love, and a Happy Fourth of July with sparklers galore. Before I forget, do get and read a marvellous book on India called *An Area of Darkness* by V.S. Naipaul. It's very funny as well as moving, and it will save you a great deal of money, because you will most certainly never go to India after reading it.   Yours,

OGDEN NASH

Erwinna, Pa.
July 12, 1965

Dear Ogden,

     •   •   •

Laura and I will be delighted to stop by on our way back from Martha's Vineyard, but as experienced old-time wayfarers, we insist on putting up at the motel you spoke of. We'll have Misty, our 3-year-old poodle bitch with us — the one who toured the Balkans, and she's so used to travel that she generally runs ahead and gets the ice-cubes ready. I think she may remind you of Spangle; she likes children, and should you have any grand-children frolicking about, they might like to see her. . . .

We have a dinner date on July 20 at the Vineyard with Frances and Albert, and will toast you all in a bumper of mead. Until we see you, then, and with love,   Yours,

Local journalistic trivia enclosed. Why do we scribes toil to invent anything?*

*Two clippings, describing the awarding of a diploma to Daniel Odor of Upper Black Eddy and the auction of household goods and restaurant equipment belonging to Mrs. Julia Penis.

JAY MARTIN *

134 West 11th Street
New York City
December 1, 1965

Dear Mr. Martin,

Thank you for your note of 25 November. I received a day or two back a carbon of the letter Farrar Straus & Giroux had sent you, and trust that you'll be able to conclude an amicable arrangement with them when you meet. I think they're a vigorous house with a strong flair for merchandising their books, and their list comprises a good many writers of serious reputation — Eliot, Edmund Wilson, West, and others — with only a few horrors like Tom Wolfe (of whom I suspect they're secretly ashamed).

I am writing in this self-same mail to the Guggenheim Foundation and the American Council to the effect you indicate, and hope that my paltry words may be of some consequence in aiding your candidacy. You must be prepared for the eventuality that my notes may fall into the hands of someone who detests my work and believes that I'm only a pale carbon copy of Max Shulman. De gustibus, etc.

More than likely, Mrs. P. (now very much recovered, thank you) and I will push off for our place in the country Thursday, 23 December, so as to make a start for Florida two days later. It would be best, therefore, if you came down to New York sometime in the week 16–22 December to help get your project started. I'll meanwhile contrive to bring up as much material as I can from the country relative to West; and when we meet I can begin providing you with a list of people you will want to sound out. I already have a couple of suggestions of folk who I believe were never approached, one of them with some interesting material.

With cordial regards to yourself and Mrs. Martin, and my sincere pleasure that you're able to undertake West's biography.

Sincerely,

*At the time, associate professor of English and American studies at Yale. His biography *Nathanael West: The Art of His Life* was published in 1970.

CHRISTIAN, LADY HESKETH *

Erwinna, Pa.
October 8, 1965

Dearest Kisty,

. . . I'm presently extricating myself from a wretched cold I picked up

*A friend from Scotland, living there and in London.

in Boston about ten days ago, and am dividing my time between trying to work on a piece for this magazine that eludes me and trying to dodge the spate of information pouring out of radio and TV on Mr. Johnson's gall-bladder. I must say that while one realizes that we live in a thermonuclear age where our chief executive's sanity and health are essential to our continued existence, it's going a bit far to have to be conducted through himself's innards morning, noon, and night. I well remember the dismaying trips we Amurricans were obliged to take through Dwight Eisenhower's bowels — I almost wrote "Dwight Eisenbowel's howls" and I don't think it would have made a particle of difference...Anyhow, such dreary considerations are actually of minor importance inasmuch as the country is turning very beautiful at the moment. The autumn foliage should be pretty rapturous to behold within another week, and fortunately we've just had a couple of soaking rains that have repaired the drought situation partially. This place is fairly alive with deer and pheasant just now; we have a fawn who can almost be said to be tame, it can be observed several times a day eating apples under the trees, and the gentlemen pheasants take their *passegiatta* (spelling?) all day long, to the accompaniment of anguished squeals from Misty, our silver standard poodle.

•   •   •

CHRISTIAN, LADY HESKETH

Erwinna, Pa.
December 1, 1965

Kisty, my love,

•   •   •

The cat-and-mouse game my London agents play with me still goes on; there has been a series of midnight calls, such as only a very bad playwright could have conceived, assuring me that negotiations to make a movie out of *The Beauty Part* are proceeding like wildfire, that I am momentarily on the verge of being called overseas, etc., etc. These then give way to periods of woolly, impenetrable silence as they retreat into their burrows where, without doubt, they spend all their time deflowering their typists. I am sick unto death of the whole gruesome saraband, and am also equally sure that the moment I get to Key West — where I hope to spend January and February — a peremptory command to fly to London will be forthcoming. Maybe the mere fact that I'm revealing this to you — the first to know — will act as a catalytic agent and bring the whole tiresome business to a head. . . .

Yours always,

OGDEN NASH

1005 Flagler Avenue
Key West, Fla.
January 26, 1966

Dear Ogden,

Laura and I were sorry not to be in the city during your visit. It would have been good to drain a bowl of sack together and get an interim report on life in Baltimore. I hope it has worked out, and especially that you are feeling better than when we talked last.

After years of touring, we finally had our rendez-vous with that mindless idiot who apparently lies in wait for every motorist: in this case, a 20-year-old cretin who, at 5:45 p.m. on Tuesday, 28 December, and five miles below Orangeburg, South Carolina, impulsively swung his Fairlane across our right of way, demolishing our Peugeot and dispatching us to the hospital. Four days thence, he was found guilty of criminal negligence in court, but being a local youth and a naval trainee, the charge was dismissed. Laura sustained a broken fibula alongside her left knee, a monumental blow in the coccyx, and a gash in the temple; I a chipped left elbow and a series of contusions on the knees resembling one of Bernard Buffet's views of the Seine. Misty, our poodle, received only psychological damages. Laura spent two days in the Orangeburg Hospital, and on Friday, the 31st, we continued onward to Miami aboard the Seaboard R.R. . . .

       •   •   •

. . . I trust the foregoing will satisfy the Parcae in charge of our invisible weavings for 1966. My message service informs me that Leah phoned my office on 14 January; has there been any activity re *Venus*? The accounts I read in the *N.Y. Times* down here of the Broadway season make me think we're missing nothing in the theater. The description of Harry Tugend's little offering two weeks ago, involving artificial insemination and the merry mix-ups resulting therefrom, confirms my sense of thankfulness that the Nashes and the Perelmans fled Hollywood when they did.*

Our love to you both, and see that you drive thirty miles an hour (we were going forty) and buckle your seat belts.

Ever,

Addendum:

I know you will forgive me for suggesting an idea for a lyric for some future musical, but is there anything in a song with the title of "Proximity" that details what proximity does: i.e.,

*The Wayward Stork.

Prox-IM-ity, it makes the bees to buzz,
Prox-IM-ity, it makes the beard to fuzz,
Prox-IM-ity, it makes the bells to chime,
It causes moon and June to rhyme, etc., etc.

Plus all kinds of scrotum-tickling double entendres, of course.

On rereading above, maybe I also sustained a concussion in South Carolina. But I think there's an idea lurking around in it.

I .   J .   K A P S T E I N

1005 Flagler Avenue
Key West, Fla.
January 27, 1966

Dear Kap,

This replies far too belatedly to Stella's very sweet note way back there enclosing the Kodachromes of you and Ben and myself at Commencement last June. I was very happy to receive them, and thought, what a distinguished grouping of *alte kackers* before I zeroed in and discovered I was easily the most decrepit. (Just funning, of course, show me a pretty woman and I immediately break into a lively hoedown, followed by Cheyne-Stokes breathing.)

Twice you all have been in my thoughts — just before Christmas when I was about to catch up with my correspondence, and again on your birthday (January 14th) when I was on the verge of sending you the following Armenian greeting recalled from our boyhood: "Inch possess you shoo sawk shoon shahm vawti; paragvamadji qvatchumah djaw daw" — understandable to even the most illiterate as "Come up my room, coffee cake." I thought this might evoke memories of that grimy drugstore next to the Empire Burlesque where you and Harry Galvin used to poison the citizenry with raspberry floats.

.   .   .

During this past autumn I was asked to give a talk on Nathanael West by a fellow named Jay Martin who teaches a popular course in American studies at Yale. As an outgrowth and because we found him so conversant with and appreciative of Pep's work, Laura and I decided to grant his request to do a decent biography, on which he's now embarked, and which will be published by Farrar Straus & Giroux. I gave him your name among others as a possible source of information, so I hope you won't mind if he gets in touch with you. I believe you will find him likeable and smart, and devoid of the idiotic ingenuousness-plus-vaulting ambition that distinguished previous so-called scholars. Martin did what is regarded as a very creditable biography of Conrad Aiken some time ago.

I enclose a clipping from what is surely the worst newspaper in the U.S.A. with the exception of the *Los Angeles Herald-Examiner*, namely, the *Miami Herald*.* You won't have to look at it overlong without realizing that the impulse that led me to add my flourishes was engendered by Marjorie Day, late unlamented teacher of English at the Classical High School. To this I append the title, steeped in venom, "A Jew Never Forgets."

And don't forget Sidney the Penman, which he, together with his bride, the fair Lorraine, sends you and Stel his love. Please mention us both to Ben and Elsie, with whom we spent a most enjoyable evening on the Vineyard last July.   Ever,

*A photo of five female professors, standing around a bust of Shakespeare. Perelman has given them Bardic facial hair.

KARL FORTESS

1005 Flagler Avenue
Key West, Fla.
January 30, 1966

Dear Karl,

The road to hell being paved with good intentions — a scientifically proved fact — I had every noble resolution to reply to yours of 3 January with dispatch. Unluckily, it found us in somewhat seedy condition, inasmuch as our Peugeot and ourselves were demolished en route here in Orangeburg, South Carolina. A 20-year-old naval trainee, as the evenings shadows were falling on 28 December, swung impulsively across our right-of-way as we were proceeding down Highway 301 to Allandale, S.C., motivated, no doubt, by eagerness to purchase a tin box of condoms in the Amoco station on our right. The car, in the vernacular, was totalled; we, Gott sei dank, got off alive. My own injuries were relatively minor, but Laura got a broken fibula alongside one knee, a massive blow in the coccyx, and so forth. However, we are fairly well mended by now, and are presently in the grisly insurance stages, with no belief whatever that we're going to catch even. The car was a sentimental loss, inasmuch as we had driven many trusty thousands of miles through the Balkans in it and it had served us well, if not long. I certainly hope to be able to afford another.

. . . I ought to tell you, since you mentioned the possibility of my having another book, that Simon & Schuster will be publishing a new collection later this year — title, *Chicken Inspector No. 23*. I suppose the title derives from some nostalgic twitch in my past, my father having at one time been a poultry farmer. (No, not Rhode Islands Reds as you might suspect — White Leghorns. To this day I cringe at the sight of a gizzard.)

As I write this, Laura is in the other room of our paltry sub-let listening

230

to the radio playing a song called "Cry Me a River." This seems to be cue enough to ask whether you have yet heard a song with the well-nigh incredible title, "Pardon Me, Miss, but I've Never Done This with a Real Live Girl Before." I was so startled at hearing it while shaving that I almost sliced off the end of my bugle. My first thought, of course, was that the minstrel was a necrophile, but the argument as it emerged was that he previously had adored only pictures in the girlie magazines or some such *schweinerei*. Anyhow, it is a peach of a lyric and not to be missed.

•   •   •

. . . Let's foregather over a smoking pastrami when you're next in the Big City. I should be back soon after March 1. Till then, and with all best,

Yours,

JAY MARTIN

134 West 11th Street
New York City
May 4, 1966

Dear Mr. Martin,

•   •   •

Your progress on the West biography sounds quite phenomenal, and I was happy to hear that the grants will permit you the time to continue working on it. I think you will like to hear that I also have come across further West material, while ransacking my files, that should be of interest to you. Inasmuch as I have it bundled up in my office here against the time when I see you, I'm too slothful at the moment to undo the wrappings and particularize, but my memory, at the time I looked it over several weeks ago in the country, is that it will definitely fill in various gaps. Owing to the various complications of our Florida trip, not the least of which was that our car was demolished in an accident on the downward trip, that we wound up in the hospital, and that we spent the ensuing two months recovering, the winter and early spring have been rather confused, what with insurance high-jinks still in flux, but everything is sorting itself out and we are getting back to some semblance of the normal.

•   •   •

I'm happy to hear of the interest that the biography has aroused; it's indeed refreshing to contemplate that a complete and accurate book about West may one day be available. Thank you, parenthetically, for sending along Malcolm Cowley's letter from West. I heartily agree with you that it's a good letter, and I well remember West's feelings about the current political activity in Hollywood. The noble piety of the Hollywood folk, as they immersed

231

themselves in the plight of the migratory workers and the like, was pretty comical. One couldn't fault them for their social conscience, but when you saw the English country houses they dwelt in, the hundred-thousand-dollar estancias, and the Cadillacs they drove to the protest meetings, it was to laugh.

Mrs. P. and I expect to be here in the city until May 15th or 20th, after which we'll be spending most of our time in Erwinna. Let me hear from you as matters develop, and if you have any thoughts regarding the extra material I spoke of above — i.e., when you would like to collect it — I'll be glad to cooperate. I don't think it would be feasible to mail it to you, for fear of its being lost, and also it's a bit bulky — five or six pounds perhaps.

With cordial best to Mrs. Martin and yourself,

Yours,

OGDEN NASH

Erwinna, Pa.
August 7, 1966

Dear Ogden,

We're just back from the Vineyard after our customary two weeks at Gay Head, as bronzed and battered as any of the celebrated boatsteerers and harpooners aboard the *Pequod*. Most of the bronze and battery was welded on due to our determination not to repeat the journey up via the Connecticut Turnpike (on which, parenthetically, we passed two collisions graced with firemen). We therefore tried to sneak back through mid-Connecticut over what we thought were rural roads, dreaming farms, lowing kine, etc. — and wound up in misery-ridden little manufacturing towns where we ate something called grinders, drove endless miles along 2-lane highways behind sand trucks, and finally took nine hours to reach New York. Megalopolis, you is my bane. Outer Mongolia, here I come. I don't know what they eat in those felt yurts, but it can't be worse than grinders.

The Vineyard this year seemed to be taken over by Cabinet officers, no doubt hiding from LBJ and his gaudy nuptials. (Incidentally, am I mistaken in thinking that many of the newscasters pronounce this "nuptuals" as in "voluptuals" or Eisenhower's "nucular" as in "nooky"?) Both Katzenbach and Stewart Udall were sojourning there, the latter with seven children who undermined their dad's attempts at conservation by sliding down the South Beach cliffs. One of these evenings, also, I intend to get out my Ouija board and try to call in H.D. Thoreau to convey a bit of information I picked up around the Chilmark post-office. It seems that Michael Straight (lately owner of *The New Republic* and now a summer resident of the Ponds) paid $37,500 for a little swatch of acreage roughly 2½ acres in size, and on this built himself

232

a rambling summer cottage — cost $250,000. What a yurt you and I could have in Outer Mongolia for this kind of spinach.

I was delighted to pieces when Dave Scherman of *Life* told me that you had fractured your resolution not to review another book, and had consented to comment on *Chicken Inspector*. Naturally, I had rather hoped that he would assign it to someone of real stature like Max Shulman (of the School of Creative Writing at Westport), . . . , or Tom Wolfe, but in this life we must take the rough with the smooth. Speaking of smooth, I read in some blat recently (Lewis Nichols in Book Review?) that my talented neighbor Mr. James Michener sold the paperback rights to his current Hubbard squash for — hold your hat — $600,000. Let's see where we stand now:

    $ 37,500 — cost of Michael Straight's acreage
       250,000 — cost of erection on same
       600,000 — Michener's *The Source*, paperback rights

$887,500 — What I haven't got now or don't ever expect to have. I've just finished paying a hillock of bills 3 and ⅓ inches high, and by living on dried prunes, catsup, and hot water, Laura and I may be able to stretch till Labor Day.

This letter would be incomplete without telling you that midway through our stay on the Vineyard, Leah Salisbury dragged me off the beach with an excited call to the effect that I must read a forthcoming novel on the cosmetics industry; Harold Rome had just agreed to write the music for a musical comedy version thereof. Knowing Leah's taste, I whimpered, but she twisted my arm. So the very next day, the prospective producer, an off-Broadway character named Whitelaw flew up to Edgartown bearing a copy, but I made him mail it to me. Well, friend, I want to tell you. I've read some trash in my time and so have you, but this was tops. Published by Crown and written by two Jacqueline Susanns named Libbie Block and Sue Ginch or something. Dealt with the rivalry between Revlon and Helena Rubinstein, and funny comical preparations for the bath named Aphrodite's Nightie, etc. O.K. — save this letter, and when, eighteen months hence, Harold Rome is deriving $600,000 per week in royalties from *Hot Skin* or whatever he'll call it you can show it to me.

To compensate for everything foregoing, I enclose some tear sheets from the *Irish Times* — reruns of columns written in the past by Brian O'Nolan, who also wrote under the pseudonyms of Myles na Gopaleen and Flann O'Brien. (Under which last he wrote a book called *At Swim-Two-Birds*.) He died last year, and I should say it was a loss, because I think these are really first-rate. I'd appreciate your mailing them back when you finish with them, as I don't know whether they can be had in book form.

It seems a hundred years since we've seen each other. Did I mention anytime in the past few months that Laura and I are giving up the flat in New York come Sept. 30th and moving here for what may be keeps? I cleared out of the web at 513 Sixth Ave. June 1st and we're going to try using this as complete headquarters with patches of travel. That air pollution and tension turned the trick...Maybe you and I can arrange to meet episodically at the Rittenhouse Club in Philadelphia and finish *White Rhino* — unless Harold Rome is garnering all the grosses with *Hot Skin.*

With all love to you and Frances,

OGDEN NASH

Erwinna, Pa.
September 21, 1966

Dear Ogden,

I assume this will find you and Frances back in Balto, burnished the color of Hickok belts and vibrant with health from all that New Hampshire ozone. At least I hope so, because this 35-m.p.h. gale and rainstorm whistling around our chimneys would be dismal up in North Hampton. However, we aren't minded to complain at the onslaught of what newspaper cartoonists used to call Ole Jupe Pluvius because we sure need it in the Dust Bowl here. It was another one of those summers that more and more resemble life in the Imperial Valley of Southern California. We're even getting to look like wetbacks.

I can't tell you — and therefore won't even fail gloriously at attempting to indicate — how flattered I am at your review in *Life* of *Chicken Inspector No. 23.* Some numskull up at Simon & Schuster's who showed me an advance copy the other day observed, with that foot-in-mouth grace publishers are famous for, "You might have written that review yourself." He was wrong; only you could have, and could have said it so aptly and pungently. I know your aversion to prose, and I am therefore doubly grateful for your employing it in this instance. Dave Scherman recently told me that the arrival of the review in the *Life* office produced a temblor. People went around showing it to each other and commenting that this was what their reviews should be like. So perhaps, in addition to my gratitude, you will have shaken up those torpid critical columns.

We are poised on the brink of folding up our flat in New York and moving our stuff down here, which tribulation takes place the 30th of this month. A snootful of pollution, combined with a second burglary of the apartment

234

a month ago, heightened our discontent with New York, and consequently we're back to country living for a while. At the moment, though, there will be a hiatus, inasmuch as I am going off to London on October 5th. *The Beauty Part* is scheduled to go into rehearsal Oct. 10th with Bert Lahr in the lead. After three years of chivying, Bert finally has come around to appearing in England, where he's never played, so I'll be sojourning there, by present expectations, for about six weeks. No doubt it will be something of a blood bath, with everyone slipping in localisms about Nottingham and reading the lines in those cold porridge accents, but I am in the situation of a man shaking out a pair of trousers because he's convinced that a nickel is lodged in a remote seam in the waistband, and I also have to confess I'm curious about the reaction of the English theatergoers to the idiom in the play. If the venture goes to term, as the obstetricians say, Laura will be coming over for the opening. So keep your fingers on the pulse of the British press, and with your others, ignite a good will candle.

.   .   .

I do hope that you and Frances will be coming up to New York in December so that we can see each other. . . .

Yours,

C A R O L I N E and W I L L I A M Z I N S S E R

Erwinna, Pa.
December 15, 1966

Dear Caroline and Bill,

.   .   .

My name on the free list of *TV Guide* assures me a front row seat at goodies indescribable, but none to compare with the enclosed clipping. Study the photograph with care; note Mme Shulman's freshly marcelled hair and expensive bangle, the Weimeraner pointing an offscreen pheasant, the heavily-encrusted English silver tea-pot, but above all, the typewriting table. The only way Slapsie Maxie could ever get his hairy little legs underneath to pound out his prosechuckles would be to extend them straight out. That is, unless he twisted his trunk whilst keeping his feet in the pool, which might lead to a hernia. On second thought, maybe a hernia is no worse than the bad cold Maxie's prosechuckles have always given, Yours ever,

P.S.   Please return this tidbit when you've had your fill of it, will you? Everybody thinks I make these things up, and sometimes, in years to come, I like to furnish proof.

235

JOSEPH BRYAN III

Erwinna, Pa.
January 19, 1967

Dear Joe,

.   .   .

. . . If I had a Xerox machine, I'd forward one of the *Times* of London's unparalleled law reports, issue of Jan. 14, 1967 — you must try to look it up. The B.B.C. commissioned a TV play from a chap named Terence Frisby, called "And Some Have Greatness Thrust upon Them," and then refused to air the two final lines as being too shocking. I quote: "The play contained a line by a female character, spoken in relation to sexual intercourse, 'My friend Sylv told me it was safe standing up,' followed incidentally by an ejaculation 'She — eh?' by another character, a television interviewer. Mr. Frisby said that the idea of the play came to him after hearing about a girl in real life who spoke an almost identical line and that the line was essential to, and indeed the climax of, the play." You will be enraptured to know that the courts insisted the B.B.C. include the lines in their production. And one needn't be H.W. Fowler to state that this is an outstanding and upstanding instance of British justice — not to mention British reporting. Anybody who can weave "ejaculation" and "climax" into the account so smoothly (and how about the title of the TV play itself?) is a greater newspaperman than Walter Burns.*

With all best,   Yours,

*From Kentucky, Burns worked on papers in Missouri, Chicago, and San Francisco, fought in the Spanish-American War, and made a whaling voyage to the South Seas (d. 1932).

CHRISTIAN, LADY HESKETH

Erwinna, Pa.
February 7, 1967

Kisty, my darling,

.   .   .

I was fascinated by your vision of Erwinna as a Gothic structure buried deep in pinewoods and arum lilies and encircled by Amish villages, and somehow think that you conceive of me as a jazz-age Horace Walpole. The reality is somewhat different. At the exact moment, a blinding snowstorm that has been falling since last night has piled up roughly 13 inches and is due to continue until late tomorrow morning. (Time now — 2 p.m.) This house, situated on a hillside below a stone barn, is reached by a steep and twisting lane from the county road, and at the first snowflake becomes impassable. I called during lunch to find out when the man who operates the snow-plow thought he might clear the lane, only to learn from his wife that he's marooned by the same snow in Pittsburgh (at least 200 miles distant). She thought it unlikely he'd be back within three days. So I may as well settle down, pile another armful of John O'Hara's novels on the fire, and listen to the distant howling of the wolves.

On the assumption that you're consumed with curiosity about my activities these past several months—to think otherwise would be damaging to my ego—I'll proceed to quickly sketch them for you. Most of my time's spent in a small outbuilding about 14 feet square removed from the house, full of arctic draughts, arduously yoking words together into a seemly and (one hopes) commercial pattern. Until recently throughout the autumn, I varied this dismal routine by a number of trips to New York and Philadelphia to participate in radio and television interviews and panel shows aimed at publicizing *Chicken Inspector No. 23*. . . . In one week not long ago, I was dragooned into appearing at (a) an hour's literary interview at a Philadelphia FM station, (b) a lecture at the Philadelphia Art Alliance, and (c) a book-and-author luncheon before 500 old ladies at the Warwick Hotel, sandwiched in between Gerold Frank, author of *The Boston Strangler*, and Garson Kanin, author of *Remembering Mr. Maugham*. (*Dis*-membering would be closer, if you come to read it.) When I subsequently asked my publisher's press officer if he thought these appearances of mine sold any books, he replied coolly, "Listen, chum, nobody knows why anyone buys books." . . .

●   ●   ●

ERNIE ANDERSON*

Erwinna, Pa.
March 5, 1967

Dear Ernie,

I trust you won't quiver with repulsion if I say that you are a veritable doll. Nobody else would have taken the trouble to hunt down and send along *The Hard Life*, *The Dalkey Archive*, and *At Swim-Two-Birds*—to say nothing of the Cruiskeen Lawn columns you've forwarded and which continue to give me such pleasure. You will want to know that the package containing the last two above-mentioned titles arrived with stunning appositeness on my birthday—almost as if you were leaning over the edge of a cloud.

I'm enclosing a note that came in a few days later from a publisher which is self-explanatory. The circles seem to be widening, and maybe before long the cult will spread to the Thirteen Colonies. Speaking for myself, I find Brian Nolan at his best in the columns, though there are of course great things in

*American press agent based in London who recommended Perelman to Mike Todd, one of his clients.

237

the books. Do you share this view? Somehow, in the columns, he wrote with such freedom, a kind of go-to-hell gaiety, as few writers ever manage to capture on paper...I was very interested in what you said in your letter of 8 January about his Jekyll-and-Hyde personality, B.C. and A.D. booze. Obviously a tortured man about whom I want to ask you much more when we eventually come to see each other.

Am trying to work up a three- or four-week hop over to London within the next month, so don't be at all surprised if you hear my muffled accents over the blower. Keep (as they say) your pecker up and go with God until we meet. And muchas gracias again.   Yours ever,

KARL FORTESS

Erwinna, Pa.
March 5, 1967

Dear Karl,

Your heavily rubber-stamped *brievel*, followed in due course by the tape you struck off of my appearance on the Merv Griffin show, arrived in this winter wonderland during an extended painting siege we underwent: which is why this reply is tardy. A fat butterball with a fake Amish accent from Chalfont, Pa., was engaged in schmeering our upstairs with latex vinyl, generating a smell (or *rauch*) unequalled outside the 11th Avenue abattoirs. His favorite shade was aqua, and every ten minutes I had to eavesdrop on the son-of-a-bitch to insure that we didn't wind up with something out of *The American Home.*

The Griffin show was such a blood bath that I shrink at the mention. He is actually (or was a couple of years ago) a nice fellow, but they load the show with these borscht comics and coozies with emparaffined busts and the whole thing zips along with such urgency—not to speak of Griffin's failure to look at any of the books he's puffing—that one can't even pretend to relax. (And that audience of j.d.'s they pull in off 44th Street.) Well, I tell you, my friend. I did a lot of TV in connection with *Chicken Inspector No. 23* (and wrote a piece for *TV Guide* about my experiences that wasn't as fictional as it may have seemed).* And I made a discovery in the course of it—viz., that publishers have found in TV a way of putting their authors to work hawking their stuff, thus eliminating the necessity of advertising. The minute I began to comprehend this, I arrived at a decision that wild horses, etc. It's all very well for folk like Woodie [Broun] who enjoy these shenanigans, but hereafter I'm strictly Herschel Hermit and nothing's going to lure me out from behind my machine.

*"Now Silent Flows the Con," collected in *Baby, It's Cold Inside.*

238

Viz. your melancholy reflection that Boston's Boston and a good pastrami but 220 miles away, how many corned beef sandwiches do you think I manage to get out here now that we live full-time in the sticks? One must journey e'en to Philly for a smell of a sour tomato. And yet, I can't say my eyes moisten at the memory of that unlovely rabbit warren I left behind at 513-A Sixth Avenue. With three concrete-mixers roaring at once on that subway construction, the steam boiling up from the tailor's pressing machine next door, and the hoarse arguments of Morris Jaffe's photo apprentices, a man could hardly hear himself pleading with a lady friend to slip into something less confining...

If I manage to get up your way this spring, as I've been long intending to, let's have a soiree at Locke Ober's or Durgan & Park's. Meanwhile, zei gezunt, keep thy foot out of brothels, thy name off lenders' books, thy hand out of ladies' plackets, and defy the Foul Fiend.

Yours ever,

I . J . K A P S T E I N

Erwinna, Pa.
September 1, 1967

Dear Kap,

Well, I guess I've seen everything now, thanks to your kindness in sending along that issue of *The Brown Jug*, which I deduce you felt needed no comment. I must say that had someone described it to me, I really wouldn't have credited it, but now that I *have* seen it, about all I'm capable of is a plaintive, despairing "Oy vay!" and an impulse to scrub out its editors' and contributors' mouths with laundry soap. . . . Well, maybe it's better to print it for general circulation, lavatory walls ought to be a damn sight cleaner henceforth.

Of course, one is inevitably borne backward on Memory's tide to the St. Patrick's Day Show in 1924 and the terrific dust-up it caused because of a few trifling double-entendres. And the hoo-ha across the land because Percy Marks's character in *The Plastic Age* inadvertently contracted a dose. And similarly pallid references to soul kissing *und zo weiter*. But all that was like we used to say "kindergartner" stuff. This is really the end, and above and beyond the dreary smut, it goes without saying, is the dreadful amateurishness of it all, text and drawings. There isn't the remotest speck of humor visible anywhere in this *torchecul*, and if I were Mr. Philip A. Press, '68, who proudly styles himself Editor, I'd flush myself down the nearest toilet.

O.K., O.K. — what else is new? It's a dog's age since we've seen each other, and I hardly know where to start recapitulating. We live in the country altogether, perhaps you've heard; after several burglaries of our New York apartment, the air pollution, and the increasing frenzy of metropolitan life, Laura and I packed it in and moved to Pennsylvania about fifteen months ago, and we haven't felt a twinge of regret to date. The winter was a mite rugged what with so many snows, and as for the local society, we prefer talking to the cardinals and nuthatches, but the aim is to intersperse living here with a maximum of travel, and that's coming to pass. We had six or seven weeks in England and France this spring, and I'm going back to London in mid-October for a spell, after which there's some more activity outlined in Italy and East Africa. I find working in the country more productive and satisfying, and we do increasingly appreciate the serenity and slower rhythm of life here. It's pretty wonderful not to have to pay three sets of utility bills, cleaning women, and similar obligations as we did when there was an apartment, my office, and this house...

.   .   .

... Laura and I send you and Stel our affection, and need I say that if you're contemplating a visit to Princeton as in the past, I'll think ill of you if you don't let us know so that we may rend a schmaltz herring together.

As always,

CHRISTIAN, LADY HESKETH

Erwinna, Pa.
September 25, 1967

Darling Kisty,

Your so-welcome letter of 29th July didn't evoke the instant response it deserved for reasons beyond my control — viz., a fortnight's sojourn in hospital that began 2nd August and thereafter a month of convalescence. I quickly add that I'm in fine health again after a surgical interlude concerned with the dear little gland we boys cherish and which has been afflicting His Most Catholic Eminence. In the course of this ordeal, I had the distinction of being nursed (among others) by a colleen named Captain Winifred O'Gara of the Queen Alexandra Royal Army Nursing Corps (Kenya) who, it emerged, was there during the Mau-Mau emergency and was not minded to tolerate any nonsense from *me*. Furthermore, I learned from my experience that almost the entire nomenclature of prostatic surgery is Irish — for example, the Foley catheter, the Toomey syringe, and the Kelley clamp. Now, I am a great partisan of the Irish, Kisty, as you doubtless know, but when Captain O'Gara,

240

in one of my moments of spasm, snarled "Pull yourself together, man" and came at me with her Toomey syringe, I would have traded the Emerald Isle and every hairy Hibernian on it for one moment's surcease.

•   •   •

Yours always,

KARL FORTESS

Erwinna, Pa.
April 4, 1968

Dear Karl,

•   •   •

. . . Spring is moving into Bucks Co. apace and the air is fragrant with cow manure being grubbed into gardens. I myself am off to Ireland on the 26th, having rented Earl Mountbatten's castle near Sligo for a week — object, copy for *Holiday* magazine. Probably will be the first Jew ever to contract oatmeal poisoning.

All best to yourself and Lillian,   Yours ever,

MONICA and RONALD SEARLE*

Erwinna, Pa.
April 8, 1968

Dear Monica and Ronnie,

This is a somewhat overcast, rainy day with the buds bursting in every direction and very much what I imagine the Irish countryside is like, so that's a direct cue into telling you that my journey to the Irish castle has come about after all. There was a lot of back-and-forthing, and it was finally worked out that I'm to spend a week there. I go to London for a week April 26th and on May 4th snuggle into Classiebawn Castle, as it's known. In the course of the negotiations Earl Mountbatten showed up in New York and I had a drink with him, apparently to demonstrate that I wasn't a burglarious type. So somewhere in the months to come you'll be faced with the obligation to portray this eminent bit of real estate with me rattling about inside of it.†

The Black Museum piece was tip-top, you caught every sinister possible facet.‡ It will be interesting to see what happens as I approach the entry wicket at London Airport. I fully anticipate that the man examining my passport will

---

*See note, p. 148.
†"Shamrocks in My Head" appears in *Baby, It's Cold Inside*.
‡"My Life in Scotland Yard," also in *Baby, It's Cold Inside*.

say, "Would you mind stepping into this adjoining room, Mr. Perelman? A gentleman from Scotland Yard would like to have a word with you." I shall spend the six-hour flight over thinking up some nimble answers.

· · ·

Well, this must be all for now, as I have to drive Laura over to a hardware store to buy a frying-pan or some equally improbable article de cuisine. Why these modern women need such refinements is beyond me; her mother cooked the meat in her bare hands held over the glowing embers and it was goodylicious. However, I suppose you can't have everything. Take care of yourselves, lots of love, and do write.

Yours ever,

CHRISTIAN, LADY HESKETH

Erwinna, Pa.
May 14, 1968

Kisty darling,

I hated leaving the warmth and good fellowship of Derek Hill's that Sunday afternoon for my trek back to the marmoreal surroundings of Classiebawn — master, though I was, of all I surveyed there, with practically power of life and death over my three varlets. You have been so long accustomed to being lapped in luxury, Kisty, that I don't think you realize the breathtaking, the awful authority those of us who rent an Irish castle for a week can wield. I had only to arch my eyebrows in displeasure over a soufflé and Mrs. Kennedy, the cook, would fall into a deep trance of apathy. I could multiply the foregoing endlessly, but I think this example will serve. Anyhow, drenched to the skin I finally regained the battlements and I can tell you that the two hot water bottles Mrs. O'Grady, the housemaid, thoughtfully slipped into my bed felt super. Of course, had Mrs. O'Grady herself thoughtfully slipped into the bed instead, it might have been even more super, but maybe you only get that with a three-week lease.

The remainder of my stay extended the frontiers of boredom beyond anything thus far known to science or letters. That part of County Sligo is rich in megalithic remains, containing hell's own quantity of cairns, dolmens, covered and uncovered graves, etc. With the sea in an absolute froth — for some reason, my presence whipped up Father Neptune into an unparalleled rage — and the rain pouring down in buckets, Lord Mountbatten's many advertised diversions were impossible, so I maundered into weedy tombs and necropolises, stabbing weakly at the earth in the hope of uncovering a Bronze Age jawbone or the shapely pelvis of some forgotten beauty, but no dice. I ultimately became so desperate that I even visited a tweed factory and a carpet manufacture,

242

both reminiscent of sweated labor in your Industrial Revolution. One day I engaged a stout fishing smack and set off for the fabled island of Inishmurray, but the waves were mountainous, and rather than have the skipper prostrated with mal-de-mer, I ordered him back to Mullaghmore. In any case, by the Friday after I saw you, I had what we colloquially call a snootful and returned to Dublin, skilfully timing matters so that Aer Lingus lost one of my bags en route to New York. (Recovered fortunately since.)

•　　　•　　　•

Pennsylvania at the very moment has skies quite as lowering as Sligo's, the weather coolish and rainy and the grass breast-high. (Sophia Loren's, that is. I recognize no other unit of measurement.) I am currently seeking a horse to borrow to crop 6½ acres of pasture around the house, the previous cropper having been struck by lightning last July. I wish you would ship me a Clydesdale by air express, I look quite smashing in snapshots with my hand carelessly toying with their fetlocks. If none is available, then see if you can find a ruminant version of Sophia Loren. They too have lovely fetlocks.

•　　　•

All my love,

OGDEN NASH

Erwinna, Pa.
September 10, 1968

Dear Ogden,

How very good to hear from you, and to find that you've successfully survived this humid and insanely turbulent summer, even at the cost of becoming an Episcopalian councilman. From your description, I will henceforth envision you as a modernique version of Praisegod Barebones down on his marrowbones.* We ourselves are mildewed and bored in equal parts from the bucolic existence, broken only by a brief week at the Vineyard and a subsequent shorter visit to Jerry Salinger in Vermont. In between, I've been draped over the typewriter trying to determine which *mot* is more *juste* than the pedestrian ones I can think of. Incidentally, your poem in *The New Yorker* about the French ones speckling the language was a daisy. I wish they'd hang Donald Barthelme to a sour apple tree and give you all the space he consumes.

The proposals you extend that we meet in San Francisco, at Chasen's, or in London are each of them delightful, but I don't anticipate being in those

*Praise-God Barebone, or Barbon, a fanatical Puritan and preacher whose name was given in jest to the ineffectual and soon dissolved Barebones Parliament of 1653 (of which he was a member), set up by Cromwell. "Down upon your marrowbones" is a phrase in Yeats's "Adam's Curse."

243

latitudes at the times you signify. We *are* getting ready, Laura and I, to make a brief trip to Europe, sailing Sept. 26th on the *France* to Southampton and spending approximately five weeks between England, France, and Switzerland. This is in the nature of a thin substitute for that trip to East Africa we've dallied with, now dissipated by economic retrenchment at *Holiday*; you've undoubtedly seen mention in the papers of Curtis Publishing's anemia. Anyway, we both need a little stimulus, a recharge of the batteries, to face the winter, so, improvident as it is, that's our program. The next voice you hear will be that of the Friendly Finance Corporation.

We saw Frances and Albert up at the Vineyard, occupying an absolute dream of a house owned by Kingman Brewster; they appeared to be in good shape, but of course that was before the political conventions. The Vineyard has evidently become the new literary water-hole, judging from the names I heard bandied about that evening and from a piece I saw afterward by Lewis Nichols in the *Times*. Speaking of the *Times*, but the London *Times*, there was a very nice paragraph about you dealing, I think, with *Peter and the Wolf*. I extracted it to send you, but it disappeared in a violent house-cleaning.

In the interval of turning this page, I've been visited by a man styling himself a security expert, i.e., one who sells burglar alarm systems and proposes to install one for us costing close to eleven hundred dollars. (How much is that in your American money?) There's been a rash of housebreaking throughout this township, apparently by expert antique thieves. Nary the Heppelwhite lowboy or Hitchcock chair do we own, but it's been a very unsettling situation. We remember when you didn't even bother to lock your door, etc., etc.

At any rate, let's not give up on this matter of seeing each other; perhaps we can frame something after we're back from Europe and before you depart for San Francisco. Meanwhile, both of us send love to Frances and yourself, and here's hoping that the lesser of two weevils wins the election, though at the moment I couldn't tell you who he is.   Ever yours,

R O N A L D   S E A R L E

Erwinna, Pa.
December 10, 1968

Dear Ronnie,

·   ·   ·

I must tell you at once how pleased I was to receive the books you sent us, *Take One Toad* and *The Square Egg*. *Take One Toad* is a strikingly original job, I was much impressed with the way you handled the period costumes and the whole conception of the book. This is not to downgrade *The Square Egg* in any sense; you have some marvellous drawings in that, it goes without say-ing. The first one, naturally, has a unity that the other as a collection doesn't. At any rate, here's hoping that *The Square Egg* has more than the modest sale you foresaw in your note to me...As for my dealings with George Wei-denfeld, I had the usual high-society dinner *chez lui* that I expected, with all sorts of face cards ranged at the tables and my own name spelt as· "Mr. Pearlman" on the place-card. George apprised me that he is thrilled (he's always thrilled, natch) at the resumption of talks between us, and said he'd be com-ing to New York today — December 10th — for a 5-week stay, when we could sit down and hammer out a design for living without the hysteria he's subject to in London. I suspect, as the song has it, that he shall have hysteria wherever he goes...By the way, I found a perfectly lovely letter from Tony Godwin awaiting me, and he, after all, is the one I shall be working with.

Before getting into *Holiday* news — which is bleak — I must tell you that Laura and I have taken a 2-month's lease on a flat in New York for January and February, those being the so-difficult ones in the country. It's at 136 East 76th Street, corner of Lexington Ave. . . .

As to *Holiday*, they're really quite impossible. At the moment, I have one firm assignment — the Sûreté, which involves a trip to Boston for certain research. I discussed with them three other ideas that ignited them, only to have them inform me a week later that all were no good. It's as plain as can be that deep austerity's on — constant references to cutting back, let's wait on that, too rich for our blood, etc. *The New York Times* has twice recently run ads for *Holiday*, full back pages with splashy drawing by Hirschfeld, pro-moting the new *Holiday* — which, looking at the two last issues, appears to be a cheap and frantic imitation of *Playboy*-cum-*Esquire*. All kinds of tits bobbing into the reader's eye, and text that has no perceptible flavor. This last issue is full of off-register photographs of Las Vegas, and if Vegas is news, God help us...

•   •   •

Yours ever,

PAT KAVANAGH*

Erwinna, Pa.
December 17, 1968

Patricia darling,

•   •   •

Everybody and his brother over here are down with aspects of what is

*Perelman's British agent from 1977 until his death.

245

now pin-pointed as flu that originated in Red China — natch — but is, more visibly, delayed reaction to Nixon's victory. Old Shovel-Nose has picked himself a cabinet that could only exist in the imagination of Saul Steinberg. Last week, on TV, he presented his wooden-faced cohorts, who had been strongly briefed to keep their God-damned mouths shut while this everlasting nudnick chanted on for a whole hour about their qualifications. All sound business men, etc., etc. No wild-eyed eggheads, thank you. Oy, what a four years we're in for. Gevalt, as they say everywhere but at American Embassy parties.

·   ·   ·

Yours,

OGDEN NASH

136 East 76th Street
New York City
January 5, 1969

Dear Ogden,

This is the first letter, and deservedly, emanating from our two-month sub-lease here, where we will be roosting while the north wind doth blow and the painters in Pennsylvania paint. And I write it with profound apologies; it's been on my conscience for weeks, as far back as when I returned from Europe and found your newest book awaiting me. Thereafter, in rather swift succession, both Laura and I were felled by almond-eyed 'flue; now recovered in some degree — she's still pretty depleted — but in any case, here we are on the threshold, as we like to think, of a new life. Whatever the adventurous aspects of pushing a shopping cart through an Acme supermarket and then toting a hundredweight of taties across snowdrifts to a car whose battery has expired in the meanwhile, I'm looking forward to the warm, steamy atmosphere of the Carlton House bar.

Getting back all too laggardly to *There's Always Another Windmill*, I need not tell you but will that you've given me again the peculiar pleasure that only you are capable of. The verses I had not seen were nuggets to be read and lingered over, the ones I had to be read with envious admiration of how you'd done them. Your wit and erudition are my despair — in the sense that I don't think you're sufficiently appreciated and honored. You are the ornament of our age, my friend, and it gave me a special warmth when I saw ourselves — you and Frank Sullivan and me — in the holiday issue of *The New Yorker*. (Question: where were Donald Barthelme and the other kooks? Answer: where they belonged, behind the arras. The devil fly away with them.) Anyhow, thank you very much for us both.

As I recall your late autumn plan, you were shortly off to San Francisco for your appearance there, and I trust it went off tiptop. There have been two luncheon meetings of The Deep Six at the Lobster,* only the first of which I was able to attend, but am told that Brooks showed up for the second, and now that I'm here, I hope to reactivate the custom. . . .

Laura's and my trip to Europe was a very enjoyable one; we spent some lovely days in Zurich and Basle (Bale, Basel—all kinds of spellings) looking at sensational gorilla collections in the latter and wonderful dittoes of Impressionist paintings in the former. Milan, Florence, and Rome thence, all first-rate, and back to Amsterdam for a week, finally returning to London. There are a couple of interesting movie projects brewing in England, one of them Evelyn Waugh's *A Handful of Dust* in which I've been trying to mingle myself for a long time. At the moment also, I've been holding extended conversations with the Sunday *Times re* some assignments they'd like me to undertake. The money is piffling by our standards, but I find a very receptive audience there, and have been shown great kindness increasingly.

Well, here's hoping that you and Frances are untouched by those Red Chinese bacteria, and furthermore that you're planning to come up here in the next few weeks, so that we may have a reunion. . . . With all love to you from us, and looking ahead to seeing you soon,

Yours,

*An informal luncheon club organized by Harvey Orkin that met weekly in the backroom of a seafood restaurant on West 46th Street (since closed). The core "membership" consisted of Orkin, *New York Times* theater critic Brooks Atkinson, *New Yorker* writers Joseph Mitchell and Philip Hamburger, Al Hirschfeld, and Perelman. The group disbanded at Orkin's death.

RONALD SEARLE

Erwinna, Pa.
May 15, 1969

Dear Ronnie,

•   •   •

. . . [I]n reference to *Holiday*, I haven't written anything for them, which is to say, the Sûreté piece, because there really wasn't enough to write about. I'd hoped to be imaginative when I finally squared off at the typewriter and invent sufficiently to piece it out. But after several tries, I at last had to admit that the crime museum I saw in Paris was a pale echo of the Black Museum, and other than my slight brush with French officialdom, I had *nyet*. You know, this whole idea of the Sûreté was actually a *Holiday* editor's brainstorm to begin with, and that kind of notion rarely works out. As witness the couple of ideas spawned at our lunch at the Lobster with Merrill Panitt. I spent the better part of an afternoon with the White Owl girl—3½ mortal hours, in

247

fact — and found merely a professional model quite devoid of interest. I ultimately did a piece for *TV Guide* on a totally different subject, i.e., nudity rather than Miss White Owl's feathers.

.   .   .

Before I forget, Laura asks me to relay to you the information, given her by some friend, that the Shakespeare Book Shop in the rue de l'Odéon is offering my autograph for sale priced at $30. She says if you're going by there, drop in and check on the accuracy of this tale. It sounds wholly improbable to me.

Other than these bits of thistledown and assorted fluff, I fear I don't have very much news. It's two months now since we returned to the country, where almost nothing happens — as Chekhov so eloquently demonstrated. The high excitement each week is the Wednesday arrival of the laundry truck. Latterly, various artisans have been crawling about refurbishing the screened porch at fees so astronomical that it'll take years to pay them off. In short, life at Cold Comfort Farm is very pedestrian these days, and would that there were enough loot to take us travelling again.

Well, my boy, I must bring this rustic ramble to a halt, as I have to fetch daughter Abby from the bus at Frenchtown, so here are affectionate squeezes from us both to you and Monica. . . . We wish you could be here, or us there, it matters not so long as we could be together. Meanwhile, and with all love,

Yours always,

PAT KAVANAGH

Erwinna, Pa.
August 15, 1969

Pat dearest,

.   .   .

You spoke in your letter of the pleasure you'd derived from reading *An Unfinished Woman*, extract thereof in *The Atlantic Monthly*. I should tell you that I saw Lil Hellman on the Vineyard several times, and one evening at dinner we talked for a long while about Leo Huberman, who was a close friend of hers. Although I knew they were friends, I was surprised by the depth of her regard for him, and I'm sure you would have shared it if you had been there. As to her complete book, I felt reading it that the best thing in it was her chapter on Dorothy Parker; I don't think anyone thus far has caught Parker's quality as accurately. . . . Hellman's words about Dashiell Hammett in her book are naturally colored by her 30-odd years of association with him, and it strikes me are rather portentous. She keeps building him up and promising wisdom that doesn't come forth...I attended a publisher's party for the book about five weeks ago where the entire literary establishment turned up. Craning my ears, or neck rather, to overhear what Philip Roth was saying to Styron, I expected to pick up juicy bits left out of *Portnoy's Complaint*, but all I heard was some complaint about overdue royalties. Oh, yes, and somewhat later, a threatening lady in black leather named Susan Sontag loomed over me, but I managed to escape with my virtue intact.

•   •   •

With much love,

OGDEN NASH

Erwinna, Pa.
August 20, 1969

Dear Ogden,

```
Food Basket Broadway Bangor..........581-8052
HEARD & SWEET 501 S Main Bangor....581-7195
Hungry Ed The Pocono Lake............646-2779
```

Heard melodies are sweet, but Unheard & Sweeter would be news of yourself and Frances. How was your trip? I read not long ago in my surface mail copy of the *Times* (London) an interview with you in what they call their Times Diary by PHS, but wasn't able to discern where you had been up till then or where you were going. Laura and I, in a 10-day trip to the Vineyard from 18 July till 28th, spent a weekend of it with Frances and Albert Hackett, who reported you as going to Ireland for a spell during your stay. No doubt you put in most of your time there roistering in the shebeens with John McCarten?*

We are all well here, even if covered with verdigris from the blasted and unending humidity and rain. Our plight, fortunately, doesn't compare with a neighbor through whose floors mushrooms have been springing up daily. On the above-mentioned trip to the Vineyard, we were able to swim only one day of the ten, the other nine it rained cataclysmically. The Hacketts, as you probably know, are in London now, and at the end of the month go to a house they rented in the Vaucluse near Avignon. We'd have liked to join them there as they proposed, but we now hope to go to England in late September for a couple of months, mingling it with a bit of France and Italy.

I should tell you as well—as a sort of footnote to the Kennedy contretemps,† which occurred during our weekend at the Hacketts'—that the Frank Sinatras and the Bennett Cerfs arrived on the former's yacht right in the mid-

---

New Yorker writer then on assignment to Ireland (d. 1974).
†Chappaquidick.

dle of the whole thing. Influential as is Bennett, however, he didn't seem to be able to cool it...

If you have any cleaning problems with rugs or upholstery, you may want to refer them to:

KNEEBONE LLOYD J
SPECIALIZING IN
RUG & UPHOLSTERY CLEANING
WALL CLEANING

I believe these snippets from our local Yellow Pages should effectively silence our readers who think we make up these funny names. In any case, love from Laura and myself, and do let us hear from you. With all the best,

Yours,

I R E N E   K E M M E R *

46 Green Street
London
November 24, 1969

Dear Iaina,

You write enchanting letters, and I will dispatch a steely-eyed Maltese torpedo, armed with a razor in the best tradition of Graham Greene's *Brighton Rock*, to menace you if you dare to stop.

.   .   .

The somber news from home *re* mass exterminations in Vietnam, Spirochete's jeremiads against the networks, and his latest tilt at the *Times* and *Washington Post* — all of it gleefully highlighted in the British press — gives one the impression here of being in that hall of twisted mirrors at Coney Island, I guess because everything local seems so sane, polite, and reasonable. To be sure, there's plenty of violence (*vide News of the World, Daily Mirror*, and their gutter press) happening daily, but it's unquestionably safe for any citizen, of whatever sex, to walk the most isolated areas at any hour, and the burglaries (it's called "being silvered" because the thieves carry jewellers' loups to examine the watermark on the plate they abstract, and they take only premium stuff) are swift, unobtrusive, and free of damage. I hope I have been here often enough so that I don't view the scene through rose-colored specs, but it does seem to me a relief from the life we live in Megalopolis. And there *are* delightful moments, as when, the other morning, I came up Mount Street past a deluxe bath shop specializing in those circular tubs, fancy johns, and super-fleecy towels. Propped up against a loofah that probably cost fifty pounds was a

*A friend of the Perelmans, who often visited in Bucks County. *Vinegar Puss* (1975) is dedicated to her.

250

printed card bearing a verse—a paraphrase of Andrew Marvell's celebrated couplet. "The bath's a fine and private place," it read, "And some, I think, do there embrace."I doubt whether Crane or American Standard would put anything like that in their show-windows, even if they were capable of thinking of it.

•   •   •

break for lunch

I know you'll forgive me for snapping the thread when I divulge where and with whom I had the meal. Twenty years ago, on our way home from the Far East (*Swiss Family P.*, etc.), we met an extraordinary man named Solly Zuckerman, already then a famous zoologist and additionally celebrated for his services to the R.A.F. in the war. In the interim, he's been knighted and is now secretary of the London Zoological Society. Well, endeavoring to get a note to the curator of the Basle Zoo to facilitate a story I'm doing on the baby gorillas up there for *Life*, I renewed our acquaintance and he gave me lunch in the members' diningroom. And of course I learned more, over a bottle of Beaune and from the subsequent visit to his office, about anthropoids than a week spent with encyclopedias. Do you wonder that I like this country?

•   •   •

Love,

AL HIRSCHFELD

Erwinna, Pa.
February 11, 1970

Dear Al,

Muchas gracias for sending along Prof. Panowski's brievel to Jerry Chod.* It is a lollapaloosa and indeed typifies the norrischkeit rampant in higher education. I've put my intestinal flora to work on it and possibly may be able to convert it into easily digestible prose.

I too am somewhat batttered by an experience in the theater, though nothing as wrenching as Jerry's, obviously. Night before last, I was sped by Rolls-Royce and uniformed chauffeur to the bedside of a sick musical called *Minnie's Boys* at the Imperial in W. 45th St. Arthur Whitelaw—or Outlaw— its producer, thought that my genius could effectively save the patient.

Knowing me as a truthful reporter, you will not doubt me when I say that it was a scalding descent into a tub of such merde as hasn't been seen outside a Catskill summer camp show. Shelley Winters wasn't appearing that

---

*Jerome Chodorov, playwright (*Junior Miss, Wonderful Town*, etc.) and director. Panowski was researching a book on musical comedy failures and had written to Chodorov asking why one of his had flopped.

251

night, doubtless taking refuge in a supposed laryngitis. Her replacement read the whole part off some onion-skin pages that kept curling up in shame. The five hoodlums representing the Marxes as children kept crawling through each other's legs and armpits to evidence joie de vivre. Plot there was none, and laughter less. Groucho, whose son Arthur wrote this — with a collaborator yet — is listed on the house boards as technical consultant. As the patrons were handed their programs they found enclosed a mimeo'd message from Groucho, asking them to pretend that they were in Philadelphia watching a break-in of the show and to exercise compassion because admittedly there were some weak spots. (This was the official 13th preview.) In his postscript to the foregoing, Groucho said with elephantine humor that if anyone in the audience raised his hand, he'd be permitted to leave the room. He needn't have; the recipient was already in the toilet, and numbers of them left for it throughout the performance.

I'll be seeing you, but not at the Imperial. Love to Dolly.

MONICA and RONALD SEARLE

Erwinna, Pa.
July 6, 1970

Dear Ronnie and Monica,

I don't know any way of apologizing to you for taking so long to reply to your letters, which I needn't tell you came at a time that was very painful indeed.* I also needn't add that the reassurance of your friendship and your love for Laura and me provided me with what solace I could glean in the circumstances...How stodgy and inept these sentences sound now that I've written them. I would so much prefer to be saying them to you and to be able to clasp your hands as I did so. But failing that, I can only ask you to believe that my thoughts have been with you so often these past months. Unhappily, I've allowed preoccupation with my own situation to overshadow that of my friends to the degree that I've ignored their welfare, and for this I do ask your indulgence. . . .

There's obviously no point in attempting to recapitulate things here, but you'll understand that during Laura's illness, I was kept busy whenever she was at home and visiting her when she was hospitalized, and all the machinery of daily life had to be tended. Once that period was over, though, the illusion of activity ceased, and, I suppose, the predictable reaction followed. Daughter Abby was a comfort, and the few neighbors hereabouts went through the motions, but in this solitary rural locale and with too many memories on every

*Laura Perelman died on April 10, 1970.

hand, it wasn't easy. Anyway, I spent some weeks with friends in town, returning here inevitably because the house needed looking after (not to mention the dogs and the horse). It became clear eventually that I can't — and don't want to — live here by myself, and I therefore put the place in the hands of a real-estate agent for sale. Thus far, no takers, and in the present state of our American economy, it may be a long pull…I wish I could brighten the picture by adding that I'd been able to immerse myself in work, but no such luck. So there you have it (except for endless legal complications straight out of Pickwick), and I defy you to show me a Russian novel half as bleak.

Oh, well, it's fundamental that one has to take the rough with the smooth (a phrase I've filched from Somerset Maugham), and no doubt affairs will improve. It's a beautiful summer afternoon in Bucks County, the foliage is lush beyond belief, and who wants to sit indoors composing letters whose gloom it'll take half a dozen Pernods to dissipate?

Ronnie, I never did thank you for sending me those blow-ups of the photographs you took here — they're beauties…I wish that this could be a longer, let alone a livelier, letter, but it's the best I can offer at the moment. Essentially it's a request for news of you both — please do write soon, and I trust that all is well with Monica and yourself. I send you my deepest affection.

Yours always,

JOSEPH BRYAN III

Erwinna, Pa.
July 29, 1970

Dear Joe,

Thank you for your screed *re* mynahs, and herewith answers to your questions.

Yes, they're great fun to have, and definitely worth the trouble, which I'd say is minor (no word-play intended). The only care they need is the effort involved in preparing their food (and that's little enough) and keeping their cage clean. They eat chiefly rice, bits of fruit, hard-boiled egg, etc. (Handbooks, generally for sale in pet shops, will outline same.) They don't have any ugly traits; they become surprisingly attached to individuals, mine used to wriggle around ecstatically whenever I appeared.

As to where to buy one and how much they cost. We bought ours in Bangkok from a firecracker store, and since they're very common out there, he and his cage came to about eleven dollars. I really don't know how much is charged for them here. It obviously depends upon how good their talking ability and range is. In general, the best plan is to buy as young a bird as you can. They're supposed to be able to learn words best between the ages of three and eight months — they can live to be thirty, by the way. To teach them, you have to cover their cage with a dark cloth and endlessly chant some word until they repeat it. This is now facilitated by records that you put on a player.

Regarding where to buy them, I know that the Belmont Pet Shop in Radio City carries them, but I'd imagine that's an expensive place. (Next time you're in NY, visit that shop, they have one or two celebrated talkers.) Several years ago, I saw some very healthy and glossy mynahs in a cobbler's shop that I used to patronize when I lived in the Village. It's on the west side of University Place between 10th and 11th Streets, closer to 11th. The proprietor, a very nice Italian gentleman, had somehow become embroiled in the bird business, and the shop was full of various genera he'd received from India. At that time he had four or five mynahs and was asking $25 apiece, which was very cheap for such good specimens.

Anyhow, and to repeat, they do become most endearing. Ours died after we'd had him about 11 years; I believe that in old age they tend to become arthritic. If any you see aren't prohibitive in price, I'd recommend buying a pair, as they do enjoy company and thrive on it; single birds of any species sometimes pine in captivity. Finally, if I were you, I'd journey down to that cobbler's shop when I was next in the city and see whether he has any for sale. If not, ask him where to shop for one. Use my name if you are so minded, though he may very well have forgotten me.

I guess that's the tale. As for Martha's Vineyard, I don't think I'll be getting up there this summer, as I'm currently negotiating the sale of this place. If it becomes final, I'll be caught up in a lot of boring legalistics, auction, etc. So I guess I shan't have the opportunity of seeing you then. But maybe in London, where I hope to go for a spell when and if this real-estate comes off. Until then, and with blessings,   Yours ever,

RONALD SEARLE

Erwinna, Pa.
August 5, 1970

Dear Ronnie,

.   .   .

Without putting a jinx on myself, I'm happy to tell you that I'm feeling worlds better than I did when I last wrote you. I've started working again (after a long drought), sold one piece to *The New Yorker* and am well along on a second. Contributing to my better mental state, undoubtedly, is the very real possibility of having sold this place (note my guarded language and crossed fingers). At least contracts have been drawn between lawyers, and I've seen the check for a down payment; one or two final details have to be ironed out, but I believe that within a fortnight I'll be able to speak definitely. What it all means, simply, is that if the sale does go through, I shall have to turn over the place on October 1, and as soon after that as I can arrange to, I'm going to London with the intention of living abroad. As you know, this has been my intention for a long, long time, and given the dire state of life in New York (which place has oppressed me for years), I very much look forward to this. . . .

•   •   •

Yours ever,

CHRISTIAN, LADY HESKETH

Erwinna, Pa.
August 18, 1970

Kisty darling,

•   •   •

. . . [A]m rushing this note off with the good news that this place *is* sold, everything signed and sealed, but not as yet delivered. Formal delivery date of premises is supposedly October 1, but I'm trying to hustle it up by a fortnight if I can, as I'd like to be in England that much sooner. So now for the next couple of weeks, I'll be busy sorting out, storing, and selling the accumulation of 38 years of ownership—which really amounts to a fearful lot of odds and ends. But this will be sheer physical activity and really not painful in any sense, because I'm truly pleased that this sale could have been arranged as it has. Because the truth is that I decided as long ago as several years that I couldn't exist much longer in this remote vale, without any contact with anyone or any sort of nourishment for the ganglia. And while the circumstances that have brought it about weren't of my choosing, it's been done and I can start a new chapter.

•   •   •

Yours always,

IRENE KEMMER

Reform Club, London
October 29, 1970

Irene darling,

At one o'clock in the morning, I approach you ball-point in hand . . . to reply far too belatedly to your two lovely letters. . . . I guess I was really depleted by the intensive pace of those 3½ weeks of publicizing my book [*Baby, It's Cold Inside*] and getting everything ready for the takeoff—the rush to tie up all the loose ends, legal disposition of the farm in Philadelphia, the mad dash to Boston and the interviews, taping TV and radio stuff, and the final four days of frantic leave-taking. It climaxed on the Wednesday night when I came aboard to find television crews from both NBC and CBS filling my cabin and waiting on the upper deck, and they really came down on me like Gangbusters: what did I think about American politics at this stage of history, was I copping out, etc., etc. By now I was reasonably fed up with all the publicity and cooked-up excitement and was a tissue of irritability and fatigue. Anyway, as I say, I just hibernated, saw a lot of dull movies of the kind that seem to be made only for ships and planes, and (as I believe the expression goes), goofed off.

. . . I was met at Southampton, after a very calm and easy crossing, by a great tan Rolls-Royce limousine with liveried chauffeur supplied by a local movie producer who's partners with Peter O'Toole; eleven pieces of luggage piled inside and whisked up to London in an hour and a half. Installed in the largest and favored bedroom of thirty such in this club and have been made much of by staff and secretary. Telephone's been going steadily since Tuesday a.m. . . . and all kinds of friends throwing invitations I'm trying to duck. Spent most of yesterday with rental agent looking at furnished flats. . . . Now I have to curb my social activities and belt out a piece I promised Shana Alexander for *McCall's*, due November 9th absolute deadline. I shall be staying on here certainly until next Tuesday, may be forced into a hotel thereafter since the Club is expected to be chockful next week. . . . Day after tomorrow (Saturday) I'm going up to Essex to spend 2 nights with Norman Lewis* at his house in Finchingfield, return Monday a.m. Invitations for future weekends coming in betimes. You know how they go for the weekend routine.

Yours yours,

*British travel writer and novelist. Perelman cites his books in the course of the letters.

IRENE KEMMER

East Grinstead, Sussex
December 6, 1970

Irene dearest,

Darling, I'm filled with remorse and apologies for being so slack with my correspondence, but the past couple of weeks have been really pretty frantic. A lot of people here I've known casually over the years have suddenly awakened to the fact that I'm now resident and have invited me to dinners, drinks, lunches, and all the time-consuming idiocies I didn't need while I was trying to sort out the flat, assemble my papers and files, get my visitor's status and tax complexities ironed out, and generally fit myself into the local social niche. Most of the hysteria has by now, Gott sei dank, simmered down, and with the exception of some unfulfilled writing promises and a couple of TV stints in the next two weeks, I'm at last beginning to lead a somewhat more rational life. . . . I don't mean to imply that all this febrile nonsense hasn't been enjoyable; it compensates for that long dreary solitude of last spring and summer in Erwinna when I behaved like a bear with a sore paw, the dark night of the soul, etc., etc. But obviously I've had to go through this manic stretch in order to attain a measure of equilibrium, and now we can look for some degree of peace and adult behavior.

Anyhow, this is to say at once how absolutely marvelous it is that you've been able to work out the trip, and I'm starting to plan a few things I hope will help you to like Britain. Or London, at any rate — I don't exactly understand how much time you'll have for the whole junket, or whether you'll want to nip over to Paris or wherever during it. Perhaps if you do have time and do want a day or two in Paris, I'll go over with you, since I yet haven't done so and want very much to see Ronald and Monica Searle, Janet Flanner, and a couple of other folk. . . . (All the [instructions concerning your arrival] will be confirmed over the phone long before, thanks to Paul Newman, whom God preserve.* Incidentally, I tried a couple of times during this past week to reach you by phone, but the international line has been clogged with business calls. It is, however, working brilliantly still; I've talked repeatedly with Shawn at *The New Yorker*, Mike Korda at S&S, and hordes of others. . . .)

Perhaps you saw, or heard of, a piece I sent on to the *N.Y. Times* and which appeared last Wednesday, the 17th, on the op. ed. page; it was called "A Farewell to Bucks." Anyway, only reason I mention it is that it's one of three I've done or am in process of doing for them. The second is appearing in today's magazine section of the *Times* in a special supplement about New York. . . . It's called "New York at a Distance — Peckings from a New Perch." (I thought I'd better not characterize myself as a pecker — too much braggadocio implied, and anyhow, there are undoubtedly enough people already who regard me as a prick.) But do read it because I've managed, I hope, to catalogue some of my emotions about the city. The third piece, which I haven't as yet written, will also be in the *Times Magazine* section (my deadline's Dec. 18th) and is supposed to deal with my first 100 hours in Britain after arriving. Prior to doing this, though, I have to telex by this coming Thursday midnight a piece for *The New Yorker*'s Christmas issue, in space they're holding open. I've got the idea outlined and know where I'm going, but only will be starting work

*Perelman had been told that the actor had taken out a contract with AT&T for unlimited overseas phone calls but had attempted to cancel it. When the company refused to refund his money, Newman gave out his credit card number on a television program.

on it tonight when I get back to London. . . . None of the preceding, I add hastily, is set down to create in your mind a picture of myself as a harassed journalist; it's merely that for circumstances beyond my control or desire, I've been pitchforked into a bunch of work I hadn't anticipated, and in my New England ethic, I feel obliged to deliver.

I should tell you additionally that I've concluded negotiations and will this week sign a deal with the Sunday *Times* here to write at least six pieces annually for them; these will appear on the first page of their second section, the news review, which is considered the honorific space in the Sunday press. Harold Evans, the paper's ed-in-chief, appears to be my most rabid fan and gave me a little dinner at the Reform with a dozen wowsers like Cyril Connolly, und zo weiter, to woo me. . . .

Finally as to where I am at the moment, this is the country house of Elaine Blond, one of the Marks and Spencer hierarchy, where I took Laura to lunch one Sunday last winter; she very much liked Nevil, Elaine's husband, who died late this spring. Elaine, who's recently been in Israel, is one of the chief spark-plugs of the Jewish community in England, raises money for Israeli causes, and entertains various dignitaries, Jewish and Gentile, here and in London. Joan and Michael Comay (he was Israel's ambassador to the UN until recently, now is their ambassador to England, and both of them people I knew in N.Y.) are staying here this w/e, also some odds and ends of minor interest. The food is super and it's a very comfy "cottage," as they call it with magnificent English understatement: a cottage with Renoirs, Utrillos, Sisleys, and other doodads of equal specific gravity. You and I should own such a cottage; it would make a Whitney salivate. You can hardly get through the front door for the Rollses, Ferraris, and Maseratis clustered about. They have all gone off to some Sunday morning nonsense at the chapel (what kind of Jews are these?) and yesterday, when they met me at the train, I was whisked around to a charity benefit for a local hospital that was right out of one of those Ealing comedies of the Thirties. I saw eleven old ladies all played by Margaret Rutherford. . . . Oh, and I forgot to say that one Saturday recently I went to the annual cat show at Olympia. The cats, while magnificent, didn't compare with the handlers and types twittering over them. Honey, I've got more stuff to write about than I'll ever get around to. I better stay healthy, and you're the kid who can help me do it.

Well, it's like 12:30, and I must descend now to the ritual that precedes Sunday lunch. A group of fresh faces (i.e., people not staying the w/e) usually attends these Sabbath formalities, and departs after a Gargantuan feed. I'll depart on the 5 o'clock rattler, be back at my flat by 6:45, and if no nudnicks interfere, should settle down to writing that *New Yorker* piece by 8:00. I hate that sort of forced draught work where there isn't time to polish as much as one would like to, but in this case it's necessary. I'm promising myself not to think of you while I'm actually working. . . .

Goodnight you lovely creature.

I R E N E   K E M M E R

15 Onslow Gardens
London
February 6, 1971

Irene, my love,

Six days of harebrained activity since I spoke to you during the last hours of Cardinal Newman's tenure (all praise to him in the highest, and I wish he'd renew his Golden Credit card), so this promised letter comes to you belatedly. The trouble has been that each time I roll a sheet into the typewriter, the fucking phone rings with someone asking whether he can accompany P. Fogg and Passepartoute from Smyrna to Epiderma and get our impressions of the trip so far.* I suppose that if nobody were interested in this globe-girdling exploit I would feel wounded, but it really seems as if I had inadvertently opened Pandora's box. King Features, Reuter's, and practically every news-scooping agency mentionable have now gone quite shrill and demand what right I have to withhold information *re* my movements. And a day or two ago, Michael Todd Jr., amid his third call explicating why he is the only person in America qualified to imprison it on film, warned me that if I didn't give him a categorical and positive reply, he could not hold off NBC much longer. I told him to hold it a while longer and then shove it up his you-know-where. Whereupon he asked plaintively, "What are you angry about?" Whereupon I hung up on him. The foregoing expains why this letter is so long in getting itself written to you. I'm busy hanging up on people.

•   •   •

. . . I've been dining out in a generally exhausting fashion, accepting invitations I'll one day have to repay with some sort of party here. I've met some nice people, some stuffy ones, and the usual range of beaky-nosed, tight-lipped hostesses and repressed Englishmen. I still enjoy London greatly. I haven't had any time, unfortunately, to explore lots of the neighborhoods through which I whiz by cab to appointments, nor to get out of the country to many places I long to see. Between now and leavetaking, I have to write a sketch for the Dietz-Schwartz revue opening in New York in April,† as well as to try to

---

*On March 5, Perelman began a trip around the world that attempted to duplicate Phileas Fogg's journey in Jules Verne's *Around the World in Eighty Days*; Perelman's "manservant" was a woman. His account appears as "Around the Bend in Eighty Days" in *Vinegar Puss*.

†*That's Entertainment*, with music and lyrics by Howard Dietz and Arthur Schwartz, opened in 1972.

do something for *The New Yorker*, and it's one month away to countdown. . . .

                    •   •   •

ABBY PERELMAN

Hong Kong Hilton
Hong Kong
April 15, 1971

Dear Abby,

                    •   •   •

It's difficult to encapsulate the events of the 41 days I've been travelling since I left the Reform Club on March 5th, but anyway: together with — —, my secretary, we went by train from Charing Cross to Paris, spent the day there with David Bruce and his wife (he the ex-Ambassador to London and negotiator with the North Vietnamese), who gave us lunch with the Searles, Janet Flanner, etc. Then by train to Rome, where spent overnight with Bob and Luisa Edwards, then by train to Naples, where sailed to Istanbul, a stormy trip with dull Krauts and French bourgeois fellow-passengers. Spent arrival day there at the Topkapi Museum, very worthwhile, also mosques, etc., and entrained that night for Erzerum in eastern Turkey. This consumed 2½ days during which we didn't know a military coup was taking place but saw lots of tanks and soldiery en route. Ominous snow and cold here made it seem dicey that our trip by car and driver through the mountain passes into Iran would work; and in the end it turned into a pretty hazardous exploit. There had been a 3-day blizzard in the mountains, and we spent a whole day toiling past stalled trucks and cars and floundering upward until, overtaken by darkness and zero cold, we had to turn back, reaching Erzerum spent in whirling snow. Our schedule was such that we had to connect with a Persian Gulf steamer in Kuwait two days later. Luckily, a plane left Erzerum for Ankara the next morning, we got aboard, stayed overnight in Ankara, and then in an exhausting day, flew back to Istanbul, down to Beirut, and across to Kuwait in time to catch the steamer. From there we sailed in the next seven days to Bahrein, Dubai, Muscat and Oman, Karachi, and disembarked at Bombay on March 26th. Some of these Gulf ports were interesting, as it was from similar ones that the dhow I sailed on in 1954 had originated; in particular, Muscat and Oman, a very remote sheikhdom just emerging into the 20th century and one very few people have ever been allowed into. Also the Sultan's mother and her harem attendants joined our ship there, which enhanced the trip.

The Indian phase — Bombay, the whole elephant journey, and that phase — became totally complex. The Indian airlines were on strike, which hopelessly confused the train system, and additionally, with true Indian inef-

260

ficiency and muddleheadedness, the agents there had messed up what advance arrangements I'd made in London. Therefore, in order to do the elephant journey—or what passed for it—we had to fly to New Delhi, drive 200 miles to Jaipur, and spend 3 nights in the rajah's palace so I could even be photographed aboard an elephant howdah prior to driving 200 miles back to New Delhi—all this in intense heat and amid great expense. From Delhi we then flew to Madras—a truly depressing place—from which we were to transit by sea to Singapore. This proved to be the worst part of the entire journey, as I had anticipated. The vessel was Indian, carrying 900-odd deck passengers, swarmed with rats and cockroaches, and the food was almost completely inedible. I loathe India and the Indians, and always have; this, however, was worse than anything I've ever undergone, and how we lived through it, I can't imagine. Mutton curries and cold tasteless chapatties, and roaches swarming over one as he lay sweating in his bunk...ugh. Two-thirds of the way across the Bay of Bengal we passed by the Andamans, the famous penal colony mentioned in *The Sign of the Four*. It was all part of the fabric.

At Penang, 2 days short of Singapore, I threw in the towel; we disembarked, flew down Malaya to Singapore, and put in three or four days recuperating from the voyage. Here we had a booking to sail by a Dutch cargo ship up to Hong Kong, a 4-day trip. But it was delayed in arrival to Singapore, and then its departure was delayed twice, which would have meant that we'd never reach Hong Kong in time for the S.S. *President Wilson* carrying us trans-Pacific. So at the last minute we had to fly up here to Hong Kong.

What I've given you above is merely a travel schedule; now comes the personal part. Throughout the Persian Gulf, India, and beyond, my female companion's true personality was beginning to unfold. Mrs. — hails from West Texas, is one of 3 daughters of a Methodist minister there. Slowly there emerged from this hitherto obedient and efficient typist of mine a bossy know-it-all who, having once been briefly a tour guide—she took a small party of whey-faced bookkeepers to Honolulu—now started to fancy herself a world traveller. If you remember how positive and contradictory — — was at her worst, you'll know just what I mean. In addition, she became such a chauvinistic Texan that on several occasions I had to restrain myself from striking her—it was like having John Wayne and Lyndon Johnson traveling with you. Carried on about what superb pecans they raise in Texas, God's country, and so forth, not to mention endless stories about the oil business there and similar fascinating anecdotes. Then, when the Lieutenant Calley business broke, she began regarding him as a martyr; the poor man was merely a victim of the military higher-ups, that kind of bilge. Well, the whole thing reached a climax in Singapore when she started to teach me how to wrap up a package of books I was mailing back to London; and I knew it was the end of the line for my prairie flower. Last night, I gave her the customary 2-weeks' notice in the form of a check and her air transportation home, and tomorrow afternoon she wings off to California by Pan-Am.

And so, 3 days from now on April 19th, I depart Hong Kong for Kobe, Yokahama, Honolulu, and San Francisco — 19 days of sea-faring. I expect to spend most of the voyage in my stateroom, working, if all the blue-haired Southern gorgons I see in the hotels here are fellow-passengers as I rather imagine they will be. The *President Wilson* is due in San Francisco on, I believe, May 7th or 8th. . . . From San Francisco I'll transit the U.S. by train, expect to arrive May 11th in New York and stay till the 14th, when I sail for Southampton aboard the *Queen Elizabeth II*. (Will be staying, as I've told you, at the Algonquin.) And, of course, looking forward to seeing you and Joe and hearing your news. So I'll conclude this overlong and too-detailed letter with the hope that you're both well, that you've survived this dismaying period of history with at least some measure of equanimity, and that we can broach a bottle of the best together when the dogwood's in flower. With best love to you both.   Yours,

NEVA PATTERSON*

Grand Hotel
Taipei
April 23, 1971

Neva darling,

Don't just *sit* there gaping in surprise at this letter from a heathen clime. I know your kind; you think Chinese are all slant-eyed yellow bastards who live on rice and rats alternately and whose women's wee-wees run sideways. Well, you may be right; I'm so confused on this, the 49th day of my 80-day trip around the world, that I'm ready to cry uncle. The only trouble is that if I did cry that, a fat nance in the next room who's been eyeing me since I checked in here would probably slip a note under my door asking whether we could rendezvous in the Jade Bar and discuss Walter Pater or flower arrangements.

Yes, I've been breasting the waves and vice versa and have come through the Persian Gulf, the Bay of Bengal, the South China Sea, and all the urine-smelling stages in between — and now comes the big surprise. I've decided to do a slight adaptation in my previous schedule, which was to proceed from San Francisco directly to New York (as in the well-known movie of the same name), and hence will be arriving in Los Angeles from Tokyo. Will be leaving

*See note, p. 207. Patterson was in the first production of *The Beauty Part* and appeared as a panelist with Perelman in 1957 on *The Last Word*, a CBS series based on viewer questions about grammar and language hosted by Bergen Evans and featuring a rotating panel of linguistic experts.

Tokyo April 30th by air and am reserving a bed at the Beverly Wilshire for four days thereafter. So call up the liquor store and whatever madam now carries on the proud tradition of that beloved brothel-keeper of my era out there, Lee Francis, and tell her that Raunchy Sid, the Terror of Onslow Gardens in London, is knocking at the door. Naturally our group won't be complete intellectually without − −, but we'll have to make Do without her. How is Do, by the way? She was the one with the big tits that used to drive us crazy back in the Jazz Age. I guess you remember those stories Scott Fitzgerald wrote about her, and Ernest, and all of us at Jimmy's Bar.

Well, it's been super visiting with you, and as a final note, just dig this: you're going to have lunch with me, alone, at the Bistro one of those four days. Three gimlets apiece and sharing a bottle of their best Pouilly-Fuissé; and scandalizing all our neighbors as we cut up touches about the people we loathe. So start thinking about what to wear and what scent − Mitsuko? Jikki? Or maybe something with a floral fragrance. I think perhaps just a touch of money at the earlobes and have done with it − that's what Jackie O. was featuring the night I met her at Annabel's. Anyhow, leave like a message at the Beverly Wilshire welcoming me − which it will warm the cockles of the heart of,

Your longtime admirer,

ABBY PERELMAN

14 Onslow Square
London
July 11, 1971

Dear Abby,

As it's about two months since we've seen each other, and if much more time elapses I may have to jog your memory to recall who I am, I'd better re-establish what the British Army calls the l.o.c. (lines of communication). So I'll start where we left off, in Cabin 2044 of the *Queen Elizabeth II*. That trip ranked high, or rather low, in the travel experiences of all time, nearly as low as the crossing of the Bay of Bengal that preceded it. The ship is a gigantic floating supermarket for English goods, crammed with shops for Fortnum & Mason, Burberry's, etc., etc. and dedicated to hawking their wares with such intensity that it's almost shameful. You keep hearing announcements over the loudspeaker, "Last call! Shops closing in twenty minutes!" and the like. The food in first class was detestable; it's said to be better in cabin class. And it's served in absolutely slap-dash fashion − the waiters have trouble resisting their impulse to yawn in your face. Altogether − the decor, the service, the entertainment − wouldn't be tolerated on a cheap cruise ship in the West Indies...My table-mates turned out to be a fellow named John Aldridge,

263

an American critic, and his wife, and Ludovic Kennedy, an English writer and broadcaster, the movie of whose book, *Ten Rillington Place*, is being shown around. They were all nice, and helped save my sanity; also agreed vociferously with all the complaints above. That bearded fool Commander Whitehead, whose picture you've seen in the Schweppes and other ads, was also aboard with his wife. He's one of the directors of Cunard, and was apparently so afraid that one of us three writers was going to put our opinions into print (as I certainly shall when I get to that part in my account) that he was constantly buying us drinks and *schmeering* us up. On the last night, he had all of us up to dinner in a sort of extra special diningroom. The food there was unspeakable, and he punctuated the meal by nervous, Uriah-Heep questions about my impressions of the trip, etc., etc.

I got back to London to find that my landlady had returned from Capetown ahead of schedule and that all my things had been brought over to my new flat: so, arriving at 2:30 in the morning with the bird and baggage in a rather jumbled-up locale was pretty peculiar. It took a long time to get straightened out, or up to the point where it is now, and that's far from complete. I had to have the room I work in, and the bathroom, repainted—they were respectively dark blue and dark green but are now very cheerful; also had to change some overhead electric fixtures and so forth. All the foregoing was complicated by the arrival of the 30 cases of books that I'd stored in Pennsylvania, which demanded bookcases being bought. So it was a big muddle for the first month. However, it was really worth the trouble, for it's a lovely flat and everyone who sees it exclaims. Also, I now have a key to the gardens in the square I face, a beautiful grassy expanse with trees and flowers from which the public is ruthlessly excluded. You occasionally see a few rather beastly little English snots in there with their nannies. So far I've been too busy working to look it over.

Tong Cha II withstood the trip very nicely. He is ensconced in the kitchen by the window, where he gets plenty of sun and air, and a commanding view of many cats going on their important errands about the neighborhood. He makes a variety of sounds, most of them earsplitting, and while I've had no complaints thus far, I live in dread. As far as recognizable speech is concerned, a species of "hello" is all I can actually claim he's learned. On the whole he's a quite nervous bird, flies about the cage precipitately when he fears you're going to reach toward him, and thus is unlike Tong Cha I, who as you remember liked to be petted. Also he refuses to bathe, and that—says the handbook—is uncharacteristic of the breed. However, maybe he will in time. He eats in unbridled fashion, consuming about one apple and ¾ of a banana, plus rice, coconut, and additives. The book says these birds have no crop, and therefore are just channels for food. The lower part of the cage seems to bear this out. He is undoubtedly a nuisance but he's good company.

After a slow start, I am working intensively on this series about the trip. It hasn't been easy; there are technical problems involved, too much dull stuff that I unfortunately must write in order to see how dull it is before I excise it. So it is one step forward and two steps back...It has been quite tiresome having to answer the eternal question from everybody, viz., "How was the trip?" For them it's an easy conversational gambit, they sit back and expect me to pour forth a stream of delicious and comical stories — which in fact are non-existent. Unlike those two other around-the-world trips, when we went as a family and the one with Al Hirschfeld, this one was hurried and mainly tedious; also the other trips lasted almost ten months apiece as opposed to 2½ months in this case. In such a short span, about all that happens is a lot of transportation. Which makes for a lot of invention when you are forced to write about it.

As regards the English and living among them, the honeymoon radiance in which I was bathed before I left on the journey has largely subsided and I see them with much more clarity. In many ways, they are the most supremely self-satisfied and smug bastards I've ever encountered. They consider that the world begins and ends here, and they're quick to let you know it. There is a phrase in the last chapter of Thoreau's *Walden* that describes their attitude perfectly: "Consider the China pride and stagnant self-complacency of mankind." For "mankind," just insert "the middle- and upper-class Englishman or woman." They all talk in a horrid sort of very fast mumble that is difficult to understand and that doesn't become easier to grasp the more you live here. This, of course, is due to the fact that they're so repressed: the males half or three-quarters fag from their schooling, the females because they've always been bludgeoned into silence. The expression "It's not done" pretty well sums up not only the state of mind of the more solvent class, but the attitude of people in shops and businesses. If they haven't got some commonplace article, their response so often is "Is that something you have in Ameddica?" accompanied by a vinegary smile. Or just a scornful "No, I wouldn't know about that," figuratively slapping you across the knuckles with a ruler like an algebra teacher. Clearly there are some definite advantages to life here as opposed to New York City, all of which you're aware of. But having lived here, I'm sure you'll have encountered some of the less attractive aspects I speak of.

This is the end of a very hot day — we've had a spell of warm ones — and as my glasses keep sliding down my nose and mingling with the typewriter keys, I'd better quit. How is everything progressing, and how are you both? I'd like to hear from you, and to feel that everything is O.K. Every so often I start to think about the farm and the last years together there, and then I

265

have to stop thinking about it...Do write. Love to Joe, and give Tasha a hug
for me.   Love,

IRENE KEMMER

14 Onslow Square
London
July 25, 1971

Irene dearest,

·   ·   ·

. . . [A] largely humdrum existence the past ten days, as I've been taking a breather since finishing the first couple of chapters of the *New Yorker*
series. . . . Groucho Marx has been here, had dinner with him several nights
ago; he's pretty frail but his mood wasn't as black as when I saw him in California. I think he was pleased with his recent appearance in New York on Dick
Cavett's show, which I've heard was good. It's rather sad to compare his present creaky self with the bounce and audacity I saw the other night in a revival
of *Monkey Business*, the first picture I did for them...I really have been leading
an exemplary life, dining out very rarely and never straying much from this
district. Michael Korda, my man at S&S, is due here in about a week, also
Harvey Orkin, so perhaps the pace will quicken, and not a bad idea. Chop-
ping up Tong Cha's food twice daily isn't calculated to set the pulses drumming.

·   ·   ·

Yours only,

RONALD SEARLE

14 Onslow Square
London
August 5, 1971

Dear Ronnie,

·   ·   ·

My flat here is now pretty shipshape; today there arrived from Hong
Kong a gigantic box containing a very handsome brass Buddha, seated,
weighing approx. 200 lbs., a pair of Buddha's hands fashioned into bookends
(sounds kitsch but actually very good-looking), and a head of Buddha so dull
that I ought to have my own examined for ever having bought it. Oh, well,
maybe I can work it off on some South Kensington interior decorator. Anyway,
I was two-thirds right in my taste. There only remains to appear from Bombay a raffia screen being woven for me, the original of which I saw in an art
gallery there. I hope it's as beautiful as I thought when I saw it...The moral

266

of all this is that the acquisitive instinct dies hard. I got rid of everything at the Pennsylvania farm, and here I go again. Whatever became of Thoreau's stern injunction "Simplify, simplify!"?

As for the account of the trip, I have been beating away at it relentlessly every day. Progress is slow, for the simple reason that essentially the trip was pedestrian — a frantic effort to get from here to there on schedule, and nothing comic or diverting happens when one travels that way. Hence I have had to invent a great deal, and that takes time. But I am encouraged by a cable Bill Shawn sent me a week ago after reading the first batch of stuff. He says that the pieces have immense spirit and drive and he believes that I will be doing my best and funniest writing in this series. I would like to feel that his judgment is correct.

·   ·   ·

Other than work, life here's been fairly unexciting — and rather pleasant for a change after much too intensive socializing last winter. I guess I'm beginning to act like a resident, and to see me with my shopping bag in the Old Brompton Road, picking up an egg at Oakeshott's, a brioche in Bute Street, and a bunch of radishes at Leguma is to see a typical South Kensington old fart. "There goes a typical South Kensington old fart," is a comment oft-heard around the tube station.

One of these weeks before long, however, I'm going to take myself a brief holiday and nip over to Paris to see you and Monica, so guard yourselves well, will you, and let me hear how everything marches. (And, of course, should you happen to come over, I'd love to have lunch or whatever.) Dear love to you both, and I hope Monica is as trim, slim, and belle as ever. With all best,

Yours ever,

IRENE KEMMER

14 Onslow Square
London
August 9, 1971

Honey bun,

·   ·   ·

This past work-week, while unbearably slow and grinding, was lightened by the presence of Harvey Orkin, who flew in with his fellow con-man, Frank Stanton. . . . Their expense account bled for a couple of very good dinners at the Connaught, etc., and I took them to a reception at the Playboy Club for Hugh Hefner under urgent pressure. The latter nauseates me, naturally, but there is something of the same fascination Las Vegas holds in the sight of the coryphées surrounding him, with their tits upsqueezed in corsets and the don't-touch ambiance. As we all agreed, the atmosphere is actually so *a*sexual that it could be a Methodist camp-meeting. The night following, we were again part of the same social whirl; there was another party for H.H. at the house of Vic Lowndes, who runs the club. We were given a cellar-to-roof tour of this 5-story mansion, which probably contains more erotica—paintings, drawings, sculpture—than the Naples Museum. The whole thing was kinky beyond belief—walls lined with closeups of every intricacy of the Sport of Kings and Queens. And in the midst of all this, hordes of Bunnies, apparently airlifted in from Chicago and elsewhere (he circulates them), each staring emptily in front of her in unimaginably woebegone misery. The noise of Musak was deafening, obviating the necessity for conversation, and anyway, nobody had anything to say to each other. Suddenly my host mumbled something inaudible about Roman Polanski, ran away, and reappeared with the gentleman. We were introduced, shook hands, and stood staring. What could I say to him? Ask him how he felt about Sharon Tate? An altogether grisly evening.

London is pullulating with tourists and therefore is best on weekends; this past one struck me as really one of the most tranquil in memory, no doubt because I'd finished another piece of the cut velvet and looked forward to a couple of days' rest. I took Orkin and friend to the New Merlin's Cave, where the musicians played with their usual dedication. Unfortunately no George Melly* or Eric Lister† to sing for them, but they reacted as enthusiastically as has everyone I've gone there with.

•   •   •

Have you read a book of Bernard Malamud's called *Pictures of Fidelman*? It's got some delicious fun in it; be sure to read if you haven't. . . .

•   •   •

Yours only,

*British jazz writer and singer and author of several amusing works of autobiography.
†British jazz clarinetist and singer, owner of the Portal Gallery in London, and Perelman's frequent travel companion in London. Author of *Don't Mention the Marx Brothers: Escapades with S. J. Perelman* (Sussex, England: The Book Guild, 1985).

IRENE KEMMER

14 Onslow Square
London
August 21, 1971

Irene darling,

•   •   •

. . . [A]s always I'm burrowing my way forward on this travel series; this has been a discouraging week, making very, very slow progress and frequently cursing myself for ever having undertaken that journey. So little actually happened that I'm forced into the position of having to invent incidents, and there's nothing harder.

. . . . . .

. . . The one real mess of an evening was this past Wednesday, when I was dragged to see a stage production of Andy Warhol's called *Pork*. Which was unquestionably the most excremental, degraded and degrading spectacle that has ever been vomited forth onto a public stage in modern time; nude fags dancing with each other, girls masturbating with egg-beaters, defecating, coprophilia, Christ knows what. If you dramatized Krafft-Ebing, you couldn't have catalogued as many perversions or assembled so much undistilled filth—all of it utterly witless, pointless, and nauseating. I was two days getting over it, and I should think it must be the greatest corrective to sexual desire since the invention of saltpeter.

. . . . . .

IRENE KEMMER

14 Onslow Square
London
November 15, 1971

My very dearest Irene,

Your special-delivery letter reached me this morning, and was so gay and exuberant that it warmed my heart. Thinking back over your visit here, as I so often have, I couldn't help feeling what a trial it must have been for you to endure my mood and to have to listen to my dispirited and joyless reactions to everything. All I can do is to ask you to understand that I do suffer from these periods of despair and frustration whose origin I can't explain and that they do pass after a time. I think I'm feeling a bit better now—at least I hope so—and I know that when, finally, I'm able to get back to work, I'll be myself again.

I can at least give you one piece of good news—that the final piece I wrote for the *New Yorker* series was okayed, which really lifted a millstone from my spirits. Bill Shawn phoned me the Sunday after you left to tell me this, and I can't convey the relief I felt, for the effort of writing it and the length of time it had taken had just about destroyed my faith in myself. Anyway, *that's* off my back, thank God, and I know you'll be glad too, for I made my anxiety all too obvious to you.

. . . . . .

. . . Yesterday . . . was a lovely day; I walked all the way to Piccadilly Circus and then took the Underground to Hampstead, where I spent four hours

269

chatting with Donald Ogden Stewart.* He's such a lovely man, and he rang up a couple of hours ago to say how much he'd enjoyed seeing me and how I'd lifted his spirits. *Imagine* me in that role...

•   •   •

Yours only,

*American humorist and screenwriter (*The Philadelphia Story*, etc.) who moved to London in the fifties after being blacklisted (d. 1980). Perelman often cited him as an early influence on his own writing.

IRENE KEMMER

14 Onslow Square
London
November 30, 1971

Irene, my darling,

•   •   •

. . . I've been solitary a good deal of the time — have seen a few people, been to a couple of parties in a rather determined, mechanical way out of a conviction that I needed to see more people. One of them was a big crowded buffet of George Weidenfeld's, my publisher, the kind he packs full of literary folk like Ken Tynan, Edna O'Brien, Cyril Connolly, etc. Everyone stands around, balancing plates and wine-glasses, and twittering. The insincerity and infighting is ferocious. — is a mean bastard, he and his wife always contrive to drip a little poison on me or whomever they encounter, and I blew the joint as soon as I could. (I should mention, as a bit of background, that I'm strictly teetotal these days, as alcohol is forbidden with this medication I take, so in fact that puts a crimp on most socializing, as you know.) Still another gathering I went to, a cocktail do, was a trifle better; here at least was George Axelrod, who, while pretty Hollywood-oriented, isn't repressed and strangulated like the British contingent; and Douglas Fairbanks, whom I'd never met before, turned out to be an appreciative fan of mine, which helped my wilted ego. Then, for contrast, there was a dinner-party, just two couples, in a grand and cheerless flat off Eaton Square. . . . — has got himself involved with a horrid old bag, some Lady So-and-So, who always gets pissed and very reactionary. On this occasion, she was all wound up on the way they've expropriated the rich in Chile. So for two and a half hours I was forced to sit there — undrinking — and listen to the hardships wreaked on Señora This and Doña That. . . . The week's social activities concluded with a luncheon for six in a freezing cold basement flat near here in Kensington. I could write, and one day hope to, a diatribe about the English hatred for heat. We sat there chewing tough little partridges with teeth literally chattering with cold; what conversation there was dealt exclusively with horse racing, of which I know nothing and care less.

I must at this point interject a quotation from this morning's *Times* that I think provides a valuable insight about this country. Richard Hoggart is delivering this year's Reith lectures. He has spent time in the U.S. and France, and was making comparisons between America and England. "Fifteen years ago, on a year's visit to the U.S., he carried over the usual stock of attitudes about the country and found that they were almost all wrong. They were not 'truths' about America but they showed truths about the British, selecting and distorting American evidence to fit their book. At the back of much American rhetoric, even when it had turned sour on itself, lay the sentiment: 'We willed this sentiment — let's make it work.'" Now comes the insight: "By contrast one of the standard English moods was unexpectancy: the small land, the unexpansive climate" — understatement of all time — "the whole lived-into social structure — especially as it has borne on the great body of working people — all this conspired to lower the imaginative sights. We were an unexpectant society, and our unexpectancy could make us illiberal, the inhabitants of worlds only penetrated, if at all, down narrow, dark brown halls lit by 25-watt bulbs."

Maybe this is only my temporary and/or current state of mind, but I think it's the foregoing attitude, combined with English smug self-satisfaction, that has bugged me increasingly and will eventually bring me back home. Also important is the uneasiness I've always felt at cutting myself off from my idiom, the American habits of speech and jest and reaction, all of them entirely different from the local variety. I hope you don't mind my running off at the mouth this way about my disillusion, but I suppose I've discovered things here that weren't obvious in casual visits across the years. Possibly if I were twenty years younger or more, none of it would matter so much. However, that hoary maxim about teaching an old dog new tricks applies. God knows I have no desire to move back into New York or live there; yet there might be some tenable existence elsewhere there — Boston, perhaps — Pennsylvania again? . . .

•   •   •

Yours only,

IRENE KEMMER

14 Onslow Square
London
December 19, 1971

Irene sweetheart,

•   •   •

I'm beginning to think very seriously about coming back to America (though mum is the word, you understand, for various reasons). It wasn't my state of mind that prompted this desire; I've been pondering the advisability over the weeks, and within the last one talked to a couple of friends here to see if my reasons made sense. Both of those I talked to are English — Vera Russell (whom you didn't meet) is actually Russian by birth but has lived here a good fifty-five years, and Rab Raphael you know. Each quickly understood why I'm disaffected with life here, especially in terms of my work, and while I think they would sincerely miss me, they agreed that my objections and conclusions are valid. I then had a meeting this past Thursday with my tax accountant, because decisions there have to be made. (It's a question of certain benefits arising from a 17-month residence.) Anyway, as it now looks, if I stick here until April 27th, I'll have fulfilled that requisite and can come home just in time for the spring weather. Wouldn't that be loverly?

•   •   •

BASIL BOOTHROYD*

14 Onslow Square
London
December 20, 1971

Dear Basil,

I was enchanted to hear about your American adventures, not to say over-awed. Anybody who does 63 interviews is not only stout-hearted, he's made of ferro-concrete. I have been through a species of that mill and I feel for you. You of course realize that this kind of activity is a wonderful gimmick the publishers discovered, a substitute for spending their own money to advertise one's books. The Author as Salesman dodge was accidentally discovered when Simon & Schuster put Alexander King — whose book wasn't even reviewed in the press owing to a newspaper strike — on the Jack Paar TV show. King, who thought he was dying of kidney trouble, felt he had nothing to lose and virulently attacked the Catholic Church, stupefying Paar and the audience. At the end of it, Paar said helplessly, "I don't know who this man is, folks, but," he went on holding up a copy of King's book, "this is a very funny book and I advise you to run out and buy it." Within a month the book was selling 10,000 copies a week, and when King died, far from his usual pauperized state, he was worth a million and three-quarters dollars. I know all this because I brought the book to Simon & Schuster in the first place.

I was also delighted to hear that Phil Hamburger† did what I hoped he might. He is indeed a nice fellow and one of the two or three colleagues on

*British humorist affiliated with *Punch.*
†Staff writer for *The New Yorker* since 1939 (*J. P. Marquand, Esquire*, etc.).

the magazine I regularly consorted with. Some of them tend to have a ramrod up their arse, acting as though they invented the paper. I well recall an occasion years ago when Thurber was going on ad nauseam about his influence and how he'd set the style for the whole enterprise, etc. I finally got a snootful and said mildly, "Come, come, it's just another 15-cent magazine." Though nearly blind, he leapt at me and tried to throttle me. It took two burly copy editors to drag him off me.

Your proposal to lunch one day suits me fine, but why don't you come to the Reform instead? Their food is something less than what you'd get at the Mirabelle. However, for sheer gloom it compares favorably with the Century in New York, and I think in this holiday season is a useful antidote to the howling Christmas cheer around Regent Street. . . .

Yours ever,

NEVA PATTERSON

14 Onslow Square
London
December 22, 1971

Neva darling,

I filched this nutsy stationery from the kidney-shaped writing desk of my hostess—had I said my hostess's kidney-shaped writing desk, it might have given you a mistaken impression—some time ago, and I know that if she and you knew each other, she would want me to write you on her classiest notepaper. . . . The wigwam you see above is set like a jewel in the middle of 10,000 acres and represents everything those dirty Reds are attempting to take away from us. Bad 'cess to them.

·　　　　·　　　　·

I'm now living in a very nice flat in what is certainly a beautiful square, and by all the rules should be divinely content. It's very far away from Needle Park, mugging, and everything we all deplore in Manhattan, but being one of those people of whom Thoreau says that they would find fault with Heaven, I am restive. The English, after a year's exposure to them (and for all their vaunted good qualities), strike me as supremely self-satisfied, provincial, and unexpectant. Their humor and their responses are so different from ours. I am used to kind of a swift give-and-take that I miss here, and which I have a definite feeling I need for my work. It's really a question of the idiom we're all used to, and whether I can function without it is still unclear to me. . . . I think the whole thing boils down to: it's a nice place to visit, etc., etc.

·　　　　·　　　　·

Yours always,

HARVEY ORKIN

14 Onslow Square
London
December 24, 1971

Harvey, mein gold,

•   •   •

. . . ['T]is my second Christmas here, and a lot of the gilt has flaked
off. . . . Sure, they like the stuff I do and all that, but I don't know how long
I can go on without whatever it is that nourishes me...Now and then you run
across something funny. . . . But for the most part, it's very dead-ass. I catch
myself walking along the Old Brompton Road with my straw shopping-bag,
buying a bunch of leeks here, a banana there, and a rock cake in the bakery,
and I suddenly ask myself, Who is this? I feel like one of those old retired
cockers you see on Lincoln Road in Miami Beach. Yeah...Next thing I know,
I'll be signing my work "Isaac Bashevis Singer."

I had a fallow spell for five or six weeks, but now, Gott sei dank, am
working again, and sent off another casual to Shawn a few days ago. In between, have watched a bunch of television and seen some pictures. Jacques
Tati's *Traffic* struck me as very thin gruel indeed. I rather liked *Klute*, thought
Jane Fonda gave a gutsy performance. . . . But the prize package is an eppis
called *The Mystery of the Organism*, a fearsome hash of Communist propagan-
da, Wilhelm-Reichian orgone boxes, and far-out sex. The big scene is one in
which a very unattractive lady, perhaps supposed to be a sculptor, toys with
the dingus of a young man until he achieves an erection and then fabricates
a plaster-of-Paris moulage of it, subsequently producing a very much larger
dildo. Well, my dear friend, I am in my later sixties but my memory is as
sound — (I almost said "as a dollar," forgive me) — as sound as Pompidou's
ass. And I can remember that when ladies used to hoist themselves up on the
summer street-cars going to Crescent Park, Rhode Island, me and my observant 14-year-old friends would catch a glimpse of three inches of candy-striped
stocking. That's STILL my idea of sex, and what's good enough for Leopold
Bloom is good enough for me.

So here it is 5:20 p.m., Christmas Eve, and I'll have to knock it off.
I'm staying here over the hols, but January 3rd am going down to Tunis for
five days dancing on the wing of a plane like Fred Astaire in Mark Sandrich's
epic. This is something Eric Lister dreamed up, there's six or seven of us motleys
in the crew and I can already feel the fleas we'll contract. But they tell me
that if you want to be a writer, you got to have various kinds of experiences.

Bless you, then, my boy, and a pinch of the Sandy Claws to weib and
kinder. . . .   Love,

L. E. SISSMAN*

14 Onslow Square
London
January 14, 1972

Dear Ed,

Thank you for your very good letter, not to mention your kind remarks about the first piece in my global travels series. I hope the ones that follow don't disappoint. For various reasons, the legal department have exercised a heavy scalpel on certain passages in the series that didn't enchant me, to put it mildly, but I've had to bear it with fortitude. This was caused by the circumstance that my Passepartoute on the journey was an actual person and they were afraid that she might hie herself to a shyster and sue: so some rather salty anatomical references and the like wound up on the cutting-room floor. Oh, well...

It must be kind of a wrench to pull out of an organization you've been involved with for so long, isn't it? But the news that you're writing verse again is elegant for me and your many admirers, and I certainly will be waiting for your profile of Dick Cavett. I've been on his show twice and think he's the best of the talk show m.c.'s by a very long shot. For one thing, he's the only one with a real sense of humor. Fred Allen always used to say of Ed Sullivan and Jack Paar and Johnny Jump-up (whatever the latter's name is, that plastic character on the Coast) that they were all pointer-outers; that is, their function was to point out talent to the watching audience, they themselves having none and no personality either. Dick reads and has read a lot, and his judgment and taste are sound. I'm not sure how long he can hold up his standards in the brutalizing punishment of five-nights-a-week performance. The last time I was on, he told me that when he finishes on a Friday night, he's absolutely drained, to such a degree that he just sits at home over the weekend trying to recover his sanity. The competition between all these guys, as you know, is fierce. I remember thinking, the first time I was on Merv Griffin's show, that he was a fairly bright and tasteful chap. He lived not far from me in the country, and soon afterward I spent an evening with him that was most pleasant—he talked with sense and point, and there wasn't any of the horsecock of the bigtime TV personality about him. Well, several years later, I did another show with him and it was all flash and filigree—the teeth, not listening to what you were saying, the David-Frost yocking it up ahead of the joke, the whole dismal syndrome. Whereas he had attempted some kind of sensible interview the first time, on the second occasion I was thrown in with a stand-up comic from the borscht circuit, some crazy little actress with big boobs, and the usual

*American poet (d. 1976).

275

pack of strays they assemble on such occasions. (Note: Please don't think I'm discriminating against crazy little actresses with big boobs — they're the cement that holds our civilization together.)

As an addendum to the foregoing, the parallel instance is Martha Deane (Marina Taylor), whose radio program over WOR at 10:15 mornings you may be familiar with. I've been on her program five or six times and it's always a pleasure; she's a cultivated, sensitive, and experienced woman who can really draw out whomever she's interviewing. The last time I was on, she told me that she never invites a writer onto her show unless she has done her homework and read his book or books, and I believe it. And I think that this may be true of Dick but not of any of the others. People like Hugh Downs merely scan a few excerpts digested by their staffs and then fudge their way through the show. The worst of the lot, and an absolute fiend, is Downs's female associate, that horrendous Barbara Walters — the most insincere, brassy nitwit in the business. Well, I've strayed off the topic, which is Cavett, and what it comes down to is whether he's got the cheap vulgarity, the Joey-Bishop tinhorn show-biz, combined with pure brute strength, to withstand the pressure of the schedule he's undertaken.

Not much news London side; everybody here with streaming colds resulting from their foul winter weather, and I'm sneezing away with the rest. I've done a little work, not half enough by far, and must beat out a couple of pieces for the Sunday *Times* shortly to follow a *New Yorker* casual I've shipped off. Trouble is there are so many pretty wenches whose keyboards are infinitely more tempting than this old Royal Quiet. I got to spend five days down in Tunisia, a rather bland experience with lots of Roman archaeology, mosaics, etc. intermixed with Arab schlock, but it served to break the routine.

Thanks for your very kind offer to visit you in the spring, and I hope it comes to pass — it'd be great to spend a couple of days straightening out a lot of traumas. My very best to you both, and do let me hear from you when you're minded to.   Yours ever,

IRENE KEMMER

14 Onslow Square
London
January 30, 1972

Dearest Irene,

Mid-afternoon of a cold, *cold* day here; last night it snowed for the first time this winter, and I'm seated here with the electric heating unit trained on me and bundled in two sweaters. Whoever called this flat centrally heated has an exquisite sense of humor. I was thinking this morning how the English always complain, whenever they visit the U.S., that they can't stand our over-heated, stifling hotel rooms, etc. They obviously are still in the Stone Age and making a virtue out of necessity. And there's also a lot of boy-scoutisme mixed in. I see men and women alike hurrying through the streets in skimpy little jackets, no mufflers, nothing, their noses blue with cold and their teeth chattering, just as though they're trying to prove they're insensible to wind and frost. It's lunatic.

•   •   •

Life around here ambles on fairly unexcitingly. This month has slipped by without any work — false starts mainly — and a good deal of dining out that featured a few quite boring evenings. One of the worst occurred this past week when I weakly consented to dinner with . . . Princess Mdivani. . . . It seems that she was previously wed to Denis Conan Doyle, the son of the celebrated Arthur, and has now become the heiress to the whole literary estate. She and the husband are determined to rope me into writing a screen play for *The Lost World*, that science-fiction nonsense of Conan Doyle's about Professor Challenger, and as a result I was dragged through two endless evenings. On the second, the Princess insisted on telling my fortune with cards, presumably hoping to foretell that I would do their screenplay. The pasteboards revealed, however, that I was not destined to stay in England. "You weel only be fulfeeled by movement," the Princess declared, her nose buried in the cards. "You are like a table — underneath you are ze real wood, but pipple see only ze veneer on top. Zey mus' penetrate through ze veneer and find ze real you, ze wood underneath." She was wrong in calling it wood, though — actually, I'd turned to stone.

•   •   •

Your own,

FRANK SULLIVAN*

14 Onslow Square
London
c. February, 1972

Dear Frank,

Ever since this book of collected pieces appeared, I've had it on my conscience to send it to you because I hoped you'd enjoy it as much as I do.†

---

*Humorist, chiefly affiliated with *The New Yorker* (d. 1976).
†*The Best of Myles*, by Myles na Gopaleen (Flann O'Brien).

I think some of the bits about Chapman and Keats that build up into awe-inspiring puns are really magnificent, and the dialogues involving The Plain People of Ireland and The Brother are just heaven.

As you have every reason to believe, I am unquestionably the world's worst correspondent, so this is a belated apology for the many times I have meant to write you. This also includes congratulations on your latest birthday, of which I can only say that I hope you break the records of those 142-year-old Turkish porters and Georgian (Soviet) gaffers that are chronicled every so often. Of course, it will involve your straining at gnats and swallowing quantities of Bulgarian bacilli, but I figure it's a price anybody would be willing to pay.

Let me finish off by quoting a sweet little West Country song, carried here by the Sunday *Times*, written by Laurie Lee, that read: "I'm dancing with wool in my eyes because the girl in my arms is a ewe."

God bless and keep you, Frank, and with much love,

Yours,

FRANK SULLIVAN

14 Onslow Square
London
March 8, 1972

Dear Frank,

Thank you very much for your letter, which brightened my whole day. I'm pleased that *The Best of Myles* finally percolated through to you, thanks to Shana Alexander, and delighted that you share my enjoyment in it. Ever since it first appeared, I'd been meaning to send it to you. I somehow felt that more than anyone I know you'd be tickled by the delicious passages about The Plain People of Ireland, the Chapman and Keats puns, and the stuff about Myles and The Brother. There's such an absence of laughter in these melancholy times that the appearance of a book like this becomes a real event. I must confess, by the way, that I personally prefer Nolan's pieces to his novels like *At Swim-Two-Birds*, *The Dalkey Archives*, and *The Third Policeman*; whether because of my ignorance of Celtic lore and some shortcoming in my nature, I just bog down when he gets into the intricacies of Irish folk history and the byways of mysticism. In any case, it warmed my heart to hear that you found the book as salty and funny as I did. He was a rare bird and one to be cherished when you look around nowadays at the bilge that passes as humor.

You speak with a certain wistfulness—your exact word is "envy"—of

Herb Mayes and myself and the dozen other friends who've been sensible enough to quit the U.S. and come over here. I wish that I could echo those sentiments and tell you that I find life here idyllic, but after sixteen months I still haven't reconciled myself to the notion that I want to spend the rest of my days in Britain. Certainly all the clichés one hears are true enough; people here are generally civil, London is quieter and cleaner and less polluted than New York. . . . And yet there's a strange listlessness about existence here, an enervating quality, perhaps due to the fact that the great days of imperial glory have faded, God knows what. Maybe this is all subjective — I'm sure it is, but anyway, at the moment I don't get the stimulus out of being here that I used to experience as a visitor. So what it boils down to, I guess, is a feeling of impermanence and perplexity as to where I really belong. Probably in Providence, Rhode Island, whence I fled like Paavo Nurmi in 1925.*

I think you may have analyzed the true reason for our general bewilderment when you said in your letter, "I don't feel I have anything in common with anything going on in the world today." It sure is a nifty world where every plane has to be searched for bombs before departure, where a tea-room full of women and children is blown to hell by gelignite in mid-afternoon, where your morning paper tells you there are 700,000 heroin addicts in our country, and where our country is ostensibly concluding a disastrous war by sending wave after wave of bombers into North Vietnam. So O.K. — let's avert our eyes from these horrors and see what else is new. This morning's *Times* carries the following dispatch from Auckland, New Zealand: "Miss Germaine Greer, the woman's lib leader, accused of saying 'bullshit' in a lecture here, today led a chorus of liberation sympathizers in chanting the word again...Miss Greer flew to Wellington today to address another liberation movement meeting. 'I guess I have forced the law into a corner,' she told a reporter. 'This is going to make New Zealand the laughing stock of the world.' " Do you remember that series of radio pieces datelined "No Visitors" that Ring Lardner wrote during his final illness, when he used to get so exercised about the double-entendres in popular songs? I wonder what he (and Ross, incidentally) would have made of Miss Greer and her liberated cohorts chanting "bullshit."

Oh, well, Frank, I hadn't meant to get off into these somber reflections. The jonquils and snowdrops are beginning to spring out of the ground in the parks here, the power cuts we sustained these past weeks are over, and pretty soon this gray murk that has hung over us for months will be dissipating. I hope that by the time this reaches you, the snow will have vanished and Old Sol will be exerting his annual witchery on the forsythia and lilac

*Nurmi was a Finnish Olympic distance runner and one of the greatest runners of the century (d. 1973).

279

buds. Again my gratitude to you for writing, and with all the very best,

Yours ever,

IRENE KEMMER

14 Onslow Square
London
March 28, 1972

Irene darling,

.   .   .

You'll be glad to know I've finally reached a decision about my future plans, and have informed the rental agents I won't be renewing my lease when it expires May 20th. . . .

.   .   .

It really will be a boost to get back home and hear the idiom again. In a strange way, it's very much like the strain of talking French to live here. I went to a dinner party last week, there were only three couples, and my hostess was American, but all the references, the itsy-bitsy crossfire, were about local happenings, politics, whatever, and the evening becomes so wearing after a while that you just lapse into silence. I wonder if because of the eighteen months I've been away I'll have to catch up on our own references? I do know that in the pieces I've worked on lately, I've had to struggle to remember slang and quick ways to phrase things, and this is precisely what I'm sure one loses by staying here.

Well, sweetheart, it's dinnertime, so I'll squeeze now and dismount from the rostrum. I haven't thanked you for calling me a week ago Sunday — it was so good to hear your voice, not to mention the moral support you gave me. It'll be a couple of months before I can thank you in person, but I want you to know how much you mean to me and have meant all along. I send you all my love, and please write. Your letters help more than you know...

Yours always,

MARY BLUME*

14 Onslow Square
London
March 30, 1972

Dear Mary,

.   .   .

. . . I plan to go back to N.Y. about May 20th for a while. South Ken-

*Journalist for the *International Herald Tribune*, based in Paris.

280

sington has finally proved a surfeit of old ladies (Anglo-Indian) and shabby genteel retirement, and I think I need a shot in the arm of Manhattan's violence, filth, disorder, but chiefly our American idiom. I really miss it, God help me, and while I may be singing a different tune soon enough, it's what I trained on for so long that this dim environment seems too much like a nursing home.

As a daily recipient of the *Herald Trib*, I now see your pieces pronto as they appear, and without wanting to be smarmy, they are absolutely first-class — economical, witty, and civilized reading. I especially enjoy them because they're about real people, and your neighbors on the left, Buchwald and Baker, are endlessly driven to writing about ITT, Nixon, Kissinger, and all those mechanical subjects that are so unfunny. I know what a hard job the two are faced with, having to get it out as they do, but the strain shows more and more, whereas you preserve a sharp edge and your prose is careful and composed. I guess I must have at some time mentioned that the biggest compliment I ever heard Joe Liebling give anyone was that he was a careful writer. I've always thought that perhaps that is the best accolade possible. . . .

Yours ever,

ERIC LISTER

220 East 73rd Street
New York City
July 23, 1972

Dear Eric,

The address northeast of these words will corroborate the rumor that I am again an ant among the eight or ten million ones that infest Manhattan Island; and had you been lounging at the corner of Second Avenue and 73rd Street this morning, you would have rubbed your eyes incredulously. Could this schlep in khaki pants, his wrinkled shirt opened at the throat and his feet in scuffed bluchers, be the fashion plate who only three months ago might have been observed in Onslow Square, out Brummeling the Beau? Yes, sir, it was the same, but today, stripped of his custom-tailored threads, he was clutching an oily bag containing cream cheese and bagels, looking for all the world like that unsavoury Jew, Uncle Fagin. What I am trying to *keckitz* out, in short, is that I am again a native of this hot, tawdry, filthy, unmanageable city, and that all the veneer I acquired in eighteen months has peeled off revealing the true schlep beneath: a Gothamite.

The flat I'm occupying here is located in one of those vast, dreary dormitories that looks like Dolphin Square strung out; it faces on the rear, overlooking some kind of Catholic institution I haven't yet figured out but I suspect is full of monks chasing nuns. Every so often I behold fat ladies tweezing their moustaches from their upper lips. I have this pad until Sept. 9th, but what my plans are thereafter I haven't quite figured out. At the moment I've convinced myself that if I parcel out the year among three or four countries, that could be a feasible existence. For instance, December through March in New York; April and May in France or Italy, June through September in England, and October and November in France or Italy. To effect this (as has undoubtedly popped into your mind) I shall certainly have to rid myself of those thirteen pieces of baggage I'm still toting around the world. Anyhow, what it all means is that England hasn't seen the last of me by a long chalk. (What the hell is a short chalk?)

The temperature must already be up to the 95-degree figure the forecasters spoke of on the radio, and even the air-conditioned bedroom I'm in is heating up, so I think I'd better conclude. I miss our little Saturday and Sunday rambles in the Porsche (useless to plead with you to slow down a trifle, old boy). Do give my best to Terry and all the lads and lasses, will you? . . .

Yours ever,

CHAIM RAPHAEL

220 East 73rd Street
New York City
September 17, 1972

Dear Rab,

It is certainly a dog's age, donkey's years, or whatever fancy metaphor you fancy since we exchanged epistles, but here is one from my own nickel-plated pistle containing some news that I trust will please you. I shall be returning to the country of my adoption in about ten days or so—I hope by 29 September. To stay, alas, for only four or five days, since I am en route to the high Himalayas, Japan, and Indonesia. Even at the remove of three thousand miles, I can envision your ears pricking up at the news, so here is what is known in the underworld as the scam.

Travel & Leisure, the magazine backed by the American Express Co. and edited by the former editors of *Holiday* (which, as you know, went down the drain), has commissioned me to do four or five pieces for them, in rough order one on the Hunzas up in the Hindu Kush, another on Hong Kong (you recall that I spoke my wrathful mind on this, but there's another angle), a third on the Hairy Ainus in northern Japan (and never mind any *chochmas* about Hairy Anus because I've already thought of that), and a fourth on Banda Neira in the Banda Sea beyond Celebes, the islet I went to in 1949 on the recommendation of Somerset Maugham, which I wrote about in *The Swiss Family P*. So quite naturally, I have to check into the Map House in St. James's for detail maps, as well as to be kitted out with Grenfell cloth windbreakers, etc. for my ascent into the high country north of Rawalpindi, Srinagar, and other storied spots.

Your swift intelligence, often compared with that of Colonel Sebastian Moran, the second most dangerous man in London, will at once tell you that the Himalayan trek lies inside the borders of West Pakistan, in what I am reliably informed is closed territory ("restricted area") because of those clashes several years ago between India and Pakistan. So it ought to be fraught, *nicht wahr*? I shall of course be carrying my press card from the *Sunday Times* but whether that will protect my *baitzim* from the Moslems is speculative. I expect to be talking with Harry Evans sometime this w/e.* It seems to me that the least his rich employer can provide me with is a gold cup as used in the prize ring.

The summer has been a hot one; I've spent it in a furnished sublet on East 73rd Street getting back into the rhythm of New York, which was barbaric and frightening at first, but I adjusted to it and now really rather enjoy it. I guess I'm a New Yorker at heart. I was born here, and despite 21 years in New England, I guess it got into my bloodstream. And I've found that my productivity returned here. I believe that I really needed the acceleration, the nervousness and pressure of New York life to stimulate my work. As you know, I always deplored the idea of writers cutting themselves off from their roots — *vide* Irwin Shaw, Stephen Crane, etc. So what I've decided to do hereafter is to parcel out the year, spending December through April in New York, my summers in England, and the autumn and spring months between France and Italy. At least I'll try that schedule for a year or two and see how it works. I've taken a pad at the Gramercy Park Hotel as of December 1, to return there after this trip and spend the winter. It's across the square from the Players Club and halfway from my old haunts in Greenwich Village and the frenzy of midtown, and needless to say, whenever you come over there will be a hot grog steaming in my kitchenette for you. . . .

Yours ever,

*Harold Evans, editor of the London *Sunday Times* from 1967 until 1981 and editor of the daily *Times* until 1982.

ERIC LISTER

Gramercy Park Hotel
New York City
January 2, 1974

Dear Eric,

Well, I guess the advent of a new year makes it time to send forth white

283

doves with messages of good will in their beaks, so I am loosing a dove with a Hebraic nose in your direction, bearing kindly thoughts. From the stories we get over here about power cuts, three day work-weeks, and similar emergencies in Britain, it sure sounds grim, and I daresay you will do a lot of your fucking this winter clad in thermal underwear. Thus far, the restrictions seem to be affecting only motorists here; there is a lot of weeping and wailing from drivers because petrol stations are closed on Sundays, but the weather has not been drastic as yet, so home heating and industry haven't been touched. (But of course there have been massive layoffs of labor in the automotive and airplane fields.) What the energy crisis *has* done — and maybe it has been used for the very purpose by the Administration — is to shove the Watergate scandals off the front page, and one has the uncomfortable feeling that that son-of-a-bitch in the White House will end up staying there till the end of his term. This is a very strange land.

Anyway, turning to more personal matters, I think my last little trip to Britain in early October did me some good: I have been working pretty steadily ever since and enjoying decent health, and just now getting ready for a winter holiday. A couple of friends and I have just decided to lease a place in Sarasota, Florida, as of now until April 30th, and will be spending varying amounts of time there during the next 16 weeks. It's on a place called Long Boat Key, and comes equipped with a motor boat, a pool (in addition to sea-bathing), and even a car. Hence I expect to go down there around the 20th of this month and live thereafter in a pair of bathing trunks and a ragged shirt. Haven't done this kind of thing for years, and am looking foward to a little beachcombing.

.   .   .

Yours ever,

HAROLD EVANS

Gramercy Park Hotel
New York City
January 6, 1974

Dear Harry,

The news brought you by a messenger with a cleft stick — and palate to match — that I'd done an autobiographical piece for *The New Yorker* was correct, and I enclose tear-sheet of same.* It appeared about a month ago, so whenever their statute of limitations allows reprint, I'm sure they'd grant the *Sunday Times* permission and I happily accede. The quid pro quo can be arranged in the usual manner — i.e., Deborah and you seize each other's wind-

*"Ready, Aim, Flee!" is collected in *Vinegar Puss.*

284

pipe and the first one who turns blue is loser.* I hope you like it — the piece, that is, not Deborah's windpipe.

I don't know why I'm being so cordial to a man who wrote me way back on November 1st that a beautiful blond playwright called Tina (who had won your drama award) was coming here and would phone me. The only blond I have seen around here is a Polish maid with fat thighs and no chest who persistently spills ammonia on my suede shoes. This can't be the woman you meant, Harry, or else you have a low opinion of me as a judge of feminine sexuality. Was Tina real or merely the product of an erotic opium dream? . . .

It now looks certain that I'll be coming over in late February as part of another global swing for *Travel & Leisure* carrying me to a number of places I've never been. So if you want to redeem yourself, dust off Tina (whom you no doubt have sequestered for yourself in a *garçonnière* in St. John's Wood) and we'll let bygones be bygones. Wouldn't it be creepy if that were really her name — Tina Bygones? She sounds kind of Hungarian.

Enough of this passementerie. Love to you and Enid, and my best wishes for the new year.   Yours ever,

*Deborah Rogers was Perelman's British agent from 1969 to 1977.

KARL FORTESS

Gramercy Park Hotel
New York City
January 8, 1974

Dear Karl,

A *farginiggin* to receive your greeting with your mynah-like grackle croaking from what I take to be your blasted oak. (Blasted not in the pejorative sense — the Shakespearean.) Abby told me that she had seen you, and a week or so earlier, when I saw Woodie and Jane [Broun] after far too long a separation, I learned from W. that you had stricken the gyves of Academe from your wrists and ankles and were now rusticating in Woodstock. I immediately asked if this were a way stop en route to Bristol and was told that you still nurtured that particular dream. We'll discuss that in depth when we forgather for our salt beef and lemon tea; for the time being, I presume you are reading what goes in England, and if you have a groat's-worth of *saychel* (my, how one returns to the mother tongue in the sere and yellow leaf!), you harbor no regrets about being here instead.

Well, as you see, I am the Ancient Mariner who not only stoppeth one of three (from emigrating to the U.K.), but like Captain Billy Bones checking into the Admiral Benbow Inn, I've anchored myself here in a general way;

and until they tip me the black spot and set me travelling again, I propose to ride out the coming crunch in this vicinity. This doesn't mean that I wouldn't be off to the Dordogne or thither Indonesia like a shot if given the opportunity, but I think a little physical inaction, combined with an equally small amount of writing, is indicated. I should confide—on what I'll elaborate more fully in person—that when I was in the Far East a year ago, I got all het up about building a schooner at Dobo in the Aru group (Indonesia, where it's very cheap to build piratical black schooners) and turn myself into a Jewish version of R.L. Stevenson. They practically had to tie me down with restraint straps to prevent this dream from maturing; I kept chanting hysterically, "But they told me they could built it for $11,000 to my order! With a Yamaha engine we'd import from Tokyo!" I even opened a small free yen account in the Chartered Bank in Tokyo—that's how serious I was...Lookahere—I was just smitten with a thought. Everyone knows that Bristol is the very place for this kind of *meshuggahis*. Why not build it in Indonesia and fit it out in Bristol together? Work it out along those lines. . . .

All best to yourself and Lillian, and a splendid New Year for yourselves from   Yours ever,

IRENE KEMMER

Sarasota, Fla.
February 26, 1974

Irene dearest,

Three weeks today since I left New York and desolated that I haven't written you before, but I've had my nose firmly affixed to the grindstone; and yesterday mailed off the piece I'd finished. At the moment it's freezing cold here, temperature midway in the forties and a wind off the Gulf warranted to freeze the proverbial brass monkey's etceteras. Most of the stay thus far, though, the weather's been very pleasant and people have been swimming, both pool and sea, and in the relentlessly optimistic forecasts one hears over the radio, they promise divine weather the next day even if it does turn out to be a howling rainstorm, as it has three or four times.

The house turned out to be a fairly comfortable one that takes you a full week to figure out. It's the oldest one in the section, situated on several acres thickly planted with orange, grapefruit, mango, coconut, and other fruit-bearing trees. On one side it fronts one of the many inlets of Sarasota Bay, and on the other it's a block's walk from the Gulf of Mexico, which is lined with motels, condominiums, etc. The side facing Sarasota Bay has the pool, a free-form job, all screened so no insect life gets at you. The 3 bedrooms each open on a small, also-screened patio. Big livingroom with dining alcove at one end. The whole place is so crammed with furniture that it looks like Lawner's auction galleries on University Place, and every available inch of wall and shelf space is dotted with statuettes, pictures, books, and the accumulation of a family's residence for God-knows how long. The owner, I discovered shortly, had been in the CIA for ten years, and according to the Ouija board I worked one night with Peter Feibleman, . . . the house is still bugged. (Never underestimate the power of a Ouija board.) Living on the place, in a flat over the garage, is a young couple . . . , former students at the local college. Both are poets — that is to say, they both have "poems" in a mimeographed magazine issued by the university.

•   •   •

. . . Miss H. . . . spends impressive periods of time on the phone, conversing with her secretary in New York, Renata Adler, and Mike Nichols, who is apparently a very close friend. Miss H., under protracted inspection, is a curious mixture, part imperious yenta who throws her weight around and part amusing old friend when she and I and the Hacketts talk about old times in the movie biz and Broadway. She has a very concrete sense of her importance that frequently burns your ass, and the Hacketts, who are manifestly very grateful to her for minor advice she gave them on *The Story of Anne Frank*, are very worshipful. They themselves are wonderful in every way — unassuming, sweet, really dear people and as close to the Christian ideal as any you've ever met. We all get on together without the least friction though every so often I'm tempted to order Lillian to knock it off. (Should say that I got here right in the middle of her being filmed by Bill Moyers. . . .)

The chief part of the cooking has been done by Hellman, with alternating trips to restaurants, which are lousy. Our staff — i.e., cleaners and one limited cook — is composed of a Mennonite lady [and] . . . one of the most frightening creatures to behold, with an orange wig and a complexion like a spoiled citrus fruit, and an Armenian student friend of the young poets. The latter's principal talent seems to be baking chocolate cakes which consume eight to ten hours of his time at $5.00 per hour. We have now cut him down to coming 3 times a week for four hours at a clip. Hellman is a good cook on spaghetti, boiled beef, and fish. A pot roast she attempted day before yesterday tasted like a shag rug (a dish which as you know we are all familiar with). Unfortunately, she does not regard herself as a good cook merely, but as a Brillat-Savarin, and requires fulsome compliments...The rest of the population here is to be seen circulating turgidly around a shopping circle four blocks distant named St. Armand's Key. Nobody here is less than 75 and many walk supported by two metal canes, resting at frequent intervals on concrete benches outside the shops. There are countless dress and shoe shops, all infernally expensive. Nobody talks about anything but the gas shortage, and every

287

program on television is concerned with the same topic. Until now—today it's reported better—there has been a very tight distribution of gasoline. The only glamorous note supplied thus far consisted of a visit by Bill Blass, the dressmaker. L.H. spent the visit raving about some garment she had bought from Blass, and he indicated in seigneurial fashion that he would be pleased to make her a copy in corduroy or sisal or some recondite material. Blass informed us that business in ladies' wear is now poor and that he has to hustle to make his former profits. He also disclosed that he keeps up his tissue tone by twice a year immuring himself in a physical-health spa near San Diego called The Golden Door where the establishment bars its female clientele every so often and admits only 15 hand-picked men. . . . He is very bronzed and (according to L.H. and Frances Hackett) good-looking. . . .

Otherwise, except for a fairly routine afternoon spent fishing with L.H. and the male poet in a motorized skiff, the net catch being a shrunken flounder and two poisonous herrings, life here has been pretty quiet. We all go to bed circa 10 p.m. and then sit around the breakfast table listening to Lillian's account of how puny her sleep was and what gossip she learned from a 2-hour chat with her secretary in New York. . . .

·   ·   ·

Love and kisses,

I R E N E   K E M M E R

Sarasota, Fla.
February 30, 1974

Irene darling,

It's a languid and warm Saturday afternoon, 3:45 to date it exactly, and my mess-mates are up forward, grouped around their game of Scrabble which they've been voraciously involved with the past couple of days. I in my turn, having completed my day's work, feel more like writing you than joining them by the pool. . . .

·   ·   ·

. . . [I'm] in a cold rage at La Hellman, who I really think deserves to have her ass kicked roundly. Of all the imperious, arrogant spectacles I've witnessed in a long time, her behavior this evening takes the cake. To put you in the picture fully—it turned out that all of us, the Hacketts, she and [Steven] Marcus, and I were dining at a supposedly chic restaurant-hotel called the Colony. . . . Blass had told the hotel that she might be coming over one evening, she'd had Albert Hackett mention her name when he reserved on the phone, so there was a big tzimmas when we arrived. Swarms of fag headwaiters descended, we're swept to a table cheek by jowl with the Gulf of Mexico, and

Hellman's beaming as the owner and manager of the hotel come to pay court. The food, like that in all the restaurants hereabouts, proves to be indifferent to lousy, and the noise is earsplitting. It emerges gradually by the end of the meal that the management has presented our two bottles of second-rate Italian wine as freebies—total price circa $10. During the early ass-kissing of Miss H., I neglected to say, the headwaiter told her that Senator Lowell Weicker was in the house and would join us at the end of the meal. Well, no Weicker shows up, and I suspect that this is what curdled Hellman's milk. So—we're back in the car driving home and she in hoity-toity fashion declares that we should never have accepted the wine. "I *told* you that we should pay for the wine," she reproaches Albert Hackett four times, "I *told* you we shouldn't be beholden—I make a point of never accepting anything in restaurants for free," etc. etc. Well, I stood it as long as I could, and at last I said, "Oh, Lil, stop leaning on it, will you?" "I *will* lean on it," she snapped. "I don't want some fag going all over Florida telling people I accepted free wine." "Why, was the reservation in your name?" I asked. "Yes, it was," she says with all the grandeur of Queen Isabella, Empress of Spain, the Indies, Mexico, and the Iberian Air Line. "And Albert, I want you to send a check tomorrow to those people for twenty dollars for the wine." (Ten dollars being its cost, as I said before.) "I'm not going to be indebted to them for a lousy twenty dollars."

I think, of course, that it wasn't this incident solely that has got my dander up; rather, it's that people have been feeding her vanity to the point where it's becoming insufferable. The hoopla that has gone on about her TV appearance with Bill Moyers, the compliments which she's forced out of us to buttress her self-esteem because she was afraid she hadn't made a good showing that night, the phone calls from her publishers congratulating her, and all that sort of rot piled upon the hosannas about her book have puffed her ego out of all recognition, and four weeks of it have begun to give me a snootful. The present schedule is that the Hacketts leave here for N.Y. on March 8th and Hellman on the 12th or 13th. As of the close of today's business, my motto is "God give me strength." . . .

· · ·

PAT KAVANAGH

Gramercy Park Hotel
New York City
March 30, 1974

Dearest Pat,

· · ·

. . . My digs are beginning to take on a semblance of hominess, now that I have decided to convert these rooms into a more or less permanent pied-à-terre. Hanging on the walls near the couch on which the pillows are strewn is that superb portrait of Queen Mary by John Deakin which I bought from Eric Lister. Facing wall contains a lovely *New Yorker* cover by André François—a bistro scene—that he gave me, and flanking it a rare photo portrait of Toulouse-Lautrec given me by Ronald Searle; next to it a photo of Maharani, the Washington Zoo's superb white tigress, next to whose thrilling flanks is a woodcut by John Held Jr. adjacent to a drawing by William Steig from *The New Yorker*. Over my desk hangs a brass ship's clock I acquired in Hong Kong and a Victorian nude painted on porcelain that I picked up in the Caledonian Market. In the bedroom, a nice new record-player plus assorted bric-a-brac (but regrettably no nudes, Victorian or otherwise. I am, however, taking applications for the post and you lead the field, *ça va sans dire*).

.　　　　　.　　　　　.

Your picture of London at the time you wrote made it sound pretty ghastly, but I presume from what I read that life is a bit more tolerable now. This morning's papers, though, should start a big westward tide of America-bound business folk and expatriates—e.g., the new government's taxes on world-wide income. I guess the salad days are over. Hereabouts all one hears is the usual speculation about Nixon's impeachment and/or resignation. His TV appearances cause such apathy mixed with nausea that I can barely watch the idiot box.

As for myself, I go along at snail's pace doing the mixture as before; wrote a couple of *New Yorker* pieces in the Southland just to stave off ennui, and very shortly will have enough of them for another collection. A producer who has been fiddling with my last play, *The Beauty Part*, for the past 18 months has now reached the contract stage, and I'm keeping my fingers crossed that it may be done next season. Also, Jason Epstein of Random House is murmuring sweet nothings in my shell-pink ear, he wants me to tell him that he can publish my autobiography—of which I've had four chapters gathering moss for three years. I keep telling him that I've been doing autobiographical bits for the past 45 years, but he refuses to listen and says he has pots of money to advance for such a project. I suppose one should never turn down money offered one for whatever reason, but my feminine intuition tells me it could easily turn into a semblance of handcuffs, what you literary fellows call a succubus or incubus (I never could tell which is which).

Well, my dear, I must stop running off at the mouth like this and curry my frame for dinner with a lady. Who knows—she may be overtaken by libido in the midst of dinner, and hurling her mashed potatoes to the floor, tear off my garments and ravish me on the tablecloth? I've often read about such things in the novels of Ouida (and more often in publications of the Grove Press), but it's well to be equipped for any eventuality. So I enclose herewith all my love and hopes for good tidings, and please write if all else fails and you can't come over.   Yours always,

WILLIAM ZINSSER

> Gramercy Park Hotel
> New York City
> May 8, 1974

Dear Bill,

.   .   .

. . . Al Hirschfeld and I have just returned from a dizzying 1600-mile trip to Louisville, Kentucky — not to the Derby (which took place on Saturday as well) but to see David W. Maurer, our old friend and author of *The Big Con*, etc. I don't recall whether we spoke about it, but if you have seen *The Sting*, you'll have instantly spotted the chilling resemblance: so much so that I wouldn't be at all surprised if an action for plagiarism isn't forthcoming soon. The parallels are too striking to be merely accidental.* It is also good news that Dave has embarked on an autobiography, which will certainly be compulsive reading, since at one time or another he has known every practitioner of the light and heavy rackets with the possible exception of Richard Milhous Nixon and his grisly crew.

At the moment a couple of major enterprises are hotting up on the front burner, i.e., my own autobio and a revival of *The Beauty Part*. It's more than likely that I may be embarking on the first on a full-time basis before too long, and several producers are seriously talking about the second as an early entry next season. My fingers are crossed so tightly that I'm having trouble doing much typing otherwise. . . .   Yours ever,

*"In 1974 Maurer filed a $10 million suit charging that the movie *The Sting* and a book by the same name were substantially copied from *The Big Con*, which he wrote in 1940. The suit was settled out of court two years later" (*Louisville Courier-Journal*, June 12, 1981).

MARY BLUME

> Gramercy Park Hotel
> New York City
> May 27, 1974

Dear Mary,

.   .   .

. . . I haven't budged out of this old Confederate stash very much since

291

I returned from the Far East back in mid-January of '73. He whom you rightly call Boswell Shenker chronicled that tiresome Florida junket of this past winter, and last fall I took a week's trip to London that was so depressing as to be indescribable. I guess I must have received some portent of the rigors to come, because the 22-to-45 day excursion I'd bought suddenly turned to ashes in my mouth and I paid a premium to vacate it. Anyway, even New York seemed jolly by contrast when I returned. In actual fact, this part of town, everything considered, makes life a bit more supportable. I have a two-room pad on the 16th floor of the hotel's annex, from which I look down on the leafy expanse of the square bordered by the Players Club, the National Arts Club, and Ben Sonnenberg's imposing pavilion, and I've managed to abate the hotel furniture's cheerlessness with some of my books and pictures, etc. . . . As for current plans, I've taken a house for July and August up at Martha's Vineyard, adjacent to my friends the Hacketts, so I should dodge a portion of that furnace-like New York summer heat. Also, as announced in this past Sunday's *Times*, an outfit called the American Place Theater will be reviving my play, *The Beauty Part*, as their first production of next season; rehearsals in September and due to open October 1. (This was the play Bert Lahr starred in that was felled by the great newspaper strike of 1963.) This outfit has a very pretty, newly built theater on West 46th Street, and the whole project delights me because — IF it succeeds — it may evoke a bit of the moola I've stubbornly believed lurks in its seams. Light a candle for it in some small unassuming church.

•   •   •

. . . [Ronald Searle] did half a dozen nice illustrations for the *Travel & Leisure* series I wrote about the Far East, which pieces, parenthetically, will be part of a collection I'm about to turn in to S&S. At present I'm also dickering with them about resuming an autobiography I've twitched at spasmodically. Later this week will tell the tale whether they're willing to put up the money necessary for me to take a year off and finish it.

•   •   •

Yours always,

ERIC LISTER

Gramercy Park Hotel
New York City
June 2, 1974

Dear Eric,

•   •   •

. . . I'm sorry to hear about the melancholy state of business, not to mention the scaffolding of Asprey's that shrouds the gallery. Perhaps it'll give you a laugh to hear of a business venture of mine that has just wound up to a dazzling climax. Maybe I told you that during the course of my last trip through Indonesia, when I was sailing among its remotest islands, I picked up nine old Chinese plates totaling about a hundred dollars. I had these with me when I was hijacked in Australia and schlepped them all over the Far East and Europe agitatedly guarding them with my life. Well, in due course I took them up to Parke-Bernet-Sotheby, where one of their so-called experts thought they would fetch about $450. Anyhow, they were sold last week for a grand total of $140, which, deducting their commission of 22%, means that I lost four bucks on the transaction. The sale catalogue described them as Japanese, with a clear inference that they were schlock. I think I had better stick to writing.

•   •   •

Yours ever,

PAT KAVANAGH

Vineyard Haven, Mass.
July 19, 1974

Pat dearest,

Delighted to receive your letter of the 10th yesterday advising that you will be arriving on the 2nd of August. . . . And if you have the hardihood to survive the dullness and questionable food hereabouts, I'm sure you'll emerge from the experience as finely-tempered as Damascene steel. I myself am getting there rather slowly; at the moment I have all the snap and spring of a hank of dental floss. It hasn't anything to do with the house, which is very comfortable and is indeed equipped with every convenience — a lovely kitchen with washing machine, dishwasher, masses of pots, pipkins, double boilers, cutlery, basters, boilers, etc. and six — count them — bedrooms, two downstairs and four up. There's a lovely enclosed garden, ideally situated for sun-bathing with a minimum of clothing, a sun-deck, and a library, livingroom, and sun-porch, all tastefully furnished. And the beach where you'll swim is approximately 75 yards distant, approached by crossing the yard of my lifelong friends, Albert and Frances Hackett. . . .

Anyhow, rest assured that it'll be a pleasure to have you here for the skimpy eight days at your disposal, and I'll give you the requisite guided tours of the island in my (rented) fire-red Dodge Colt. My dialogue may not be as crisp as Sean Connery's nor my sinews as resilient, but any unprejudiced observer will testify that I have a heart and belly as big as all outdoors. And with that thrilling prospect, I bid you welcome. With much love,

Yours ever,

RONALD SEARLE

New York City
November 4, 1974

Dear Ronnie,

John Locke* has told me that you are now back in Paris, so I settle down on my hams to indite this long overdue letter. First of all, to thank you very much indeed for your drawing of myself being inducted into the Chinese tailor shop in Hong Kong that illustrated the fourth piece in that *Travel & Leisure* series. As soon as it's framed, it goes up on the wall of my stash here to brighten the inflationary winter solstice ahead. . . . Anyway, it'll make a peachy companion piece to one of André [François]'s covers for *The New Yorker*, a café scene he did a couple of years ago; and it will also be cheek by jowl with that marvelous photograph of Toulouse-Lautrec you once gave me.

•   •   •

The New Yorker has seven pieces of mine backed up which, for incalculable reasons, they haven't yet run, and as they're part of a new collection which will be published in March — title, *Vinegar Puss* — I trust will shortly appear in its pages. Meanwhile, my forever itching foot is longing to carry me to some distant clime, as it seems an aeon since I've gone travelling. I'd like very much to spend a bit of time in the department of Corrèze (visions of cassoulets in Perigord and so forth) and would like to racket around Macon and some other spots I saw on previous trips. As distant clime, I realize these don't qualify as compared to Indonesia, Japan, and the East, but I don't know whether I can summon up the moxie to pack up my effects, stow them in the hotel's basement, and subject myself to all the requisite medical shots. I guess, therefore, that one of these days very soon, I'll contrive a lunch with Caskie Stinnett† and see where the power and majesty of Amexco can dispatch me.

•   •   •

Yours ever,

*Searle's American agent.
†Dean of American travel writers; travel editor, *Holiday*, 1965–67, editor in chief, 1967–70; editor in chief, *Travel & Leisure*, 1971–75.

ERIC LISTER

Gramercy Park Hotel
New York City
December 1, 1974

Dear Eric,

•   •   •

I've been working as little as I possibly could of late, feeling a strong desire to do some extensive travelling, and last week presented a project to *Travel & Leisure* magazine—for whom I did that last trip to the Far East. If, as I hope, they look with favor on it, I may shortly be embarking on it. It involves a lot of assorted spots I haven't seen, like Sweden, Israel, Russia, Siberia, Borneo, and New Guinea, and I'd be approaching them through your bailiwick, so light a candle for the enterprise and keep your fingers crossed. From the economic point of view, things being what they are currently, this may not seem like the ideal time to go a-voyaging, but then, no time really is, and at my present age, I have the feeling that I should crowd in what travel I can while the spirit moves me. There'll be plenty of opportunity to sit in that chimney corner cackling over my pint of bitter later on.

•   •   •

Yours ever,

MARY BLUME

Gramercy Park Hotel
New York City
December 16, 1974

Dear Mary,

•   •   •

Thank you for your sympathetic vibrations to the unveiling of *The Beauty Part*. Your hope that it was a triomphe and that I was borne from the theater on Clive Barnes's shoulders was wrong in one anatomical respect—i.e., he carried me out on the sole of his shoe and disposed of me (as do New York pedestrians) by scuffing said shoe against the curb. Which is to say that he scathed and roasted the play and blistered me with a particularly vindictive review that surprised everyone, and I can only suppose that he completely misunderstood the whole damn thing. However, we did get good notices from Edith Oliver in *The New Yorker*, *Newsweek*'s Jack Kroll, *The Daily News*, and some others: none of which, however, affected the play's run of five weeks. . . . So while I was denied the satisfaction of its being moved to Broadway and resultant shekels, it'll be turning up in the boondocks as it has since its original production with Bert Lahr in 1962.

As for myself, I spent a couple of boring months this past summer up on Martha's Vineyard, which literary water-hole has now exhausted its charm for me; I like some of its denizens singly, like Lilly Hellman and the John Herseys, but en masse and coagulated with the *New York Review* crowd, that type of High Bohemia gives me goose bumps. I guess you would call it the Lionel Trilling syndrome, that mixture of academe and successful-author and celebrity-chasing civilian where everyone is being so brittle and epigrammatic that your inlays loosen in your head. Personally, I just get flushed and inarticulate on a small quantity of vermouth and immediately long to be sequestered in some greasy spoon in Kincaid, Oklahoma, where they've never seen a celebrity since Stepin Fetchit left town.

Maybe all that is why—plus the fact that, as they say, I have sand in my shoes—I've recently become restless again for the far horizon. Anyway, I'm now discussing another wide-ranging travel project with *Travel & Leisure* magazine that I hope will take me ultimately to Borneo, Bhutan, the Vale of Hunza in the lower Himalayas, and some other outbacks as well as Russia, Israel, and a couple of similar fever blisters I've missed. This ambitious journey's to be firmed up before Christmas, *on espère*, and I'd like to be off in January. Owing to weather conditions, I'd probably go trans-Pacific and would like to hit Europe in late summer or early autumn so as to revisit Languedoc, Corrèze, and the Pyrenees. At all events, this is my present fantasy, and should it disappointingly simmer down to a fortnight at Rivkin's Pleasure Dome in the Borscht Belt, a boy can dream, can't he?

Well, Mary, it's very sweet of you to have given me this excuse to run off at the mouth, but it's also a license to wish you a joyous Yule and a painless 1975. I never thought I'd be typing those numerals, which in my youth were associated with images of traffic cops flying through the air with wings on their heels and citizens piloting cigar-shaped airships. I hear that scientists are now freely discussing the possibility of test-tube babies. O.K. for such newfangled ideas, but I will stick with my old-fashioned ideals. Let's have more folk like Chairman Mills and Fanne Foxe, more screen classics like *Wet Rainbow*, and more straight-shooting executives like R.M. Nixon. If you agree with that, please circulate this letter to six other persons and ask them to send it on to six others. And God bless and keep you.

Yours ever,

NEVA PATTERSON

Gramercy Park Hotel
New York City
January 1, 1975

Neva darling,

I should have written you long before this to thank you for your wire when *The Beauty Part* scampered on. Or I should have sent you a whole wheel of cheese from the Trappist monks in Kentucky, or a sable stole from Alexandre Frères, or a box of mildewed ZuZus from Loose-Wiles, The Bakery with a Thousand Windows. Anyway, it was heartening to know that your aorta was pulsating with good wishes, which was undoubtedly why none of the scenery fell out of the flies and none of the latter jammed in our male actors' trousers. Everybody—with the possible exception of Clive Barnes—voted the evening the best ever, hot cocoa was served to the audience, some of whom had to be awakened to drink it, and we all pledged ourselves to hold a reunion ten years thence and discuss all the hilarious things that had happened in the production.

If you are skilful at mathematics, you will have figured out that the dateline above is actually New Year's Day, and I am sitting here on my tushy gazing down sixteen stories into the leafless trees, thinking of my many friends out of work everywhere like myself. If we have nothing else in common, this unites us, and I say thank God we have *something* to share. I think Norman Vincent Peale would find quite a sermon in that. . . .

I thought about a fortnight ago that there was a strong possibility we might be seeing each other, as I'm poised on the ball of one foot to begin another wide-ranging journey. I expect to take off in a few weeks for a lot of dissimilar places like Tahiti, Borneo, Warsaw, Leningrad, Scotland, and Lord knows where else for *Travel & Leisure* mag. My notion was to head west so as to have the benefit of good weather in Borneo—they have bathing, head-hunting, and all sorts of jollies at this season—but for scheduling reasons, ye Editor Mans now wants me to go the other way around, so I may be a while in reaching the Grand Old Town. And many a crow's-foot and wrinkle will yez be afther seein' on this grand old countenance, I'll be bound, afther me experiences with those murtherin' pagans. Oh, shit, I can't keep up this ethnic dialogue, it's raising hell with my diphthongs.

·   ·   ·

If I had my wish, I would like to be with you folks right now—not necessarily in the City of Our Lady the Queen of the Angels, but perhaps in Paris—knocking back a bottle of Dom Pérignon and wearing paper hats. Failing that, I send kisses all around the family and love as always from

Yours only,

PERRY HOWZE*

Gramercy Park Hotel
New York City
January, 1975

Dear Perry,

Judging from your progressive-school handwriting, the content of your previous note, and the imperious tone of the message below, you seem to be

*At the time, an aspiring graphic designer and cartoonist who had written Perelman a fan letter. They later became friends.

a wilful infant who is accustomed to getting her own way. Accordingly, you may profit from a word of advice and I'll give it to you for free.

The next time you issue a demand for anything, honey, whether it's a spoonful of farina or a Christmas card, examine the name of the person you're asking and spell it correctly.

Now wipe the egg off your face and have a happy New Year.

Love,

ANNE GREGG*

Gramercy Park Hotel
New York City
February 1, 1975

Anne dear,

My birthday seems a very auspicious date to answer your letter of January 3 from the Hotel Mola in Ankara, and I respect you for being so honorable — you promised to write me in the holidays and indeed you did. I shan't attempt to conceal how downcast I was at the news that you had been abducted into the seraglio — that you had, so to speak, embraced Islam. At the same time, I was rejoiced to know (for your sake) that you had found happiness with a minion of the former Ottoman empire, and your devotion in shuttling to and fro until he completes his military service bespeaks a generous heart.

As you will doubtless gauge from the preceding paragraph, I am deliberately drawing a portrait of myself calculated to impress you. I want you to think of me as a man with a heart as big as all outdoors — a chap who, if grief-stricken that one whom he has long adored has fallen in love with another, yet has the nobility to rise above petty jealousy and express pleasure that she has achieved *her* heart's desire. Is not this foxy of me? I mean, do you perceive my infinite cunning? The point is simply that while I was initially crushed by your revelation, drenched in gloom for several days, a subsequent rereading of your letter kindled my spirits. O.K., I said to myself, so this is the situation. The lady has thrown her cap over the Golden Horn, is plighting her troth with this 30-year-old infidel who has obviously been evading the responsibilities he owes his homeland. Further, and knowing what we do about Turkish men, I continued, it is more than likely that this fellow has one or more wives tucked away while he conducts his amours. Is it not permissible to dream, therefore, that when the first frenzy of Annie's passion subsides, the scales will drop from her eyes and her cooler head will prevail? (I

*At the time, features editor of the British edition of *Good Housekeeping*.

298

predicate this on the assumption that you have two heads—anyone who falls in love with a Turk must have.) Accordingly, I concluded, I shall so conduct myself that until this *beguin* of hers wears itself out, *I* will remain fixed in her memory, like Heathcliff wrapped in his mantle—a kind, good friend to whom she can always turn, in whose arms she can sob out her disillusion with those sneaky Levantine bastards. And when she turns those magnificent orbs to me, her cheeks streaked with tears and her bosom heaving, then—*then*, I say (if you will permit me to mix my metaphors) you will be in the driver's seat, Charlie. Do you get the scenario, Anne?

> •   •   •

I still haven't forgiven you (and perhaps never shall) for neglecting to come to America this past year, but then, you are richer by a tin automobile and a Turkish beau, the value of either inestimable. In whatever case, I long to see you if only fleetingly so as to carry forward the memory of that Ulster accent and your bewitching smile. It'll be some solace in the Himalaya snows and deep-tangled jungles of Borneo. Until then, and with much love,

Yours,

ERIC LISTER

Gramercy Park Hotel
New York City
February 2, 1975

Dear Eric,

There is an old saying around the porter's desk in Brown's Hotel that one rotten apple in a barrel contaminates the whole cask and that when things look darkest, along comes S.J. Perelman to make things really *geferlich*. So it is not to be wondered at that come March 3rd, I shall be hurtling into London for a week's stay, the opening stanza in another global trek.

> •   •   •

As you see from my neat typing, I am in wonderful physical and mental condition, not a mark on me from some very bruising encounters in the sack, and as cheerful as a cricket. I am also glad to report that in contrast to my superb state, most of my friends are rolling around in bath chairs and subsisting on zwieback. If you yourself are having difficulty chewing the crust of the zwieback, I think you will find that dipping it into the cocoa prior to ingestion puts less of a strain on the dentition. I learned this trick from an old Hebrew when I was growing up in Providence, Rhode Island.

. . . With appropriate pinches to one and all,

Yours,

HAROLD EVANS

London (?)
March 24, 1975

Dear Harry,

Herewith a not unduly muddled tally of my whereabouts during the next nine months, as you requested. Subject, of course, to possible strife in some areas (such as the reluctance of one bird or another to rendez-vous with me in those locales). . . .

I dined with luscious Anne Gregg, ye features editor of *Good Housekeeping*, after our meeting at the Garrick and did my best to persuade her into some housekeeping with me, but she is still fixated on her Turk, worse luck. Anything you can do to see him sewn into a sack and dropped into the Bosphorus will be deeply appreciated. I hear on all sides in London that you are a man of infinite cunning that recalls the insidious Dr. Fu Manchu at his most devious. I challenge you (short of supplanting me in her affections) to prove it. With all the best,   Yours ever,

DIANE DANIELS*

Hotel Montalembert
Paris
March 27, 1975

Diane dearest,

•   •   •

Flew to Edinburgh [from London] on March 10, and v. much like the city & Scots' geniality & warmth contrasted with tight-assed English restraint. Most pleasant dinner & night's stay with doctor & family in Glasgow, then to Perth neighborhood to call on character named Sir Iain Moncrieff of That Ilk, friend of English friends. There met with kilted and sporraned guest of his, a chap who within the next couple of days in Edinburgh offered to guide me via motor to a nosegay of clan strongholds & impressive houses. Which began promisingly by our staying with a couple of face cards I already knew, but lost momentum; practically all the vaunted earls and barons were off in Jamaica and Madeira & we saw few interiors but some nifty formal gardens. Stayed in four rural hotels as we moved west (he driving) so indescribably cold that I don't expect to thaw out before I reach Borneo. . . .

. . [As we] progressed, I began to suspect that I was teamed with a

---

*A recent friend of Perelman's who had been introduced to him in Connecticut by his friends Max and Barbara Wilk. Max Wilk is the author of *And Did You Once See Sidney Plain? A Random Memoir of S. J. Perelman* (Norton, 1986) and other books.

300

closet lush, and was shortly proved right. He'd been on a strict diet of Guinness when we started out, but early on, his dialogue changed to quasi-scientific discussions. There were, he contended, many misapprehensions *re* the harmfulness of malt whiskey; a team of world-famous biologists had recently discovered that as long as one continued drinking, his health would be AOK, but sudden abstention could be fatal, practically insuring a heart attack. Etc., etc. And in the next bar, he took a smaller tot of Guinness and a double malt whiskey. On the third day, Guinness was a thing of the past and the malt was whistling out of his ears. This had a perceptible effect on his driving (I myself have a license and was empowered to drive, but wasn't keen to, not having driven English rules, the wrong side of the road, for four or five years). Well, by the time we reached a place called Oban in Argyll, he was looping, and when he almost mowed down two old ladies, I decided I'd had it. As I was paying for the car and our lodgings, I made noises signifying that we should return to Edinburgh. Amid this he went off to phone some laird that we were coming to stay with him, and must have sustained a blackout because he was missing for 3½ hours after I saw him enter the phone booth. I got a traffic warden who in turn alerted two constables and a patrol car went scouring the town for him. Then he suddenly turned up, swaying through the traffic like Eric Shipstad in an ice show. To cut short the whole thing, he'd completely liquefied by the next morning, having consumed most of the contents of the bar, and I decanted him back to Edinburgh on the train. What Avis will eventually charge for retrieving the heap is anyone's guess. I intend to keep moving East one step ahead of my American Express Card charges.

• • •

ANNE GREGG

Souillac, France
April 13, 1975

Anne dear,

• • •

Knowing your penchant for astrology, you might like to hear of my reading in Paris by one Mlle. Lambs, an elderly, red-haired party in the rue de Dragon I was recommended to (for purely literary purposes, of course). She was right out of Gian-Carlo Menotti's *The Medium*, domiciled on the 6th floor walk-up in a minute flat overflowing with the accumulation of years plus a fat, torpid cat. She threw the cards (Tarot, naturally), prepared charts based on my birth-date, and consulted my palm closely, all with the following predictions. I am embarked on a journey destined to be a great success, the benefits of which will become apparent next year. The next three years,

301

in fact, should prove to be the most auspicious of my life. There will be periods of relative uncertainty in June (Israel?) and August (India?), but I am not to hasten my journey, she stressed that I would be doing myself a disservice unless I took plenty of time to do what I felt obligatory. She seemed positive that contrary to my plan to extend this trip until early January, I would conclude it in October or November. (Curb whatever impulse you may have to burn this letter and save it just for reference.) She then asked if I was interested deeply in someone, and I didn't interpret this as meaning Dirk Bogarde or Curt Jurgens, so I said yes. Well, dear, she said you were undergoing a period of self-searching, hesitation, inability to decide your future, but that in time it would prove to be very favorable for me. (At that point, my hand trembled and I spilled some ashes on her cat.) She wanted to know what were my intentions toward this person, and I said they were very serious, meaning, in the French sense important, not somber. So then I inquired if this person's zodiacal sign, the same as mine, would preclude happiness. Well, you know what answer I wanted, and I got it. I felt that a hundred francs was a bit excessive for the consultation, but in view of the optimistic forecast about our future, it would be churlish to boggle. As a footnote on the foregoing, I would like to point out that at no time did this wise woman see any intimation of the star and crescent as a dominant influence on your life. Though admittedly prejudiced, I interpreted her analysis of your state of indecision as due to vague Anatolian seismographic disturbances that meant nothing on the Richter scale.

You asked that if anything useful for your page happened, I would be good enough to transmit same. So herewith an occurrence of a culinary nature . . . combined with laundry problems. When I arrived here last Tuesday I bundled up my frillies needful of washing and bore them to a laverie on the outskirts of Souillac — the only one, apparently, available for miles. As I entered its portals veiled with steam, I realized I'd forgotten to mark "NO STARCH" in French for my chemises, but had clean forgotten the word for starch though I knew it ended in "on." Determined to brazen it through somehow, I handed over the bundle to the young man in charge and with a series of sliding, uphill thrusts, said I didn't want any "dindon" in the chemises. "Dindon? Dindon?" he repeated helplessly. Then, genius that he was, he realized what this insane foreigner was driving at. "Ah, oui! Pas de *amidon*!" It wasn't till I got back to my pocket lexicon that I realized I'd been begging him not to put turkey in my shirts. It says something for the four girls bent over the vats that not one hooted with laughter.

•   •   •

Yours always,

DIANE DANIELS

Les Granges Vieilles
Souillac, France
April 14, 1975

.   .   .

On the basis of a week's stay here, I think my decision to skip Switzerland was well-founded. It's a large, square, mansard-type house — I would say late 18th century or early 19th — set in a parklike preserve of beautiful old trees & very well kept by M. Augey and wife, whose home it is. Just far enough out of Souillac, a nice small town with all needful shops, so that one can drive in 4 kilometers for newspapers, shopping, etc. I'm the sole guest, occupying what one can only call a bridal chamber with marble fireplace, great gold mirror, and double windows giving onto a balcony. And the food is really quite fabulous, in keeping with the reputation of this part of France. . . . I'm on demi-pension because if you had to eat 2 meals of the sort they serve each day, you couldn't survive it. . . . Best of all is the fact that it's very quiet and I've been able to work speedily as I have to.

A nice hilarious footnote on my motor trip through Scotland with that highborn lush. Don't know whether I mentioned it in my account, but at one point he suddenly asked me to lend him 37 pounds for some undisclosed purpose. I had to cash American Express checks to oblige him, which was rather bothersome at the moment, but I did so, and on the edge of some village, he entered a house & paid off someone, God knows who. Well, when our trip ended with his disastrous collapse, he quite reluctantly wrote out a check plus the cost of a cat basket he'd asked me to purchase. It came to something over 40 pounds, and I tried cashing it in London as he instructed me to. His bank wouldn't accept it (though his name was imprinted on it) because of a legal technicality, so an English friend of mine put it through his account & gave me the money for it. Well, yesterday I got a letter from my English friend, the check had of course bounced and I'll have to pony up. The good old Scots aristocracy with the kilt and the tartan and the sporran. The only consolation is that it might make an effective curtain for my piece on Scotland.

.   .   .

DIANE DANIELS

Souillac, France
April 30–May 1, 1975

.   .   .

Glad to hear that Lil Hellman got the award of Woman of the Year,

303

and gladder that she rapped Sinatra and Hope over the knuckles. She's a brave and feisty dame, and there are all too few of them around. Dottie Parker was another, and Janet Flanner. And maybe Bella Abzug, from the once I met her. All of them women of spirit. I suppose it takes a lot of tempering to produce that kind of mettle — a bunch of *tzorris* or *tzouris* (depending on the Yiddish you favor) mixed with a lot of sympathy for people. The odd thing is that in some women, like that awful Barbara What's-her-name on the *Today Show* — you see how readily I've forgotten her name — all it results in is hardness. End of sage discourse on the distinctive women of our time.

Well, this is the beginning of my final week here — I leave for Paris on Thursday, the 8th — and it's been a nice experience except for the loneliness. Last Saturday I drove over to Sarlat, about 17 miles, and this afternoon cruised around in the back farm country a bit. It's really the most exquisite rural scenery I've ever encountered, like Hampshire in England and the White Highlands in East Africa, and the farm buildings, houses and barns, are as much part of the earth as the foliage. Of course, it's at its peak right now; the greens and terra-cotta colors almost artificial in intensity owing to lots of rain, and the trees and shrubs all in flower. Lucky to have seen it before the tourist plague arrives.

●　　　　　●　　　　　●

. . . English is a very strange language. Here is a sentence I copied out of a recent edition of the London *Sunday Times*: "Richard Murdoch, whose *Much Binding in the Marsh* helped to keep British peckers up during the war, is 68 today." If that were read over a dinner-party in mixed company in Pelham or Rye, I'm sure the hostess would be ruffled (despite the fact that half the guests had peckers under their napkins). The word "napkin," in fact, isn't considered too genteel in English society, connoting as it does a lunar condition in the ladies. For that matter, we in America rarely say to each other, "Why don't you knock me up about four o'clock?" Etc., etc.

●　　　　　●　　　　　●

Well, I have finally finished Brendan Gill's *Here at The New Yorker*, and if a one-word descriptive review is needed, my choice is "Icky." Plus ass-kissing; the way he goes on about Bill Shawn, the editor, is enough to curdle the milk. Additionally, it's autobiographical (which I contend such a book shouldn't be) to the most boring degree. Gill comes of a rich family, father a Hartford doctor who gave the numerous children everything they wanted, and sent the author to Yale, where he made Bones. He revels in it and also the rich origins. The book is padded and strung out with endless details about the office and many of the personnel, all of it as uninteresting to the general reader (and myself in large part) as can be. O.K., so its presence as No. 4 on the best-seller list proves me wrong. . . .

There's only one place to go from this hotel, and that is straight to Lane-Bryant's. The lard starts forming on the guest even before he gets out of his car, and by the time he rises flushed from the table, he can be used to baste an ox. Here is what we had tonight: Potage Maison/Langouste Mayonnaise/Poulet de ferme Roti/Pommes de terre Lyonnaise/Salade de maison/Fromages assortis/Tartelette. Now mind you, I eat this only once a day, together with breakfast, being on demi-pension, but people come here and eat a meal like that above for *lunch* also. Fortunately, inasmuch as I'm going on to Tahiti eventually, I'll be able to pick up a muu-muu there.

More or less on the preceding, I gathered from something you let drop in a previous letter that you've pretty well washed your hands of the book you were working on. . . . Can't say I blame you. The idea of publishing a book oneself is a dud. It's what's called vanity publishing, and if you watch the small ads, you'll see an outfit called Vantage Books that deals in just that sort of thing. They collect a couple of thousand bucks from their luckless clients, run one ad to salve their egos, and then do a quick remainder job. The writer can then present his friends in what you aptly term the aluminum siding game with an inscribed copy and then sit around explaining what's wrong with Joseph Heller. . . .

.   .   .

Yours,

DIANE DANIELS

Lindos, Rhodes
June 7, 1975

.   .   .

Assuming that you'd like a quick report on what happened, I'd say it was grim and fatiguing, occasionally interesting, frequently puzzling, and an experience I'm sort of glad I had but could never be persuaded to repeat. My only venture behind the Iron Curtain, in 1964 through Jugoslavia, Roumania, and Hungary, really didn't give one a view of a planned society in the Russian sense, which I got this time. You feel as if you were one of those countless automata in Saul Steinberg's drawings in his albums, those rubber-stamp figures he repeats endlessly, moving in vast perspectives at the command of some ruthless and unpitying intelligence. Or in other words, you lose all sense of individualism such as we have. Part of that was understandable since I was travelling with a 17-person Intourist group whose every movement was supervised, but I also spent five additional days by myself after the group left; and that portion was the most unpleasant, because the single foreigner gets cold and minimum service and is made to feel unwelcome and odious.

305

At both ends of the trip in Moscow, we were put up in what must be the world's largest hotel, the Rossia — 3000 rooms accommodating 6000 people, an ant-house that took 4 days to puzzle out. Absolutely bewildering place, filled with tourists blundering about trying to find their floor, their restaurant, their group, and nobody understanding a word of English. Or French, or anything but Russian. For the smallest inquiry, they'd bark, "Tourist bureau" in a section of the maze you couldn't find a second time. The result was that everyone's stomach was knotted in frustration with hunger and irritation...The tourism in Moscow is what you'd expect. You see those portions of the Kremlin they want to show you — the museum with imperial thrones, carriages and dinner services. Also three churches of dwindling importance. Everybody snaps pictures of everything, which consumes hours. (I was the only person without a camera.) You spend an evening in a concert-hall with hyperthyroidal Georgian dancers spinning daggers out of their teeth. You're taken to a Lenin museum and another museum celebrating their conquest of outer space. Etc., etc. You're fed cucumbers with breakfast, lunch, dinner, and Kiev cutlets — those squishy things that spray you with butter when you cut into them. We had fifteen servings of Kiev cutlets in 14 days, producing surfeit, nausea, and constipation indescribable. (And nowhere in the whole fucking Soviet Union to buy milk of magnesia. They never heard of it. They also apparently never heard of toothpaste, I finally managed to procure a tube in a hardware store in Yalta.) O.K., so there *are* some handsome 18th-century buildings in Moscow. You find out that they were all designed by Italians, as was the Winter Palace in Leningrad and practically any public edifice you admire.

Well, then we flew to Kiev, where someone (whether the KGB or some nosey individual in the hotel) jimmied open one of my bags but I believe didn't extract anything. Lots of churches in Kiev, also war memorials. Lousy rooms, lots of super-realistic Soviet sculpture of workers and masses of Lenin statues. Then flew on a hot and overcrowded Aeroflot plane to Simpferopol, from which an endless bus trip to Yalta. Lots of sanitoria and resthouses for workers, who sit on the sea front and gape at the American tourists. Here, as in Moscow, Kiev, and Leningrad coming up, the tourist is persuaded to shop in "dollar stores," where there's nothing but those humpty-dumpty Russian wooden dolls, lacquer boxes costing 40 to 60 bucks each, and embroidered blouses purchasable on 7th Street off Second Avenue in New York. In Leningrad, their most handsome city, another huge hotel where Elizabeth Taylor is said to be occupying an entire floor. I went over to the studio where she's being filmed in *The Bluebird*, watched a take, and after some drinks with her and this new male plaything of hers, Henry Something, in her dressingroom, went back to the Leningrad Hotel, where our tour was also staying. We had some more to drink in her quarters, which in fact consist of three tiny rooms. She also told me what she's being paid for the job — eleven roubles a day, about $15, which is standard movie pay there. Apparently, she's doing it solely as a sentimental gesture toward Mike Todd's memory; he was the first one to conceive the idea of a joint U.S.-Russian production, which this is....Our group then went to Peter the Great's castle on the Gulf of Finland, which has trick fountains that spray the unsuspecting. As most of those we saw being sprayed were German tourists, we had a slight obscure pleasure.

·   ·   ·

Yours always,

IRENE KEMMER

Lindos, Rhodes
June 25, 1975

Dearest Irene,

I surface again in this most delightful corner of Christendom to say how sorry I am that we didn't connect in Moscow, but I guess Intourist tours are never fated to meet. . . .

It was a spooky feeling that your group was trailing us and I kept wishing it would catch up because it would have been a boon to talk and cuddle with you. Of the twenty in our party, there were only a couple of individuals who weren't squares of the most geometrical sort. As viz one evening when we attended a sort of glorified vaudeville show in Moscow — lots of exuberant Georgian dancing, etc., and stimulating it was. The opening number of the second half, though, was sheer corn, drum majorettes marching up and down the stage backed by a sort of Lawrence Welk conducting a 46-piece band in selections from *Blossom Time* or some such hoary musical comedy. Well, next a.m. at breakfast I remarked to my table in the Pectopah at the Hotel Rossia that this itty-bitty scene could have been lifted in its entirety onto the great stage of the Radio City Music Hall. My seven fellow-diners said blankly, "Where?" I had to explain that we had an amusement temple by that name in Manhattan, none had ever heard of it. They were all from Independence, Kansas, Sausalito, Cody (Wyo.), and similar places. But many had heard of Richard Milhouse Nixon and were still fiercely loyal.

Anyway, apart from the tour itself — about which you will get my reactions eventually in print, since I'm too tired of the subject to repeat — I had some interesting side encounters. Stevens and the press corps in Moscow were very matey; I attended 2 or 3 parties where I met Yevtushenko and Vosnesenski, and got to know several extremely nice diplomatic folk like Ford, the Canadian ambassador, etc. Yevtushenko in particular became v. friendly — washed along on a tide of vodka — and gave me a free palm reading climaxing with

307

the intelligence that I would live 12 years more. "I know this because I was trained by Siberian gypsies," he announced rhetorically. "Are you not made happy by the news?" I replied that I had a Ukrainian girl friend in America who, according to the stars, was slated to meet a young man, younger than herself, and fall deeply in love with him. He answered that I need have no fear, as I grew older I would become ever tenderer and sweeter like a ripe fruit and thus continue to win my fair Ukrainian's regard.

. . . After returning to Moscow, I had two meetings with people who gave me details of the life intellectuals lead nowadays that weren't quite as velvety as those handed out by our Intourist guides; and from what I could see and judge, it's *molto* grim. This was confirmed by my press friends who of course have to live with it and have become adjusted to its Byzantine nature.

In whatever case, my spirits soared upward instantly even during the hour's pause at the Belgrade airport, and Rhodes, which has some very appealing features, proved to be just the sort of ambiance I wanted to work in. . . . This house has an excellent livingroom, bedroom, second bedroom containing a first-rate library, kitchen, and patio, and believe it or not, it was stocked with liquor and groceries of every description. One could stay here six months just to enjoy the books in the library, but at my back I seem to hear time's winged footstep hurrying near—not to mention the blow-torch Caskie Stinnett is applying to my backside.

· · ·

Yours,

IRENE KEMMER

Hotel Merlin Cameron Highlands
Tanah Rata, Pahang, Malaysia
August 7, 1975

Dearest Irene,

· · ·

This letter would ordinarily have been datelined Kashmir, India, had I adhered to my original schedule, but I guess you're fully conversant with Indira Gandhi's antics the last six weeks and in particular her high-handed suppression of the press. When I first learned in Israel of her invoking powers to arrest foreigners and hold them for two years without explanation, and shortly thereafter of the press censorship and expulsion of correspondents, I realized that in view of my repeated slurs about India (viz., in "Around the Bend in 80 Days" in *Vinegar Puss* and elsewhere), I was especially vulnerable. So I decided to overfly India and spend the time I'd allotted to writing about Israel and Iran up here instead.

. . . / .

. . . Israel was drudgery; I disliked the country and, for the most part, the people — found them aggressive, self-centered beyond all excuse, and (despite their mixture of homelands and origins) as parochial as small-town Kansans. The Tel Aviv Hilton is a nightmare, as garish as Grossinger's or the Concord Hotel in the Catskills and as full of the same all-rightnicks; and Tel Aviv is the Grand Concourse and Rivington Street rolled into one without the rough heartiness of Manhattan. As for Jerusalem and its holy sites, both the Hebraic and Christian religious ethics have always bored me and I just saw a lot of sunbaked masonry in a parched and stony, terribly uninviting hilltop desert. I stayed in East Jerusalem, the Arab quarter, in a hotel called the American Colony favored by journalists, and it was a diametrical opposite of the T-A Hilton: a cool, dignified place, originally founded by an American Baptist family and still run by their descendants, which was at one time the residence of a Turkish pasha. It was really an oasis during my two weeks in Israel. Did some touring while there down to the Dead Sea and saw Masada, the fort where 900 Jews committed suicide rather than surrender to the 11th Roman Legion, also saw the place where the Dead Sea Scrolls were found. The one worthwhile evening in the whole trip was a dinner I had with Isaac Bashevis Singer, who happened to be in Jerusalem after being given an honorary degree in Haifa. A remarkable and interesting man; I hope you like his stories in *The New Yorker* as much as I do.

. . .

DIANE DANIELS

Hotel Merlin Cameron Highlands
Tanah Rata, Pahang, Malaysia
August 10, 1975

. . .

I guess that it's just about this stage of the trip, having completed 12,000 of the 24,000-mile girth of the globe, that I always start to get homesick. All I read about New York (*Newsweek* had a very complete takeout on its financial problems, civic breakdown, and general melancholy future) doesn't sharpen my appetite to return there, but I do miss friends and companionship and fluent communication with English-speaking people instead of talking pidgin with taxi-drivers, hotel clerks, and waiters. As for the thrill of seeing new places, that's pretty well worn off in five or six globe-girdlings, and I very much doubt I want to make any more. An occasional jaunt to Europe, yes, and *schluss*.

. . .

309

ISRAEL SHENKER *

Hotel Merlin Cameron Highlands
Tanah Rata, Pahang, Malaysia
August 18, 1975

Dear Shenk,

This is a long overdue brievel, I have been scrawling your name with my lipstick on hotel bedroom mirrors from here back to Kiev . . . but you know how we travelling men are, writing up our reports to the firm at night, chasing with grips in hand to the station to catch the 8:30 for the next town, and the day fritters away like matzo-wasser. . . .

Have spent the past fortnight in this pleasant hill station two miles above the coastal fry-pan, hocking out a piece on Israel that I'm sure will bring down *pech und schwebel* on my head from the indigenes. It went off to *Travel & Leisure* today and I hope its Gentile editors have the courage to run it. Everybody is so fucking pious about the place, the inhabitants and visitors both, that nothing lively gets into print (or nothing that I've seen). I take the liberty of saying that the piece referred to will be an exception. . . .

> •   •   •

. . . Would like to get back to N.Y. for the holidays to be mugged, all the people who count are Gotham-bound. Also, I simply must not be missing those society group shots in *W*, that glossy supplement of *Women's Wear Daily*. "Countess Tessa Rospigliosi, and on her right, flanking Mrs. Herman Schtampf, Mr. Sidney Ferelkamb." I always wind up that way, me and my flanken.

Gee, it's been great visiting with you folks. Please go across the street and have a Broadway soda on me at Schrafft's (choc. and coffee syrup mixed, coffee ice-cream). I burst into tears as I wrote that down, do you realize it's six months nearly since I had one? I wonder if you New Yorkers realize how luxuriously you live — it's like Rome under the decline. If I were Juvenal, I could write such a satire — I said Juven*al*, not the other word.

Cheers,

New York Times journalist who most often covered the Perelman beat.

AL HIRSCHFELD

Bandung, Java
Indonesia
September 14, 1975

Dear Al,

> •   •   •

. . . To get back to my serpentine movements since I last wrote . . . I spent 10 days in Iran between Tehran, Persepolis, Shiraz, and Isfahan. Then, instead of working in Kashmir, I overflew India because of Mme. Gandhi's convulsions and my vulnerability *re* published anathemas about her country, and went direct to Bangkok. Spent a week at the Oriental Hotel there . . . then flew down to Penang. I did quite a lot of moving around in Malaysia. Went up to a place called Pulau Langkawi where I hoped to work, but it was too hot, so backtracked to Penang, flew to Ipoh, and drove up to Cameron Highlands (which was where Jim Thompson disappeared) and had a cool work stretch for 2 weeks there. Then went to Malacca for a long weekend, over to Kuala Lumpur for several days, and flew up to Hong Kong. Stayed at the Peninsula this time, surely one of the world's great hotels, and saw a lot of old pals. Then to Kota Kinabalu in Sabah (North Borneo) and successively to Brunei and Kuching in Sarawak, concluding in Singapore as mentioned previously. I now plan to spend 2 weeks here at Bob's and write my 5th piece, on Iran, before heading for Tahiti.* What with a couple of weeks there, and 10 days or 2 weeks in Hollywood, I'd offer a rough estimate that I should be back in Fun City sometime during the second week of November.

· · ·

I picked up a marvellous anecdote about Alma Mahler in Greece that I'll save for your festal board, but I think you should know the following. On the waterfront of Hong Kong Island, there's a huge skyscraper called Connaught Center with circular windows which, when it was being built, was advertised to be the tallest building in Asia. When I was last in H-K, it was being referred to as the Hong Kong Stilton. Returning this time, I was told that the Chinese now refer to it as "The House of a Thousand Ass-holes."

· · ·

Yours ever,

*Robert Mörzer-Bruyns, longtime chief representative in the Far East for KSM, the Dutch shipping lines, and, later, KLM, the Dutch airlines.

DIANE DANIELS

Bandung, Java
Indonesia
September 17, 1975

· · ·

. . . Since I last wrote, I've been doing some pretty concentrated travel — to various places like Malacca and Kuala Lumpur in Malaysia, Hong Kong, Kota Kinabalu and Brunei and Kuching in Borneo, and Singapore. You can find all these fly-specks on any decent map of Southeast Asia. . . . I will say for publication, however, that Hong Kong was the high spot in the foregoing catalogue; I dwelt in unimaginable luxury in the Peninsula Hotel there, which certainly has to be one of the world's greatest, and my pleasure was intensified when the final bill revealed that the manager had given me freebies on the room rent. (No small item at $58 per diem plus service and tax.) The average, however, was less glorious, inasmuch as I got to stay in some pretty crummy lodgings like Chinese hotels in Borneo and the ever-depressing Hilton in Singapore. I think the most hilarious Hilton experience of my life took place in the Jakarta Hilton here in Java. It's the most awful schlocky establishment you've ever seen — still unfinished building, but they installed me in one of what are called their Executive Lanai cottages. Indescribable decor obviously beamed at pleasing American businessmen and inflating their egos. Well, these lanais must have been finished as recently as two months ago, and God knows what swindling the contractor indulged in. Anyway, I have just risen from the loo, stepped into the shower, and started to soap myself when there's a sound like a piece of linen being torn (but amplified 10,000 times) and one whole tiled wall falls in on the john — just where I'd been enthroned. Smashed to smithereens on the floor; it really would have lacerated me rather dramatically. I had great pleasure in summoning the manager, the assistant manager, and the p.a. dame when I was dressed, and pointing out what a cockamamie structure they had. The p.a. dame confided to me afterward that it was the third episode of the sort, and the hotel hasn't even formally *opened* yet.

•   •   •

NEVA PATTERSON

Papeete, Tahiti
October 1, 1975

Neva darling,

I wrote you something like six weeks ago from Cameron Highlands in Malaysia in reply to your own letter, arrival of which was indeed a Bright Spot in my wayfaring, and hope it reached you in due course. Subsequently wayfared up to Hong Kong and had a darlint time there, largely because ye host at the Peninsular cuffed me the cost of superb room, whose price was also superb. After that week, I did another in North Borneo, hemstitching three places called Kota Kinabalu, Brunei, and Kuching in Sarawak, all of them turning out to be tedious, hot, and of dubious value copy-wise. Thence to Singapore for a couple of days, one wasted in being taped by a Canadian but did unexpectedly bump into Carl Mydans, the w.k. *Life* photographer and an old friend; he looks the dead spit of Claude Rains to the point where I always have to refrain from bursting into that theme song from *Casablanca.* . . . Well, then, I hied me on to Jakarta in Indonesia and up to Bandung in the hills, where I spent 2 weeks writing a segment on Iran, and then did the broad jump Jakarta-Sydney-Nadi (Fiji) to here, a very fatiguing flight. Am just recovering from jet lag and a common traveller's complaint called hotel rage; on getting here, I checked into (without knowing the ropes) a frog establishment called The Maeva Beach Hotel which soaked me $44-plus per diem and luxury taxes besides. However, soon recovered my equilibrium after seeking out the *syndicat initiative* supplying info to tourists, and am now in the Royal Papeete, which is regal right down to the size of the cockroaches in the shower. Shake this letter carefully before stowing it under your nighties.

At the moment, it looks as if I'll stick here until Wednesday, Oct. 8, and then fly by Pan Am to L.A., arriving next morning, the 9th. . . .

So what I'm leading up to is this: Would you be a true darling and ring up the Chateau Marmont on Sunset Boulevard to make a reservation for me? I've stayed there a number of times in the past and much prefer it to the Bev. Wilshire, etc., which just charge hayseeds the earth to rub flanges with personalities like Rosemary Theby and Bryant Washburn. . . . If it occurs to you to wonder why I'm basing myself that far away from Beverly, etc., I'll be checking out a lot of the Hollywood of my period — Musso-Frank's, the bookshops, the Vine St. Derby, etc., etc. for the piece I'll have to write eventually. . . .

I don't know how I can further impose on you, other than to ask you to lunch with me as soon as you can after that — provided of course you're not hips-deep in a job. We've so much to talk about and I do want to hear your opinion on Cassius Clay's new romance and whether you feel Rona Barrett is really sincere or merely out for "filthy lucre"? (And is there really a head underneath that coiffure or just straw.) Also, why, with the dearth of good leading men, is everyone overlooking Troy Donahue? . . .

Well, a roach has just appeared on the platen of this typewriter and as I went to demolish him, he held up one of his three hundred feelers and cried, "Stop, my name is Archy!" So I'll have to quit now and have a little confab with him about Mehitabel and Don Marquis and all that. Take care of yourself until you enwrap my spavined figure in your arms, and with love to James and Megan and everyone,   Yours ever,

ANNE GREGG

Santa Barbara, Calif.
February 15, 1976

Anne dearest,

By now you are completely recovered from the pox, mid-Asiatic cholera, yaws, pellagra, and whatever sinister diseases you contracted in your ill-advised junket to Turkey last month, so I presume you are strong enough to withstand the shock of a letter from this benighted place. What in the world is he doing out there, I can hear you ask? (I can't hear you ask at all; it's just that I hear all kinds of imaginary voices these days.) Well, I'll thank you to feign some respect, even if you don't feel it; I am a Regent's Lecturer at the University of California in Santa Barbara for the month of February. And a month in Santa Barbara is no longer than any six-month sentence in Wandsworth on bread and water. The very name "Santa Barbara," as your knowledge of Spanish has already told you, means The City Without Restaurants, and truer words were never spoken. Souvenir shops by the thousand, laden with pin-cushions, plastic doilies, worry-beads, and shell necklaces there are; bookshops piled high with Christian Science tracts, plaster replicas of the Madonna, and catechisms bound in broderie Anglaise line the streets; but restaurants and laundries there are none. The philosophy, obviously, is that since everyone here is 92 years old, he is practically dead anyway, so why feed him and wash his undies? . . .

In whatever case, my presence here lacks all sense, since (a) the veal-faced students to whom I'm being exhibited haven't any notion of who I am or what I do, and (b) I would realize my true potential so much more fully if I were where you are. I miss you, Anne; why are we not — at this very moment — snuggled in a booth at Annabel's, holding hands and (with difficulty) stifling our yearning for each other? These are the thoughts sloshing through what is left of my mind on the Pacific Slope this dreary Sunday afternoon, and I hold you directly responsible. Because if you didn't exist — which is unthinkable — *I* would be responsible and therefore riddled with guilt, so it's an easy cop-out to blame you. You get the picture? You fill me with an equal mixture of craving and resentment — in other words, true love. Anne, I adore you. Look, let's be sensible about this. London and San Francisco are only eight hours distant from each other by the polar route. We'll meet at the Mark Hopkins in San Francisco next Friday the 20th. By Monday the 22nd, our blood tests will have been completed, we marry on Tuesday, honeymoon at Pebble Beach Wednesday and Thursday, divorce on Friday, and by Saturday you can be back in London with 24 hours to rest up before getting back into your office at *Good Housekeeping* on Monday. Or, alternatively, I'll meet you halfway at Anchorage in Alaska, which will give us a three-day honeymoon before we divorce. Could anything be fairer than that, I ask you? Nobody, certainly, can accuse me of pettiness in this affair; and furthermore, if this letter is ever produced in court, any judge would rule that the defendant (that's me, you'd be the plaintiff) acted with magnanimity at all times and refuse to award you a penny. No, Anne, search your heart and ask yourself, "Am I dreaming? Am I foolish enough to turn down a paladin such as he?" I think that after two minutes' reflection, you'll ring up British Airways...Wait a second. Now that I've had a moment to ponder, I withdraw the whole thing. California has a community-property law whereby you'd automatically get 50% of everything. Let's get married in Andorra, where I can skip into Spain at the least sign of discord in our union. I'm being my own lawyer in this matter, and you know the old saying, "He who acts as his own lawyer has a fool for a client."...Well, I'm certainly glad I didn't give way to a rash impulse. Still, I wish you and I were holding hands at Annabel's.

•   •   •

Anne, I trust you are well, though it is inconceivable that you can ever be happy, or even approximate total contentment, until you are mine. To which ultimate objective you can be as sure as you are that the sun will rise in the morning that I am devoting myself. And it is with that thought that we take leave of beautiful Anne Gregg and Costa Rica, the Land of the Coffee Bean. Write me, sugar.   All love,

ERIC LISTER

Santa Barbara, Calif.
February 23, 1976

Dear Eric,

I think I'm in arrears as regards our correspondence; just before leaving New York for this benighted place on Feb. 2, I looked over a sheaf of mail that had piled up and recall an unanswered letter from you that tormented my conscience. Since I can visualize the expression of stupefaction on your face at the address above, I'd better explain I've been spending this month as a so-called Regent's Lecturer at the University of California, Santa Barbara Branch. Before you fall apart with laughter at the thought of me in cap and gown, my duties have been minimal; I did two public appearances and otherwise have sat in on some classes in journalism, "creative writing" (whatever the fuck that is), and the like. Nothing to cause any ruptures or prolapse of the uterus, inasmuch as my auditors have been veal-faced scholars of both sexes — and all too few of those leggy, deep-bosomed sirens for which this coast is celebrated. Meanwhile I've been quartered in a hotel that I suspect is actually a senior citizens' retirement village, for the average age of the guests is between 87 and 92. Meals in the diningroom are served as follows: lunch between 11:30 a.m. and 12:30, dinner from 5:15 to 6:30. Do you get the picture? These hours are arranged so that the clientele can hobble swiftly back to their rooms and catch Mary Tyler Moore and the talk shows on TV prior to tucking themselves into bed at 9:30. So I have been going reasonably bonkers for the past three weeks, but come Friday, thank God, will be winging down to L.A. for three or four days prior to departing for New York. A couple

315

of my lady friends down there in Hollywood don't know it, but they're going to be confronted by a sex-mad Jewish chap with little steel-rimmed specs who may well tear their clothes off. There's nothing to fan the sex urge like a month in the geriatric ward.

·　　　　·　　　　·

Life in New York in the interim has been standard and unremarkable; the city's bankruptcy is visible in pot-holes in the streets, general cut-back of services like garbage collection, reduced numbers of police and firemen, and increased savagery of taxi-drivers. I'm back in my old digs at the Gramercy Park Hotel, schlepping myself around the dinner parties as that extra male hostesses frantically phone at the last moment, and wolf-whistling the odd shapely female. Haven't seen the Wilks, Max and Barbara, since returning, but recently exchanged letters with Max, who I gather was in London not long ago, so you must have foregathered at Bloom's in Foubert Place for the yummy Yiddish fare. (I leave it to your imagination what the corned beef is like in Santa Barbara, where they haven't seen a Jew since DeMille's *King of Kings*. The only chopped-liver known hereabouts is what these cigar-colored retired bank presidents contract from drinking too much bourbon.)

·　　　　·　　　　·

The octogenarian waitresses in the diningroom are ringing their cow-bell to indicate that unless I get in there pronto (it's now 6:18 p.m.) I will get no chopped carrot-and-raisin salad or any of that spurious fodder you retail at the Nut House—this whole ordeal is revenge on me for downgrading the subject of health foods. So I will have to draw to a close on this melancholy vignette of a man ready to sell his soul for a whiff of a potato *lotkeh*. A pinch of the claws to Wally, Lionel, and everyone, and I enclose some newsprint from the *L.A. Times* that may interest you. With love and kisses,

> Yours ever,

PAT KAVANAGH

> Gramercy Park Hotel
> New York City
> March 29, 1976

Dearest Pat,

Eric the Lister speaks the truth; I *am* back in New York but only within the past ten days, having been addlepated enough to let myself be cajoled into a month's so-called lectureship at the University of California in Santa Barbara. Never had been sucked into academe before, but had heard all that swill about what marvelous feedback one receives from the students, "you learn more than they do," etc., etc. Also, I was probably impressed by being told

316

that Aldous Huxley and Christopher Isherwood had been Regent's Lecturers too. Well, to compress the whole experience into a capsule, I can tell you (if you don't already know Santa Barbara) that it's the White Man's Grave, the place where the elephants go to die. . . . As for the students, lots of denim, beards, and dirty hair, and none of those tanned, long-stemmed American beauties my erotic dreams had previsioned. There were 15,000-odd students and they had heaps of apathy. All their questions (the few who had any) ran, "How does a person get hold of a good agent? How does a person break into writing for television? Could Harpo Marx really speak? Why is *The New Yorker* such a lousy magazine nowadays?" I told this to Lil Hellman, who has done a lot of lecturing, last night at the Hacketts'. She said, "I'll tell you how I always start with classes. I say to them, 'Now listen, you. I'm not going to tell you how to become famous.'" I wish I'd known that before I went out.

Well, anyway. The global trip took 7½ months, and I hope I don't have to do any more of them. This was No. 6, and I think I've squeezed the lemon dry. . . . Meanwhile I'm getting busy on some things for *The New Yorker*, which after all is the box stall I rightly belong in.

•   •   •

All love,

CASKIE STINNETT*

Gramercy Park Hotel
New York City
October 3, 1976

Dear Caskie,

Any man who takes the trouble to write me from the old E. & O. in Penang deserves a quicker answer than this.† But I have been hors de combat (that steed in the next stall to hors concours) with a rotten cold that I'll probably have to go all the way to Penang to get rid of. This is the first cold that has refused to yield to 1½ packs of Kents a day. Just goes to show that more resistant strains of bacilli develop whenever the scientists at American Tobacco think they're winning.

Glad to hear that the words are spouting out of the typewriter. Down here the effect is more that of gum boots being sucked out of a marsh heavily infested with algae. Also the sentences are very curious — they all can be read backward, like a palindrome. Able was I ere I saw Elba — you know. Maybe I should really be working for Parker Bros. who manufacture those games and puzzles instead of this journal and *T. & L.* Speaking of the latter, Pamela

---

*See note, p. 294.

†The Eastern and Oriental Hotel, an old colonial establishment where Somerset Maugham wrote.

F[iori], in thanking me for the 8th and final piece (on Hollywood) in the series, wrote: "A grizzly finish to a splendid series." Do you think I should give her a bear hug for the compliment? Obviously the secretary she dictated it to was one of those Sarah Lawrence literati who'd never seen the other word.

I guess you saw our Lil breathing fire on the front page of the *Times* in that hair-pulling match with Diana Trilling, and repeated likewise in yesterday's (Sunday's) entertainment section. Maybe the girls should book with the Pond Lecture Bureau as a wrassling act for Chatauquas and county fairs. Or the best seven out of nine falls at the next Authors' League social. I'm sure Halston could run up something real nifty in the way of red and blue rosettes for their trunks. Then the winner could be matched against your fave Bella Abzug.

I guess on these frosty mornings you're probably finding moose tracks around the woodshed and the Log Cabin Maple Syrup coated with a thin film of ice, so it won't be long before you're back in F. City. If such is indeed your program, I hope you'll let me buy you lunch — at Pearl's, maybe, or wherever? Meantime, all best, and looking forward to seeing you soon —

Yours,

PAUL THEROUX *

Gramercy Park Hotel
New York City
October 18, 1976

Dear Paul,

.   .   .

My air-mail subscription to the *Times* of London brought me your review of Tom Dardis's *Some Time in the Sun*, by a coincidence a day or so after someone unsuccessfully sought to inveigle me into a radio talk show about it. The honest truth (as opposed to the dishonest truth) is that I now have a snootful about this subject. I'm sick of these innumerable books about Fitzgerald's Sturm und Drang in Hollywood, both by his gossip columnist mistress and the flock of young guys who hope to create reputations by exhuming some tiny phase of his life there. (You may also have read Caroline Moorehead's column in the self-same *Times* stating that Sheilah Graham has another book coming out on further unknown aspects of Scott's life with her.) To what purpose all this crud, anyway? Generally speaking, all the parties concerned (except Agee, who was movie-struck and a determined self-destroyer) worked in Hollywood because it was the decade of the Great Depression and

*American novelist and travel writer living in London. Perelman sought him out after Theroux had written a favorable review of *Vinegar Puss* in *The Spectator*.

they couldn't earn a living elsewhere. They none of them made any real money in the Hollywood sense out of it—only the screenwriters on the inside, whose names wouldn't mean a thing to the public, except Ben Hecht's, made the big dough—people like Robert Riskin, Norman Krasna, Harry Kurnitz, Bright & Glasmon. These last were the Roman candles, the Catherine wheels of that epoch of movie writing, and their names now are writ in water. They've been superseded by the Robert Townes (*Chinatown*), Steven Spielbergs, and other infant geniuses who demand and receive $400,000 per script, and who in turn will be replaced in a couple of years by other unrecognizable names. If you want to know who's turning out the present movie feces—i.e., what writers—just read *Variety* for a couple of weeks; I guarantee you won't recognize the name of any writer you ever heard of, even on the *Playboy* level...But just to wrap it all up—I say as I've said for years: if you want to know what writing for the movies is like, just read Raymond Chandler's two pieces on the topic in *Raymond Chandler Speaking*. I think of very few others who have been able to capture the disgust and the boredom of dealing with the Yahoos who run that industry. Their names are no longer Louis B. Mayer, Irving Thalberg, and Darryl Zanuck, but their mentalities are the same, or I should say even baser, because today's tycoons are all agents, ten-per-centers whipped and worn smooth by the hot blast of television...

Ah, well, forgive me for running off at the mouth on this score, it's really brought on by the Tom Dardises and other neo-Joycean Ph.D's rooting around in the Hollywood debris. I suppose I actually *should* have agreed to do that radio tape I spoke of earlier and got all this stuff off my chest.

Re H.P. Lovecraft who you mentioned—I was dimly aware that he was alive and unwell in Providence while I was being forcibly educated there, but what little work of his I came across was in quasi-horror pulps, kind of sub-Edgar Allan Poe stuff, and seemed pretty spurious to me. The only person I ever knew who had any knowledge of him was a spaced-out freak who worked with the Brown Dramatic Society. . . . From what I read in the alumni magazine a couple of years ago, his red corpuscles gave out and he occupies a headstone somewhere in the verdure near Pawtucket. Mention of that part of the world reminds me—you and I never got around, that afternoon at Brown's Hotel, to discussing George V. Higgins and his novels about small-time hoods in southern New England. I enjoyed those—did you care for them?

Pat Kavanagh writes me she'll be coming over shortly before Thanksgiving, and mentions that you've seen each other recently. Give her a pinch in the Sitzfleisch for me—we've been Platonic friends (more's the trouble) for years. All the best for now, and do write again when the spirit moves.

Yours ever,

PAT KAVANAGH

Gramercy Park Hotel
New York City
October 18, 1976

Dearest Pat,

. . .

Frances Lindley may undoubtedly be accurate in describing the lull in publishing, but it's part of a much larger Lull — everyone's brain has ceased operating while these two clowns, President Jerry Ford and Aspirant Jimmy Carter, flail away at each other with panty-hose filled with Nembutal. This is the most numbing, footless, and foolish Presidential election in anybody's memory. Ford is an utter numskull all of whose ganglia are working like crazy just to keep him from bumping into sharp objects that might pierce his carapace; Carter, a religious caterpillar and a holy man, is so busy flashing that ghastly death's-head grin that he doesn't have time to get any conviction into what he's saying, just recites what his advisers have told him by rote. It's really the most dispirited spectacle to live through that I can remember — no longer a choice between the lesser of two weevils, you now know that you can't win, and that's why 70,000,000 Americans are going to stay away from the polls, as the papers keep on repeating. I don't know if the BBC is showing these three so-called Presidential debates, but if so, then I'm not telling you anything new. All I hope is that the report I've heard — viz., that your telly has started to run *Mary Hartman Mary Hartman* — is true. Have you seen any of them? Some of the series is really magnificent spoofing of life in America — Mary Hartman's life in that kitchen, spraying the interior of her oven, brewing coffee for every disaster domestic or otherwise, the venereal disease threat overhanging her marriage, the love clinic, the funeral exercises of the luckless man who drowned in her soup, etc., etc. I prophesied from the moment I'd seen the second instalment that when this was shown in Britain it would become an all-out sensation, so do keep tabs on it and let me know, won't you?

. . . [After a visit to Martha's Vineyard in August] I ended up spending a night with Jerry Salinger, up on the Vermont border, in his eyrie. We hadn't seen each other for six years, and I'm glad to report that he looks fine, feels fine, and is working hard, so you can dispel all those rumors, manufactured in Hollywood by the people to whom he won't sell *Catcher in the Rye*, to the effect that he has taken leave of his senses.

The intervening white space that precedes this paragraph indicates a lapse of time, wherein I went down to Walsh's Chop House on East 23rd Street. I had a whiskey sour on the rocks, closely followed by Virginia ham steak,

320

glazed, with sweet potato and corn niblets, two salt-stengels (a form of bread-roll), and 2 cups of coffee. Throughout the foregoing, I finished reading Lilly Hellman's *Scoundrel Time*, and it is my considered opinion that Lil has begun to confuse herself with George Sand. I see all the preliminary symptoms of *folie de grandeur*; she regards herself as a historical character, and as someone who has known her since 1928 or thereabouts, I am becoming alarmed lest those men in the white jackets armed with butterfly nets suddenly appear and entice her into their wagon. In all fairness, I quite realize that Lil may often have mused to herself that *I* am barmy also; that is the prerogative of old friends; but honesty compels me to say that in this book she has finally told the presumptive reader more than he wants to know about Dashiell Hammett and her fine old Southern background. Have you read it? And, having read it (or not), what's your opinion?

Well, the two clocks plus one wrist-watch plus one travel clock that regulate my life tell me that it's 12:05 midnight, so I shall now lay myself down and continue reading *By a Stroke of Luck!*, Donald Ogden Stewart's auto-biography which he forced on me this past summer. I'm sorry that the fruit machine has to register two slightly wormy apples, one after the other, but honesty (which compelled me to say something candid above) again compels me to say that this one wins all the winter fatuity sweepstakes. Quite obvious-ly this must have been published by a vanity press which couldn't afford to pay for a copy editor; I've already marked 37 typos, instances of misinforma-tión, mistaken attributions, really a horrendous job; and as for the content — well....

Pat, darling — let me know well ahead of time when you'll be coming, won't you? So we can make plans. Until then,

Dearest love,

MEL CALMAN*

Gramercy Park Hotel
New York City
October 25, 1976

Dear Mel,

The legend atop your stationery read "Mel Calman Ltd.," whereas I have always thought of you as Mel Calman Unlimited, so I see that the years since I (sadly) left Onslow Square have hedged you in. This is in direct contradic-tion of the first principle of capitalism, which is balloonism, or unrestricted expansion. Where would the Rockefellers be today if sainted old John D. had

*British cartoonist.

321

gone on selling short-weight kerosene (paraffin to you) to widows and orphans instead of wisely deciding to mulct the whole country? No, my boy; you are sailing by false charts (false-chartism) which defies the very essence of capitalism. Of course you will assume a soapy smile and tell me that you are living in a welfare state run in terms of the social contract, and my reply to that is, well, you're better off than I am, Buster. I am living in a state of single blessedness where I have to schlep my own laundry to the Chinaman's, nobody to sew on a button or make me a hot meal at nightfall and nary a warm body to snuggle up against in those cold sheets. Jesus Christ, what's happened to all those wonderful broads that used to be around when I was a boy? They tell me the whole world is pullulating with sex, but all I see are hoarse-voiced lesbians in denim and giggling hair-dressers with toupees and 22-inch cuffs on their pants. All these environmentalists are complaining about erosion and a shortage of oxygen, but do you want to know what the real trouble is? The world is suffering from a shortage of nooky. Nobody is getting laid any more. (Well, not in the last couple of weeks.)

Now, I know you won't believe this, but I am a man who always speaks the *emmis* (the truth in our Jewish patois, how is it that I should be explaining such a thing to a Jewish lad like you, but that shows how the world is going nowadays). The *emmis* or truth is that I was in London this past summer for a fortnight, and one day I found myself somewhere vaguely in the neighborhood of Lambs Conduit. So I figure, I'll pop around to your gallery and we'll split a pint of plonk or something. The only trouble, I didn't have my little black book with me, it was lying on the dresser at Brown's Hotel. So by the time I got back to Dover & Albemarle Sts., the temperature was 95 degrees and I was a limp rag and spent the rest of the afternoon hovering between life and death in the bathtub. And that was pretty much the pattern of my whole two weeks in London. It was practically the greatest non-visit anyone ever made in the summer of 1976. Somewhere in there I did catch up with Harold Evans, but he was so surrounded by deputy editors, department heads, and assorted flunkeys that we hardly exchanged two words.

Anyway and notwithstanding, I am O.K. or rather shouldn't complain because nobody is listening in any case. (Least of all one of those big, beautiful broads above-mentioned. And apropos of that doesn't it strike you as curious that there should be such a shortage of big, beautiful broads? The birthrate figures show that twice as many girls are born as boys. Is someone killing them off before they attain puberty? This would make an interesting study for sociologists, and when the sociologists are finished with it, they could maybe explain to me why two or three weeks have to pass before a person gets laid.)

Well, the radio has just blared out the happy news that the pound fell six cents to a total value of $1.56 this morning, so I assume that you and Karen are lolling back in your drophead Bentleys with bodywork by Mulliner and swigging Krug '53 champagne like mad. Tonight you will enjoy a fine dinner at Ecu de France in Jermyn Street, both of you divinely clad in your glad rags from Laura Ashley and Turnbull & Asser, and afterward pop into The Talk of the Town to hobnob with Sir Lew Grade, Sir Charles Clore, and all your society friends. So be it. Just don't forget 220 millions of us over here — plain people, good people — going to the polls with furrowed brows faced with the decision to choose between a Michigan football player and a Georgia peanut farmer.

So this is the thought I'd like to leave with you if I may. The next time I'm in London, I shall carry my little black book with me whenever I walk out of Brown's Hotel. In the meantime, give some thought to the following. Why is it that a man should spend his whole life writing or cartooning as the case may be, plug away at his craft, wearing himself to skin and bone (or fat and gristle as the case may be), and yet sometimes two or three weeks should pass ere he gets laid? Is this right — is it just — is it democratic? I mean, if you read it in a book you wouldn't believe it — and yet everything we know supports this tragic state of affairs. Christ Almighty, look at Harold Evans wasting his time fighting the thalidomide decision and the Crossman diaries, when here is a real issue affecting literally thousands of people like

Yours ever,

WILLIAM A. DYER, JR.*

Gramercy Park Hotel
New York City
November 2, 1976

Dear Bill,

It will undoubtedly strike you as bizarre that ten months should elapse before your letter to Pamela Fiori of *Travel & Leisure* about me gets a response, but for openers let's absolve Pamela of guilt. She, good girl, did forward it, but I was off somewhere and the robots who handle the mail at the Gramercy Park Hotel here, where I'm more or less based, must have used it to decrease the sweat-band on their Panamas or bake a fish in, because it turned up ages later in an assorted bundle of old L.L. Bean catalogues, threats from collection agencies, and vilifying letters from factory girls who claimed I had de-

*Brown University alumnus and editor of *The Brown Jug* before Perelman.

flowered them and left them in an interesting condition. To compound the whole thing, I have been offshore at intervals this year—not, as you ungenerously suspect, as an operative of the CIA, but merely roving in quest of copy—so, what with constitutional inertia and reluctance to discharge even the most elementary functions, it has taken all this time to pick up the quill.

Anyway, I was so pleased to hear that you had read and liked the Russian instalment of that *Eastward Ha!* series they've been running. It terminates with the Hollywood chapter in their December issue, and by a coincidence, Simon & Schuster called this morning to signify that they'll publish the whole thing in book form early next fall. So Mummy is lying here in her flower-filled room at the Lying-In Hospital, wan but radiant, with that little bundle of manuscript nestling close to her, and the next person who dares to propose another trip around the world to me is liable to get a poke in the snoot. I wouldn't even go as far as Apponaug, not if they promised me a bucket of free quahogs.

If that Rhode Island localism fails to evoke a nostalgic sob from you, perhaps this will: the Graham Gallery on Madison Avenue has just sent me an announcement of a show of John Held Jr.'s work, Nov. 3 through Nov. 27, and if you're looking for an excuse for a quick trip to New York, no better one exists. What's more, I'll spring for what our British cousins call a slap-up lunch, and we can cry our eyes out over the purported good old days, though I doubt that the bartender at "21" still remembers how to mix a pousse-café.

As you see, this letter was begun on Election Day, but somewhere during it, I became frozen in front of the idiot box, watching David Brinkley and John Chancellor call out the results, and now that I resume, we have a new Chief Executive. God grant that having made it, he can now dispense with that dental display; I haven't seen so many teeth since Jeanette MacDonald quit singing those operettas. I guess neither of us has ever lived through such a boring campaign. There were moments during the so-called debates when I fell into a catatonic state where my breath hardly frosted a mirror and I awoke to find my legatees gathered around me, rubbing their hands expectantly as they waited for my will to be read.

Quite obviously, Bill, it would be fatuous to attempt to review the events of the past half century in a paragraph, so I won't yield to the temptation. However, I will say that I do get to Providence occasionally and gape in wonder at the changes wrought by the years at Brown. Is this big important institution the same cozy little college where Sammy Walsh used to beat out Zez Confrey's "Greenwich Witch" on the piano in the Brown Union while everyone's sheepskin coat steamed on the radiators? Have these hairy, bearded youths ever heard of relentless martinets of the stature of William Herbert Perry Faunce and Otis G. Randall whose one casual glance would cause a grown

324

man to pee in his pants? Is there anyone still alive who remembers that immortal burlesque production called *Red Hot Martha*?

Oh, well, here I am, beginning to sound like one of the older members of the Grand Army of the Republic, so let me cease and desist. Do send me a line when you have a moment, and, if there's any likelihood you might be in town, I expect to be here all winter. With all the best,

Yours ever,

CASKIE STINNETT

Gramercy Park Hotel
New York City
December 4, 1976

Dear Caskie,

If you're still on your rocky fief in Maine, which I somehow doubt, you're probably a cross between a sunburned icicle and one of Marsden Hartley's granite-faced fishermen, but I'm sure this will reach you thanks to your Wiscasset postal connection. I also assume you're in touch with wide-ranging Mme. Hellman, whose visage bundled in dark Russian mink has now become as familiar to readers as that Scott's Emulsion person bundled in oilskins was in our youth. The hair-pulling match with Diana Trilling, in my view, lacked the zing of true drama; it would have been much more effective had it climaxed with the two contestants, naked and coated with chicken fat like Gertrude Ederle, wrestling for the best two falls out of three at the New York A.C.* Anyhow, Lil got plenty of publicity out of it, which of course she needs like a hole in the head. . . .

The other two clippings, out of my air-mail edition of the *Times* of London, nicely illustrate what some of our British cousins consider true hilarity, i.e., pissing and farting. In two years there, I tried unsuccessfully to elicit from them what they thought was so wrenchingly comic about farts. The mere mention of wind (*vide* Bea Lillie's song "Wind under My Heart") was enough to set audiences rolling in the aisles. And I would be a rich man today if I had a nickel for the countless newspaper stories about that Frenchman who was able to play the Marseillaise or whatever by rhythmically discharging his gas. From Mrs. Trollope onward, English visitors to America have been lambasting us for our crudity in spitting everywhere, but no American observer has ever taken them to task on the above subject, as far as I know.

The only alleviating factor in the onrushing descent into Christmas horror at the moment is the presence of Pat Kavanagh, who's here till the 14th

*Ederle was an American Olympic swimmer and the first woman to swim the English Channel.

or so. (She's likewise the only gift South Africa ever made to the gaiety of nations.) She is coming around in a few hours to sup with me on Virginia baked ham and candied sweets at Walsh's, that reliable East 23rd St. saloon, perhaps the one oasis left in this district.

Speaking of girls (who was speaking of girls? I'm obviously shoe-horning this into the text because it has intense meaning for me), do you know one named — —? She was married to — —, but they are now divorced. This creature made a considerable dent on your correspondent in months past and has reciprocated not at all. It puzzles me beyond endurance, and if you have any subterranean information or means of obtaining same, kindly furnish details. I speak, naturally, under the rose, as one member of Interpol to another.

· · ·

Yours ever,

ERIC LISTER

Gramercy Park Hotel
New York City
December 23, 1976

Dear Eric,

. . . [L]et me thank you for sending over the reconstituted green cardigan. You'll never know what *nachis* surged through my veins as I gazed upon it, nor what it did for British-American relations. Everywhere I roamed for three weeks I hymned endless praises to the workmanship and pride of craft in the U.K. I was constantly stripping off my jacket in restaurants to show diners my new fluffy woolen elbows and once or twice was almost arrested as a flasher, when I absent-mindedly started to remove my shorts. . . .

Well, anyway, autumn has drifted by in a more or less humdrum manner; I've been out to Bucks County, Pa., several times in connection with getting my MG restored to service, and after wide search managed to find someone who's currently awakening it from its six-year sleep. I stayed overnight twice with the Mushams in my old house, and can tell you that the Indian screen looks terrific as the headboard of their nuptial bed. Also, your wheelbarrow—the one you sold Leila M., is in their livingroom, burdened with plants. The whole farm is a hive of activity; . . . everywhere you look bushes and trees are being planted, people are quarrying out rocks and substituting brick walks, baby peacocks and guinea hens are cackling, and their accumulated six offspring are strewing wet towels about. But it's a lovely place and I occasionally have to repress pangs that I own it no longer—though it made sense to sell it, all considered.

Pat Kavanagh has been and gone, she says she's developing an affection for New York but I can't guess why, the streets have pot-holes like mine craters, veritable Alps of garbage stand neglected sometimes for days, Lexington Avenue and others teem with black hookers and their pimps, and at night the roads are empty of life for fear of muggers. And if anyone's looking for nasal pollution, brother, we have 17 kinds of sulphur-laden chimney exhaust going day and night...Have talked with Hellman a few times since her return, she said she enjoyed seeing you and that you talked of nothing but money, which I dismissed as a playful and affectionate distortion of your meeting. Thanks, incidentally, for the Alphonse Allais collection. I read several reviews of it in the London *Times* and elsewhere and had been planning to order it.

.   .   .

As ever,

P A U L   T H E R O U X

Gramercy Park Hotel
New York City
December 24, 1976

Dear Paul,

Between the constant repetition of "White Christmas" and "Jingle Bells" on station WPAT and the increasing frenzy of Saks' and Gimbel's newspaper ads as these fucking holidays draw near, I have been in a zombie-like state for weeks, totally incapable of rational thought or action. I must have arrived at near-paralysis yesterday afternoon when I was in the 4th-floor lingerie section ("Intimate Apparel") in Saks 5th Avenue. I had just purchased two such intimate garments for gifties to a couple of ladies of my acquaintance, a tall blonde and a somewhat shorter brunette. For the former, I had chosen a black lace chemise in the style known as a teddy back in the Twenties (familiar to you as the scanty garment worn by Rita Hayworth in the war-time pinup). For the shorter brunette, a similar peach-colored job. Both of these real silk, parenthetically, and as I signed the charge slip, I knew that when the bill comes in after January 1st, I would kick myself for my prodigality. Anyway, while the hard-featured saleslady was wrapping them up with appropriate mash-notes to each bimbo, I went upstairs to the men's dept. to buy myself a cheap tie-tack. When I returned for the feminine frillies, I found (a) that the saleslady had forgotten to identify which box was which, and (b) that she had switched the notes. In other words, the blond Amazon would find herself with the brunette's undershirt and some steamy sentiment addressed to the latter, and vice versa. I broke out into a perspiration — it's tropically hot in those department stores anyway — and insisted on the saleslady clawing open the boxes, which meant destroying all the fake holly berries, silver cord, and mish-mash they were entwined in. This of course put her in a foul temper, and meanwhile a waiting queue of customers became incensed. The upshot was a group shot of seven or eight people leering and cackling obscenely as I stood there holding the two chemises and the notes appropriate to the recipients. Given the savoir-faire of Cary Grant I might have risen above it but the only savoir-faire I possess is Oliver Hardy's, and little enough of that.

Other than this, I am well, and better for having read your story "Dependent Wife" in the London *Times* the other day; your description of Ayer Hitam revived my sense of claustrophobia in similar Malaysian locales. . . . Some months ago, when lunching with Caskie Stinnett, who edited *Travel & Leisure* before Pamela Fiori, we got to talking about Ipoh in Malaysia and the grisly Station Hotel there. And he said that once, when he also passed a night there, he saw the most beautiful woman he had ever beheld in his life, a Eurasian, whom he didn't get to meet but who he still dreams about in his lonely island off the Maine coast. This is the kind of fantasy that only three people in the whole world understand — you and I and Caskie Stinnett.

⋅   ⋅   ⋅

Yours ever,

CASKIE STINNETT

Gramercy Park Hotel
New York City
December 26, 1976

Dear Caskie,

⋅   ⋅   ⋅

Your fortnight in Switzerland, despite rain and snow, sounded enviable; the only thing that has fallen on Gramercy Park during your absence was black soot from the pants factories surrounding. As for the beauty you picked up in the Modigliani room of the Berne Museum, do not despair. One day she will tire of her fat, bald, impotent, and rich spouse and turn up on your doorstep. I also discern from my crystal ball that in 1984 you will inherit eleven million dollars and become president of Liberia. My talent for divination is still spoken of with awe in Providence, R.I., where I grew up.

I went to see *Comedians* night before last and reaffirmed why I have stopped going to the theater. It's a vaudeville show chock-full of ancient wheezes, shellacked over by Mike Nichols's direction and dealing with a pack of dingy English crumb-bums in Manchester longing to become stand-up comics. I know I'll be accused of fascist leanings, but I wish to God somebody would write a witty comedy about clean and hairless middle-class people, if indeed any such folks still exist. They must; I see them going in and out of Grand Central and Radio City, and even a few at Abercrombie & Fitch. (Well, not so many at the latter; perhaps that's why Abercrombie is bankrupt.) I was also rather astounded by the garb of theatergoers seated around me. Less than half the men wore ties; lots were clad in sweaters or what we used to call beer-jackets and three or four guys had ropy fur coats of Russian pony and raccoon. Where these derelicts got the $15 per ticket, don't ask me.

Your notion of an apartment in Boston for a while seems like a good idea. But watch out for those hoods that George V. Higgins writes about. Have you read his novels?

Cheers and all the best for 1977.   Yours ever,

LEILA   HADLEY

Gramercy Park Hotel
New York City
January 13, 1977

Leila darling,

Thought you might be interested in this shopping column on Hong Kong in today's London *Times*. Very knowledgeable, and as for the bit I've encircled, perhaps you may want to consider acting as supplier for Seh Wong Yuen's Restaurant. After all, a few gross of copperheads picked up in the woods could lessen the taxes on the farm appreciably.*

Incidentally, and while I'm writing, I wonder if you could dig up that plastic fried egg from Japan I loaned you (when we talked about converting it into a compact)? Someone I know is interested, and I'd be obliged if you could post it when you have a minute.   All love,

*In May of 1976, Hadley had married William Musham, the buyer of Perelman's farm in Bucks County.

ERIC   LISTER

Gramercy Park Hotel
New York City
March 6, 1977

Dear Eric,

. . . I really am not interested in going to China, since I've already been there. And since I have seen Communism in Russia and its satellites, I am

329

less than ever interested in seeing China again. Your projected tour is obviously a good opportunity and in your shoes I would grab it.

As I think I mentioned in my last letter, I expect to be coming over to London during the first 2 weeks of May—date so far indefinite—and am pleased you'll be there then.

Finally managed to contact Bob Gill & he sent me the snaps of ourselves. One of my lady friends promptly stowed the picture of me eating soup in Lindos in her corsage, where, of course, I was too much a gentleman to try to retrieve it. So you know that your handiwork hereafter will be in safe tits.

All regards, and do write at more length when you have more length. Which I hope will be always.   Always,

KARL FORTESS

Gramercy Park Hotel
New York City
April 11, 1977

Dear Karl,

Please forgive this belated reply to your brievel of 22nd March. I have been torn up between finishing off a piece for the superscribed blat and trying to get my old '49 MG Tourer back on the road. It's been sitting on blocks at a neighbor's in Erwinna ever since I gave up my place in 1970. Last October I finally found a mechanic in New Hope—appropriately named Armand A. Legg—who contracted to put it into shape to pass inspection. Thereby hangs a tale; he has been flicking rust off it with a Brillo pad ever since, now and then teasing wax out of its gozzle with a Q-tip, and between-times sending me bills large enough to put a down payment on a Lamborghini. Well, if those fuckers in Harrisburg ever issue me license plates, it should be in service by the end of the month—just as I'm getting ready to leave for England.

The last half of the foregoing sentence ties in with your statement, "and as for N.Y.C. all I miss are those salt beef sandwiches." Other than those— currently best obtained at the 2nd Ave. Deli corner of 10th Street—Christ only knows why I remain here. For one thing, I just paid my NY State & City taxes and find that it cost me roughly $5500 to live here—i.e., for the *privilege* of living here. For the privilege of dodging muggers, breathing the sulphur of its smokestacks, stepping on dog-scheiss, etc., etc. This will explain why I'm now going over to have a second look at a darling little town called Ludlow, midway between Shrewsbury and Hereford, in Shropshire. I saw it last June and promptly got an erection. I'm not issuing any large statements to the effect that I intend to spend the rest of my days there, but maybe there's a small house on the outskirts, etc. I rather fancy myself as an *alte kocker* with a knobbed stick, attended by standard gray poodle, thrusting kids out of my path and exchanging greetings with Miss Marple, who delivers my mail on a bicycle. Who is that old eccentric, Uncle Jim? Why, he is that elderly Hebrew gentleman who bought Dr. Kinsolving's house which they say it's haunted. And so forth.

Anyway, that's the phantasmagoria I'm figuring to pursue come May 10th. But should you be planning to come down to N.Y. anytime before that, I certainly will be delighted to trip over to the 2nd Ave. Deli and cut up touches with you over a hot salt beef. Meanwhile, with all best to yourself and Lillian, a happy New Year and bad 'cess to the enemies of the Crown.

Yours ever,

P.S. And what is by no means a coincidence: On April 21, my two Ben Shahns, one Stuart Davis, and one Horace Pippin go on the auction block at Sotheby Parke Bernet. They too have lain in storage since 1970 and I can't see any virtue in holding them any longer, what with the prohibitive cost of insurance. After the auctioneers and Uncle Sam take their cut, the remaining bubkess would far better be employed in a bit of soil in Shropshire or the equivalent.

CASKIE STINNETT

Gramercy Park Hotel
New York City
April 15, 1977

Dear Caskie,

.   .   .

Your description of the animal alert button at Salt Lick Lodge is an eloquent testament to what's happened to tourism in our time. I thought the night I spent in the old Treetops in '53, the day before the Mau Mau burned it to the ground, was the summit in organized luxury, but this computerized snooping makes everything else pale.

I assume that you must have missed the Academy Awards broadcast and thereby Lil's ovation from the celebrants; she must have been gratified indeed at their tribute, and she got in some good rabbit punches in her speech. The high-light of the evening for me was Norman Mailer, who never fails to provide pure horse-cock. In case you missed it, he began thus: "It is related that on one occasion, Voltaire was taken to a male bordello in Paris." (A hush fell over the assemblage; after all, who other than Proust—who operated one—has ever been associated with such a filthy enterprise?) "On emerging," he continued, "he was asked how he had enjoyed the experience. He replied,

'Once a philosopher, twice a pervert.' The award for the most distinguished cinematography by second cameramen," he said, fumbling open the envelope, "goes to Milton Zeltzberger for *She Opened His Drawers.*"

Boston as a winter niche for your activities sounds very worthwhile. This city is giving me increasing migraine, there are just too many rats in this cage and the human scale by now has just about diminished to zero. I'm going off to London about May 7 and soon after to Shropshire to see some more of it, perhaps nosing around for a simple pad there where I can wear a Tolstoyan blouse, stump around with a gnarled stick, and mystify the rustics. . . .

From present plans, I ought to be back in town along about July 1, and I'd be delighted to visit your island; it sounds blissful. So all the best for now, and watch those sidecars at St. Botolph's, man, or your cheeks will sparkle like pippins.   Yours ever,

I S R A E L   S H E N K E R

                                        Gramercy Park Hotel
                                        New York City
                                        April 29, 1977

Dear Shenk,

Thought the enclosed would interest you, forwarded by a lady friend who teaches at the Sorbonne.* The classification of my work as dementia praecox dates back to an introduction to an early book of mine whose preface was written by Robert Benchley; he thus described the field we both worked in. Today, for the first time, I looked up the definition of d. p. in Webster, and got a schreck.

I enjoyed our recent evening together greatly, and even more your piece on the 2nd Ave. Deli when I perused it with my peruser next morning. What geschmack! What poesy! And what price Joe Liebling's eulogia to food? You am de bestest in the field.   Best,

*Program from a congress sponsored by the Association Française d'Etudes Américaines. Lectures included "S. J. Perelman et la 'dementia praecox school of humor' " and "Paroles de Schlemil."

C A S K I E   S T I N N E T T

                                        Gramercy Park Hotel
                                        New York City
                                        June 29, 1977

Dear Caskie,

                •   •   •

London was rampant with Jubilee fever — whipped up, the Left press contended, to merchandise British goods, and the royals did their roles manfully. Everybody was up to his ass in fireworks, parades, and panoply. Have you, by the way, heard what the disrespectful call the Queen, Princess Margaret, and Prince Philip? The first is referred to as Brenda, the second as Yvonne (both good dreary suburban names), and the last as Phil the Greek. There were 400,000 tourists in the city, it was claimed, and most of them Arab; in any case, I was moved around like a checker piece at the hotel I stayed in at South Kensington, occupying six different rooms that month. Otherwise, I trudged around Shropshire and Herefordshire looking at real estate, none of it particularly enthralling, and then proceeded to Cork and vicinity which I hadn't ever visited, and did like that. Saw a hell of a nice Georgian house at Shanagarry, Co. Waterford, but my delirium has since cooled. The complexities of split residence between New York and Southern Ireland are too much to undertake at my patriarchal age. It's O.K. for striplings like Richard Condon, Donleavy, etc., but forty years in Bucks County have winded me.

•   •   •

I couldn't agree with you more about hatred of rock music and the whole rock scene—totally mindless, a cult dedicated to outdoing each other in ugliness, noise, and swinemanship. I remember Al Hirschfeld once describing a lecture Al Capp gave him on how to succeed in cartooning. "You have to think of something so disgusting that it'll cause people to throw up," he explained. "If you draw a wart on someone's nose, always put hairs on it. I've just created a character called Bathless Groggins who hasn't bathed since childhood—he stinks so that nobody'll go near him. It's going to make me a fortune." The same formula Rat Scabies and the Punk Rock crowd operate on—the more emetic, the bigger the applause.

On which oppressive thought, I pinch your claws.

Yours ever,

PAT KAVANAGH

Gramercy Park Hotel
New York City
July 10, 1977

Dear Pat,

Thanks for your note, attesting arrival of copies of *Most of SJP* and galleys of (sic) *Eastwood Ha!*. Update your secretary *re* title lest she start converting that into *Yeastwood Harooch!* or *Breastfed Yech!* or something equally raunchy.

Regarding your query, "Do you specifically *not* want to be published by Lord Weidenfeld from here on?," I have to explicate. They . . . fucked up the first one, *Baby, It's Cold Inside*, by timorously printing an edition of 2500 copies which, when it got lovely reviews, promptly was exhausted. With booksellers clamoring, it then took them something like 11 weeks to get back into print, by which time the book was a dead issue. They then published *Vinegar Puss*, which also got a very warm acceptance from the press, and never once bothered to contact me, though I've been in Britain twice, other than to demand cash payment for the few copies I've ordered for friends.

In other words, the four-year courtship dance that Lord George executed around me to snare me onto his list was just so much hogwash, and I would therefore think that on the old principle that a new broom sweeps clean, let's try elsewhere. . . .

•   •   •

Love & kisses,

E . B . W H I T E

Gay Head
Martha's Vineyard, Mass.
August 24, 1977

Dear Andy,

Your welcome letter reached me in this curious house I rented sight unseen by phone when I was in London back in June. I had gone to Britain with the notion that I might possibly buy a rose-bowered cottage, a tumbledown shack in Athlone, to punctuate the dullness of life in a New York hotel suite. My search wound over a good part of Shropshire, Worcestershire, and eastern Wales, and turned up some of the most depressing huts left over from the industrial revolution. I then remembered that Joe Liebling had proclaimed Cork and vicinity God's country, so I hastened there and was shown a series of Georgian houses with stabling for fifty horses, minstrel galleries, pipe organs, and vats for brewing one's personal mead. Hardly had I crept back dejected to London when some false friend alerted me to this opportunity on the Vineyard—an erection by a Harvard economist with sweeping views of the Elizabeth Islands, from which, on a clear day, one could get the scent of fried clams and salt-water taffy in Oak Bluffs. Well, it is all true. It is also true that the economist or his architect contrived a dozen fiendish clerestory windows, as they're called: so designed that when tilted, they funnel in all the rain-water on the roof and the mosquitoes in the entire neighborhood. The furniture is largely built in and cunningly lit so that a person barks his shins if he moves without planning half an hour before. From the knees down not one inch of skin is visible on either leg, just band-aids. I look like one of Koren's drawings in the grand old magazine.

334

As for the social life here, you can well imagine. The survivors of the '40s and '50s, when Laura and I summered here, haven't developed the Dickensian sweetness I acquired with old age. They seem bitter, crabbed, and their faces are yellow with Angst, but in one respect they haven't changed; their jokes are the same. They are still using the jokes out of the Dartmouth *Jack o' Lantern* and the Princeton *Tiger* they started life with. Sample: "He: Are you fond of Kipling? She: Yes, but I haven't kippled lately." Another: "She: Why did you kiss me on the chin just now? He: My error, dear. I should have remembered that Heaven's above."

The task you described of organizing Katharine's papers for eventual dispersal sounds overwhelming, and very saddening. There aren't any consolations at a time like this, and the assurance of friends that time will lessen the pain tends to sound glib, but it does happen very, very slowly. I just wish it were possible, though, for the dead to stay out of one's dreams...

My thought, Andy, was that Katharine's letter to me did belong with the material going to Bryn Mawr; I had a Xerox made for myself, and I know it will move me just as much in the future as when I received it.

With all my best,   Yours,

PAUL THEROUX

Gramercy Park Hotel
New York City
October 16, 1977

Dear Paul,

I swan (which I guess is the first person singular of the verb "to swan" — e.g., I swan, you swan, we all swan) I should have written you ere this to thank you for the *N.Y. Times* review of *Eastward Ha!*. It was a peach, and so regarded by many, who were impelled to ring up and congratulate me, when, of course, they should properly have lauded *you* because it was written with such felicity, humor, and affection. It was Lillian Hellman's eagle eye in particular that spotted this last attribute. And, of course, it was of inestimable value in launching the book, which, parenthetically, isn't officially released until this next Wednesday. Apparently, the *Times* jumped the gun, deciding they could give your review better space that week than if held till later, and fortunately, S&S had copies out in the trade by then, so it all worked out nicely. Anyhow, I'm now being put through the usual neuralgic gymnastics, the TV stuff, interviews, and crapola that attend the birth of a book, wherein the writer is besought to make an ass of himself to the greatest possible number of captives. If only some genius could come up with statistics to confound the publishers, proving that the more a writer is exposed to the public, the less his book sells!

Other than this, I've hardly done a lick of work except a piece for your Sunday *Times* in its Pleasures of Life series. But from afar I hear thorns crackling under the pot; Pat Kavanagh writes me that Methuen will publish *Eastward* in the U.K. and maybe will reissue *The Most of SJP*, so I'm not yet stiffening into rigor mortis. (Oh yes, a little stiffening in one part of the body, thank God, else why bother to get up in the morning?)

Well, I'll conclude this unsprightly pavane while the outworn typewriter ribbon still functions and then hop into the sack, as I have to be up with the lark. Why, you ask? Because tomorrow a.m. I am off to Cherry Hill, New Jersey, to address 300 female librarians gathered in conclave by Baker & Taylor, the book wholesalers. Your natural question: will there be so much as a single cherry among those 300 Cherry Hill librarians? My answer: quien sabe? My second answer: Who cares? It is all for the greater glory of Simon & Schuster, a Gulf & Western affiliate.

Keep well, amigo. Yours ever,

MORLEY SAFER*

Gramercy Park Hotel
New York City
November 9, 1977

Dear Morley,

So stiffened with horror have I been ever since absorbing those reports from Nigeria you sent along that my floor maid, Isosceles, was overheard to remark to one of her colleagues, "I swan, dat gemmun in Suite 1621 done remind me ob Thaddeus Sholto in *De Sign ob de Four*, which he was transfixed wid de poisoned thorn by dat no-good Andaman Islander. He eben got dat dread *risus sardonicus* on he visage, sho nuff."

The poor soul was right, and now that I am again ambulatory, wild horses ain't gwine drag me anywhere near Lagos or West Africa. Granted that we merry-andrews are obliged to search out difficulties and dilemmas to sharpen our nails on, but I'd say Nigeria is beyond the call of duty.

So thanks for the warning, even though you acted from the best of motives.

Keep the faith. Yours ever,

*Television journalist, most recently associated with *60 Minutes*.

MEL CALMAN

Gramercy Park Hotel
New York City
December 18, 1977

Dear Mel,

    •   •   •

   . . . I have been pulled hither and yon with quote promoting unquote
my recent volume, *Eastward Ha!*, the usual circuit of interviews, speeches,
and similar bed-wetting that ensues with a new book. Luckily, it's all finished
now and the book can go straight into the remainder bins. Should you wonder
why you haven't received a copy, it's on account of my discovery some time
ago that books mailed to Britain never get there. However, this is my prom-
issory note for one, and if I can fasten on some London-bound friend, I'll
entrust him or it to mail it onward...It was not until last week, by the bye,
that I received your Penguin from Al Hirschfeld, who is so absent-minded
that I had to phone him four times dunning him for it. Still, it was worth
the wait, you have some delightful things in it I hadn't ever seen.

   . . . Pat Kavanagh, my luscious agent, has sold *E. Ha!* and *The Most
of S.J.P.* to Eyre Methuen, who will be launching them circa May 25 and I've
consented to come over for this same exploitation swill. How this will fit in
with the Great MG Motor Project, I haven't yet figured out. Harry Evans
of the Grand Old Paper, when last I heard, is due to be here in January and
has promised to discuss it some more in depth, so I'll know later. Now as to
the all-important problem of a tall companion on the adventure, half woman
and half mechanic (or all woman and ⅓ mechanic), since you have so stringent-
ly withdrawn Karen from the sweepstakes—bad 'cess to you for a Puritani-
caltight-assedjewbastard, wouldn't give a man the time of day if he was dying
of hunger—I have to tell you that in the interim I have decided to broaden
the search to include tall *Americans*. (The only ones I am excluding are tall
Albanian girls, never having seen any.) Well, stap my vitals, two days after
I made this resolution and passed it around to a few households, I get a tug
on my line like a marlin striking—yes siree. The new contestant is an enravish-
ment named Delta Willis, a photographer by profession, which she's already
travelled in Africa and God knows where else, but WAIT! WAIT! Six feet of
sheer loveliness, hails from Pine Bluff, Arkansas, I tell you I thought I was
dreaming. And now comes the spooky part. Do you know that the very night
before we met, this lady had a dream that she was riding in a 1949 YY-MG
Tourer, right-hand drive with a canvas top, red leather interior, and who was
at the wheel but a man with little pebble glasses and an unruly moustache!
I tell you, it sent shivers up my spine. This person I'm speaking of has had
to run down to Pine Bluff, Arkansas, for the Christmas hols but is scheduled

to be back in Manhattan right afterward; so hopefully we shall meet in a garage built into the Plaza Hotel, with cozy leather banquettes and tinkling glassware, where Delta and I can discuss just what sort of becoming jump-suit and goggles she should wear. ARE YOU LISTENING, KAREN? You could have been in that front seat if it wasn't for a tightassedPuritanicaletcetc whose name I needn't mention. Oh, it's enough to curdle the milk in your veins, some people's idea of friendship.

At the present time—to be candid, I've lost all track of the time, sitting here and fondling my typewriter—it's 5:37 of a rainy Sunday afternoon and the realization has just been borne in on me that I'm starving, I haven't eaten anything but a raisin bun since lunch. So I must regretfully take leave of you and huddle with that half a barbecued chicken I left in the fridge. I also have some frozen strawberries, plus a few brownies my ungrateful daughter mailed me, to pad out the meal, but what shall I read whilst I engulf these goodies? Well, fortunately, I still have six unconsumed articles in *The Best of Forum*—"Bestiality: Why Not Do It with a Schnauzer?," "Sado-Masochism, a New Approach for School Leavers," and four sparkling others in similar vein. A merry Xmas, then, *mes petits*, and a gorgeous New Year to you both as well as love to the girls. I wish you were all here, but failing that, I'll drink a toast to you next weekend.   Yours ever,

PAT KAVANAGH

                                                 Gramercy Park Hotel
                                                 New York City
                                                 April 16, 1978

Dear Pat,

                    •   •   •

Whether or not word has sifted back about the National Book Awards of the past week I don't know, but I'm enclosing a couple of photo-copies. As no specifics are mentioned, I am compelled to reveal blushingly that the medal reads: "Special Achievement Award to S.J. Perelman for a sustained and exceptional contribution to American writing." It was tendered to me at Carnegie Hall and afterwards ensued a vast drinks party given by the massed publishers at that most hideous of all hotels, the Americana, following which Simon & Schuster threw one of its own at The Four Seasons for approximately 500 well-wishers of Gulf & Western, the conglomerate that comes closest to being as large as Michael Korda's ego. Far from inflating my own (my own ego, that is), I have to report that in consequence of all the photographers' flash bulbs, mine has shrunk to pea size. I just want to get into that MG and head for the capital of fried rice and won ton soup.

•   •   •

Much love,

HOWARD KISSEL*

Gramercy Park Hotel
New York City
April 19, 1978

Dear Howard,

Thank you so much for your gracious copy of Simon Leys's book, *Chinese Shadows*. I remember thinking, at the time it appeared, that this was one book I really wished to read, and now I can do so.

. . . What is all this fuss about *An Unmarried Woman*? I have just laid FOUR DOLLARS per ticket on the barrelhead to see it and am fuming. After all, I can watch *Another World* or any similar soap opera on the box and injure my eyesight for free...

I didn't see *WWD*'s coverage of the dinner at the Whitney on the night Saul Steinberg's retrospective opened, but I did see that Woody Allen attended bravely in mufti whereas all the nobs were in full regalia. That's the kind of pluck that deserves an Oscar from J.M. Rothman and all the other cut-rate men's clothing firms.

Yours in the bond (Bond suits?)

*At the time, a journalist for *Women's Wear Daily*.

VERONICA GENG*

Gramercy Park Hotel
New York City
April 22, 1978

Dear Veronica Geng,

Hope you don't mind my talking behind your back. I did say "Veronica," but the reporter was so busy getting your last name right that he blew the first half.†   Best,

*Humorist and, at the time, *New Yorker* fiction editor.
†"[Perelman] thinks Chris Chase, who co-authored Rosalind Russell's autobiography, and Victoria Geng, a *New Yorker* staff writer, are 'emerging talents' " (*Minneapolis Tribune*, April 9, 1978).

MARY BLUME

Gramercy Park Hotel
New York City
April 26, 1978

Dear Mary,

. . .

I am . . . coming over to London for a month that begins with 3 days
of enforced TV and related garbage in behalf of a couple of books Methuen's
publishing there. . . . My principal errand is to sort out a project that Harry
Evans . . . and I have been cooking, wherein I drive my 1949 MG from Paris
to Peking. As you can gather, it's got a lot of bugs, not the least of which
is furnishing me with a support system, in effect a pursuit or backup car to
carry some vintage replacement parts, petrol, and band-aids I might need.
Carefree, adventurous Harry Evans thinks this would detract from the romance
of the adventure, and fearful, jittery SJP thinks it might hearten the occupants
of the front seat. The other occupant is a blond Amazon hailing from Pine
Bluff, Arkansas, who was recommended as a knowledgeable mechanic. This
person is fully aware that $99\,^{44}/_{100}$ of her role is to serve as the target of my
raillery—so she says. As I recall, my companion on that 80-day circuit of the
globe said the same thing. This tour may end equally disastrously. Nevertheless,
as Metternich or Maeterlinck or Manischevitz, the Father of the Modern
Matzoh, observed: "You cannot make an omelet without breaking eggs."

. . .

It will give you some index of my activities that last night the lady on
my left was 90 years old (albeit her name was Lynn Fontanne) and that the
reason I am terminating this letter now is because I am going to a cocktail
party celebrating the 85th birthday of a lady writer (albeit *her* name is Anita
Loos). My purpose in telling you this, I needn't assure you, has nothing to
do with name-dropping. Rather it is that now I'm in the sere and yellow leaf,
I tend to be numbered increasingly among the geriatrics. Perhaps this is why
I'm striving to drive from Paris to Peking—one last chuck of the dice.

Love,

ROLLIN VAN N. HADLEY*

Gramercy Park Hotel
New York City
May 14, 1978

Dear Mr. Hadley,
Do forgive me for not responding earlier to your very kind note of April

*A friend of Lady Christian Hesketh.

1st. I've been immersed in trying to get some work finished before going to Britain next week; and, in fact, have just written to Kisty, telling her of your letter and hoping that I may get to see her. She is indeed one of the most remarkable and lovely people I've ever known, and so many of her admirers have become friends through that circumstance that we threaten to grow into a very considerable political force. Our platform: to extirpate feminist writers seeking to out-gross *Fanny Hill.*

Thank you for your amiable reference to "Sherry Flip." The real name of that doomed musical revue, I may now reveal, was *Walk a Little Faster*, starring Beatrice Lillie and Bobby Clark-Paul McCullough, and "Sherry Flip" was a title proposed in its early stages by Dorothy Parker. It was my first meeting with Mrs. Parker and a quite horrifying one about which I will tell you some day when I come up to Boston. Which I certainly shall before too long, and it would give me great pleasure to meet you. Thanking you for having written, and with kindest regards,   Yours sincerely,

HAROLD EVANS

London
June 10, 1978

Dear Harry,

It seems to me that our project for the drive from Paris to Peking is now befogged by such muddle that I really must clearly define my interest in it and the basis upon which I want to proceed with it. Since I shall be returning to New York next Monday the 19th, it is vital that you and I have a complete understanding if the trip is to take place at all.

Let me say at the outset that from the beginning I have viewed the journey as taking place from Paris to Peking and that it is the *journey* and not the *arrival* that matters. It is the trip and its vicissitudes, the dilemmas and imbroglios, that will furnish me with the copy you want — *not* the fact that at its conclusion we may be able to reach Peking. Hence, the proposal advanced that the trip begin at Peking has the following disadvantages and weaknesses:

1. It will be difficult, if not altogether impossible, to arrange Chinese consent. In whatever case, it will be time-consuming at this juncture, when time is of the essence.

2. The trip will be infinitely more costly, since it will involve shipping my MG and the Land Rover from Britain.

3. Above all, it will be *anti-climactic*, and I strongly stress this. Even if the Chinese accede to the idea, the rest of the trip becomes merely an exercise in endurance and of subsidiary importance — whereas the reverse, starting in Paris with the hope of achieving Peking provides an objective, a *goal.*

341

I have said above that time is of the essence, and here is why. With Paris-Peking, I can very shortly ship my MG to Britain for necessary checkup and adaptation of springs, etc., the Land Rover can be outfitted with essential supplies, and the trip be started on September 1, when the weather is most ideal for the journey. Additionally, throughout the trip, efforts can go forward to convince the Chinese to permit us to drive to Peking.

Finally, I must mention that the reverse course — Peking to Paris — carries one dire possibility: it demands that I ship the MG to Britain with no certainty whatever that the trip will take place. Weeks, and perhaps months, may elapse while permission from the Chinese is awaited. And if that permission is denied in the end, your belief in the project and my enthusiasm will dwindle and I shall be left with an MG in Britain.

Accordingly, Harry, I'm compelled to speak very plainly. I must have a decision from you before I leave London next Monday the 19th. If it is Paris-Peking, I'll do it as agreed. If not, let's forget the whole thing, and no hard feelings. I'll merely insist that *you* buy me lunch at "21" on *my* birthday next February 1.

With all the best, and urgently awaiting that decision,

Yours ever,

MARY BLUME

Gramercy Park Hotel
New York City
June 28, 1978

Dear Mary,

It was very good seeing you in London, and I hope you've recovered from the experience of eating in that bizarre nookleteria we lunched at.

This is just a short note to confirm that the giant swing is going ahead as planned after sorting out some minor, bothersome bugs. We're scheduled to start from Paris on Sept. 1, and I hope to come over to London August 15 to crisp up final details. Shipped the MG off to Southampton earlier this week, and now busying myself getting visas, etc., also endeavoring to get permission to drive across China (which will take some doing, I believe).

Overwhelming heat here and everyone whey-faced; the Glorious Fourth weekend starts tomorrow, and I'm committed to finish it with 2 days chez Glorious Vanderbilt at her Southampton beach house. How I got myself into such a pickle I don't know, unless it's that my first name coincides with that of her one-time hubby, Sidney Lumet. Could she be suffering from pro-semitism? On the other hand, she may be pro-geriatric; I'm not as stunning as Stokowski but I'm almost as old. Wish me luck. Yours in the bond,

Love,

ARTHUR H. ROSEN*

Gramercy Park Hotel
New York City
July 17, 1978

Dear Sir:

I am in receipt of your boorish little note in which you dub me "an alte knacker" (whatever you conceive that to mean) and a "meshugener" (misspelled though the intent is clear), and equate me with folk seeking to perform rock on the Great Wall and to canoe on the Yangtse. Not content with these gibes at a person unknown to you, you then demand with a cackle whether I consider myself a comedian. All the foregoing, please note, on the basis of a telephone inquiry reported to you by a subordinate, the details of which you know nothing about.

Let me, therefore, reply as succinctly as I can. I have never before heard of you, but if the above is indicative of your skill at furthering relations between the United States and China, you are lamentably miscast. You belong on the borscht circuit — not at Grossinger's, the Concord Hotel, or even at Kutscher's, but at some lesser establishment where the clientele is as gross and chuckle-headed as you are. It defies reason that the promotion of cordiality between two great nations should have been entrusted to an asshole.

Yours, etc.

*At the time, president of the National Committee on United States–China Relations, Inc.

MEL CALMAN

Gramercy Park Hotel
New York City
July 26, 1978

Dear Mel,

Thanks for yours of the 18th inst. I'm writing this as headlines blaze about the first test-tube baby, and we both know what that means — adieu to fucking. From here in, it's all Bunsen burners and agar-agar plates and glass pipettes. No more of that delicious wrassling around on couches, "Look what you've done to my hair, naughty boy!," and capsized eyeballs and thigh-balls. Not to mention the spate of jokes we're going to be inundated with on radio and telly.

I'm exhausted from running around acquiring visas, medical shots, carnets, all the preliminaries for that giant spin, but hope to cram all preparations in by 15th August. The curvaceous Mrs. Kerz rang up a few minutes ago, tanned and restless from a week in New England, and wanted to be remembered to you. Says she has an adorable new green sweater that stopped traffic on West 42nd Street this noon. I don't know what she means by this, but she said you'd understand.

•   •   •

Fondly,

DIANE DANIELS

Islamabad, Pakistan
September 30, 1978

Diane darling,

Arrived here the 28th, day before yesterday, after 21 days of relentless driving from London—all three of us (knock wood) in seemingly good health and the little old girl, as colleague Syd Beer affectionately calls my 1949 MG, somewhat dusty but in fine shape. We are ensconced—if that is the term for three men occupying a double room and bath, the odd man out sleeping on a mattress on the floor—at the town's newest and most garish hotel, over which there hangs a silent pall of bankruptcy. There cannot be more than two other guests in the joint. Islamabad is a newly created "city" a few miles distant from Rawalpindi containing all the embassy posts of various nations, and the only reason we're here is the gigantic series of floods inundating India, the country we're about to enter. The U.S. Embassy is being very helpful in furnishing advice and sending signals ahead to New Delhi that will enable us to transit those sections of India not under water. The situation at the moment in Bengal (eastern India) and Calcutta is so grave that it's being called the worst flooding in recorded history, but we are being assured of routes toward Madras (where we'll leave by ship across the Bay of Bengal to Singapore with the car and its trailer) so that we shouldn't have too much difficulty.

. . . Thus far the high point of the trip (in every sense) was Afghanistan—the people are the nicest, most colorful, and filthiest, but after the Iranians and Turks with their devious natures, they were a pleasure. I met some nice Iranians, as you may remember from *Eastward Ha!*, but you can tell Bob Breitbarth that I'll curl his hair with my account of what it's like to enter and leave that country by road.

•   •   •

MARTHA SAXTON*

The Peninsula Hotel
Hong Kong
November 7, 1978

Martha dear,

It would be rather lunatic to apologize for a lapse in our correspondence, mine having consisted of a postcard from Afghanistan or somewhere and yours being non-existent, not through any dereliction but only a Ouija board could acquaint you with my whereabouts. That I happen to be in this heavenly hotel, in good enough fettle and with no visible scars — never mind the mental ones — is proof enough of the existence of divine intercession.

Unless you've seen the *Sunday Times* (London) since 1 September, you won't have known that my two colleagues and I (the others named Eric Lister and Sydney Beer) took off on that date and reached Bombay 25 driving days thence, having logged 7700-plus miles. The only thing our trio agreed on was that it was the worst endurance test each had ever had. I filed several telexes to the paper during the trip and I guess no reader had to peruse between the lines. The car behaved magnificently, even if its occupants didn't. Generosity impels me to say that considering we were a mixed bag, none of us laid hands on each other. Of course, you must remember that I will have the last word inasmuch as I'll be writing about it, though I may have to fictionalize their names, British libel law being rather more intolerant than ours. Nuf sed.

Conan Doyle recounts that when Sherlock Holmes's chronicler encounters a friend (at the beginning of "A Study in Scarlet"), the friend exclaims, "Why, Watson, you are as thin as a lath and as brown as a nut!" I, thanks to a couple of weeks of Chinese food, have won back a few lbs. and no longer resemble a parboiled lobster. Granted that the local sing-song girls still give me a wide berth; nonetheless, I'm slowly becoming identifiable as hominoid. By the time we see each other there may even be vestiges of my former self.

Just when that will be, in Wolcott Gibbs's apt phrase about Henry Luce, knows only God. I'm enmeshed in negotiations that can only be called Byzantine, and you may hear more ere long. Meanwhile, I can merely seize this moment to pledge my devotion as always. Dear love to you, and please give my best to Enrico.

*American travel and history writer (*Jayne Mansfield and the American Dream*, *Louisa May Alcott*).

ISRAEL SHENKER

The Peninsula Hotel
Hong Kong
November 8, 1978

Dear Shenk,

．　　　　　．　　　　　．

The enclosed swatch of newsprint is based on the assumption that you haven't meanwhile read previous reports in the *Sunday Times* (London). You certainly didn't see the interviews in the Pakistan *Times* or the Bombay papers because we burned them as they came hot off the press. Otherwise, our trajectory through fourteen or fifteen countries created about as much comment as if a bullock circling a water wheel had farted.

Currently the wiseacres of the Hong Kong press corps are convulsed with giggles that an old Jewish upstart believes he can get into China with a vehicle almost as old as himself, but I say to them, "They all laughed at Jean-Jacques Rousseau when he said man was perfectible, yet today we have people like Jody Powell." So I am out to show them, and if my Byzantine negotiations with the Celestials pay off, there will be some chopfallen visages in the fourth estate. (Of course, it could go the other way too, so like any smart gambler, I've sprinkled a few bets around that I'm not going to make it.)

I guess this brings you up to date on my activities; hence will close with best to you and your good wife, Mary. She is a patient, long-suffering woman—no, no, I'm not implying anything. I never listen to gossip, and if a man wants to beat his wife, that's his own business, etc.

Yours ever,

DIANE DANIELS

Hong Kong
November 9, 1978

．　　　　　．　　　　　．

. . . [The journey] was the worst endurance test, mental and physical, in any travel I've done. If you've seen any of the successive telexes I filed to the *Sunday Times* in London, you'll get an inkling. . . . My erstwhile colleagues, the two Brits, have now departed to resume their sordid pursuits and malign me; I am naturally grief-stricken at their anguish, but stoutly continue my Byzantine negotiations with the mighty empire to the north, which are—I say this guardedly—extremely promising. You might like to light a couple of joss sticks in my behalf, but it's barely possible that you'll receive news of interest via the media.

Thanks to the superb Chinese groceries available here, I've recovered some of the flesh that evaporated during the trip. I fortunately escaped even a headache or stomach qualm throughout, though my chauffeurs spent lots of time in the excusado en route and kept swallowing handfuls of Lomotil. The car behaved magnificently, even if they didn't, and I visit it daily in the garage a block distant and caress its fenders. . . .

•   •   •

PRUDENCE CROWTHER

Gramercy Park Hotel
New York City
January 5, 1979

Dear Prudence Crowther,

That was a very nice letter you wrote me back in September enclosing this manuscript, but I didn't get to read it until Christmas Eve (which perhaps was more timely) when I got home from Asia. The usual response when a lady says she loves you is to send her a dozen long-stemmed American Beauty roses. You would have received them but for the fact that my excess baggage costs from Hong Kong totalled $285. Of course, if you'd like, I can send you my excess baggage receipts, which could be worn in a locket and might make a stunning accessory.

I liked "Writer at Work: Geoffrey Stiles" and was just debating how to tell you so without wounding your sensibilities when two things happened in swift succession: a) Your name jetted out of *The New York Review* masthead as being clearly implicated in its type production, and b) "Writer at Work" etc. turned up in *The New Yorker* renamed "Frank Grange, Fictionator." Even to one stupefied by travel, it was plain that your career was already in full orbit and that any advice I'd offer would be presumptuous.

So many thanks to you, then, and one biographical point — are you an offshoot of Bosley and Florence Crowther, by any chance?

Sincerely,

ANNE GREGG

Gramercy Park Hotel
New York City
January 28, 1979

Dearest Anne,

Thank you so very much for your lovely letter of 3/2/78 with its crest of your voluptuous kiss imprinted on the salutation. I shall tell you straight off that though it didn't reach me in the Far East or wherever you initially

347

addressed it, it must have exercised a beneficent effect on me, because I am (knock wood) altogether recovered from the pneumonia that struck me down in Peking. (They diagnosed it as bronchitis, but the X-rays here in New York disproved them.) Furthermore, in a display of will such as I never believed myself capable of, I haven't had a cigarette in 4½ weeks. Of course the brain has dried up completely as a result, but I'm assured by reformed smokers that it *sometimes* resumes functioning...

The trip was a very, very difficult one — not because of the car, which behaved brilliantly — but just fearful roads, accommodation, food, and weather conditions (floods, heat, earthquake, rebellions). And worse than all of these, my colleagues, who turned out to be unspeakable. On the other hand, the Chinese proved to be fine. They agreed to let me bring my car into China but it would have taken about six weeks due to complexities of transportation, and at that point I had just come out of the hospital and hadn't the strength to stay on in freezing Peking. The brass were very disappointed that they couldn't be photographed in Tien An Men Square grouped around my '49 MG.

So now I am laboring on the account promised to the Sunday *Times*, though all is up in the air there due to the suspension. I'm happy to read that you didn't fall victim to *your* industrial dispute; but the news from England sounds so dire — strikes, food shortages, etc. I hope it really isn't as grim as our press here makes it sound. The truck strike now touches me personally, inasmuch as I believe that my car is resting inside a container at the Southampton docks. I shipped it back to the U.K. by sea to have some modifications changed before it's returned to the States.

I hope you're serious about your hope to come over to New York this year. It might be the very tonic you say you need, and I'm sure it's the one I do. Meanwhile, bundle up that stiff upper lip, much thanks again for your letter, and with oceans of love,   Yours ever,

PRUDENCE CROWTHER

Gramercy Park Hotel
New York City
February 4, 1979

Dear Prudence Crowther,

Thank you belatedly for clarifying your non-relationship to Bosley C. (than whom few film critics are more pompous) and particularly for your Abilene Aunt Daisy's "oats" card.* It had a certain timeliness in that 1 February chanced to be my birthday, having been dropped neatly 'twixt FDR and James

*From a turn-of-the-century parlor game to do with grains.

Joyce, who I hope you will agree are a nifty set of parentheses. Now, I am not quite sure what these grain cards betoken, but the illustration on the face of the card seems to portray feverish activity in something like the Chicago wheat pit; so uniting this thought with the hooves reference in your colophon, the union of Kansas and California in your genealogy, and the classy reference to Poussin in Ingres' *The Apotheosis of Homer*, I end up with a mosaic that I don't mind admitting is altogether baffling. Just who are you, Crowther? Are you Irene Adler, the fascinating, elusive creature of *A Scandal in Bohemia* celebrated in its opening line, "To Sherlock Holmes she is always *the* woman"? Are you Cigarette in Ouida's *Under Two Flags*? Or are you (by some unimaginable magic) a recreation of that greatest of all Eurasian enchantresses, Jetta Goudal, whose slave I have been since the age of fifteen? Or maybe you're the Countess de Winter, that mad, bad, glad sorceress of Dumas. Well, no doubt you are an amalgam of them all.

Anyhow, this is to tell you that while you have never received a dozen red roses (much less a single deadly nightshade), the next time I come down to Balducci's to have my wallet sheared, I will pop into that basement florist's next to Bigelow's drugstore and dispatch a few bedraggled sweet williams for your window ledge. Pending that, accept meanwhile, I beg of you, dear Mademoiselle, my assurances the most distinguished,

Yours,

PRUDENCE CROWTHER

Gramercy Park Hotel
New York City
February 13, 1979

Dear Miss Crowther,

Delighted to receive your update on wallet shearing in the Village, and particularly enraptured by the Degas-like fillette in a tutu erupting from a suede chukka boot. In writing about Balducci's and the Elite Shoe Repair, you are dealing of course with one block of Sixth Avenue that has deep sentimental associations for me. Halfway along it, where now stands some so-called "Jamaica" restaurant, once stood Siegel's, also a restaurant but in the Twenties and early Thirties a haunt of writers like Philip Wylie, Finley Peter Dunne, Junior (son of Finley Peter Dunne, Senior), your present correspondent, etc. One evening I was dining there with Nathanael West, when Phil Wylie came in with a Park Avenue gland specialist named Dr. Berman. (As you doubtless suspect, I can never forget anything really unimportant.) "This is Dr. Berman, the gland specialist," Wylie introduced him to us. "Mention any writer you like and Dr. Berman will name the physical shortcoming responsible for the

349

man's idiosyncratic style." "O.K.," said West. "James Joyce." "Humph," returned Dr. Berman. "Poor eyesight." "Dostoievsky," I said. "Epilepsy," said Dr. Berman. There was quite a long silence, then Dr. Berman asked, not without irritation, "Well, how about it?" "We can't think of any other writers, Doc," West apologized. "Goddam snobs," the Doctor muttered. "Come on, Wylie, let's sit over in the back."

It is indeed spooky that around 11:05 you were watching that film on flossing just when I was opening my birthday presents, but the facts are spookier still. As you were watching that film on flossing, I was *not* opening my presents; I was in the Gramercy Pastry Shop on Third Ave. buying a rye bread with caraway seeds. And that is so much more significant, isn't it, when you come right down to it? I mean, there you were (so to speak) undergoing a rebirth, inaugurating a new day by flossing the seeds out of your teeth, and there was I, beginning a new year by acquiring a set of whole new seeds for mine. You can't tell me there isn't a pretty significant meaning in that contrast, sister.

Before we leave this ever-so-romantic subject of flossing, here is a paragraph from a story by Georgia Dullea, *N.Y. Times*, as contained in a clipping in the *London Free Press*, London, Ontario, sent to me by some wrecker and diversionist: "Flossing was in fact the high point of a small dinner party that Judy and Robert Fresco gave in their Park Avenue apartment. As the guests looked on, the hostess maneuvered dental floss around the mouths of her two sons, aged 3 and 8, with the same dexterity she employs on her own teeth every night while watching the late news on television. Everybody clapped. Mrs. Fresco blushed and said she owed it all to 'Marvin-With-the-Satin-Lips.' She meant Dr. Marvin Mansky, her 'very hip' dentist. He has a huge pair of satin lips hanging on his office wall, along with his name in neon. He also has a hygienist who reminds Mrs. Fresco of Bette Midler. 'She taught me everything I know about dental floss,' Mrs. Fresco said."

Would you like to collaborate on a musical, to star Bette Midler, about a romance between Dr. Marvin-with-the-Satin-Lips, an orthodox orthodontist, and Mrs. Fresco, a sexy young Park Avenue matron? The song they're going to go out whistling is named "Toot-toot-Toothsy, Goodbye."

Ever yours,

PRUDENCE CROWTHER

Gramercy Park Hotel
New York City
February 24, 1979

Dear P.C.,

The shorter salutation above is not meant to denote undue familiarity

350

but rather to strike a balance between the starchy, dancing-school propriety of Miss C. and the coziness of Dear Prudence. The only other Prudence I know is the proprietess of that very good restaurant in London called Prue's, who I guess still does a weekly food column in the *Daily Mail*. She's a very attractive lady who puts up a toothsome meal, but her prose style doesn't compare with yours.

It's a right smart number of years since I've ventured into the Jumble Shop, which at the time your folks were courting had two entrances, one on 8th Street and the other on MacDougal (latter now called the Shakespeare, I believe, or Shakespeare Tavern). Somewhere in my Jumbled effects, probably in that black steamer trunk yonder, are a couple of those query sheets that Harold Ross used to send *New Yorker* contributors, numbered from 1 to 95. (I say this because John Cheever once told me he actually got 95 queries from Ross on one of his short stories. I think my high score was 73.)* Anyway, the point is that I made reference to the Jumble Shop in whatever I was writing about the Village, and Ross wanted to know if it was a real name, couldn't believe there was such a place. I could vouch for it, having dwelt a stone's throw away for about a year and a half at 47 West 8th. It was a singularly charmless street then, and today is hardly a cut above Hogarth's Gin Lane. Of the restaurant I remember only that it had the traditional shaky green tables, which undoubtedly shook even more as your sire popped the question nervously. (Or your pop sired the question, if you prefer.)

Your wistful inquiry about Dr. Berman's whereabouts will have to go unanswered, but I hope you can answer one of mine — viz., how do you know you have no pineal gland? *Webster's 2nd International Dictionary* assures me that it is present in all craniate vertebrates, one of which I take you to be. Or is this an unwarranted assumption?

The flower selection guide you sent along was peculiarly relevant, inasmuch as I was indeed winding up to place an order with my local florist. However, my local florist always requests the phone number of the party receiving the order, and Information tells me yours is unpublished. So, I'll trade you my unpublished number for yours, herewith: 473-1362 (Private, ex-directory, unpub.); GR 5-4320, Ext. 1621 (Hotel).

How fascinating to watch the evolution of an image of oneself through hints in the correspondence of another when the two haven't met. For example, you calmly accept the possibility that I may have been one of fifty who were hustled out of the Infinity Disco last week† (about as likely an assump-

---

*E.g., query no. 3 from Harold Ross's notes on "Cloudland Revisited: Lady Play Your Endocrines" (November 22, 1948): "Not clear what meant here. Did he add a tangerine to the ice cream–graham crackers diet, or did he substitute the tangerine for those items."

†Refers to a fire in a building where some friends of mine lived.

tion as my being the paparazzo who photographs the gatefolds for *Penthouse* or Nelson Eddy's stand-in). Soon afterward, however, in a small blackout forming over your head aboard public transportation, I am seated on a bar stool (at some nifty nite-spot like the Park Central's Anguish Room Bar) clad in a white dress suit, smoking two cigarettes at once, and indistinguishable from Paul Henreid, when the waiter enters with the MacIlvoy Flyer you discreetly bribed him to buy me. Now, do you know what I'm going to tell you, as Myles Na Gopaleen, that darling man, says over and over? I'm going to tell you how wide of the mark your conception is. In actual fact, I am a startling combination of the fire chief supervising the clearance of the disco and the salad cook at the Park Central, a waspish Greek from Thessalonica, resembling nobody so closely as Frank Langella, whom I had the evil fate to sit up watching in *Diary of a Mad Housewife* until 1:30 this a.m.

As for you, kiddo, I have you figured out to the last hairpin. It stands to reason that anyone who is considering subletting her place and moving into a large safety-deposit box must be on the petite side—right? Kind of a Goldie Hawn type—right? Squeaky little voice, big bows on the shoes, etc. *YET—* what does the reference to the angora cloche tell us??? Whom does that summon up but lovely, restless Faye Dunaway which SHE would be ideally cast in the role of the type producer of this smart metropolitan literary journal. Aha, *now* we're getting somewhere! Who could play the male lead—do we have anyone under contract? Mr. Mayer, I don't want to raise false hopes, but have I got an idea, a hunch, it'll blow you out of your seat...What is it, speak up, man!...How about that suave worldling, that squire of dames Bernard Malamud? My God, what an inspiration—Perelman, from now on you are board chairman of M-G-M and here is a little bonus, 50,000 shares of Scripps Howard preferred...   Yours,

Janet Baker singing "Where the bee sucks" is such a total mystery that my ganglia frost over. I do, however, have a record player, and despite your reluctance to play Zeus, I can play Danae even if it means going into drag. After all, if Bernard Malamud has the gall to appear on the same screen with Faye Dunaway...

CASKIE STINNETT

Gramercy Park Hotel
New York City
February 25, 1979

Dear Caskie,
Thank you for your letter. I've been remarkably remiss about my cor-

respondence since I got back after the holidays; maybe it was an anti-typewriter syndrome brought on by the shutdown of the *Sunday Times*. More likely it was a certain faiblesse lingering on from the pneumonia siege I had in Peking. Anyhow, I'm well over that, I hope, and in the process have (I also hope) shaken off the weed. Yes, sir, not a single cigarette in two months, and sometimes a whole patch of four or five days passes without a backward glance at the habit.

To encapsulate the Paris-Peking adventure is difficult, particularly because I'm bored with having had to recount it so often, but I'll race through it. Miss Pine Bluff, Arkansas, about whom you inquire, never became part of it, inasmuch as I jettisoned her in mid-August; I discovered quite by accident that she had teamed up with an agent who was offering a putative book by her to half a dozen publishers for this coming spring—in short, Sweetie Pie was trying to beat me into print with her own account of the trip. Anyway, that required an adjustment of the participants in the exploit, and in the end I made the journey with the two Brits who were to have driven the backup vehicle, i.e., the trio in my 1949 MG Y Tourer pulling a small trailer behind us. Went through central Europe, the Balkans, Turkey, Iran, Afghanistan, Pakistan, and India in 27 actual driving days, having started Sept. 1, all the way to Bombay. Car behaved like a dream, wish I could say likewise of the Brits. Food, accommodations, and everything ghastly from Germany onward. The three of us slept in one room throughout, and *that's* for the birds once you're over Boy Scout age. Beyond Bombay, no land route, and behind us massive floods. (Also no ships nowadays, complicating matters.) So we flew the car to Hong Kong as well as ourselves. Came now the problem of permission to enter China, about which intercession at all levels had failed. Six weeks of hush-hush negotiations (after two of which my Brit colleagues went home) and I was given visas to enter together with Nancy Nash, w.k. journalist lady in HK. Flew to Peking where, within 48 hours, the cold I had caught in HK rared up into fever and I was immured in hospital for 5 days. The Chinese agreed to having the MG brought in, first by sea to Canton, then in a box-car up to Peking, all of which would have required 6 weeks. But health and cost prohibited, so after 10 days, back to HK, where I shipped car by sea to England and flew back via London. The MG, natch, got caught in the great lorry strike in Britain, was not off-loaded in Southampton but diverted to Hamburg, and is temporarily in limbo. If I know my luck, I'll probably have to go over to Germany to liberate it.

Now, whereas I get the impression that you and various popsies have been rumpling a series of beds during all these past months, you can comb the whole long paragraph above without dislodging a single thread of scarlet. I have often heard that it is fatal for a full-blooded man of mature years to go 4½ months without fucking, and this was indeed the case with me last year,

353

but the lesson is clear—I contracted pneumonia as a result. So let this be a cautionary tale. . . .

I've seen Lil only once lately, she came to the Hacketts' for a birthday drink at a dinner they gave me, and I was distressed at her appearance. I mean to get in touch with her, but I've been trying to hack out an account of the adventures for the Grand Old Paper and it's dispiriting work, particularly as the G.O.P. isn't appearing and nobody knows if it will ever. Oh, well, I suppose it's the nature of the dodge we're in—never better described than by S.J.P. as Making Bricks Without Straw.

I expect to be here, nose against grindstone, unrelievedly through the spring, so if you're coming down this way, Caskie, do let me know—it would be nice to have lunch. Meanwhile, and hoping you can get a half-nelson on the U.S. Corps of Engineers, with all the best

Yours ever,

PRUDENCE CROWTHER

Gramercy Park Hotel
New York City
March 10, 1979

Dear Prudence,

The triple parlay in your mailer earlier in the week—Florence Dora Rapp's book-jacket sneakily o'er-covered with PPC's legend, that tracing of what I take to be your bedroom slipper, and Janet Baker's record—was a great success. That is to say, I studied Miss Rapp's jut-jawed and somewhat equine features with my own jaw sagging in disbelief, and after what surely must have been the count of 15, adenoidally saw that your name was hinged to the space below the photograph. (How does one "adenoidally" see anything? Elide that.) Then, believe it or not, I slipped off my suede shoe mfd. by George Cleverly, 27 Cork Street, W.1, and placed my unshod foot on your pattern, and you will be transported to know that we could exchange bedroom slippers. And finally (but not altogether lastly) played Janet Baker, who does indeed have a lovely voice, and it was generous of you to introduce me to it. The altogether lastly was your enclosed letter, which contained several authentic nuggets. Gee whiz, to think that the person who's reading this is she who sets up the *NYR* classifieds! Hey, Crowther—yoo hoo! I read you religiously every issue. Nugget #2: In one of the most waspish denunciations since Mons. Fulton Sheen quit the air waves, you lash me unmercifully for my taste in shallow-dish tarts (Faye Dunaway, etc.), then weave in a serpentine glide into a cab driver's equating you with Jane Wyman in *Johnny Belinda*, and then with consummate gall (knowing my Achilles heel) wind up with a quote from Bernard

354

Malamud in your day-book. Nugget #3: Never before have I struck anyone of the three sexes as an amalgam of John Dewey and William Powell, though there is nothing rebarbative in that description. I *have* been told that were I locked in a room with Judge Harold Medina and only one of us emerged, it would be difficult to say positively who it was.* This concludes one of the longest paragraphs this old Royal Quiet has ever regurgitated.

And now, as though my emerging portrait of you isn't sufficiently complex, I must add the fragile tutu of the ballet dancer, muscling away a scant ten blocks from me at 32nd and Lex. Where in God's name do you find time to do your work, redecorate your friends' lofts, attend ballet school, and work on that musical of *Hans Brinker, or The Silver Skates* based on the book by Mary Mapes Dodge? AND write pieces for *The New Yorker*—forgive me for omitting that. But of course all this is explained by your letter headlined La Roseraie that arrived this morning; in which you represented yourself arriving home from work at 8:30 in a towering ill humor for a number of quite valid reasons you described graphically. Now that was a very graceful prelude to your remarks about the roses, but it found a very responsive chord because I've been in a (sustained) bearish mood myself recently. My 1949 MG Y Tourer, which I shipped from Hong Kong to Southampton on Dec. 17, was not off-loaded at Southampton because of the big truck strike in Britain; instead, it was sent to Hamburg, and now *nobody* knows where it is. . . .

Do excuse this glissando into personal *schmerz*, my dear; what I really was getting into above before I got derailed was an attempt to tell you what a *very* nice letter that was. . . .

We really should meet, you know. What do you think?

*Judge Medina became well known in 1949, when he presided over the trial of eleven members of the American Communist party charged with conspiring to overthrow the government. *Current Biography*, 1949, describes him as "dignified and debonair," with a strong resemblance to Adolph Menjou. In the photo reproduced there, the resemblance to Perelman is striking.

CASKIE STINNETT

Gramercy Park Hotel
New York City
August 2, 1979

Dear Caskie,

Belatedly, this copy of Norman Lewis's *Naples '44* which I promised so long ago. Apologies—cafard, anhedonia, bugger-all—sheer laziness in getting a book mailer is the real reason.

Finally got through with a *New Yorker* piece that kept winding around me like a fucking woodbine (and I don't mean an English cigarette if you are old enough to remember that brand). Speaking of that family periodical, did you read K. Tynan's profile of Louise Brooks? I dislike the man but I must say it was a good job—largely because Louise is such an amazing woman. If they ever return my MG I would like to drive up to Rochester this fall and see her. Also, much sorrowed last week to read Corinne Griffith had passed. She was still a beauty when I knew her in 1951. Ah, well, les neiges d'antan...

How was the weekend with Alfie?   Yrs. ever,

PAT KAVANAGH

Gramercy Park Hotel
New York City
August 12, 1979

Dear Pat,

•   •   •

What follows now is not in any sense a coherent or logical report on [the problems of writing the Paris-to-Peking narrative], because in order for you to appreciate what I faced, you would have to hear my account of the journey. In any case, I devoted about 3½ months' writing to the project, and apart from breaking my nails on it at various moments since, I don't intend to go any further with it. Of the six trips I've made around the world, this was far and away the most arduous, the worst endurance test I've undergone. It was completely joyless, devoid of incident, hopelessly unproductive, and indeed psychologically searing because of the two persons I was with. The car behaved like a dream, and they like a nightmare. I've always succeeded in the past in deriving humor from tribulations I've encountered, but you will have to take my word for it that nobody on earth could milk chuckles out of this. So—to sum it up in terms of the calendar, I invested in 1978 one month's trip to England for which I myself paid, plus 4½ months on the journey itself plus 3½ months of writing. That's nine months, which is ordinarily enough to make a baby but not in this case, stranger. Anyhow, the exigencies of earning my living preclude devoting any more time to it.

There's one other matter, totally unrelated to the foregoing, which I would like to ventilate if I may. That concerns the Eyre Methuen paperback of *The Most of S.J.P.* enclosed. Could you find out for me:

. . . Who is responsible for this? Where did he or she discover this sickening photograph on the cover, and why did whoever it was not consult me to inquire whether I had any objection? And secondarily, who assembled the text on the reverse, which is just about the most labored, foot-in-mouth job that has ever appeared on any book of mine? The cover on the Heinemann

356

paperback of the same book won two prestigious art director's awards; this one is *Pure Dreck*.

. . .

Love,

HAROLD EVANS

Gramercy Park Hotel
New York City
August 20, 1979

Dear Harry,

I received your letter of August 1 several days ago and was desolated at your charge that I had inflicted a coronary on you *via* Pat Kavanagh's report to you that I had abandoned the Paris-Peking narrative. Please believe that this was hardly my intention when I intimated as much to her a couple of months back. In any case, I very much deplore that we — you and I — couldn't have had a quiet hour together when you were here most recently so that I could have gone into the problem. Attempting to sort it out by correspondence is no good, and I'm not going to try here.

Nevertheless, I think it is not only useful but indeed mandatory for the solution to have you read what I did write. It will, I hope, serve a double purpose; it should convince you that I did my professional best to distil what humor I could out of the material at hand, and it should secondarily demonstrate the basic futility of the exploit. I venture to say that there is no comic writer, past or present, who could derive laughter from that combination of individuals trapped in a situation that was unquestionably the most repetitious, deadly boring, and savage endurance test in my experience.

Anyway, here is a copy of what eventuated for yourself and another which I'll ask you to please send over to Pat. When you've both read it, we can then discuss the dimensions of my obligation to you and possibilities for meeting it. With regards, Yours,

PAUL THEROUX

Gramercy Park Hotel
New York City
September 4, 1979

Dear Paul,

. . .

I of course have received *The Old Patagonian Express* and must salute

357

you as the winner of the True Grit Award for 1979—it is the horror epic of
the decade, far more chilling than that Amityville Horror thing or any Gothic
novel I know of. And so graphic—every smell, every heap of offal—I flinched
and regurgitated throughout the whole journey as painfully as the most im-
pressionable Foxcroft miss would have. It was exactly as I'd always conceived
all the places you visited and, as I say, my admiration for your pluck in continuing the journey was unbounded. I have to say that I shared Paul Fussell's
and the *N.Y. Times* daily reviewer's (was it John Leonard, I think so) opinion
of the book as a whole. The account of Borges was really tops, and of the
compatriots and fellow-travellers you encountered. To sum up, I thought it
was a wholly truthful, honest, and workmanlike portrait of an appalling experience, and it had a special relevance for me. I myself have spent altogether
too much time this year breaking my nails on the account of that Paris-Peking
trip I made. The major part of it was as distasteful—though not as sustained—
as your adventures, and after a lot of bleeding cuticle, I decided to abandon
it. I guess there are certain subjects—or maybe one's subjective reactions to
them—that in spite of the most manful attempts are totally unproductive. The
one I picked certainly was, and it took a lot of Sturm und Drang to make
me realize that my Sisyphean labors were getting me nowhere.

Have you had a look into Christopher Lasch's *The Culture of Narcissism*?
Some very salty pages, even if endlessly depressing. Also, did you catch an
excellent piece by Kenneth Tynan in *The New Yorker* called "The Girl in the
Black Helmet" about Louise Brooks? As one of the less fervent admirers of
Tynan, this is wrung from me, but if you haven't read it, it's worth pursuing.
Can get you a copy if you have trouble finding it.

I'm sending this to London on the general principle that if you're not
there already, your sons must be on the verge of resuming school. So here's
hoping all's well, and with best,   Yours ever,

PAT KAVANAGH

                                        Gramercy Park Hotel
                                        New York City
                                        September 29, 1979
Dear Pat,

To tackle the more recent of your last two communications—the one
of 18th September *re* Harry and his desire to send me to California:

There's something out of sync here. Harry and I saw each other on 10th
September here, at which time it was my understanding that he *had* read the
Paris-Peking material—which your letter, dated the 18th, said he still hadn't.
In any case, at our meeting I presented him with Xeroxes of 8 pieces of mine

from *The New Yorker* which will appear in my next collection and which I proposed as substitute for the Paris-Peking material — as he had suggested in the copy of his letter I sent you. (I also gave him an envelope containing Xeroxes of those pieces to pass along to you, so you would be au courant with the situation. Didn't he do so?)

The substance of the meeting with Harry, as I understood it, was that with these 8 articles he now has a body of text by me with which he can face up to his accountants — justify his expenditure of the money in question. While it is true that these articles don't deal with Paris-Peking, I got the definite impression that this was of minor importance — what was worrying him was having *some*thing to put forward as the consequence of our dealings.

Now, he then brought up this notion of his about California, to which I responded with guarded interest. It sounded *moderately* promising, and he was very enthusiastic about its possibilities; but I've done a lot of thinking about it since and I don't see what opportunities it offers me as material. I've written my fill about the freakishness of Hollywood — I've really tired of *that* subject — and try as I have to visualize what other bizarrerie lurks out there, I honestly don't come up with enough kooky aspects to promise the wordage required. So the grievous answer, in short, is no dice.

Well, Pat, so much for *that* situation. By a coincidence, on the day I saw Harry, I also received the announcement that you are now in a state of holy matrimony. What a surprise! And how becoming I'm sure it must be! I'm only sorry I'm not there to kiss the bride and wish her everything wonderful. As for your legion of admirers over here, I speak for all of them, I know, when I say that if the groom harms one hair on your head or blacks one of your eyes or so much as knocks you down even once, why the whole lot of us will rush over and deal with the blackguard as he deserves. Let him put that in his pipe and smoke it. 　　　　　　　　　　　Love,

　　　　　　　　　　　　　　　　　　　　　　　　　Sid

359

Index

Recipients of Perelman's letters are followed by **boldfaced** page numbers on which the letters appear.

Griffin, Merv, 238, 275–76
Griffith, Corinne, 108, 356
Griffith, D. W., 127
Guinness, Alec, 201
Guinzberg, Harold, 41*n*
Gulf & Western, 336, 338
Gulliver's Travels, 201

Hackett, Albert, xvi, **15–16, 54–56, 70–71,
  77–78, 83–84, 99–102, 103–104, 107, 111–
  112,** 121, **136–38, 152–54,** 173–74, 195,
  225, 244, 249, 288–89, 292, 293, 317,
  354
Hackett, Frances Goodrich, xvi, **15–16,
  54–56, 70–71, 77–78, 83–84, 99–102,
  103–104,** 107, **111–12,** 121, **136–38,
  152–54,** 173–74, 177, 195, 225, 242,
  244, 249, 288–89, 293, 317, 354
Hadley, Leila, xxvii, **80–83, 84–99,** 111–12,
  **112–13, 116–21, 123–24, 126–29,
  130–36,** 137–38, **140–44, 165–71,
  174–77, 179–83, 184–88, 191–97,
  198–202, 223–24,** 326, **329**
Hadley, Rollin Van N., **340–41**
Hahn, Emily, 74, 147, 169–70
Hairy Ainus, 282
Hamburger, Philip, 247*n*, 272–73
Hammerstein, Oscar, 54
Hammett, Dashiell, xix–xx, 248–49, 321
Handful of Dust, A, 247
Hand Made Fables, xviii
Hanna, Mark, 113, 118, 120, 134, 136,
  137, 138, 144, 173, 176, 177, 193, 194,
  196, 200
Happy Days, xxiii
Harriman, Margaret Case, 50
Harris, Jed, 58
Hart, Moss, 16, 191
Hartley, Carr, 155–56
Hartley, Marsden, 325
Hasso, Signe, 183
Hawkes, Jack, 214
Hayes, Helen, 144
Hayward, John, 147
Heart of the City, The, 54
Hecht, Ben, 319
Hefner, Hugh, 267–68
Heinemann, William, 216
Heiress, The, 18*n*, 78
Held, John, Jr., xi, 290, 324
Helena Rubinstein, 233
Heller, Joseph, 217–18
Hellman, Lillian, viii, xix, 98, 182, 187,
  199, 248, 287, 288–89, 295, 303–304,
  317, 318, 321, 325, 327, 331, 335, 354
Hemingway, Ernest, 162, 171, 221, 263
Herbert, A. P., 216
Here at The New Yorker, 304
Here Is New York, 102

Here Today, 41, 47
Herrick, Robert, 210
Hersey, John, 295
Higgins, George V., 319, 329
Hiler, Hilaire, 71
Hirschfeld, Al, xiii, xvi, 60, 62–63, 72,
  87*n*, 101, 104, 113, 119, 130, 132, 143,
  148, 164, 183, 201, 245, 247*n*, **251–52,**
  265, 291, **310–11,** 333, 337
Hirschfeld, Dolly, 183
Hitler, Adolf, 31
Hitler Gang, The, 56
Hoggart, Richard, 271
Holiday, xiii, 69, 75, 77, 78, 87, 92, 95, 96,
  100, 103, 104, 107, 120, 124, 127, 132,
  134, 168, 179*n*, 244, 245, 247, 282, 294*n*
Holliday, Judy, 53*n*
Hollingworth, , Clare, vii, xvii
Hollywood, Calif., xxvi, 8, 23–24, 59,
  62–63, 171–74, 180–81, 218, 231–32,
  313, 319–20, 359
Hollywood Knickerbocker Hotel, 19
Hollywood Reporter, 24, 63
Hollywood Ten, 103
Holmes, Sherlock, 349
"Home Is Where You Hang Yourself," 17*n*
Hong Kong, 72, 86, 164, 214, 282, 294,
  311–12
Honolulu, Hawaii, 85
Hope, Bob, 101, 107, 304
Hopper, Hedda, 174
Horse Feathers, xii, 8*n*, 54*n*
Hound and Horn, 57
Houseman, John, 200
House of Flowers, 166
Howard, Trevor, 178
"How to Fall Out of a Hammock," xv
How to Win Friends and Influence People,
  35
Howze, Perry, xxiv, **297–98**
Huberman, Leo, 248
Human Beast, The, 26
Huston, John, 128, 179, 193
Huxley, Aldous, xviii, 317

Ill-Tempered Clavichord, The, 68*n*, 105*n*,
  135
Illustrators' Club, 182
India, 97, 260–61, 308, 344
Indochina, 72–73, 112–13
Infinity Disco, 351
In Gay Madrid, 5
Ingersoll, Ralph, 98*n*
Ingres, 349
In Our Time, 221
International Herald Tribune, 98, 280*n*,
  281
Intimate Journals of Gauguin, 6
Intolerance, 127

367

371